DATE DUE			

THE HISTORIC MISSION OF JESUS

THE
HISTORIC MISSION
OF JESUS

A CONSTRUCTIVE RE-EXAMINATION OF THE ESCHATOLOGICAL TEACHING IN THE SYNOPTIC GOSPELS

By

CECIL JOHN CADOUX

M.A., D.Litt., Oxon ; M.A., D.D., London ; Hon. D.D., Edinburgh ;
Vice-Principal of Mansfield College, Oxford

HARPER & BROTHERS
NEW YORK *and* LONDON

Printed in the United States of America

SOCIIS MEIS
QVIBVSCVM IN COLLEGIIS
DE MANSFIELD
ET DE REGENTIS PARADISO
PRO REGNO CHRISTI
MOLIOR ET MOLIAR

GENERAL PLAN OF THE BOOK

DETAILED TABLE OF CONTENTS

CONTENTS

viii

CONTENTS

PART TWO

THE NATURE AND PRESENCE OF THE KINGDOM OF GOD

CONTENTS

PART THREE

The Future of the Kingdom as first
ENVISAGED

CONTENTS

PART FOUR

The Future of the Kingdom as last envisaged

CONTENTS

CONCLUSION

LIST OF ABBREVIATED TITLES

The ensuing list does not include all the works quoted in the footnotes of this book, still less all those consulted in the preparation of it, but only those designated in the footnotes by abbreviated titles needing explanation. By the use of this list in conjunction with the footnotes, the reader should be in possession of the title, authorship, and date of every work quoted. The dates inserted in brackets are those of editions or reprints not used.

Abrahams, *Studies*.	*Studies in Pharisaism and the Gospels.* By I. Abrahams. Cambridge. First Series, 1917. Second Series, 1924.
Bacon, *Beginnings*.	*The Beginnings of Gospel Story.* By Benjamin Wisner Bacon. New Haven, U.S.A., 1909.
Bacon, *Mark*.	*The Gospel of Mark : its composition and date.* By Benjamin Wisner Bacon. New Haven, U.S.A., and London, 1925.
Bacon, *Matthew*.	*Studies in Matthew,* By Benjamin W. Bacon. London, 1930.
Bartlet, *St. Mark*.	*The Century Bible. St. Mark : introduction, Revised Version with notes, index, and map.* Edited by J. Vernon Bartlet. . . . Edinburgh, 1922.
Bartlet and Carlyle, *Christianity in Hist.*	*Christianity in History : a Study of Religious Development.* By J. Vernon Bartlet and A. J. Carlyle. London, 1917, (1935).
Beginnings of Christianity, i.	*The Beginnings of Christianity. Part I, The Acts of the Apostles.* Edited by F. J. Foakes Jackson and Kirsopp Lake. Vol. i. London, 1920.
Bennett, *Social Salv.*	*Social Salvation : a religious approach to the problems of social change.* By John C. Bennett. New York and London, 1935.
Beyschlag, *Theol.*	*New Testament Theology or historical Account of the Teaching of Jesus and of Primitive Christianity according to the New Testament Sources.* By Dr. Willibald Beyschlag. Two vols. Edinburgh, 1895. (Translated from the German of 1891.)
B. J. R. L.	*Bulletin of the John Rylands Library,* Manchester.
Blunt, *The Gospels and the Critic*.	*The Gospels and the Critic.* By A. W. F. Blunt. Oxford and London, 1936.

CONTENTS

Bousset, *Jesus.*
Jesus. Von Professor D. W. Bousset. Dritte Auflage. Tübingen, 1907. The corresponding pages of the English translation by J. P. Trevelyan (London and New York, 1906) are added in brackets.

Bousset, *Relig. des Jud.* (1926).
Die Religion des Judentums im späthellenistischen Zeitalter, verfasst von D. Wilhelm Bousset. In dritter, verbesserter Auflage herausgegeben von D. Dr. Hugo Gressmann. Tübingen, 1926.

Box, *St. Matthew.*
The Century Bible. St. Matthew : introduction, Revised Version with notes, index, and map. Edited by G. H. Box. . . . Edinburgh, 1922.

Bultmann, *Jesus.*
Jesus, von D. Rud. Bultmann. Berlin, (1926); 1929, (1934).

Burkitt, *Earliest Sources.*
The Earliest Sources for the Life of Jesus. By F. Crawford Burkitt. London, 1910. See also below under *H.C.L.M.K.*

Cadbury, *Peril.*
The Peril of Modernizing Jesus. By Henry J. Cadbury. New York, 1937.

Cadman, *Last Journey.*
The Last Journey of Jesus to Jerusalem. Its purpose in the light of the Synoptic Gospels. By William Healey Cadman. Oxford and London, 1923.

A. T. Cadoux, *Parables.*
The Parables of Jesus : their art and use. By A. T. Cadoux. London, 1930.

A. T. Cadoux, *Theol. of Jes.*
The Theology of Jesus. By Arthur Temple Cadoux. London, 1940.

C. J. Cadoux, *Cathol. and Christianity.*
Catholicism and Christianity : a Vindication of Progressive Protestantism. By Cecil John Cadoux. London, 1928.

Charles, *Crit. Hist.* (1913).
A Critical History of the Doctrine of a Future Life In Israel, in Judaism, and in Christianity. . . . By R. H. Charles. Second edition, revised and enlarged. London, 1913.

Christian Worship.
Christian Worship : studies in its history and meaning. By members of Mansfield College. Edited by Nathaniel Micklem. Oxford, 1936.

Clemen, *Primitive Christianity.*
Primitive Christianity and its non-Jewish Sources. By Carl Clemen. Edinburgh, 1912. (Translated from the German of 1909.)

Congreg. Quart.
The Congregational Quarterly. London.

Creed, *St. Luke.*
The Gospel according to St. Luke : the Greek text with introduction, notes, and indices. By John Martin Creed. London, 1930.

Dalman, *W.J.*
The Words of Jesus considered in the light of post-Biblical Jewish Writings and the Aramaic Language. By Gustav Dalman. Edinburgh, 1902. (Translated from the German of 1898.)

CONTENTS

xix

CONTENTS

CONTENTS

xxi

CONTENTS

CONTENTS

CONTENTS

INTRODUCTION

Notwithstanding the vast amount of useful work—linguistic, documentary, historical, and expository—which has been done during the last fifty or sixty years on the contents of the New Testament in general and of the Synoptic Gospels in particular, we are still without any comprehensive and generally-satisfying account of the real purpose of Jesus in his public Ministry and the real content of his teaching. Expression has indeed been given recently to the opinion that, in view of the almost exclusive attention hitherto paid to the analytical study of the several strata of New-Testament literature and the various preparatory disciplines of higher and lower criticism, the time has now come for scholars to concentrate their efforts on interpreting the message of the New Testament as a whole.[1] No doubt such a unification would be very timely and valuable ; for there is unquestionably a great oneness prevading all parts of the New Testament, and the right understanding of any individual part depends therefore in no small measure upon the right understanding of the whole. At the same time it must be remembered that the dependence is mutual, and that the endeavour to obtain a complete and systematic view of the real content of Jesus' own teaching—in distinction (so far as possible) from the interpretation put upon it by his first followers—remains in consequence a vital pre-requisite for the true understanding of the whole Christian movement. Such an endeavour ought not to be thought of as rendered hopeless or unwise either by the close intermingling of record and interpretation in the Gospels, or by the new stress which many modern theologians are laying on the objective and transcendental aspects of Christian belief. Nothing that can rightly be said along these lines alters the fact that knowledge regarding the personal character and aim of Jesus himself is in large measure attainable through a critical examination of the Gospels and is absolutely fundamental to a right interpretation of the Christian message as a whole.[2]

---

[1] Dodd, *Present Task*, 12, 16, 29–38. Dr. Dodd explicitly declines (31f.) to call the desideratum a " synthesis " ; yet this term would seem to be its correct designation.

[2] Cf. Dodd, *Hist. and the Gosp.* 38, 163 (". . . what the character of preaching at its centre must always be : it is a re-presentation of the history of Jesus ").

It must, of course, be realized that, in pursuing such an inquiry, we have continually to be on our guard against the danger of reading into the records of Jesus what we most wish to find there, and of misrepresenting by our modern constructions a body of data which are throughout both fragmentary and occasional.[1] Many long-accepted opinions regarding Jesus' personal religion, social and national outlook, and dominating object in life, have been roundly declared to be the fanciful creations of scholars and preachers unaware of their modernizing proclivities. It has, for instance, been seriously argued that, in all probability, Jesus consciously pursued no plan, purpose, or programme at all, but followed quite casually what he felt from time to time to be the leading of God's Will.[2] Such a plea surely indicates that the dread of " modernizing " can go too far. Account must needs be taken, not only of the wide differences between the mentality of Jesus' age and that of our own, but also of those great unities which pervade and embrace all human experience and which alone render possible any real knowledge of the past.[3] In particular, it is inconceivable that one who was conscious of fulfilling the rôle of Messiah, and who frequently referred to the purposes for which he had " come ", could have been without a fairly definite and conscious " object in life ".[4] As for the danger of systematically classifying his unsystematic utterances,[5] the analogy of such a science as botany or zoology (which largely owes to its classification of unsystematic material its power to explain that material) should encourage us to believe that the danger is not very serious. The mind of Jesus was, after all, a unity ; and as a human mind it presents likenesses to our own. In classifying and interpreting his utterances, therefore, while we

[1] These difficulties have been very forcibly put by Dr. H. J. Cadbury in his *Peril of Modernizing Jesus*, passim. Cf. Bultmann, *Jesus*, 7–9, 18 ; Manson, *Teaching*, 116f. ; D. W. Riddle in *J.R.* xiv (1934) 154, 162, 164 ; *Times Lit. Suppt.* 15 Oct. 1938, 656 (" the temptation to portray the Christ more in accordance with the writer's own personal ideals than in keeping with the data . . . is one that is not easily resisted ").

[2] Cadbury, *Peril*, 120–153, esp. 140f,, 153. Cf. Schweitzer, *L.J.F.* 404 = *Quest*, 356 (J. Weiss's insight " schaffte alle ' Aktivität ' auf das Reich Gottes ab, und macht Jesum zum lediglich Abwartenden ").

[3] Bennett, *Social Salv.* 73f. Dr. Cadbury recognizes, of course, the existence of these unities (*Peril*, 4, 31f., 48, 148f., 191) ; but he makes a minimal use of them (e.g., 48 : " . . . the aim of this book is to minimize the modernness of Jesus ").

[4] Dr. Cadbury (*Peril*, 130–137, 208f.) discusses these items of evidence, but depreciates their historical value as owing too much to the later thought of the Church. His quotation of Bultmann in this connexion, however, betrays too ready an acceptance of that scholar's excessive scepticism.

[5] Cf. Holtzmann, *Theol.* i. 176–178 ; Denney, *Jes. and the Gosp.* (1913), 214.

may at times confuse the conscious and explicit with the sub-conscious and implicit, we are not likely to misrepresent his intentions simply through being too methodical in our quest for them.

The first result of the application of modern methods of criticism to the Gospels was the production of a series of books describing the life and teaching of Jesus in the manner that has come to be known as "liberal". The discovery of the fact that, in the successive documents making up our four Gospels, an increasing amount of doctrinal adornment and interpretation had been introduced, encouraged the assumption —natural enough to Christian devotion—that, if these unhistorical doctrinal accretions were stripped away, there would remain a "Jesus of History", whose teaching the modern Christian idealist could heartily accept, and whose leadership he could unreservedly follow. This teaching, it was felt, would be found to consist mainly of such inspiring doctrines as the universal Fatherhood of God, the Brotherhood of Man, the supreme duty of lovingkindness, the Kingdom of God as an ideal of social righteousness, and so on. There must have been countless Christian ministers, teachers, and workers, who drew their main inspiration for service from such a reading of the Gospel-story.[1]

This "liberal" account of Jesus was not so far astray from the truth as many modern theologians would have us believe— certainly not so far astray as is the version which some of them are recommending us to substitute for it. It represented, at least, an honest and intelligent attempt to disentangle the essential and abiding realities from the less-essential vehicle in which they were conveyed. But it erred through over-confidence in its presuppositions and over-simplification in its treatment of the material.[2] It was accordingly destined to undergo a very severe shaking-up at the hands of those who, seeing the mistake of assuming the identity of the morally-acceptable with the historically-true, transferred the whole stress to that part of the Gospel-teaching which is least easily assimilated by the modern mind—the eschatology.

It is widely known how in 1906 the theological world was faced with Albert Schweitzer's substantial work, 'Von

---

[1] Grateful mention may be made of Josiah Strong's book, *The Next Grea Awakening* (1903), as a fine sample of a class of literature to which many were deeply indebted.

[2] Cf. Weinel in *R.G.G.* iii (1929) 153 f., 160, 168f. ; Manson, *Teaching*, 15.

Reimarus zu Wrede '. In form a history, mainly, of the critical work done on the life of Jesus during the previous century-and-a-quarter, it culminated in a theory of Schweitzer's own, in which the eschatology was used as the key to everything else. This theory had, in a sense, been anticipated in Johannes Weiss's ' Die Predigt Jesu vom Reiche Gottes ' (1892) and a couple of other German works, and especially in Schweitzer's own sketch of Jesus' life, entitled ' Das Messianitäts- und Leidensgeheimnis ' (1901). Schweitzer's views were introduced to English and American students by Sanday's ' Life of Christ in Recent Research ' (1907), and were brought before a still wider public a little later (1910), when an English translation of his great work appeared under the title of '' The Quest of the Historical Jesus '. A second and revised edition of the German was published in 1913 as ' Geschichte der Leben-Jesu-Forschung ' ; and this has been several times reprinted (1921, 1926, 1934). It was not till 1925 that his 1901-sketch appeared in an English dress with the title, ' The Mystery of the Kingdom of God '.

Schweitzer's theory was briefly as follows. Jesus' mind was absolutely dominated by the fixed dogma of an eschatological programme, according to which the Messianic birth-pangs, the appearance of the Son-of-Man-Messiah on the clouds, the resurrection of the dead, the Last Judgment, and the supernatural inauguration of the Kingdom of God, were destined quickly to succeed one another in the very near future. From the time of his baptism onwards, Jesus was conscious of being himself the Messiah. But he kept this conviction a profound secret ; and both the imprisoned John and the cheering crowds at Jerusalem thought of him as simply the Elijah-herald— a view which Jesus himself did not correct beyond saying that John was Elijah. Yet he spoke much of the Son of Man in the third person, and of the birth-pangs through which he and others were to go prior to his now-imminent coming. He thought this coming of the Son of Man, i.e., of himself, would take place before his Disciples had been able to call all the cities of Israel to repentance (Mt. x. 23). His ethical teaching, therefore, in so far as it bore on social conditions, was simply an '' interim-ethic '', devised only for the short interval which remained before the Kingdom should finally come. But neither birth-pangs nor Parousia took place ; and it was their non-occurrence (not any imaginary loss of popularity) which caused him to re-mould his forecast. He concluded that the birth-pangs would befall himself alone, and that, in order to

4

usher them in as the prelude to his own later reappearance in Messianic glory, he would have to die. He went to Jerusalem deliberately for that purpose : not historical conditions, but dogmatic necessity, occasioned his death. The secret of his claim to be the Messiah, revealed at Caesarea-Philippi to the Twelve, was still carefully hidden from the public : but it was betrayed by Judas to the High Priest, and acknowledged by Jesus himself before the Sanhedrin. The Resurrection of which he spoke was identical in his own mind with the whole process leading up to the Parousia. To sum up, Jesus " lays hold of the wheel of the world to set it moving on that last revolution which is to bring all ordinary history to a close. It refuses to turn, and He throws Himself upon it. Then it does turn ; and crushes Him. Instead of bringing in the eschatological condi-tions, He has destroyed them. The wheel rolls onward, and the mangled body of the one immeasurably great Man, who was strong enough to think of Himself as the spiritual ruler of mankind and to bend history to His purpose, is hanging upon it still. That is His victory and His reign ".[1]

No attempt can be made here to summarize or even enumerate the many valuable contributions which have been made to the problem since Schweitzer first really convinced scholars that the eschatology of the Gospels must be taken seriously.[2] Comparatively-few writers were found to express complete agreement with him. The general feeling was that he had gone too far ; but every grade of difference between almost complete concurrence with his view and complete repudiation of it was represented. Of the attempts to refute the eschatological view in its entirety, perhaps the most note-worthy was that of the Rev. C. W. Emmet in ' The Lord of Thought ' (1922) : he argued that the distribution of apocalyptic matter in the Gospel-documents showed that much of it was erroneously ascribed to Jesus by early Christian writers, and that the remainder ought to be interpreted figuratively. The apocalyptic teaching, particularly that part of it which dealt with the future punishment of the wicked, Emmet judged to be so inconsistent with the doctrine of the fatherly love of God that one or other of them must be rejected as not having really emanated from Jesus ; and the apocalyptic teaching was

---

[1] Schweitzer, *Quest*, 369 (not in *L.J.F.*). Schweitzer's own views are stated by him, rather unsystematically, in *L.J.F.* 368–443 = *Quest*, 328–395, and in *Mystery*, passim. Cf. also, Leckie, *World to Come*, 39–41.

[2] The more significant of them are noted in R. N. Flew's art. in *E.T.* xlvi. 214–218 (Feb. 1935), C. J. Cadoux's in *E.T.* xlvi. 406–410 (June 1935), and W. D. Niven's in *E.T.* l. 325–330 (Apl. 1939).

accordingly rejected as the less original of the two. But most scholars, while believing that Schweitzer had overdone his thesis, accepted in principle the plea that Jesus did entertain some apocalyptic expectations which were never actually fulfilled in the literal sense ; and on this assumption they have expounded and illustrated various phases of the problem with great skill and success.[1] But all these valuable contributions leave the mind of the reader still worried over certain unanswered questions. If Schweitzer has gone too far, how much farther has he gone than he ought to have gone, and why ? Still more seriously, if Schweitzer is not wholly wrong, how are we to reconcile the resultant limitations in Jesus' knowledge with our Christian trust in him as Lord and Saviour ?

Schweitzer's work has been incautiously welcomed in one quarter where it might have been expected to rouse the strongest disapproval. I refer to those who, in the interests of a more conservative Christology, regarded the liberal inter-pretation of Jesus as heterodox and dangerous. To see the Jesus Christ of the Church's Creeds represented as a pious human reformer, from whose words idealists could demon-strate the truth of pacifism, socialism, and other aberrations of a modern age, was so revolting to many with strong theological and ecclesiastical sympathies, that they felt grateful for any argument which demonstrated such a representation to be historically untenable. So we find them again and again observing with evident satisfaction that Schweitzer has at least demolished the liberal picture of Jesus—as if that demolition in some way helped to re-establish their own credal position.[2] They apparently did not realize that to flee to Schweitzer for deliverance from liberalism was (as the saying goes) only to leap from the frying-pan into the fire. For if it is hard to see the Christ of tradition in the Jesus of liberalism, how much harder is it to see him in the deluded visionary whom Schweitzer put in his place ? Instead therefore of welcoming the new school of " konsequente Eschatologie " as a valuable ally of orthodoxy, these modern scholars should have heeded the warning which Hecuba gave to her husband :

" Non tali auxilio, nec defensoribus istis,
        Tempus eget ".

---

[1] A good example is Mackinnon, *Historic Jesus*, 196–207.
[2] See, e.g., Relton, *Study in Christol.* 105f., 236f., 266 ; Blunt, *The Gospels and the Critic*, 46, 48, 69f. ; V. Taylor, *Sacrifice*, 272f ; *E.T.* xlviii. 148f. (Jan. 1937) and lii. 322f (June 1941).

For you cannot consistently rejoice over Schweitzer's defeat of liberalism, and at the same time quietly ignore the positive arguments and conclusions on the strength of which he bases his claim to victory.

Since the end of the last Great War (1914–18), the arena has been entered by two fresh forces, which have indeed contributed help along certain lines, but which—because more value has been claimed for them than they really possess—have in some ways increased rather than assuaged the already-existing confusion. I refer to Form-Criticism and the Barthian Theology.

Form-Criticism investigates and classifies the various forms (parable, anecdote, miracle-story, etc.) in which the material included in the Gospels has been preserved, compares these forms with one another and with the analogous forms found in non-Christian literature, and endeavours in this way to give an account of that obscure process by which oral tradition, devotional imagination, and primitive records bridged the gap between Jesus' own lifetime and the composition of the canonical Gospels. Much has been done by Form-Critics to illuminate this dark period of development : but it must be remembered that the conclusions they reach are in the nature of the case bound to be almost wholly conjectural, and are consequently very precarious. When one asks how exactly the new study has helped us to distinguish better between factual record and legendary accretion, the answer is meagre and disappointing. Its most eminent exponents differ very widely among themselves as to the historical inferences to be drawn from it, and some of them use it to defend an extremely-sceptical attitude to the Gospel-records generally.[1]

The advent of the Barthian Theology has been of value in guarding us against the danger of ignoring or under-estimating the numinous and transcendental elements inherent in the Christian religion : but as regards the quest for a better understanding of the historical Jesus, it has hitherto proved a hindrance rather than a help. Though laying stress on the historical character of the Incarnation, atoning Death, and Resurrection of Christ, as ensuring the particularity of these

[1] Good accounts of the work of the Form-Critics and of the literature dealing with it are accessible in B. S. Easton's *The Gospel before the Gospels* (1928), V. Taylor's *The Formation of the Gospel Tradition* (1935), E. F. Scott's *The Validity of the Gospel Record* (1938), and E. B. Redlich's *Form Criticism* (1939). Cf. also Lightfoot, *Hist. and Interp.* 27–56 ; Blunt, *The Gospels and the Critic*, 54–68 ; and Dodd, *Parables*, 40f. n.2 (". . . I do not think it has yet provided us with a trustworthy criterion for the historical value of the reports in the Gospels . . ."), and *Hist. and the Gosp.* 78ff.

vital moments in the Gospel-message,[1] it takes little interest in historical evidence as usually understood and still less in the character and doings of Jesus as a human being.[2] Its strong antipathy to liberalism and all that liberalism stands for renders it unfavourable to any painstaking investigation of Jesus' life and teaching, except in so far as such investigation can be used to reveal the untenability of all liberal conclusions or to bring out the close conformity of Jesus' teaching with the theological opinions of Dr. Karl Barth.

Allusion has just been made to the unnatural blessing bestowed by certain conservative writers on Schweitzer as their great stand-by against liberalism. We have yet another exemplification of the truth of Trinculo's remark, that " misery acquaints a man with strange bed-fellows ", in the extremely-negative critical position taken up by certain Barthian scholars. Drs. Karl Ludwig Schmidt and Rudolf Bultmann, two of the most sceptical of the Form-Critics, have strong sympathy with Barthian views.[3] And there is discernible in the writings and utterances of certain other doctrinally-conservative theologians a growing sympathy with the stand-point of Barthianism, an increasing tendency to use its catch-words, and a willingness to make, like the Barthians, generous concessions to the negative arguments of Form-Critics and other radical theorists. Whether these concessions can be harmonized with the transcendental Christology maintained by those who make them, I do not wish now to discuss. I wish only to repeat that, whatever be the merits or demerits of the Barthian Theology generally, one cannot but regard its attitude to the historical Jesus as erroneous and regrettable, while the use of Form-Criticism in order to demonstrate the legendary character of the greater part of the Synoptic narrative seems wholly unjustified.

Dr. Vincent Taylor recently stated at the conclusion of an article summarizing the work of the last fifty years on the

[1] Cf., e.g., Karl Barth, *Credo* (1936), 79f.
[2] See some extraordinary words used by Emil Brunner, in *The Word and the World* (1931), 87f.
[3] Cf. Schmidt's art. in *R.G.G.* iii (1929) 112--119 ; and Bultmann's *Geschichte der synoptischen Tradition* (1921, 1931), *Erforschung der synoptischen Evangelien* (1925, 1930), and *Jesus*. Bultmann expresses his distrust of nearly all that the Gospels tell us about the life and personality of Jesus : he believes however that the main lines of Jesus' *teaching* are correctly preserved, and he expounds it in a strongly-Barthian sense. For a criticism of this attitude, see Weinel in *R.G.G.* iii (1929) 166f., and V. Taylor, *Tradition*, vi, 14f., 17, 36–38, 84–87, 105–113.

8

Gospels, " We are, I believe, on the eve of fruitful developments in that study of New Testament theology for which the present generation has waited so long ".[1] The object of the present study of ' The Historic Mission of Jesus ' is to contribute in some small way to the production of these developments. There is no idea of attempting to do over again what has already been fully and competently done by others. Moreover, a painful dilemma besets any one who undertakes a fresh treatment of the subject indicated in my title. The amount of good work recently produced on the various divisions and aspects of it is so enormous that the process of garnering and utilizing its results is in danger either of omitting some important contributions or else of becoming over-loaded with literary references and distracted with side-issues. No attempt at a complete documentation therefore has been made : but possibly the author may take a little comfort from the thought that a whole life-span would barely suffice for such completeness ; and so—believing that usefulness does not necessarily depend on omniscience—he has accepted the risks involved in his limitations, and offers his work to the sympathetic scrutiny and judgment of his readers.

It may prove helpful if at this point the principles which will govern the investigation here undertaken are outlined.

The use of the literary sources will be, as far as it may be, objective. Not that it is possible for any historical inquiry to be wholly objective. Without some subjective sense as to what is possible, probable, credible, and the reverse, we could not carry through any effort to reconstruct the past : there is therefore no need for us to apologize for introducing to some extent subjective considerations. Nor can it be denied that subjective considerations always bear some impress of the " personal factor ", and that there is no absolutely-reliable rule-of-thumb whereby we can make sure that our subjective machinery of judgment will never in any way mislead us. But the discipline of historical science in general enables us to see, at least roughly, what the requirements of objectivity really involve. They involve, over and above a serious and honest desire to arrive at the truth, a laying-aside of all conscious preferences as to the results to which the investigation shall lead. In studying the eschatological teaching of Jesus, for

---

[1] *E.T.* l. 12b (Oct. 1938). In *Tradition* (21), he expresses his " belief that the task of our generation is a renewed, untiring investigation of the problems of Gospel Origins ".

instance, we must not be swayed (so far as we can help it) by a natural desire to discover that he was wholly immune from the intellectual limitations of his day and never foretold an event which did not occur. The greatness of the Christian movement and the authority of its Creeds must not be brought in to block plain and simple inferences from the Gospel-evidence as it lies before us. Just as we unhesitatingly and trustfully use our innate subjective sense of what is probable and improbable in arranging and dating our documents, in determining their original wording, in translating them from Greek into intelligible English, and in interperting their meaning by what we know of the Aramaïc language in which their ultimate sources, both oral and written, were couched, so are we fully entitled to use that same subjective apparatus in taking account of the idiom of Oriental thought and the habits of the Oriental and particularly the Jewish mind. We must not therefore assume in advance that Jesus' words will be wholly free from inconsistency and from features that may seem to us moderns highly-coloured and bizarre : nor must we evade all evidence of a certain kind by the ready plea that Jesus was " above the heads of his reporters ". The record must be allowed to speak for itself. In the needful work of sifting it, we may rightly use our sense of probability and its opposite, but we must keep that sense as free as we can from all admixture of personal preference.

In regard to the historical credibility of the Synoptic Gospels themselves, I incline to take a more conservative and trustful attitude than has prevailed in many circles since Form-Criticism became known. I realize, of course, that the comparison of one Gospel-document with another reveals the fact (which inherent probability and internal evidence in any case suggest) that the Synoptic record has in numerous places been more or less radically affected by the thoughts and needs of the Christian Church of the first century.[1] Yet I hold that the oft-adduced primary religious interest of the Evangelists, which certainly prevented them from treating their subject as objectively as a modern historian would aim at treating his, did not prevent them from seriously endeavouring to narrate what had really happened.[2] For a very large proportion of the Synoptic matter the hypothesis that it is a substantially-reliable record

[1] What Dr. Cadbury calls " modernization " is already visible in the Gospels themselves (*Peril*, 17–20, 178f.).
[2] " Their historical interest is not to be placed third or fourth, but first " (E. F. Scott, in *H.T.R.* xix. 163 [Apl. 1926]). Cf. Holtzmann, *Theol.* i. 179–182 ; H. D. A. Major in *Mission*, etc. 10f.

of what actually happened is far more likely to be true than the hypothesis that it has been piously invented in order to serve some purpose about which the early Church was concerned—and this notwithstanding the fact that a certain amount of such pious invention did take place.[1]

In regard to the structure of the Synoptic Gospels and the dates of their component parts, the present writer professes himself a grateful and whole-hearted disciple of the late Dr. B. H. Streeter. Dr. Streeter's Four-Document-Hypothesis gives a far more probable account of the facts as we find them than does any of its alternatives. There is appended to this Introduction a list of the several documents concerned, with brief notes regarding their date and character. It has not seemed necessary to enter either there or here into a discussion of the grounds on which the conclusions regarding these documents and sources are based, or to give references to the relevant literature. The interested reader can easily find ample material of this kind for himself. It will be sufficient to assure him that the conclusions here tentatively adopted are based on years of detailed study, and that the absence of discussion and documentation must not be interpreted as indicating any arbitrary dogmatism on the numerous controversial questions involved.

There are only one or two more documentary matters on which comment is needed here.

In the opinion of a large number of scholars, Mk. xiii embodies a short Jewish-Christian document, usually called " the Little Apocalypse ", which was produced in Palestine about 60–65 (some would say about 40) A.D. It is thought to have included at least those portions of Mk. xiii which foretell wars, tumults, the desecration of the Temple, tribulation, and the appearance of the Son of Man in the clouds (xiii. 7–8, 14–20, 24–27), as distinct from the warnings against false Messiahs and against persecution, which may well have come for the most part from the lips of Jesus himself. The theory cannot be pronounced impossible, despite the fact that its supporters are not in entire agreement as to the limits of the supposed document. One may plead in its favour that Mk. xiii is the only lengthy discourse included in this Gospel, and that it contains inconsistencies which render its complete unity improbable. It is not, however, easy to imagine how Mark,

---

[1] In particular, the unique character of the *parables* is strong evidence that for the most part they must have originated with Jesus himself (A. T. Cadoux, *Parables*, 13f., 43, 252f. ; Dodd, *Hist. and the Gosp.* 88f.).

writing at Rome, either could or would have incorporated in his book an alien document produced (ex hypothesi) in Judæa, possibly within a few years of the time at which he himself was writing. It is almost equally difficult to see how such a document could have been embodied in the Gospel after Mark had finished it. Moreover, some of the verses assigned to " the Little Apocalypse " have close parallels with other passages in the Gospels where the use of no such extraneous document can reasonably be suspected. It seems on the whole preferable to explain such discrepancies as the chapter contains partly by the natural tendency of Mark (as of the other evangelists) to put in close proximity to one another sayings originally spoken on quite different occasions, and partly to the tendency of the early Church to modify radically certain remembered sayings of Jesus and even to ascribe to him (without any dishonest intent) some sayings which in point of fact he never actually uttered. In any case the specific contents of the passages assigned to " the Little Apocalypse " must be treated as of somewhat doubtful authenticity.[1]

Another documentary topic demanding notice is the question of the use to be made of the Fourth Gospel. With the exception of one or two sporadic allusions, the Johannine discourses have not been utilized in the ensuing discussion. It is perfectly clear that, as it stands, the Fourth Gospel (which, contradicting the Synoptists, represents the Messianic claim of Jesus as publicly known from the commencement of the Ministry) cannot possibly be the work of one of the Twelve. Taken as a whole, the discourses it ascribes to Jesus differ strikingly, both in subject-matter and in style, from the earlier and better-attested Synoptic discourses, and to a considerable extent resemble in both respects those portions of the book in which the Evangelist is quite clearly speaking for himself and not even professing to be reporting the Lord's words. Here and there we find him apparently borrowing a saying from one or other of the Synoptists ; and it is by no means impossible that there may be preserved, especially among the numerous short pithy sayings which he describes Jesus as uttering, some other

---

[1] Cf., among others, Stanton, *G.H.D.* ii. 115–121 ; Moffatt, *I.L.N.T.* 205, 207–209, 221, 225 ; Charles, *Crit. Hist.* (1913), 379–385 ; Meyer, *Ursprung*, i. 125–130 ; Bartlet, *St. Mark*, 348–351, 369 ; Rawlinson, *St. Mark*, 179–182 ; Burkitt in *H.C.L.M.K.* 245f. = *Jesus Christ*, etc. 49f. ; Manson, *Teaching*, 260–263 , 275 n. 5, and in *Mission*, etc. 616f, 628f. ; Major in *Mission*, etc. 158–161 ; Busch, *Zum Verständnis der synoptischen Eschatologie ; Markus 13 neu untersucht* (Gütersloh, 1938) ; L. O. Bristol in *E.T.* li. 301–303 (Mar. 1940).

genuine words of his. But we have no other means than guess-work of separating such genuine sayings from their context ; and the possibility of their existence does not alter the fact that the Johannine discourses as a whole are quite clearly Johannine interpretation, not reports of Jesus' own words. True it is that certain recent movements in criticism have challenged the soundness of refusing to treat the discourses as, like the Synoptic sayings, sources for Jesus' teaching : but the arguments advanced strike the present writer as singularly unconvincing. Like Thucydides and most other ancient historians in furnishing the speeches of historical characters, like Plato composing the Socratic Dialogues, and like certain Christian hymn-writers in framing words addressed by Christ to the believer, the Fourth Evangelist has quite clearly given himself a free hand. He has made use of sundry historical situations in which he knew Jesus to have from time to time found himself, in order to put into his mouth utterances of varying length, which he had no authority for believing that he had ever actually said, but which he felt to set forth vital and unquestionable Christian truth. That being so, it seems useless to try to discover real sayings of Jesus in his Gospel.[1] We must, of course, take account of the significant fact that Jesus lived such a life that seventy years after his death his followers were willing to put such discourses into his mouth. That fact throws light on the problem of his life and person ; but it is indirect light, and the investigation of the use we are to make of it belongs to another department of inquiry than the one on which we are at present engaged.

Another movement of modern criticism is sometimes appealed to in this connexion—I mean, the strong feeling that Mark, the earliest of the canonical Evangelists, told his story from the standpoint of so high a Christology that the old clean-cut between the Synoptics and the Fourth Gospel, as between history and theological interpretation, ought no longer to be recognized.[2] Those who appeal to this recent movement of

---

[1] For a moderate defence of the theory that the Johannine discourses contain much of the real teaching of Jesus, see W. F. Howard, *The Fourth Gospel in Recent Crit.* etc. (1931), 215–229, 267–270, and in *E.T.* xlvi. 486–491 (Aug. 1935) : also V. Taylor, *Sacrifice*, 80, 195, 218–220, 238–249, 270. Cf. however Bacon, *Matthew*, 428 ; Lietzmann, *Beginnings of the Christ. Church* (1937), 297f. ; Dodd in *Hibbert Journ.* xxxvi. 473 (Apl. 1938).

[2] Cf. Hoskyns and Davey, *Riddle*, 240 (" . . . is what he [the Fourth Evangelist] says so different from what Mark had said or from what is involved in the whole material which composed the earlier Tradition ? ") ; Lightfoot, *Hist. and Interp.* passim, esp. 98, 208–225.

scholarship ought, however, to realize that its tendency is not to increase our sense of the reliability of the Johannine reports, but to decrease our sense of the reliability of the Synoptic reports. However that may be, the undoubted community of interest which characterizes all the four Gospels does not suffice to close up the palpable qualitative gulf which yawns between the Synoptic and the Johannine versions of Jesus' teaching.

A word only is needed by way of reference to the so-called "Agrapha", i.e., sayings attributed to Jesus elsewhere than in the canonical Gospels. These are found partly in the early Apocryphal Gospels, partly scattered up and down early Christian literature, partly in dubious or ungenuine variant readings in old manuscripts of the Gospels : one of them occurs in the genuine text of Acts (xx. 35). As we are almost wholly without the means of testing the genuineness of these supposed sayings otherwise than by their inherent suitability (which is often very hard to judge), and as most of them are undoubtedly not genuine, no attempt has been made here to use more than a very few of them.[1]

In the drawing of this broad distinction between the Synoptic Gospels on the one hand and the Fourth Gospel, the Apocryphal Gospels, and the Agrapha on the other, as it should not be thought that the possible existence of genuine sayings of Jesus in the latter group is denied, so it should not be supposed that the presence of a certain amount of fictitious material in the former is forgotten. Nevertheless the line of distinction referred to is justified by the difference in the general character of the material on this side of it and on that. The task of distinguishing between the more and the less reliable portions of the Synoptic record will to some extent be facilitated by our designation of the documentary source of each passage quoted and by the consideration of the character of these several sources as described in the appendix to this Introduction. The collection of the evidence on each point is meant to be complete, so far at least as the Synoptic Gospels are concerned. The less-reliable testimonia thus included will be readily recognizable as such, and will serve in a subordinate way to confirm or clarify what rests on stronger evidence. For it needs to be borne in mind throughout, that even a historic-

[1] The literature dealing with the Agrapha is extensive, and includes that dealing with the important early apocryphal *Gospel according to the Hebrews*. Suffice it here to refer to Preuschen, *Antilegomena*, 2–9, 22–31, 135–141, 151–155 ; Menzies in H.*D.B.* extra vol. 338b–343a ; Ropes, *ibid*. 343a–352b; James, *Apocr. N.T.* 1–8, 10–12, 25–37.

ally-ungenuine report of what Jesus said may yet have some historical value for us, as revealing what his words were at a very early date understood to mean, and what perhaps they do in point of fact imply.[1]

To turn now from the documents to the facts of which they speak, reference must next be made to certain pre-suppositions on which it is here suggested the Gospel-story ought to be studied.

It will be provisionally assumed that the primary interest of Jesus was with the actual lives and needs of the individuals and communities of his own day. He was, before everything else, a real man, " made like unto his brethren ", with a human heart, a human understanding, human passions and sympathies, human faith in God. Those among whom he dwelt were leading real human lives ; their virtues and vices, their joys and sorrows, their needs and dangers, were such as belong to the race at large. Jesus' chief concern therefore was with beings of flesh and blood ; and his plans and efforts had reference in the first place to them and their needs. In particular, he had to consider his fellowmen as placed in a certain historical situation ; and it was primarily with them in that situation that he undertook to deal.

This concern with the special, as a feature of the outlook and activity of Jesus, needs to be constantly kept in mind, the recognition of it being threatened from two quarters.

The normal Christian view of Jesus as the Saviour of the whole human race is indeed an essential item in the content of the Gospel. The Father-God revealed by and in him is the only true God, the only worthy object of the faith of all mankind. No revelation concerning Him can ever over-ride that manifestation of His righteousness and His love which is vouchsafed to us in Jesus Christ our Lord. But the eternal truth of this conviction does not imply that, within the limits of his earthly life, Jesus consciously dealt only with the eternal and the universal, to the exclusion of urgent issues that lay right at his own door and pressingly beset the men of his own race and time.[2] The service he rendered to them was indeed founded on eternal truth, and his fulfilment of it was fraught with

[1] Cf. Winstanley, *Future*, 125 (à propos of " the Little Apocalypse "—see above, pp. 11f.) ; V. Taylor, *Sacrifice*, 81 : also, from a more sceptical point of view, D. W. Riddle in *J.R.* xiv (1934) 157f., 167.
[2] Cf. Liberty, *Political Relations*, 2f. ; Simkhovitch, *Understanding of Jes.* 2–4 ; Bultmann, *Jesus*, 14 f. ; A. T. Cadoux, *Parables*, 26, 50, 56, 58f. ; Dodd, *Parables*, 24–28, 135 n.1, 195, 197 ; *Doctrine in the Ch. of Engl.* (1938), 32.

eternal consequences for us all. But its eternal and universal significance does not blot out of existence the temporary and particular setting which was its vehicle. When a lately-deceased Roman Catholic wrote, " It is extraordinary how very little there is in the recorded words of Christ that ties Him at all to His own time ",[1] he was overlooking the important fact that the great work which Jesus did " for us men and for our salvation " he did as a Jew of the first century, grappling directly and in the first place with the needs of those in the midst of whom he lived.

A second circumstance which often obscures from Gospel-students the human realities of the situation is their knowledge of the wide prevalence of eschatological beliefs among the Jews of Jesus' own day and the certainty that his ideas were to some extent affected by those beliefs.[2] For the purpose of estimating, however, the extent to which his thinking was influenced or controlled by contemporary eschatology, it has to be borne in mind that, prevalent as this latter was, we have no warrant for believing that it was either universally accepted or sharply defined. The greatest possible uncertainty and variety of opinion existed as to what precisely was destined to happen and in what sequence the several events would occur. A modern scholar's " systematische Darstellung " includes the following paragraph-headings : Final Oppression and Confusion, Elijah as Forerunner, Appearance of the Messiah, Final Onslaught of the Hostile Powers, Destruction of the Hostile Powers, Restoration of Jerusalem, Assembling of the Dispersed, the Kingdom of Glory in Palestine, Renewal of the World, General Resurrection, Last Judgment, Eternal Blessedness and Condemnation : an Appendix deals with the idea of a Suffering Messiah (almost certainly a post-Christian conception).[3] But this account is " systematic " only in the sense that the scholar in question has scientifically classified the evidence for us. There was nothing systematic about the way in which these items in the programme were regarded by

[1] G. K. Chesterton, quoted in *Times Lit. Suppt.* 30 June 1932, 472. Cf. also Bennett, *Social Salv.* 78.

[2] Good accounts of Jewish eschatological literature and ideas are available in Charles's articles in H.*D.B.* i. 741b–749b, and in *E.Bi.* 213–250, 1335–1372, and his *Crit. Hist.* (1913), 1–361 ; Schürer, *G.J.V.* ii. 579–651 ; W. V. Hague in *J.T.S.* xii. 57–98 (Oct. 1910) ; Holtzmann, *Theol.* i. 44–47, 85–110 ; Strack-Billerbeck i. 6–11, 63–74, 467f., 481–485, 585f., 597, 602f., 747, 835, 949–961, ii. 273–299, iv. 779–1212 ; Bousset, *Relig. des Jud.* (1926), 202–301 ; Gloege, *Reich Gottes*, 29–48 ; Moore, *Judaism*, ii. 277–395, iii. 195–206 ; Manson, *Teaching*, 151, 158, 246–260 ; Volz, *Die Eschatologie der jüdischen Gemeinde*, etc. (ed. 1935).

[3] Schürer, as in last note.

the Jews themselves.[1] Certain of them (not infrequently the very idea of a personal Messiah) are completely missing from some Jewish forecasts.[2] It is this total lack of unanimity and uniformity which seems to rule out absolutely any such theory as Schweitzer's, according to which Jesus' mind is supposed to have been dominated by a fixed, though purely imaginary, apocalyptic programme.[3] To say this is not to deny that his mind was to some extent influenced by the eschatological interests and thoughts of his people.[4] To what extent it was so influenced, only a painstaking study of the actual evidence can tell us. The investigation is rendered harder than it would otherwise be by the fact that our several informants were themselves affected by the eschatological outlook and that in different degrees.[5] The view here urged as inherently probable is that, in the case of Jesus, eschatological beliefs were strictly secondary to the practical situations he had to face and the personal human realities with which he had to deal. In thinking about his task, his mind naturally found a place for this and that general eschatological conception : but to suppose that he faced life with the idea that eschatology had told him precisely what world-events were destined to occur, and when and in what order they would occur, and that his whole life and thought turned on such foreknowledge, seems to me intrinsically unlikely and not borne out by the actual evidence.[6] On the same ground one must reject the view that he shaped his course and framed his speech at every turn—that he even forced on his own death—with the main intention of fulfilling this or that supposedly-Messianic passage in the Old Testament.[7] Had he done so, he

[1] Cf. Moore, *Judaism*, i. 162, 170. I doubt whether Schweitzer's phrase " dies oder jenes der Räder der eschatologischen Maschinerie " (*L.J.F.* 249 = *Quest*, 255) is justified.

[2] Cf. Lightfoot, *Hist. and Interp.* 59f.

[3] Cf. D.C. Simpson in *H.C.L.M.K.* 165 ; C.C. McCown in *J.R.* xvi (1936) 36–39.

[4] Cadbury rightly urges (*Peril*, 69f.) that Jesus would never have roused the opposition that he did, had there not been much in common between himself and his opponents.

[5] Cf. Holtzmann, *Theol.* i. 417 ; Streeter in *Stud. in the Syn. Prob.* 423–436 ; Sanday in *Hibbert Journ.* x. 90–94 (Oct. 1911) ; Moffatt, *Theol. of the Gospels*, 72–75. H. Preisker has an interesting art. in *Z.N.W.* xx (1921) 199–205 on the extent to which the Synoptists knew and used the Jewish apocalypses.

[6] Cf. Holtzmann, *Theol.* i. 164–166.

[7] That largely is the interpretation of his life given by the late Sir E. Hoskyns in *Myst. Christi*, 67–89, and *Riddle*, 84, 87–94, 160. Per contra, cf. Holtzmann as in last n. ; also *Times Lit. Suppt.* 16 July 1931, 556 (critical review of Hoskyns and Davey, *Riddle*) ; Manson in *Mission*, etc. 477 (" That Jesus Himself . . . cared very much about fulfilling the current Jewish Messianic expectations, is most unlikely "). See also below, pp. 249–251.

would surely have reduced his great redemptive contest to childish and meaningless stage-play. His choices in word and deed doubtless recalled to him at times what looked like Scriptural foreshadowings of them ; doubtless they even seemed to be at times the execution of a providentially-ordained destiny. But such interpretations of them were, I believe, strictly secondary to the practical moral and religious demands of the situation which faced him from time to time. The manifest originality of his mind and the stern realism of his aspirations constrain us to assert no less than this.

Two consequences seem to follow from this priority in Jesus' life of the practical demands of the situation. Full evidence for them will be furnished later in the body of the work (see below, pp. 163ff., 183ff., 266ff.) : at the moment, however, it is needful to mention them, because the recognition of them is not general among New-Testament scholars, and yet it will affect very profoundly any reconstruction we may make of the purpose and forecast of Jesus. The two facts in question are these : firstly, Jesus' expectation, at the beginning of his ministry, that he would be accepted and followed as Messiah by Israel, not repudiated and martyred ; and secondly, his deep interest and concern over the dangerous mutual attitude of Israel and Rome, and his strenuous effort to avert the threatened clash of arms between them.

It is in every way probable that the ensuing investigation of the teaching of Jesus will raise extremely-serious questions in the minds of many of my fellow-Christians. The issues involved have, in fact, entered into my own spiritual pilgrimage in a rather special way. In my early twenties I found refuge from spiritual negation and despair in the teaching of Jesus as presented in ' The Twentieth Century New Testament ' translation of the Synoptic Gospels. The detailed study of that teaching, coupled with the fellowship of others in practical Christian work, brought me a faith in God for the continuance of which I can never be sufficiently thankful. But it gave me more than a religious foundation : I got from it an ethic to act by. The reading of Tolstoy confirmed me in my belief that I had not misunderstood the teaching of Jesus. Like many other Christians, I took it for granted that a complete and sufficient social ethic lay before us in the Synoptic sayings of Jesus, very little (if at all) below the surface. I was vaguely aware of attendant difficulties, both practical and theoretical ; but they did not trouble me, and I even became a little impatient with those who thrust them upon my notice. Not long after the commencement of my more technical theological studies, I wrote for a College-prize an essay on ' The Eschatological Teaching of Jesus in the Synoptic Gospels ', wherein, by the lavish use of the plea " Jesus above the heads of his reporters " and of E. Haupt's and G. B. Stevens's methods of interpretation, I found the Master's words free from all admixture of human error, and fully consonant at every point with modern scientific and historical knowledge. For many years after that, I was fully prepared to argue for the direct application of his teaching to modern ethical problems, in particular the problem of war and violence, and to defend in detail the pacifist solution as both historically Christian and morally sound. Later on, I learned to face more frankly the conditions and limitations from within which the teaching of Jesus was delivered, and I strove to work out a theory of his ethical and religious authority as Lord which would not involve a tacit evasion of critical problems. I had come to realize very clearly that, whatever the consequences might be, the relevant facts of history in their entirety must be honestly faced. Perhaps that is one of the simple moral lessons which Jesus himself constrains us to learn—a passionate love of truth for truth's sake. Such a love is by no means the whole of Christianity, but it is a very essential item in it.

My endeavours to deal truthfully with the history and authority of Jesus brought me into occasional collision with some of my Christian friends, though I was encouraged by the approval of others. Still more recently the need for a return to the Jesus of History has come home to me with fresh clarity and force, as being the only means of conserving certain religious and ethical values which the traditional Christology (unintentionally, no doubt) threatens to obscure. Now I take up again, as I did thirty years ago, the problem of the eschatological teaching in the Synoptic Gospels. I do not now, as I did then, approach it with the hope that I shall find all the details of Jesus' teaching to be credible according to the modern standards of scientific truth, still less with the subconscious intention of pressing his thoughts into any modern mould. I am more prepared than I was to find that we cannot to-day just take over for ourselves as it stands the whole of the teaching he is recorded and may be believed to have given. On the other hand, two considerations encourage me to go forward in good heart. One is that, whatever else may be uncertain, this is certain—that God approves of our quest for truth at all costs, and may be trusted to see to it that that quest brings us nearer to Him, and never parts us from Him. The other is that Jesus' saving power, though in large measure mediated through his recorded words, rests ultimately on some deeper foundation, which it is very hard for us to discover and is beyond our power to define, but which links a blessing with every real advance in our knowledge of his earthly life, even though such advance may at times be fraught with some surprise and pain.

I ask the indulgence of my readers for having thus waxed to some extent autobiographical. It seemed the directest means of indicating the view-point taken throughout this book. The aim of the book is not to solve the deep problems of Christology, but only to contribute some materials for solving them in the form of a clarification of certain aspects of our Lord's teaching, along with an assessment of the historical trustworthiness of the Gospel-reports of its various component elements. If at the close of it some few elementary conclusions suggest themselves in those parts of the fields of ethics and theology which lie just beyond the province of history proper, the statement of them will constitute the furthest reach of my hopes and expectations.

APPENDIX TO INTRODUCTION

(See above, p. 11.)

Q = a collection of Jesus' sayings and discourses (including an account of John the Baptist and one or two incidents, but no Passion-story), probably composed in Aramaïc by Matthew the Apostle at Antioch in Syria between 30 and 50 A.D. Two slightly-differing Greek versions (or editions of one Greek version) of Q were used in the composition of our Gospels of Luke and ' Matthew '. Passages common to these two Gospels, but not drawn from Mark, were taken from Q. Being the work of a personal follower of Jesus, Q possesses extremely-high historical authority.

M = a collection of Jesus' sayings and discourses and of stories concerning him, compiled at Jerusalem about 55–60 A.D. by the leaders of the Jewish-Christian Church in that city, who disapproved of the distinctively-Pauline version of the Gospel. Its origin gives it considerable authority ; but this is very often impaired by its anti-Pauline bias, by an exaggerated taste for the marvellous, and by an uncritical eagerness to match the Gospel-story with Old-Testament prophecy. Passages peculiar to our Gospel of ' Matthew ', which are not simply editorial, presumably come mostly from M.

L = the narrative and teaching-matter (including a complete Passion-story) peculiar to the Gospel of Luke (other than merely-editorial touches). It was probably collected in Greek by Luke himself, when staying at Cæsarea during Paul's imprisonment there, 57–59 A.D. As the fruit of personal inquiry in Palestine at this date, L possesses high historical value. The first draft of Luke's Gospel (" Proto-Luke ") consisted of a combination of Q and L.

Mk. = the existing Gospel of Mark, written in Greek at Rome about 66–67 A.D. by John Mark, who had earlier been the companion both of Paul and of Peter. It was based on the author's recollection of narratives and sayings reported by

Peter, perhaps also on certain written documents (see, e.g., above, pp. 11f.). As reflecting Peter's personal recollections, it has high authority; yet having been for the most part written down after Peter's death by one who was not himself a disciple of Jesus, and who had strongly-marked theological interests, it is at certain points misleading.

Lk. = the existing Gospel of Luke, written in Greek about 80 A.D., in Greece (Boeotia ?) or possibly at Ephesus, by Luke the physician and the former travel-companion of Paul. He fashioned it by inserting nearly the whole of Mark's Gospel in large batches at select points in his already-existing draft, " Proto-Luke " (see above, under L), and by prefixing to it the birth- and infancy-narratives of John the Baptist and Jesus.

l is used in the present work to designate editorial touches from the hand of Luke. See also below, under m.

Mt. = the existing Gospel of ' Matthew ', written about 85 A.D. at Antioch in Syria. It was composed in Greek, and was not a translation from a Hebrew or Aramaïc original. It is the work, not of Matthew the Apostle, nor of any other eye-witness of Jesus, but of a learned Jewish-Christian, who wished to reconcile the two parties which looked to James of Jerusalem and to Paul respectively, by setting forth *Peter* as the leading Apostle. He took the Gospel of Mark as his framework, prefixing to it his special birth- and infancy-stories, and weaving into it large portions of Q and M, which he re-grouped at will and often conflated with one another and with Mark. His historical authority, as distinct from that of his sources, is decidedly low, for he constantly evinces a willingness to abandon historical accuracy in the interests of edification.

m is used in the present work to designate editorial touches from the hand of this final compiler of Mt. Both m and l thus sometimes indicate, not the whole verse referred to, but only the word or words in it relevant to the topic under consideration.

OTHER EXPLANATIONS

In quoting from the Gospels, I have translated direct from the Greek, bracketing words which are needed in English, but which have nothing corresponding to them in the original.

Passages occuring in Mk., and reproduced from Mk. in Lk. and Mt., are translated from the *Marcan* wording ; Q-passages are translated from Lk. or Mt., according as the one or the other seems to give the more original version. References to the parallels are always added ; but the sign used to introduce them (=) should not be understood to mean that the verbal equivalence is exact : it is often only approximate. Verbal differences between the different Synoptic versions of a saying are ignored, unless they are significant for the point at issue.

Here and there I have preferred to paraphase briefly rather than furnish a direct translation. In such cases, of course, inverted commas are not used.

It must be borne in mind throughout that, where a saying is not explicitly and closely linked with a particular incident in the Gospels, we can rarely be sure of its occasion and context.

Sayings described as having been spoken by Jesus after his Resurrection must necessarily, on account of the special character of the post-Resurrection narratives, be regarded as historically more dubious, on the whole, than sayings reported to belong to the time before his death on the Cross.

In the case of every Gospel-passage quoted, what has seemed after investigation the most probable original reading has been followed. Textual problems are, however, not discussed ; and reference to them is made in a few cases only, where the adoption of a particular variant might otherwise cause perplexity.

Each chapter opens with a summary of its conclusions, set out in bold-faced type, and divided into numbered clauses corresponding to the numbered sections of the rest of the chapter. It is hoped that this device will assist the reader to keep his hand on the thread of the argument. The categorical form in which these summaries are worded is not intended to imply a claim to have authoritatively settled all disputed questions, but is adopted only for the purpose of putting in as clear and simple a form as possible the constructive conclusions reached.

PART ONE

THE BRINGER OF THE KINGDOM OF GOD

As is well known, the great theme of Jesus' teaching was the Kingdom of God. It is not, however, proposed to begin with that theme, because back of it lies the question of his own person, character, rank, and function. It was his personal presence which involved the presence or nearness of the Kingdom.[1] Part One of the book will therefore be devoted to a consideration of Jesus' teaching about himself. In regard to the title here chosen for it, it is true that Jesus is nowhere in the Gospels said to bring the Kingdom of God ; and to speak of him bringing it has by certain scholars been pronounced erroneous, on the ground, apparently, of his having explicitly ascribed the coming (or giving) of the Kingdom to God Himself.[2] Nonetheless it is submitted that the designation here used is not inaccurate, since Jesus was in point of fact the person through whom the Kingdom became a new reality among men.[3] The appearance to the contrary rests only on the familiar Jewish custom of reverently ascribing the cause of all things—particularly all good things—to God, a habit of thought by no means inconsistent with a vigorous sense of personal responsibility and initiative. The failure of several modern scholars to assess this habit of thought accurately has, as I hope to show later, vitiated their interpretation of the teaching of Jesus at more than one point (see below, pp. 43, 66 n. 1, 178f. [5], 188f. [7], 203–207).

[1] Cf. H.-D. Wendland, *Eschatologie*, 200–211, 247–249.
[2] Cf. Burkitt, *Earliest Sources*, 63 (" The Christ does not bring in the Kingdom,—that is the work of God Himself ; . . . "), and in *H.C.L.M.K.* 205 = *Jesus Christ*, etc. 8 (similar) ; Otto, *Kingdom*, 103f. (" It is not Jesus who brings the kingdom— a conception which was completely foreign to Jesus himself ; on the contrary, the kingdom brings him with it . . ."). This passage in Otto is quoted with approval by Dodd (*Parables*, 45 n. 1), Manson (in *Mission*, etc. 378), and Flew (*Church*, 127 ; cf. 73).
[3] Dr. Dodd thus rightly speaks of " His work as bearer of the Kingdom of God " (*Hist. and the Gosp.* 129).

CHAPTER I

THE SON OF GOD

(1) Jesus regularly spoke of God as the Father of the Disciples and the Jews generally whom he was addressing, (2) and of their Sonship to Him as a privileged status to which, by fulfilling certain ethical conditions, they might attain. (3) He taught them to use in prayer the more intimate and homely form " Father ", instead of (or as well as) the customary Jewish address " Our Father". (4) He also thought and spoke of himself as " Son of God ", (5) frequently referred to God as " My Father ", (6) and addressed Him intimately as " Father " in prayer. (7) But he never said " Our Father " on behalf of himself and others : (8) on the contrary, he sometimes spoke of God and himself as " the Father " and " the Son ", as if he were the Son of God in some absolute or unique sense.

(1) The formula " thy Father " or " your Father " (once " their Father "), with or without some adjunct referring to " heaven ", appears in the following documents :

Q : Lk. vi. 36 = Mt. v. 48 ; Lk. xii. 30 = Mt. vi. 32. The following may possibly have belonged to Q : Mt. v. 45 (but probably M or m ; contrast Lk. vi. 35) ; Mt. vi. 26 (unless m ; contrast Lk. xii. 24) ; Mt. vii. 11 (but probably m ; contrast Lk. xi. 13) ; Mt. x. 29 (unless m ; contrast Lk. xii. 6) ; Mt. xviii. 14 (unless we should read " my Father " : but possibly M or m ; contrast Lk. xv. 10).

M (in addition to the possibilities just noticed) : Mt. v. 16 ; Mt. vi. 1, 4, 6 (bis), 18 (bis) ; Mt. vi. 8 ; Mt. vi. 14, 15 (unless we should assign these to m ; see below, under Mk.) ; Mt. xiii. 43 (unless m) ; Mt. xxiii. 9 : by implication also, the parable in Mt. xxi. 28–31.

L : Lk. xii. 32 (but possibly l) : by implication also, the parable in Lk. xv. 11–32.

Mk. xi. 25, on which Mt. vi. 14,.15, if not drawn from M, are based.

m (in addition to the possibilities noted above under Q and M) : Mt. x. 20 (contrast Mk. xiii. 11, Lk. xii. 12, and Lk. xxi. 15).

The phrase " the Father ", in the third person, with or

27

without reference to " heaven ", appears once probably in Q (Lk. xi. 13 : the " your Father " in Mt. vii. 11 is probably from m, just possibly from Q), once in a very doubtful reading of a verse in an extract from M (Mt. xxv. 41 : see below, p. 32 top), and in Lucan two post-Resurrection sayings in Acts i. 4, 7.

The conception of God as the Father of Israelites was, of course, no novelty :[1] but it will be better to hold over any discussion of its meaning in the teaching of Jesus, until we have the rest of the evidence before us.

(2) The evidence regarding the attainment of Divine sonship consists of three passages :

Q (also M ?) : Lk. vi. 35 = Mt. v. 45 : the wording is different in the two parallels, and Mt. may be conflating Q and M, but the notion that those who love their enemies " will be ", or " may become ", sons of God must have been represented in some form in Q.

M : Mt. v. 9 : " Happy are the peacemakers, for they shall be called ' sons of God ' ".

Mk. iii. 34f. = Lk. viii. 21 = Mt. xii. 49f. : Jesus declares that whoever does the Will of God (Who in m is here referred to as " my Father in heaven ") is his " brother and sister and mother ".

It seems arbitary, in view of the last-quoted passage from Mk., to refer this Divine sonship (which the evidence directly connects with obedience and ethical likeness to God) to the state of the good after death, because these are called in Lk. xx. 36 (l, possibly L) " sons of God, being sons of the Resurrection ".[2] With Jesus, Divine sonship is clearly a moral attainment : it is not, as with the Stoïcs, a natural possession of all men, whatever their character, however true it be that it is a *potential* reality for all.[3]

(3) The Lucan version of the Lord's Prayer begins " Father " (Lk. xi. 2 L), the Matthæan version " Our Father " (Mt. vi. 9 M). Mk. xiv. 36, Gal. iv. 6, and Rom. viii. 15 make it clear that the Aramaïc equivalent of the nominative ὁ πατήρ, when used as a vocative, was אבא (Abba) ; and the same must be true of the actual vocative πάτερ here used by Luke. Attention

---

[1] Cf. Dalman, *W.J.* 184–189, 268–273 ; Bousset, *Relig. des Jud.* (1926), 377f. ; Moore, *Judaism*, i. 116, ii. 201–211, iii. 190f. ; D. C. Simpson in *H.C.L.M.K.* 162f. ; Manson, *Teaching*, 37, 89–93, and in *Mission*, etc. 581 ; Strack-Billerbeck i. 371f., 392–396, 919.

[2] Cf. Windisch in *Z.N.W.* xxiv (1925) 241 ; Easton, *Christ in the Gospels*, 134f.

[3] Cf. Ben Sirach iv. 10 : Stevens, *Theol. of the N.T.* 70 f. ; Bultmann, *Jesus*, 177f.

has recently been drawn to the interesting fact that this form "Abba" was an intimate and homely form of address (such as would be used by children in Jewish homes : cf. Lk. xv. 18, 21 L), and was therefore, as a form usable in prayer to God, mostly avoided as unduly familiar, in favour of the more customary formula " Our Father ". Jesus apparently envisaged a closer fellowship between man and God than did his Jewish contemporaries.[1]

(4) That Jesus thought and spoke of himself as son of God in the sense in which every pious Israelite was a son of God is involved a fortiori in his claim to be " Son " in a unique sense, and is also implied in his frequent designation of God as " my Father " and his occasional designation of the Disciples as his " brothers " (Mk. iii. 34f. = Lk. viii. 21 = Mt. xii. 49f. ; Mt. xxv. 40 M ; Mt. xxviii. 10 M ; John xx. 17). Yet it is hard to find a single passage in the Gospels in which he is certainly called " a son of God " in this general way. The clearest case is the exclamation of the centurion at the Cross, " Truly this man was God's son" (or "a son of God ": Mk. xv. 39 = Mt. xxvii. 54) ; and even here the words *could* mean "the Son ",[2] and the Evangelists doubtless understood them in this sense, and read into them a Gentile's confession of Jesus' Messiahship (cf. Lk. i. 32, 35 fin.). In every other instance, even where the definite article is not used in the Greek, the reference is to Jesus' unique Sonship, in his capacity as Messiah. We shall discuss this reference later : but for the sake of simplicity and completeness, the evidence is summarized here.

We begin with three important Marcan passages.

Immediately after his baptism, Jesus felt aware of the descent of God's Spirit into him, and heard a voice from heaven, saying to him, " Thou art My Son, the Beloved ; in thee I delight " (Mk. i. 10f. = Mt. iii. 16f.). The term " the Beloved " is almost equivalent to " the Only ", and was a current Messianic appellation. There are some grounds for believing that, in the Lucan parallel (Lk. iii. 22 Q ?), the original wording ran, " My Son art thou ; to-day have I begotten thee "—a quotation of Psalm ii. 7.[3] If that be so,

[1] Cf. Strack-Billerbeck i. 919, ii. 49f. ; A. L. Williams in *J.T.S.* xxxi. 42–47 (Oct. 1929) ; Manson in *Christian Worship*, 41f., and in *Mission*, etc. 460. Montefiore concedes (*Hibbert Journ.* xxviii. 104 [Oct. 1929]) that Jesus spoke more habitually about the Fatherhood of God than did the Rabbis.

[2] As Wellhausen points out (*Mc.* 132f.).

[3] The case is best stated and argued by Streeter, *Four Gospels*, 143, 188, 276 ; but the originality of this Western reading is not universally accepted (see, e.g., Creed, *St. Luke*, 57f.).

it is probable that we have here the version given in the document Q, on which Luke (who in other respects here shows independence of Mark) is drawing.

At the Transfiguration, a voice from heaven says, " This is My Son, the Beloved ; listen ye to him " (Mk. ix. 7 = Lk. ix. 35 = Mt. xvii. 5 : Luke, possibly employing another source beside Mark, substitutes for " the Beloved " " the Chosen ", another quasi-Messianic title [cf. Lk. xxiii. 35 L ?], while m adds from the story of the Baptism the words " in whom I delight ").

I submit that it is natural and justifiable to interpret the words said to have been spoken from heaven at both Baptism and Transfiguration [1] as expressing the consciousness of Jesus himself.

During his hearing before the Sanhedrin, Jesus is directly asked by the High Priest, " Art thou the Messiah, the Son of the Blessed ? ", i.e., of God, and answers, " I am " (Mk. xiv. 61f. = Mt. xxvi. 63f. [m substitutes " God " for " Blessed ", and " Thou hast said (it) " for " I am "] : Lk. xxii. 66–70 gives a rather different version, but one which like the Marcan implies Jesus' acknowledgement that he is " the Messiah " and " the Son of God ").

This Marcan evidence is supplemented by Q, not only in its conjectural parallel in Lk. iii. 22 to Mk. i. 11, but in the story of the Temptation—another reflection, surely, of Jesus' own mind—where he is twice approached by Satan with the words, " If thou art God's Son " or " a Son of God " (Lk. iv. 3 = Mt. iv. 3, and Lk. iv. 9 = Mt. iv. 6). The words could equally well mean " Since thou art the Son of God " ; and they refer in all probability to the consciousness of a special Messianic Sonship which had just previously come to Jesus at his baptism.

In the Parable of the Wicked Vinedressers, recorded by Mark, the " beloved son " of the Owner, the one messenger he had left, is clearly meant to represent Jesus as Messiah (Mk. xii. 6 = Lk. xx. 13 = Mt. xxi. 37 : l omits the word " one " and m " one " and " beloved ").[2] In Mt. xxii. 2, m has converted the " man " who " was giving a great dinner " (Lk. xiv. 16 Q ?) into " a king who gave a marriage-feast for his son ".

m makes explicit the Divine sonship implied by the Messianic office in his version of Peter's confession at Cæsarea-Philippi, " Thou art the Messiah, the Son of the Living God "

---

[1] Cf. Dalman, *W.J.* 276–280.
[2] Cf. Menzies, *Earliest Gospel*, 216f. ; Rawlinson, *St Mark*, 161f. ; Manson, *Teaching*, 104.

(Mt. xvi. 16 ; contrast Mk. viii. 29 = Lk. ix. 20), and of the mocking words addressed to Jesus on the Cross, " If thou art Son of God " (Mt. xxvii. 40 : contrast Mk. xv. 29f.), and " He trusts in God : let Him rescue him, if He cares for him ; for he said, ' I am God's Son ' " (Mt. xxvii. 43 : contrast Mk. xv. 32, Lk. xxiii. 35 L).

Finally, we must note the ascription to Jesus of Divine Sonship (in the Messianic sense) by persons who were possessed by demons—an ascription which Jesus usually met with an emphatic injunction of silence.   The passages are Mk. i. 24f. = Lk. iv. 34f. (' . . . " . . . we know who thou art—[thou art] God's Holy [Son] ! " And Jesus rebuked it, saying, " Be muzzled ! . . . " ') ; Mk. i. 34 (' he would not allow the demons to speak, because they knew him ' [Lk. iv. 41 l makes the allusion explicit by adding ' to be the Messiah ']) ; Mk. iii. 11f. (' And the unclean spirits, whenever they saw him, fell down before him, and screamed out, saying " Thou art the Son of God ".   And he warned them repeatedly not to make him known ' [Mt. has a parallel to this last sentence in xii. 16]) ; and Mk. v. 7 = Lk. viii. 28 = Mt. viii. 29 (the Gerasene maniac calls out, " Jesus, thou Son of the Most High God ").   There is nothing improbable in the view that psychic sensitives like the demoniacs may often have discerned in Jesus a person of special character and peculiarly-exalted rank, and that Jesus declined their public testimony because it did not harmonize with his own plans.   That seems a more probable hypothesis of the significance of the Marcan data than the theory that the injunction of silence is an after-thought brought in unhistorically by the Evangelist in order to account for the strange failure of Jesus' fellow-countrymen to recognize him as the Messiah (see below, pp. 51f., 55).

In Mt. xiv. 33 m (contrast Mk. vi. 51f.) the Disciples are unhistorically represented as saying to Jesus after the stilling of the storm, " Truly thou art God's Son ".[1]

(5) Jesus refers to God as " my Father ", with or without some adjunct referring to " heaven ", in the following documents :

Q : Lk. x. 22 = Mt. xi. 27 : " All things have been handed over to me by my Father ".   The reference to " my Father in the heavens " in Mt. xviii. 14 (if this is the right reading : certain authorities have " your Father ") may come from Q or M or m ; see above, p. 27.

M (in addition to the possibility just referred to) : Mt. vii. 21

---

[1] Cf., on the whole question, Dalman, *W.J.* 274–276, 280–282.

(possibly m or even Q: contrast Lk. vi. 46); Mt. xv. 13; Mt. xvi. 17 (possibly m); Mt. xviii. 10; Mt. xviii. 19 (possibly m); Mt. xviii. 35 (quite probably m); Mt. xxv. 34; Mt. xxv. 41 (but the true reading probably had no explicit reference to God: see above, p. 28 top); Mt. xxvi. 53.

L: Lk. xxii. 29; Lk. xxiv. 49 (conceivably l: a post-Resurrection saying). We may note here also Lk. ii. 49, from the Lucan Protevangelion, where Jesus is said, when twelve years old, to have referred to the Temple at Jerusalem as " my Father's (House) ".

m (in addition to the possibilities referred to above, under M and Q): Mt. x. 32, 33 (contrast Lk. xii. 8, 9); Mt. xii. 50 (contrast Mk. iii. 35 = Lk. viii. 21); Mt. xx. 23 (contrast Mk. x. 40); Mt. xxvi. 29 (contrast Mk. xiv. 25); Mt. xxvi. 39 (contrast Mk. xiv. 36 = Lk. xxii. 42); Mt. xxvi. 42 (contrast Mk. xiv. 39).

In Mk. viii. 38 = Lk. ix. 26 = Mt. xvi. 27, God is referred to as the Father of the Son of Man. How far we may consider " the Son of Man " to be here a self-designation of Jesus is a question we must consider later (see below, pp. 90ff.).

(6) The prayers in which Jesus addresses God by the familiar title " Father " (see above, pp. 28f. [3]) are recorded in

Q: Lk. x. 21 (bis) = Mt. xi. 25f.

L: Lk. xxiii. 34; Lk. xxiii. 46: I incline to believe that the former of these passages is part of the true text of Lk. (the latter is not disputed), and that both of them are historically reliable, though I should regard the latter as somewhat more dubious than the former.

Mk. xiv. 36 = Lk. xxii. 42: the Lucan parallel here may be from L (m in Mt. xxvi. 39 [cf. 42] substitutes " my Father ").

(7) The only passage in which the words " Our Father " are placed on the lips of Jesus is Mt. vi. 9, the Matthæan version of the Lord's Prayer. Even if this were the most original form of the prayer (see above, p. 28 [3], and below, p. 166), the phrase would not be used by Jesus on behalf of himself among others, since the prayer is meant for the use of his Disciples. Nor is the absence of other evidence here simply accidental, for (as has been seen) there is an abundance of other evidence to the effect that Jesus was conscious of being God's Son in a special sense.[1]

(8) The absolute use of the terms " the Father " and " the Son " is attested in three passages:

Q: Lk. x. 22 (bis) = Mt. xi. 27 (bis), the so-called " Johan-

[1] Cf., however, Holtzmann, *Theol.* i. 341–343; Weinel, *Theol.* 146–151.

nine " saying : " No one comes to know the Father except the Son, . . ."

Mk. xiii. 32 = Mt. xxiv. 36, where Jesus says that " not even the angels in heaven, nor the Son ", know the day or hour of the future coming of the Son of Man, " but the Father only ".

M or more probably m : Mt. xxviii. 19, Jesus' post-Resurrection injunction to the Disciples to baptize converts " into the name of the Father and of the Son and of the Holy Spirit ".

Setting the third of these passages aside as almost certainly a creation of the early Church, we can confidently accept the other two as historically-reliable records of what Jesus said. The Marcan passage is guaranteed, not only by the fact that it has Marcan attestation, but because it is of such a character that no early Christian could have ascribed it to Jesus unless he had undeniable authority for doing so. The Q-passage is guaranteed to us by the fact that, standing as it does in Q, it has as high documentary authority as any passage in the Gospels—in all probability the authority of Matthew the Apostle. Admittedly the contents of the passage are exceptional ; but it is not accurate to say [1] that " there is no sure parallel for his speaking of himself as ' *the* Son ' in a special sense ", for the Marcan passage is a sure parallel of this kind, not to mention the great mass of less-decisive evidence just considered under (4). To disbelieve a statement so attested, simply on the ground that it is exceptional in content, seems to me unscientific and indefensible.[2]

From the foregoing study of the Divine Sonship of Jesus it will be seen that the concept is closely linked with that of his Messiahship. For reasons that will presently be made plain, the discussion of his Messianic consciousness must be postponed to a somewhat later point in our study. As already mentioned, however, the whole of the evidence regarding his Divine Sonship has been collected in this chapter for the sake of simplicity and convenience, even though it has involved anticipatory allusions to the Messiahship. Our next immediate task is to discuss the basis and the most vital outcome of Jesus' conviction that he was in some special sense Son of God.

[1] As Montefiore does (*S.G.*[2] II. 173, cf. 175, 181).
[2] Cf. Manson, *Teaching*, 110. There is surely nothing " strange " in the recognition, on the part of liberal scholars, that the Divine Fatherhood as Jesus viewed it applied to men generally, and also in a peculiar sense to himself (Cadbury, *Peril*, 204 top). Such recognition is forced upon us by the evidence.

CHAPTER II

THE LOVING AND INTIMATE SERVANT OF GOD

(1) Jesus' claim to be the Son of God in a unique sense rested in the first place on his experience of unique filial intimacy with God—(2) a sense which dated even from his boyhood, (3) became strikingly real to him at his Baptism and again at his Transfiguration, (4) was manifested in the frequency and the familiar language of his prayers, (5) and was given open expression in his so-called " Johannine " utterance. (6) It owed much to the affectionate and harmonious relations which had existed between himself and his human father. (7) It led him to feel the insufficiency of the idea of God as " King ", and so in his teaching to lay unprecedented stress on God's Fatherhood. (8) It carried with it the ideal of loyal and unreserved obedience to the Divine Will, after the manner of " the Servant of the Lord " depicted in Deutero-Isaiah. (9) Jesus acts for God : his doings are God's doings. (10) As the basis of his claim to unique Sonship, it was more fundamental than the consciousness of Messiahship, which resulted from it.

(1) and (10). That Jesus did actually claim to be both *the* Son of God and the Jewish Messiah is historically undeniable. It is argued by some that the latter claim was the basis of the former and exhausted its significance.[1] That the two were closely allied is doubtless true ; but that the consciousness of Messiahship was prior to that of Sonship is most improbable. The ground for believing that the sense of Sonship was prior is cumulative, and will become clearer as we proceed. I would here observe only that spiritual status is inherently likely to have been the cause of a sense of official vocation, rather than its consequence.[2]

---

[1] See, e.g., Montefiore, *S.G.*[2] I. cxxiii, 19, 85–87, II. 181.
[2] For the filial consciousness of Jesus, see, e.g., Holtzmann, *Theol.* i. 173–175 ; Bartlet in H.*D.C.G.* ii. 700 ab, 704 ; J. A. Robertson, *Spiritual Pilgrimage*, Sections I and II. Dr. H. J. Cadbury, on what seem to me quite insufficient grounds, apparently views positive speculation regarding the " religious experience " of Jesus as unwarranted and illusory, and denies— or at least sees no reason to believe—that Jesus enjoyed any exceptional sense of God's presence ; he refers in this connexion to the largely-conventional character of references to the Deity customary among Moslems (*Peril*, 9,

34

(2) At the age of twelve, Jesus speaks of his presence in the Temple at Jerusalem as " being in my Father's (House) ", to which therefore it was only natural for him to resort (Lk. ii. 49). His words, taken by themselves, could be translated, " (engaged) in the (affair)s of my Father " ; but as the question under discussion was one of locality, the former translation is more likely to express the meaning of the original. We do not know how Luke came by the story ; but there is no reason to doubt its substantial accuracy (incidentally the reference to Joseph and Mary as Jesus' " parents " [ii. 27, 41 ; cf. 33] if not Mary's allusion to Joseph as " thy father " [ii. 48], indicate that it ante-dated Luke's acceptance of the doctrine of the Virgin Birth). However translated, Jesus' reply reveals an extraordinary sense of the close relation between God and himself,[1] which could not, of course, at that early age have had anything to do with a claim to Messiahship.

(3) For the evidence regarding the Baptism and Transfiguration, see above, pp. 29f. While the Divine Sonship here attested undoubtedly has reference to the Messianic office, the forms in which it is expressed make it unlikely that it stands for Messiahship only. At his baptism Jesus " felt that he stood—and now he realised as never before the Messianic meaning of the fact—in that perfectly filial relation to God which was the destiny of man as originally created ' in the image of God ', though it had been lost by Adam and never recovered until in his own experience and person ".[2]

(4) For the significance of Jesus' use of the word " Abba " in addressing God in prayer, see above, pp. 28f. (3), 32 (6). The frequent allusions in the Gospels to Jesus praying are easily found, and do not need to be adduced here : cf. especially

---

162–164, 176–181, 186–190). Cf. Bultmann, *Jesus*, 141f. (Jesus knew nothing of any mystical relation to God).

The filial consciousness of Jesus is believed to have been the basis of his claim to Messiahship, and not simply its consequence or equivalent, by Wendt (*Teaching*, i. 180f., 191, 393f., ii. 123f., 130), Holtzmann (*Theol.* i. 339, 352f., 413–415 : " . . . Sein Messiastum war demnach die geschichtlich gebotene, die unvermeidliche Anschauungsform, in welche sich für seine Vorstellung der Erfahrungsgehalt seines religiösen Lebens, also sein Sohnesbewusstsein gekleidet hat "), Bartlet (*St. Mark,* 56, 93), Bartlet and Carlyle (*Christianity in Hist.* 26), Meyer (*Ursprung,* ii. 444), Box (*St. Matthew*, 30, 97), Peake (in *B.J.R.L.* VIII. i. 58f. [Jan. 1924]), Major (in *Mission,* etc. 112 : " This theo-centric egoism is the very core of the Messianic consciousness of Jesus "), and others. See below, p. 52.

[1] Wendt, *Teaching*, i. 95f. ; Holtzmann, *Synopt.* 323, *Theol.* i. 175 (" Für solche Intensität des religiösen Lebens schon im Kinde mag immerhin Lc 2 49 ein bezeichnender Zug erhalten sein ").

[2] Bartlet and Carlyle, *Christianity in Hist.* 22. Cf. Manson, *Teaching*, 102–104.

Lk. v. 16 l (his custom), Lk. vi. 12 l, possibly L (a whole night spent in prayer).[1]

(5) The precise wording—like the historical reliability and the exact interpretation—of the so-called " Johannine " saying of Jesus in Lk. x. 22 = Mt. xi. 27 Q has been the subject of much discussion. A probable form of the original saying is, " All things have been handed over to me by my Father ; and no one comes to know the Father except the Son and any one to whom the Son desires to reveal (Him) ".[2] I have argued above (p. 33) for the originality of this passage as an actual saying of Jesus. Whatever form of words we choose as most likely to be what Jesus, according to Q, really said, the utterance very clearly implies a uniquely-close intimacy between him and God.[3]

(6) That Jesus' stress on the Fatherhood of God owed much to the happy relations between himself and Joseph is, of course, a conjecture, but a very reasonable one. It is inherently unlikely that he could have drawn the parallels he did between the human and the Divine paternal benevolence, if his own human father had not in earlier years meant much to him. Between him and his mother, on the contrary, there does not seem to have been anything like a close understanding (Mk. iii. 21 [unparalleled in Lk. and Mt.] ; Mk. iii. 31–35 = Lk. viii. 19–21 = Mt. xii. 46–50).[4]

(7) Without in any way undervaluing the importance of the conception of God as Father among the Jewish contemporaries of Jesus (see above, p. 28 n. 1), we can be in no sort of doubt as to the greatness and the novelty of the emphasis which he himself placed upon it. While using it at times in the way that had apparently become familiar to devout Jews, he made it in a new fashion a basis for delineating the nature and the ways of God, and charged it with a fullness and depth of meaning which for his hearers had no precedent.[5] With him it was no mere theological commonplace, but a fundamental and all-important reality, founded upon his own direct experience of communion with God, and becoming more sacred and

---

[1] For the prayer in Gethsemane, cf. Manson, *Teaching*, 104f., 198.
[2] Cf. Holtzmann, *Theol.* i. 345–351, and McNeile, *St. Matthew*, 162–166, where the literature on the subject is summarized.
[3] Cf. Dalman, *W.J.* 282–287 ; Dodd in *Myst. Christi*, 63 ; Manson, *Teaching*, 109–113.
[4] Cf. Holtzmann, *Theol.* i. 162 ; Klausner, *Jes. of Naz.* 235, 280 ; Montefiore, *S.G.*[2] II. 119 ; W. H. Stubbs in *E.T.* xlii. 425–428 (June 1931) ; L. Weatherhead, *His Life and Ours* (1932), 63f. ; S. Pearce Carey, *Jesus* (1939), 22f.
[5] Per contra, Cadbury, *Peril*, 94 : " Even religiously the fatherhood of God is neither a novelty nor a new emphasis with Jesus ".

more full of meaning as his life-course brought him nearer and nearer to its tragic climax.[1]

(8) If God the Father be the supremely-real Presence and the supreme object of trust and love (Mk. xii. 28–31 = Mt. xxii. 34–40 : cf. Lk. x. 25–27 L), it follows that life must be lived in strenuous and unqualified obedience to Him.[2] Jesus must be, not only the beloved and chosen Son, but the loyal and submissive Servant, of God. Only those who, like him, did the Will of God, would he recognize as his true kinsmen (Mk. iii. 33–35 = Lk. viii. 21 = Mt. xii. 48–50). This sense of being engaged entirely in God's service led him to apply to himself, and enabled him to derive support and guidance from, the Deutero-Isaianic passages portraying the Servant of the Lord and describing his experiences (Isa. xlii. 1–4, xlix. 1–6, l. 4–9, lii. 13–liii. 12, with the addition of lxi. 1ff. as similar in spirit, although not using the actual word " servant "). The evidence that Jesus applied these passages to himself is not abundant, and has been felt by some to be inadequate ; but cumulatively it is quite sufficient to warrant belief. It is as follows :—

(a) Isaiah xlii. 1 (like other phrases in the same book— xliv. 2, lxii. 4) is echoed in the voice from heaven at the Baptism and the Transfiguration (see the passages from Mk. and probably also from Q and L quoted above, pp. 29f.).

(b) Isaiah lxi. 1f. was read by Jesus in the synagogue at Nazareth ; and after reading the passage he added, " To-day has this Scripture been fulfilled in your hearing " (Lk. iv. 17–21 L).

(c) Isaiah liii. 12 was explicitly applied by Jesus to himself

---

[1] Cf. Dalman, *W.J.* 189–194 ; Manson, *Teaching*, 24f., 93–115. The latter gives the most detailed study I know of the teaching of Jesus on the subject. Ignoring for the most part the distinction between " my Father ", " your Father ", etc., classifying the references according to the Gospel-documents to which they belong, and allowing for the tendency of Mt. to insert the word in passages where the sources did not warrant it, Dr. Manson comes to the conclusion that, before Peter's confession at Cæsarea-Philippi, Jesus hardly ever, if at all, spoke of God as Father. He further argues that, even after Cæsarea-Philippi, he used the term " Father " for God only in prayer or in speaking to his inner circle of Disciples. Bearing in mind the custom of contemporary Judaism, Jesus' consciousness of special Sonship from his baptism onwards (not to mention his boyhood), and the condition of our Gospel-sources, I feel doubtful as to whether the chronological distinction holds good quite as definitely as Dr. Manson believes, and still more so as to his restriction of the utterances to those made in the presence of Disciples. But these points do not seriously affect the main issue with which I am here concerned ; and I fully agree with Dr. Manson in his insistence on the meaning of the language in question, as I have represented it in the text above. " The question is at once posed ", he says (94), with reference to the New-Testament teaching generally, " What did Jesus do to this old belief in the Fatherhood of God to give it such power and influence over the lives of men ? "

[2] Cf. Manson, *Teaching*, 105, 115, 168, 197f.

at the Last Supper : " I tell you, this which has been written must be accomplished in regard to me, ' And he was reckoned among the transgressors ' " (Lk. xxii. 37 L).

(d) Isaiah liii. 11f. (" My servant will make *many* righteous ", and " he bore away the sin of *many* ") are twice clearly echoed in the words of Jesus—firstly, when he said that " the Son of Man came to give his life as a ransom for *many* " (Mk. x. 45 = Mt. xx. 28), and secondly, when at the Last Supper he said that his blood was " being poured out on behalf of *many* " (Mk. xiv. 24 = Mt. xxvi. 28).[1]

(9) The quasi-identification of himself with the Deutero-Isaianic Servant of God and the entire self-dedication to God's work involved in this identification carried with it the implication that his own activities are virtually the activities of God Himself. Thus it was that, when he expelled the demons, he expelled them " by the finger of God " (Lk. xi. 20 = Mt. xii. 28 Q : the latter has " spirit " for " finger "),[2] and when he dismissed the cured madman in the land of the Gerasenes, he bade him tell his friends " how much the Lord has done for thee, and how merciful He has been to thee " (Mk. v. 19 = Lk. viii. 39 : by " the Lord " Jesus certainly meant God, as Luke's parallel actually states ; but the following verse in Mk. seems to show that Mark thought " the Lord " was Jesus himself. Cf. Lk. v. 17 l ; Mk. ii. 12 = Lk. v. 26 = Mt. ix. 8). Thus too he declares that whoever receives or rejects him receives or rejects in so doing the God who sent him (Mk. ix. 37 = Lk. ix. 48 = Mt. x. 40 ; Lk. x. 16 L or possibly l or Q). The three parables of the Lost Sheep, the Lost Coin, and the Prodigal Son, particularly the sentences with which they severally close (Lk. xv. 7, 10 Q or L [cf. Mt. xviii. 13f. Q or M or m] ; Lk. xv. 32 L), bring God's concern over wayward human lives into a very close relationship with Jesus' own activity (cf. Lk. xv. 2 l ; also Mk. ii. 15–17 = Lk. v. 29–32 = Mt. ix. 10–12, 13b, and see generally the following chapter). In Lk. xxiv. 49 L or l, Jesus says he will send upon the Disciples the Spirit promised them by God : but as a post-Resurrection saying, this is likely to be a creation of the early Church rather than an actual saying of Jesus : in any case, it does not refer to his earthly ministry.

(10) See above, p. 34.

---

[1] Cf. Moffatt, *Theol. of the Gospels*, 139–149 ; Rawlinson, *St. Mark*, 254–256 ; Otto, *Kingdom*, 250–253 (he sees another quotation of Isaiah liii in Mk. ix. 12 = Mt. xvii. 12) ; V. Taylor, *Sacrifice*, 46–48.
[2] Cf. Otto, *Kingdom*, 168f.

CHAPTER III

THE FRIEND OF SUFFERERS AND SINNERS

(1) Out of his loving obedience to God, conceived of as Father and therefore as merciful, (2) sprang Jesus' passionate and loving concern for men, (3) both as individuals, (4) and as social groups. (5) This concern found emotional expression in the compassion he habitually felt for those who were in any kind of need or trouble, (6) in his fondness for little children, (7) and in his longing to " save " men. (8) It took concrete form in his willingness to cure their physical and mental disorders, (9) his stress on the duty of love and mercy, (10) and his efforts, by means of his teaching, (11) his personal friendship, (12) and the agency of his Disciples, (13) to lead them into the true and lasting happiness of filial intimacy with God.

(1) However the conceptions of fatherhood may differ in different ages and places, and however unidealistic and conventional the title may sometimes tend to become,[1] the connexion with it of the ideas of love and compassion is fairly widespread. In Jewish thought at all events this connexion was clear and close. The Old Testament abounds in stress on the mercy of God ; and the comparison in Psalm ciii. 13, " As a father has compassion on his children, so Yahweh has compassion on those who fear Him ", enshrines one of the standing religious convictions of Judaism. It so happens that nowhere in the Gospels does Jesus say explicitly that God loves men ; [2] but he does say, " Your Father is merciful " (Lk. vi. 36, probably Q, possibly L or l ; but the parallel in Mt. v. 48 [" Your heavenly Father is perfect "] is almost certainly secondary—m, perhaps M, improbably Q) ; and he speaks of God as the lavish bestower of gifts and benefits of every kind.[3] This mercy and generosity of God are not confined to those who are at least moderately good, but extend to the undeserving. " He is kind to the unthankful and evil " (Lk. vi. 35, probably Q, possibly L or l ; the parallel in Mt. v. 45 [" Who lifts up

---

[1] Cadbury, *Peril*, 9.
[2] Cadbury, *Peril*, 150.
[3] The evidence for this statement is so familiar and abundant that references hardly need to be given. Cf. Holtzmann, *Theol.* i. 220f.

His sun over evil and good men alike, and rains upon righteous and unrighteous "], which refers specially to the indiscriminate gifts of God *in Nature*, probably comes from M). Especially is God's compassion moved for those who through wrongdoing have drawn suffering on themselves. Just as, in the Old Testament, Yahweh's " soul was impatient over the misery of Israel " (Judges x. 16), so for Jesus the " joy before the angels of God over one repentant sinner " (Lk. xv. 10 Q or L: cf. Mt. xviii. 14 Q or M or m) clearly implies the Divine sorrow over the unrepentant sinner. In the father who " was moved with compassion " for the returning Prodigal (Lk. xv. 20 L), and in the King who was " moved with compassion " for the insolvent debtor (Mt. xviii. 27 M), we have unmistakable pictures of God's attitude to the penitent. Nay more, while the Parable of the Prodigal Son represents God as welcoming the penitent on his return, the Parables of the Lost Sheep (Lk. xv. 4–7 Q, possibly L : Mt. xviii. 12f. Q + m, possibly M) and the Lost Coin (Lk. xv. 8f. Q or L) represent Him as actually going forth in the effort to reclaim him while still impenitent. This is a new and striking element in the delineation of the Divine character—one anticipated indeed in the Old Testament (cf. Hosea and Isaiah lxv. 1f. in some correct translation), but to some extent forgotten in Rabbinism, at least as regards its practical implications.[1]

(2) It so happens that the only person whom Jesus is explicitly said in the Synoptic Gospels to have " loved " is the Rich Man who asked him what he must do to procure eternal life (Mk. x. 21 : the parallels omit the notice). But he who pronounced the injunction " Thou shalt love thy neighbour as thyself " to be the second greatest commandmeut in the Law, second only to the supreme requirement of love for God (Mk. xii. 31 = Mt. xxii. 39f. : cf. Lk. x. 27 L) and similar to it (m), must himself have been a great lover of men. The way in which he links these commandments together, taken in conjunction with his belief in the love of God and in his own close relationship to Him, points to that love of God as itself the foundation and cause of the passionate love he himself felt for men.[2] Be that as it may, nothing other than such a love must be presupposed as the ruling motive of one who " came

---

[1] Cf. Montefiore in *Hibbert Journ.* xxviii. 101, 104f. (Oct. 1929), and *S.G.*[3] I. 55, II. 249, 520f. ; also *Rabbinic Lit. and Gosp. Teachings* (1930), 221–224, 372f. (per contra, 356) ; Easton, *Christ in the Gospels*, 151 ; Otto, *Kingdom*, 393–395 (he regards this representation of God as that special truth which Jesus as Son alone knew [Lk. x. 22 = Mt. xi. 27]).

[2] So A. T. Cadoux in *The Lord of Life*, 67f., 69f.

not to be served, but to serve, and to give his life as a ransom for many " (Mk. x. 45 = Mt. xx. 28 : cf. Lk. xxii. 27 L).

(3) The parables describing the shepherd's eager search for the one sheep that strays from his flock of a hundred (Lk. xv. 4–7 Q or L : Mt. xviii. 12–14 Q or M), and the woman's eager search for the one drachma lost out of her ten (Lk. xv. 8–10 Q or L), set forth the urgent concern of God and of Jesus as His representative for each individual person, as is indeed expressly brought out in the Matthæan conclusion to the former parable : " Thus it is not will(ed) before my Father in the heavens that one of these little ones should be lost " (Mt. xviii. 14). The same conviction regarding God is presupposed by Jesus in his declaration that even every sparrow that falls is remembered and observed by God (Lk. xii. 6 Q [or l] = Mt. x. 29 [m or Q]). In a pictorial description of the Last Judgment, kind actions are reckoned as having been done or not done to Jesus himself according as they had or had not been done " to one of the least " of his " brothers " (Mt. xxv. 40, 45 M). Each individual life was thus of priceless worth to God and therefore also to him who seeks before all things to serve God.[1]

(4) Whether the phrase " corporate personality " be philosophically sound or not, it does reflect a mode of thought thoroughly familiar to the ancient world, and by no means unknown even to-day. In the historical development of Jewish beliefs, this mode of thought preceded the realization of the value of the individual ; and even after the rise and establishment of individualism in the Exilic and post-Exilic periods, the collective interest remained the normal concomitant or background of personal religion.[2] In the Synoptic record of Jesus' teaching, it shows itself in the way in which he apostrophizes Khorazin, Bethsaida, Kapharnaum, and Jerusalem, and refers in the third person to Tyre and Sidon, Sodom and Gomorrha, as if each of these were a moral unit. His personal concern for the communities thus addressed comes out in the terms in which he addresses them. " Alas for thee,

[1] Cf. Bartlet and Carlyle, *Christianity in Hist.* 16 ; Montefiore, *S.G.* [2] I. cxvii (". . . He is much more the teacher of the individual than was Amos or Isaiah . . ."), 17, II. 325 (" A more sublime reply can hardly be conceived " than Mt. xxv. 40. " The worth which Christianity assigned to every human soul brought a new feature into the Roman and heathen world. Even the poorest and most wretched creature—a gladiator, a prostitute, a slave— had separate, distinct value in the eyes of God ") ; A. T. Cadoux in *The Lord of Life*, 68 (". . . He did not treat men in mass, but gave His whole mind to the man or woman before Him, setting an absolute value on the individual human soul . . .").

[2] See the full discussion of the idea of corporate personality by Dr. H. Wheeler Robinson in *Beihefte zur Z.A.W.* lxvi (1936) 49–62.

Khorazin! Alas for thee, Bethsaida!" (Lk. x. 13 = Mt. xi. 21 Q) is doubtless to be understood as an expression of pitying grief,[1] as also in all probability is the cry to Kapharnaum: "And thou, Kapharnaum, wilt thou be exalted to heaven? thou wilt go down to Hades!" (Lk. x. 15 = Mt. xi. 23a Q). Certainly in the familiar appeal to Jerusalem, the tone of disappointment and grief is unmistakable: "O Jerusalem, Jerusalem! . . . How often have I wished to gather thy children together, as a mother-bird gathers her brood of nestlings under her wings, and ye would not come!" (Lk. xiii. 34 = Mt. xxiii. 37 Q). And similarly on the last ride into the city: 'And as he drew near, having caught sight of the city, he wept over it, saying, "O if only thou hadst come to know, even at this (late) day, the things (needful) for thy peace! But now, they have been hidden from thine eyes! . . . thou knewest not the season of thy visitation (from God)!"' (Lk. xix. 41–44 L).

Of course the corporate unit which was of special importance to Jesus and his fellow-countrymen was Israel itself; and we shall have to consider later what was his personal attitude to the nation as a moral and religious whole. Here we have to note that his concern for men was not confined to his ministry to individuals, important as that ministry was, but that it included an interest in sundry social groups, principally (as we shall see) in the people of Israel and in humanity at large (see below, pp. 136ff., 147ff.).

The realization that Jesus had an eye for corporate, as well as for individual needs, and that the Kingdom of God was itself, in part at least, a social conception, led liberal scholars of a bygone generation to think of Jesus as primarily or at least largely a social reformer, aiming at the gradual establishment of a sort of Utopia by means of the inculcation of a code

---

[1] It is important to remember that οὐαὶ is an expression of agonized horror on behalf of those over whom dire calamity is pending, whether the calamity be deserved or not (cf. Strack-Billerbeck i. 778f.). It may, of course, imply anger and threatening, but it may also imply sympathy: only the context can indicate which. See, for instance, Mt. xviii. 7 ("Woe to the world because of offences; for it is needful that offences should come: only woe to him by means of whom the offence comes!" [apparently Q; but the parallel in Lk. xvii. 1 differs a little and omits the first "woe"]), and Mk. xiii. 17 = Lk. xxi. 23 = Mt. xxiv. 19 ("But woe to the women who are pregnant, and to those who are giving suck in those days!"). It is extraordinary that Montefiore apparently did not realize this, but regarded οὐαὶ as a curse or at least as an expression of unloving scorn (S.G.[2] II. 167f., 415f.).

The allusions to Tyre and Sidon occur in the same context (Lk. x. 13f. = Mt. xi. 21f. Q), those to Sodom (and Gomorrha) in Lk. x. 12 = Mt. x. 15 Q and Mt. xi. 23b, 24 (Q or m).

of sociological ethics.[1] The more recent realization that such a description of him is anachronistic, and that the unmodern notions of cataclysm and Divine intervention entered in no small measure into his calculations, has led recent authors to pour scorn on the views fondly entertained by their predecessors in the field, and to wipe the whole idea of social betterment completely out of their picture of Jesus' plans and expectations.[2] The reaction was, no doubt, in a measure justified. The idea of a gradual or evolutionary betterment was certainly alien from the ancient mind ; nor can we think of Jesus as a social reformer in the same sense as that which the words would suggest to-day. But, as so often happens, the corrective has been overdone. The customary prominence of Divine agency in the speech of devout Jews did not at all imply that human initiative and activity were excluded ; and modern scholars are therefore mistaken in inferring, from allusions to God as " giving " the Kingdom and from prayers for its " coming ", that we misrepresent the mind of Jesus if we speak of his followers working for, or establishing, or extending the Kingdom on earth. In the matter of winning a battle or raising crops, the devout Jew did vigorously all he could, and ascribed the result, whether good or bad, to God. So too, we may suppose, with Jesus' thought and speech about the Kingdom (see above, p. 26, and below, pp. 66 n. 1, 178f. [5], 188f., 203–207). And when we remember that the Kingdom was, beyond all question, in part a social concept, and that the thought of it was in some way or other the background of all his ethical teaching, we shall perhaps see that he may after all be rightly described as a social reformer, in the sense that he was concerned with the social good of men as well as with the good of the individual, that he was devoted to the realization of an ideal into which social values very largely entered, and that much of his teaching had reference to the way of life which would both subserve and characterize the ideal in question.[3]

[1] Cf. the literature referred to in Holtzmann, *Theol.* i. 265f. n. 1.

[2] Cf., e.g., Bultmann, *Jesus*, 37f., 97f., 113f. ; Easton, *Christ in the Gospels*, 132f. ; Manson, *Teaching*, 117 ; H.-D. Wendland, *Eschatologie*, 37f. ; Alan Richardson in *The Student Movement*, xxxix (1937) 122f., 147f., 175f., cf. 182 ; Cadbury, *Peril*, 9, 86–119, 197 (3), 202f. (1), 207 (19). In an interesting article on ' The Social Translation of the Gospel ' in *H.T.R.* xv. 1–13 (Jan. 1922), Dr. Cadbury anticipated, though in a more constructive spirit, much of what he says in *The Peril*.

[3] Cf. N. Schmidt, *Prophet of Naz.* 298, 303 ; Holtzmann, *Theol.* i. 265–268 ; Shailer Mathews, *Social Teaching of Jes.* (ed. 1910), 3ff., 40ff., 53–59, 69, 72 ; Bultmann, *Jesus*, 45f. ; C. C. McCown in *J.R.* xvi (1936) 45f. The most recent thorough-going attempt to exhibit Jesus as a revolutionary mainly concerned to establish social justice is Mr. Conrad Noel's *Life of Jesus* (1937).

(5) Jesus is several times said to have been ' moved with compassion ' for persons in trouble—for the hungry crowd (Mk. viii. 2f. = Mt. xv. 32), for the bereaved widow of Nain (Lk. vii. 13 L), and for a blind man (Mt. xx. 34 m).[1] He behaved with compassion towards a leper, even touching as well as healing him (Mk. i. 41 = Lk. v. 13 = Mt. viii. 3),[2] and towards the father of the epileptic boy, who cried to him, " Have compassion on us " (Mk. ix. 22). He comforted the anxious Jairus with the exhortation, " Fear not " (Mk. v. 36 = Lk. viii. 50). But the most significant passage is Mk. vi. 34 and its parallels. In Mk. it runs, ' And having gone out (of the boat), he saw a large crowd, and he was moved with compassion for them, because they were like sheep that have no shepherd ; and he began to teach them many things '. The Lucan parallel (Lk. ix. 11) has nothing about compassion ; the Matthæan (Mt. xiv. 14) just mentions it : and both substitute cures for teaching. There is another parallel in Mt. ix. 36, clearly dependent on and closely following Mk., but adding the observation that the crowds were ' worried and depressed ' (m). The reference to shepherdless sheep is an echo of Numb. xxvii. 17, 1 Kings xxii. 17, and Ezek. xxxiv. 5.[3]

We must next note the familiar words, " Come hither unto me, all ye who are toiling and burdened, and I will give you rest. Take on yourselves my yoke, and learn from me, for I am gentle and humble in heart, and ye will find rest for your souls ; for my yoke is kindly, and my burden light " (Mt. xi. 28–30 M). This passage probably did not stand in Q (though it immediately follows a Q-section)—otherwise Luke would almost certainly have included it. It therefore lacks first-class documentary authority. Moreover, in its tone and terms it so

[1] The phrase does not occur in the parallels to the last-mentioned passage, namely Mk. x. 52 = Lk. xviii. 42. In Mt., therefore, it is clearly an editorial touch, having no more documentary authority than the gratuitous Matthæan manufacture of two blind men out of one. Yet it is not necessarily untrue to fact : cf. Bartlet, *St. Mark*, 309 (on Mk. x. 49 [" Jesus stood still "] : " The piteous appeal fell at last on ears ever open to all human need ").

[2] The true reading in Mk. i. 41 is almost certainly ὀργισθείς, not σπλαγχνισθείς (" was angry ", not " was moved with compassion ") : cf. 43. Opinions differ as to what was the cause of Jesus' anger : possibly it was because the leper, in coming into a house, was breaking the Law (so Rawlinson, *St. Mark*, 21f., cf. 256) ; but if so, why then did Jesus touch him ? Dr. E. R. Bevan's view (in *J.T.S.* xxxiii. 186f. [Jan. 1932]), that Jesus was angry with the evil power behind this terrible disease, seems to me on the whole less difficult than any other. In any case, the consent, the touch, and the healing were compassionate (so Montefiore, *S.G.*[2] I. 39).

[3] Cf. J. A. Robertson, *Spiritual Pilgrimage*, 126f. ; Montefiore, *S.G.*[2] I. 125 (suggests that originally the compassion was simply for those who were hungry), II. 141.

closely resembles certain passages in Proverbs (i. 20–33, viii. 1–36) and Ben Sirach (xxiv. 19–22, li. 23–27), in which the Divine Wisdom invites needy men to come and receive her gifts, that many modern scholars declare confidently that we have here a quotation from some lost Jewish Wisdom-book, put fictitiously into Jesus' mouth. There is, however, no real reason why Jesus should not himself have spoken thus, perhaps being influenced by the language of Ben Sirach in doing so. He was voicing his compassion for those who were groaning under the burdens of the Law as interpreted by the Scribes (Lk. xi. 46 = Mt. xxiii. 4 Q), and offering to provide them with a more comforting alternative.

To the same general effect we may quote his benedictions, " Happy are ye poor " (Lk. vi. 20b = Mt. v. 3 Q, where m adds the gloss " in spirit "), " Happy are ye who hunger now " (Lk. vi. 21a = Mt. v. 6 Q, where m has " those who hunger and thirst for righteousness "), and " Happy are ye who weep now " (Lk. vi. 21b = Mt. v. 4 Q). He was concerned, not only for those who felt the Law to be a burden, but for those who suffered from unjust social conditions, and, as the humble rank-and-file of the nation, were looked down upon by the wealthy and the strong.[1]

Nor finally can we believe that one who felt such strong compassion in the presence of suffering was immune from pain when he faced the glaring and pervasive fact of human sin.[2]

(6) The tenderness of Jesus towards little children is clear from Mk. ix. 36f. = Lk. ix. 47f. = Mt. xviii. 2–4 and Mk. x. 13–16 = Lk. xviii. 15–17 = Mt. xix. 13–15. It is significant that Mt. and Luke avoid saying, as Mark does, that on both occasions Jesus ' folded ' the children ' in his arms '. " Hardly anything is more characteristic of Jesus than his attitude to children. It is unparalleled in ancient literature, though Paul's tone in Col. iii. 21 . . . has caught something of it ".[3]

[1] Cf. Sanday in *H.D.B.* ii. 608a ; N. Schmidt, *Prophet of Naz.* 298f. ; Holtzmann, *Theol.* i. 162–164 ; Marriott, *The Serm. on the Mount* (1925), 169–173 ; G. Murray in *H.C.L.M.K.* 46–49 ; Bacon, *Matthew*, 423–425.

[2] Cf. A. T. Cadoux in *The Lord of Life*, 69f. We may not inaptly quote here one of the Oxyrhynchus *Logia of Jesus*. It is not historically genuine, but it illustrates the impression which the spirit of Jesus had left on men. " I stood in the midst of the world, and in flesh did I appear to them : and I found all men drunken, and none found I athirst among them : and my soul is grieved over the sons of men, because they are blind in their heart, and see not (? their poverty)".

[3] Bartlet, *St. Mark*, 292 (cf. also Burkitt in *H.C.L.M.K.* 235 = *Jesus Christ*, etc. 39). While Dr. Bartlet's statement is broadly true, it ought perhaps to be added that there are in ancient literature sporadic traces of a sense of the value of childhood and the respect due to it. Cf., e.g., Juvenal,

(7) Jesus is several times represented as earnestly desiring to " save " men. " The Son of Man has come to seek out and to save that which had been lost " (Lk. xix. 10 L : a saying doubtless genuine, but not necessarily spoken on the occasion on which Luke reports it, for the story about Zacchaeus reaches a perfect ending without it). Very similar words are found in Mt. xviii. 11, a verse which has " Western " attestation only, and is probably no part of the original text of Mt. In Lk. ix. 56 L certain textual authorities have the words, " The Son of Man has come, not to destroy men's lives, but to save them " : they are indeed omitted by many important early manuscripts, and are therefore often regarded as a gloss suggested by Lk. xix. 10, the passage quoted at the beginning of this paragraph ; yet motives for the deliberate omission of them and of other words that go with them can easily be imagined. Quite possibly therefore they formed part of the original text of Lk.[1] Since the two concepts of " salvation " and " loss " (or " destruction ") are—as the passages just quoted indicate—exact opposites, it is very pertinent to add here a reference to Jesus' mission-charge to the Disciples, " Go rather to the lost sheep of the house of Israel " (Mt. x. 6 M), and to his reported declaration about himself, " I was not sent to any but the lost sheep of the house of Israel " (Mt. xv. 24 M or possibly m). His purpose to save the lost is set forth also in the Parables of the Straying Sheep (Lk. xv. 4–7 [Q or L] : Mt. xviii. 12–14 [Q or M or m]) and the Missing Coin (Lk. xv. 8–10 Q or L) ; his use of the Disciples for the same purpose comes out again in his designation of them as " fishers of men " (Mk. i. 17 = Mt. iv. 19 : cf. Lk. v. 10 L), and in his words to them, " The harvest indeed is large, but the workers are few. Beg therefore the Owner of the harvest to send out workers to (reap) his harvest " (Lk. x. 2 = Mt. ix. 37f. Q). We shall have to discuss later what precisely Jesus meant by " salvation " : but the stress he laid on it testifies clearly to his deep and loving concern on men's behalf (see below, pp. 49f. [13], 215–217 [5], 236f. [15].).

(8) We are not here concerned with many of the interesting questions raised by the record of Jesus' healings ; we need

---

Satir. xiv. 44–49 (". . . Maxima debetur puero reverentia : si quid | turpe paras, nec tu pueri contempseris annos, | sed peccaturo obstet tibi filius infans ") ; also the Rabbinic saying quoted in Moore, *Judaism,* iii. 104, and in Cohen, *Everyman's Talmud* (1932), 183 (" The world exists only on account of the breath of school children ", etc.).

[1] Cf. Montefiore, *S.G.*[a] II. 455f. ; Major in *Mission,* etc. 277.

to note only the broad facts that he did cure a number of those who were physically and mentally ill, and that he did so primarily out of compassion for the sufferers.[1] While non-mental illnesses are sometimes referred to as if they were due to demonic power (Lk. iv. 39 [contrast Mk. i. 31 = Mt. viii. 15], Lk. xi. 14 = Mt. ix. 32f. = Mt. xii. 22 Q ; Lk. xiii. 16 L), they are as a rule clearly distinguished (e.g., Mk. i. 32–34 = Lk. iv. 40f. = Mt. viii. 16) from those mental and nervous disorders, which were definitely attributed to demon-possession, and which necessitated for their cure the actual expulsion of the demons.[2] There are some grounds for believing that Jesus regarded the latter as the more serious and urgent type, and that after the first few months of the Ministry he was compelled to restrict very drastically his healing treatment of cases of non-mental sickness, lest his teaching-work should be crowded out.[3] It also seems likely that his healings had significance for him as indications of the real presence of that Kingdom of God which he proclaimed as Messiah (Lk. iv. 18f. L ; Lk. vii. 18–23 = Mt. xi. 2–6 Q ;[4] Lk. xi. 20 = Mt. xii. 28 Q) : but the evidence makes it clear that they were in the first place deeds of mercy done out of sympathy for the actual sufferers.[5]

(9) We may note the following passages (see also below, p. 120 [7]) :

from Q : Lk. vi. 36 = Mt. v. 48 (see above, p. 39) ; possibly also Mt. xxiii. 23, though the Lucan parallel (Lk. xi. 42) does not mention mercy, and the Matthæan wording may be due to M or m.

from L : Lk. x. 27b ; Lk. x. 30–37 (esp. 33, 37) ; Lk. xv. 25–32.

from Mk. : Mk. xii. 31 = Mt. xxii. 39.

from M : Mt. v. 7 ; Mt. xviii. 33 ; Mt. xxv. 31–46.

(10) It is not necessary to collect the passages from which we learn that Jesus gave himself assiduously throughout most of the period of his ministry to the work of teaching and preaching in public. Only a few sayings need to be noted.

---

[1] On Jewish beliefs regarding the connexion between sickness and sin, see Strack-Billerbeck i. 495f., and cf. Héring, *Royaume*, 22f.

[2] Menzies, *Earliest Gospel*, 69b, 97ab, 135ab ; A. T. Cadoux in *E.T.* xxxvi. 491 (Aug. 1925), and *Theol. of Jes.* 23–25, 60.

[3] Cf. A. T. Cadoux in *E.T.* xxxvi. 490ab, 491b (Aug. 1925).

[4] Unless we are to understand the healings here referred to as *figurative* (A. T. Cadoux in *loc. cit.* 490f.). On the Messianic significance of the miracles, cf. Gloege, *Reich Gottes*, 115–126 ; Hoskyns in *Myst. Christi*, 74 ; Hoskyns and Davey, *Riddle*, 163–177 ; Major in *Mission*, etc. xxviii ; Otto, *Kingdom*, 162, 348.

[5] See above, pp. 38, 44, and cf. Montefiore, *S.G.*² I. 36 ; Otto, *Kingdom*, 348.

The Parable of the Sower (Mk. iv. 3–9 = Lk. viii. 5–8 = Mt. xiii. 3–9), when considered apart from the allegorical and probably-ungenuine interpretation of it which Jesus is represented as having given (Mk. iv. 13–20 = Lk. viii. 11–15 = Mt. xiii. 18–23), is now widely recognized, not primarily as a pictorial description of different types of listeners, but as an encouraging analogy between preaching and agriculture : just as the farmer, despite the sundry risks of waste and failure attending his work, can yet be sure that nature will yield him a fine crop, so Jesus, as preacher of the Kingdom, has confidence that, despite a percentage of unresponsive hearers, he can yet count on convincing a substantial majority.[1] Again, we have Jesus' regret that there were not enough workers to gather in God's harvest (see above, p. 46)—a sentiment which m directly connects with his compassion for the worried and depressed crowd (see above, p. 44, and cf. also Mt. xiii. 15 fin. m for Jesus' desire to effect spiritual and moral healing). In Lk. x. 22 fin. = Mt. xi. 27 fin. Q, he speaks of the Son's willingness to reveal the Father to men. Lk. vii. 22 = Mt. xi. 4f. Q may refer figuratively to the effects of Jesus' teaching rather than to his actual healings (see above, p. 47 n. 4) ; and in any case the Lucan version of it concludes with the words, " the poor have good news preached to them ". Finally, we have Jesus' application to himself of the words of Isa. lxi. 1, 2a, which in the original Hebrew ran as follows, " The Spirit of the Lord Yahweh is upon me, for Yahweh has anointed me ; He has sent me to give good news to the afflicted, to bind up the broken-hearted, to announce liberty to captives and release to prisoners, to announce a year of Yahweh's favour . . .". The Greek of L (Lk. iv. 18f.) is a little different ; but in the synagogue at Nazareth Jesus would read and interpret the Hebrew text. Despite the early reference to anointing (with its tacit hint at Messiahship), there is no real reason why Jesus may not have quoted the words and applied them to himself (see below, p. 57).

(**11**) Jesus scandalized the Scribes and Pharisees by his willingness to associate in table-fellowship with persons whom they regarded as irreligious, disreputable, and negligent of the Law (Mk. ii. 15f. = Lk. v. 29f. = Mt. ix. 10f.). " Look ", they said, " a glutton and a tippler, a friend of tax-collectors and sinners ! " (Lk. vii. 34 = Mt. xi. 19 Q). Jesus frankly admitted the charge, and defended himself by urging that, as

---

[1] Bacon in *Hibbert Journ.* xxi. 132f. (Oct. 1922) ; A. T. Cadoux, *Parables*, 154–157 ; Dodd, *Parables*, 180–183 ; B. T. D. Smith, *Parables*, 126, 128.

it is the sick, not the healthy, who need the doctor, so these "sinners" are the very ones to whom he must offer his hospitality (Mk. ii. 17 = Lk. v. 31f. = Mt. ix. 12, 13b).[1] He further appeals to the results in the lives of those who accepted him : God's "Wisdom is vindicated by her children" (Lk. vii. 35 = Mt. xi. 19 fin. Q : 1 says "all her children", and m replaces "children" by "works").[2]

(12) See above, p. 46 (7).

(13) The nature of the change which Jesus hoped to effect in men by means of his teaching and influence is, as has already been indicated (see above, p. 46 [7]), summed up in the term "salvation". Only a more comprehensive study of his teaching as a whole would suffice to give us the full content of this great term (see below, pp. 215-217 [5], 236f. [15]). At the moment, however, we may—without risk of undue modernization—perhaps venture to say that a central element in its meaning was the attainment by men of a filial relation towards God such as that enjoyed by Jesus himself—a relation of trust, obedience, and intimate communion.[3] Alternatively, Jesus' objective might not inaccurately be described as the maximum felicity of man. So far from implying a light or lenient view of sin, such an objective involved the gravest condemnation of it as that which renders lasting happiness impossible. The Messianic Age was in Rabbinic thought mostly envisaged as sinless.[4] But it was also looked forward to as a time of joy and plenty, of physical as well as spiritual and moral well-being.[5] And it was natural that Jesus, the compassionate Saviour and friend of men, and the foe of their misery as also of their wrongdoing, should spend himself in the promotion of human righteousness and joy, should speak often of the happiness of

[1] In *Congreg. Quart.* xiii. 158f. (Apl. 1935), Dr. T. W. Manson argues that l's gloss (" to repentance ") in Lk. v. 32 spoils the sense and reduces the saying to a mere platitude : " to call " in Mk. ii. 17 means not to summon to repentance, but to invite to a feast.

[2] Cf. Holtzmann, *Theol.* i. 185–190.

[3] Cf. J. E. Carpenter, *The Relation of Jesus to his Age and our own* (1895), 20–23 ; Wendt, *Teaching*, i. 100f., 192f., 203, 393f., ii. 124f., 155, 167 ; Holtzmann, *Theol.* i. 301–304 ; Manson, *Teaching*, 112 (" . . .he claims to make the Father real to men in the same sense that the Father is real to him "), 113, 115 (" . . . his teaching would make the Father have the same place and power in the life of his disciples, that they too may be heirs, heirs of God and joint-heirs with Jesus Christ "), 198–200, and in *Mission*, etc. 422 (" . . . He sees the deepest tragedy of human life . . . in their rejection of God's greatest gift ").

[4] Strack-Billerbeck i. 70–74.

[5] Strack-Billerbeck i. 607, 610 : cf. also the frequent allusions in the Messianic *Psalms of Solomon* to the coming εὐφροσύνη of Israel (x. 5f., 8, xi. 3, xii. 3, xiv. 10, xv. 3, xvii. 35).

those who would follow him,[1] and should liken the heyday of his early ministry in Galilee to the conviviality of a wedding-feast (Mk. ii. 19 = Lk. v. 34 = Mt. ix. 15).[2]

[1] I refer to the numerous " Beatitudes " scattered up and down the Gospels. There is no linguistic justification for any distinction between the renderings " Happy are . . . " and " Blessed are . . . " The Greek adjective μακάριος (Plur. -οι) used in this connexion is simply the equivalent of the Hebrew plural abstract noun אשרי used in Psalm i. 1 and many other passages with reference to the enviable state of the person or persons referred to, and meaning interjectionally " O the happiness of . . . ".

[2] What Bultmann (*Jesus*, 75f., 79f., 124–127) and other Barthians have written, about Jesus knowing nothing of any " humanistische Menschenideal ", and setting no store on the worth of humanity as such, seems to me, in view of the foregoing evidence, strangely wrongheaded—another case, perhaps, of failure to understand and interpret rightly the Semitic habit of speaking of God (see above, pp. 26, 43, etc.).

The words of Mk. ix. 19 = Lk. ix. 41 = Mt. xvii. 17 (" How long shall I be with you ? . . . ") do not expresses Jesus' real attitude : they would fit rather that of a " Gott, der nur vorübergehend in Menschengestalt erschien, um alsbald in den Himmel zurückzukehren " (Dibelius, *Formgesch. des Ev.* [1919], 87 : cf. Creed, *St. Luke*, 136).

CHAPTER IV

THE MESSIAH OF ISRAEL

(1) Jesus was certainly convinced that he was the predicted and awaited Messianic King of Israel. (2) This conviction was based upon, and was secondary to, his consciousness of being in a unique sense the Son and (3) intimate Servant of God, charged, as herald and bringer of His Kingdom, with a saving mission to men. (4) The apocalyptic features of the Messianic idea were subordinate to these primary concerns. (5) His Messianic vocation became clear to him at his baptism : (6) but he made no public announcement of it during his ministry. (7) The main reason for this secrecy was that his conception of Messiahship differed so widely from that of the Jews generally, that a public declaration that he was Messiah would have gravely misled them, and thus have impeded his work. (8) He had also to consider the risk of rousing political suspicions. (9) He did, however, lead up to the recognition of his Messiahship, by repeatedly hinting at it in word and action, both before (10) and after Peter's acknowledgement of it at Cæsarea-Philippi. (11) But it was only at the end of his life that he explicitly avowed it in public.

(1) Certain eminent scholars have doubted and even denied that Jesus thought and spoke of himself as Messiah. The main ground for this negative judgment is the unobtrusive part played by the Messianic idea in the Gospel-story, in particular Jesus' repeated injunctions that it was not to be mentioned in public—injunctions explicable (it is suggested) only as the Evangelist's method of accounting for the strange failure of the Jews to recognize him whom the Church declared to be their rightful Lord (see above, p. 31). The Church's ascription of Messiahship to Jesus is on this view usually thought to have sprung from Peter's epoch-making vision of the risen Christ.[1] It is not proposed to argue the question here : that has been done elsewhere by abler hands. Let it

---

[1] The classic statement of this view is Wrede's work, *Das Messiasgeheimnis in den Evangelien* (1901). Cf. also Bultmann in *Z.N.W.* xix (1919/20) 165–174 ; and K. G. Goetz in *Theol. Stud. und Kritiken*, cv (1933) 117–137. Dr. R. H. Lightfoot has recently written in defence of Wrede (*Hist. and Interp.* 16ff.). Cf. also, for a non-Messianic interpretation of the demons' outcries, Hering, *Royaume*, 135–140, 142f.

suffice to remark that the denial of Jesus' Messianic conscious-ness seems to rest on an unwarrantably-low estimate of the historical value of the Gospels, that Jesus' secretiveness in the matter of his Messiahship can (as will be presently shown) be more satisfactorily explained as due to the conditions of his work than as an invention of his followers after his death, and that the great number of modern scholars are therefore un-questionably right in believing his Messianic claim to be an historical reality.[1]

(2) The abundant evidence in the Gospels showing that Jesus regarded himself as the Son of God in some unique sense is collected and discussed above (pp. 29–33). There can be no doubt that, in many passages, the phrase or concept " the Son of God " appears as a virtual equivalent of " Messiah " (pp. 29–31, 33–36). It is, however, submitted (pp. 34f.) that, (a) since spiritual status naturally precedes, rather than follows, official vocation, and (b) since some at least of the evidence for Jesus' consciousness of special Sonship (e.g., his feeling at the age of twelve, and his use of " Abba " in prayer) seems to have little or no reference to the office of Messiah, we ought to think of his Messianic consciousness as secondary and subordinate to his filial consciousness, however closely the two were connected together in his own mind. This conclusion receives some support from the fact that there is not much evidence to show that the Old-Testament designation of the Messianic King as the Son of God (Psa. ii. 7, lxxxix. 26f., 2 Sam. vii. 14) was frequently used in Jesus' day—though its rarity in Rabbinic literature might possibly be explained as due to a desire to avoid a Christian expression.[2]

(3) Jesus' application to himself of the prophecies about the Servant of the Lord in Deutero-Isaiah (see above, pp. 37f.) is yet another proof that for him the conception of Messiahship was not itself primary, but was governed by other considera-tions. We have no evidence to show that these Servant-poems

---

[1] There is a good discussion by the late Dr. A. S. Peake in *B.J.R.L.* VIII, i. 52–81 (Jan. 1924). Cf. also, among others, Holtzmann, *Theol.* i. 308f.; Mundle in *Z.N.W.* xxi (1922) 299–311 ; Rawlinson, *St. Mark*, 260 ; Gloege, *Reich Gottes*, 137–142 ; K. L. Schmidt in *R.G.G.* iii (1929) 147f. ; Major in *Modern Churchman*, xxiv. 424–426 (Oct. 1934), and in *Mission*, etc. xxiii., 29 ; Otto, *Kingdom*, 159–161, 228f. ; V. Taylor, *Sacrifice*, 18–20 ; Flew, *Church*, 160f. ; H. G. Hatch, *The Messianic Consciousness of Jesus* (1939), 28–55.

[2] Cf. Dalman, *W.J.* 268–273 ; Bousset, *Jesus*, 80–83 (Eng. tr. 175–180: " . . . So war für Jesus der Messiasgedanke die einzig mögliche Form seines Bewusstseins und doch—ein unzureichende Form ; eine Notwendigkeit—aber auch eine schwere Last, . . . "), and *Relig. des Jud.* (1926), 227f. ; Swete, *St. Mark*, 358f. ; Winstanley, *Future*, 201–205, 294–297 ; Manson in *Mission*, etc. 335 ; Macaulay, *Death of Jesus*, 89–91.

were in his time interpreted by the Jews messianically ; and it is not probable (despite Isa. lxi. 1) that they were, for Deutero-Isaiah (xlv. 1) represents Cyrus, King of Persia, as Yahweh's anointed; and the lot of the Servant, who has to face contumely and even martyrdom, would hardly fit in with the idea of a victorious theocratic king, such as most Jews expected their Messiah to be. Jesus' appropriation of these passages, therefore, could not have been based on his Messianic consciousness, but was an extraneous appendage to it, added originally by himself as its true explication. Its basis could have been only his submissive devotion to the Will of God his Father and his self-dedication to the clamant needs of the men and women ‑around him.[1] Any theory, therefore, which represents Jesus' mind as dominated by Messianic notions, to the exclusion of other important interests, is clearly at variance with our evidence.[2]

(4) As with the Messianic office, so with the striking apocalyptic expectations frequently associated with it in the Jewish mind, particularly those connected with the figure of the Messianic " Son of Man " portrayed in the Books of Daniel and Enoch. We shall have later to consider the meaning of the phrase " the Son of Man " as Jesus used it : here it is needful to note only that the distinctively-apocalyptic ideas were in all probability secondary to Jesus' filial consciousness and the conviction that he came, not to be served, but to serve. The form they took in his mind was determined by these more fundamental considerations, and received special modification from the gradually-developing certainty of his early martyrdom at the hands of his fellow-countrymen. Important though these ideas were as parts of his world-view, they must not be pictured as constituting a cast-iron programme, unalterably fixed by the nation's literature and dominating Jesus' whole forecast from the commencement of his ministry.[3]

---

[1] Cf. Weinel, *Theol.* 225 (" . . . Jesus ist nicht, nachdem er sich eine Zeitlang bloss für einen Propheten gehalten hat, nach und nach bis zum messianischen Selbstbewusstsein aufgestiegen, sondern *er hat seinen messianischen Beruf als einen prophetischen* ausgeübt " : italics mine) ; Rawlinson, *St. Mark*, 253–256 ; Otto, *Kingdom*, 57, 107, 174.

[2] How grievously this fact is often overlooked may be illustrated by some editorial words in *E.T.* xlviii. 148f. (Jan. 1937). The writer counts as one of the recent factors which have revolutionized theology " the discovery of the New Testament eschatology by Albert Schweitzer. This completely disposed of the liberal portrait of Christ. . . . With the Jesus who really lived, and whom the Gospels picture, the Messiahship was not a secondary matter, but the sum total of all His activity, of His being and willing. With the picture of Christ set forth by Liberalism this Jesus has nothing in common ". But see above, pp. 3–7.

[3] Cf. Bartlet and Carlyle, *Christianity in Hist.* 26 (Jesus' use of the phrase

(5) Of those scholars who believe that Jesus viewed himself as the Messiah, the great majority hold that his consciousness of Messiahship first became definite and clear on the occasion of his baptism at the hands of John. The story of the baptism, as recorded by Mark and probably also independently in Q (see above, pp. 29f., 35 [3]), makes this the most acceptable view.[1] The modification of it preferred by some—the theory, namely, that Jesus was convinced, not that he was already the Messiah, but that he would come to be so in the future [2]—has no claim to be preferred to it. The secrecy and unobtrusiveness of the Messiahship during the Ministry can be better accounted for than by supposing that at first it was a merely-prospective dignity.

(6) When, in replying to Jesus' inquiry at Cæsarea-Philippi, Peter acknowledged him to be the Messiah, he received the confession with tacit approval, if not with the emphatic and explicit commendation reported here (unhistorically, as it would appear) by m or M (Mt. xvi. 17-19).[3] Then, ' he warned them to speak about him to no one ' (Mk. viii. 30 = Lk. ix. 21 = Mt. xvi. 20 : the last-named paraphrases, ' he commanded the Disciples to say to no one that he was the Messiah '). It follows, of course, from this important record that, prior to this occasion and at least for a considerable time afterwards, Jesus made in public nothing like an explicit claim to Messiahship. And except for an occasional unhistorical insertion in Mt. (e.g., xiv. 33 m), the rest of the Synoptic

---

" Son of Man " " set aside the conventional Apocalyptic conception alike of the Kingdom and of Messiah. For according to Apocalyptic, the Son of Man played no part in preparing his people for the Kingdom, but appeared suddenly with no prior human history—a vital contrast— . . . Such a being . . . was no true Messiah as the Hebrew prophets conceived the *rôle*. The Apocalyptic Messianic ideal cannot, then, have been Jesus' own ideal, or the real basis of the title by which he chose to hint at his own function and person. The real source of his Messianic consciousness, and therefore what moulded his own distinctive idea of Messiahship and the Messianic Kingdom, was his filial consciousness of the Father. . . . The current Messianic and Apocalyptic conceptions merely afforded forms which he used, . . . ") ; Otto, *Kingdom*, 174 (" Such a consciousness of mission did not arise and does not receive its true explanation from apocalyptic or other historical antecedents, although its forms may be determined by and contained in such antecedents . . . this form could be no other than that of a Messiah . . . ").

[1] Cf., e.g., Wendt, *Teaching*, ii. 123 ; Rawlinson, *St. Mark*, 253f. ; A. T. Cadoux in *The Lord of Life*, 58, 60 ; Manson, *Teaching*, 197, 266f. n. 2, as samples of a great host.

[2] Cf., e.g., Piepenbring, *The Historical Jesus* (1924), 116f. ; Montefiore, *S.G.[2]* I. cxxixf., 183f. (cf. *S.G.[1]* I. 58) ; Jülicher in *T.L.Z.* lix. 230 (June 1934—in review of Otto).

[3] Cf. C. J. Cadoux, *Cathol. and Christianity*, 379–384 ; Manson in *Mission*, etc. 493–497 (assigns it to M, but does not regard it as a genuine saying of Jesus).

evidence shows that no such public claim was asserted by Jesus until he stood before the Sanhedrin. When we consider the ease with which the open declaration of Messiahship might have been antedated in later Christian thought,[1] we can have no hesitation in accepting the Synoptists' representation as historically true.[2]

(7) While the current Jewish ideas as to the character and work of the Messiah were very indefinite, so indefinite in fact that some of the programmes sketched by the Apocalyptists omitted him altogether, there can be no doubt that such a Messiah as Jesus intended to be—a king without an army at his back, going about doing good, regarding lowly service as his greatest glory, facing (like the Deutero-Isaianic " Servant ") the prospect of misunderstanding, insult, and opposition—was glaringly different from the royal hero whom at least the bulk of the people expected. Under these circumstances it was obvious that for him to announce in public that he was the long-awaited Messiah would have meant, not only grievously misleading the people, but making the work on which his heart was set largely impossible through the misconceptions he would have created (see above, p. 31). There was, moreover, no necessity for him to advance his full claims. The achievement of the object of his mission would not be seriously imperilled by the intervention of some delay in the nation's recognition of his true title ; and that being so, it was clearly the wisest plan for him to say nothing about the Messiahship for the present, and to check any premature tendency on the part of over-enthusiastic persons to proclaim it.[3] It is possible that he had his policy of secrecy in mind when he spoke the somewhat obscure words, " There is nothing that has been covered up, which will not be revealed, and hidden, which will not be known . . ." (Lk. xii. 2f. = Mt. x. 26f. Q : there is a close parallel in Mk. iv. 22 = Lk. viii. 17).[4]

[1] As the lapse of time increasingly foreshortened the Christians' view of Jesus' life, it became more and more difficult for them to believe that there had ever been a time in that life when the Lord was not announcing himself as God's Messiah. Thus, in the Fourth Gospel, there is no secrecy about the Messiahship : Jesus speaks openly about it to all and sundry from the beginning of his ministry.

[2] Weinel, *Theol.* 223f.

[3] Cf. Wendt, *Teaching,* i. 179f. ; Bousset, *Was wissen wir von Jesus ?* (1906), 61f. (" . . . dass Jesus sich in diesem Punkte zunächst in Schweigen gehüllt habe, weil er instinktiv die Unmöglichkeit fühlte, seiner Umgebung klar zu machen, in welchem Sinn er sich den Messias nenne ") ; Rawlinson, *St. Mark,* 258–262 (discussion of Wrede) ; Montefiore, *S.G.*[2] I. 184f. ; Otto, *Kingdom,* 219f. For the special injunction of silence on the demoniacs, see above, p. 31.

[4] Cf. A. T. Cadoux, *Parables,* 145f.

(8) Jesus would undoubtedly have incurred grave political danger, had he allowed it to be noised abroad that he seriously considered himself to be the Jewish Messiah. " The Roman police " (and the same would be true of the government of Herod Antipas), " which had an Argus-eye for movements of that kind, and rendered them innocuous in the speediest possible way, without first making lengthy enquiries concerning character and motives, would not have tolerated for long a ' Son of David ' and ' King of Israel ', whom great numbers of the population were saluting as such—however convinced he might have been on his own account of the non-political and exclusively religious character of his mission ".[1]

(9) The plan he actually adopted was to push ahead with his teaching about the Kingdom of God and with his works of exorcism and healing, which he regarded as indications of the presence and power of the Kingdom, and from time to time to suggest by act and word that he himself, as inaugurator of the Kingdom, was the Messiah, but always to stop short of an explicit declaration to that effect. He would accustom the Jews to see for themselves the truth of his teaching and the value of his work, before he would inform them directly by what title he ought really to be known.[2] The points in the Gospel-records of the Ministry (prior to Peter's Confession at Cæsarea-Philippi), at which indirect hints of Jesus' Messiahship may be seen are the following.

(a) John the Baptist's announcement, " There is coming after me the one who is stronger than I, the thong of whose sandal I am not worthy to stoop down and untie. I have baptized you with water ; but he will baptize you with fire . . ." (Mk. i. 7f. : cf. Lk. iii. 16f. [Q + Mk.] = Mt. iii. 11f. [Q + Mk. + m]).[3] These words were probably meant to be an announcement of the early appearance of the Messiah ; but the public and explicit application of them to Jesus (who had not yet appeared before John) is not a part of the original record, though it is suggested by l (Lk. iii. 22 [" in bodily form "]) and m (Mt. iii. 16f. [" This is My Son ", instead of

---

[1] Holtzmann, Synopt. 10 : cf. D. S. Cairns in Contemp. Review, lxxix. 204–207 (Feb. 1901) ; Meyer, Ursprung, ii. 451 ; Montefiore, S.G.[2] I. 184 ; Goguel, Life of Jes. 372. John vi. 15, probably an historical touch, illustrates the danger. Schweitzer, on the other hand, is disposed to doubt the frequent appearance of Messianic claimants (but cf. Sharman, Future, 154–161) and with it the likelihood of political alarm (L.J.F. 246, 346f., 351 = Quest, 253, 315, 320 n. 1).

[2] Cf. Menzies, Earliest Gospel, 168 ab.

[3] For the substitution of " fire " for " Holy Spirit ", see Creed, St. Luke, 54a.

Mark's and Luke's " Thou art . . ." ; i.e., a declaration to John and the crowds, instead of an assurance addressed directly to Jesus]). Moreover, it forms an integral element of the story as told in the Fourth Gospel (John i. 26–34).

(b) Jesus' open application to himself (in the synagogue at Nazareth) of the prophecy of Isa. lxi. 1f. (" The Spirit of the Lord Yahweh is upon me, for Yahweh has anointed me ; . . "), with the words, " To-day has this Scripture been fulfilled in your hearing " (Lk. iv. 17–21 L). There is no need to doubt that Jesus actually did read these words in public, and did so apply them to himself. We must suppose that, despite the reference to anointing, what he said was not understood as tantamount to a direct assertion that he was himself the Messiah. But it could hardly have been less than a fairly-strong hint that he was so.

(c) Jesus' authoritative tone in teaching, his independent attitude to the Law, etc. (see below, p. 72). This might certainly suggest that he felt himself to be filling some specially responsible or exalted office.[1]

(d) His reference to himself as " the bridegroom ", presiding at what might be viewed as a kind of anticipation of the Messianic Feast (Mk. ii. 19 = Lk. v. 34 = Mt. ix. 15).[2] We cannot, however, be sure as to the *time* at which he so spoke. The Marcan chronology cannot be depended on in detail ; and the immediately-ensuing allusion to the bridegroom being taken away, if genuine, suggests a date later in the Ministry (see below, pp. 189–191).

(e) His choice of twelve personal Disciples, corresponding in number to the twelve tribes of Israel. Would not this fore-shadow the undertaking of an important *national* rôle ? (see below, pp. 143f.).

(f) The reply which he gave to the question which the Baptist sent to ask him, namely, whether or no he was " the coming one ". His reply was, " Go and tell John what ye have seen and heard—how that the blind regain their sight, the lame walk, lepers are cleansed, the deaf hear, the dead are raised, the poor have good news preached to them. And happy is any one who is not made to stumble through me " (Lk. vii. 19–23 = Mt. xi. 2–6 Q : Mt. omits the clause about the preaching to the poor). We may wonder whether the actual enumeration of the healing works was really spoken by Jesus, or whether it is an amplification by the author of Q, and

---

[1] Cf. Holtzmann, *Theol.* i. 295–307 ; Gloege, *Reich Gottes*, 132–137.
[2] Cf. Otto, *Kingdom*, 220f

whether it was meant originally to refer to physical or spiritual healings (see above, p. 47 n. 4). But as it stands, Jesus' reply strongly recalls the quasi-Messianic passages, Isa. xxix. 18f., xxxv. 5f., lxi. 1f. ; and its very ambiguity would suggest to those who heard it that the real reply to John's enquiry was in the affirmative.

(g) The occasion on which Jesus presided at a meal of a great crowd in the open air (Mk. vi. 35–44 = Lk. ix. 12–17 = Mt. xiv. 15–21 ; Mk. viii. 1–9a = Mt. xv. 32–38). This was in all probability thought of by him as an anticipation of the great Messianic Feast in the Kingdom of God. The real significance of the scene has been obscured from view even in the Gospels by the stupendous character of the physical miracle which Jesus is reported to have then worked. While, however, we may feel compelled to discredit the miracle (just as most now realize that in Mk. and Mt. the incident has been erroneously duplicated), we are under no necessity to regard the whole scene as fictitious. The explicit allusions in the Gospels to Jesus " blessing " and " giving thanks for " the food he distributed recall the same features in the story of the Last Supper ; and as this latter was quite explicitly an anticipation of the Messianic Feast, it is natural to suppose that the crowd-feeding in Galilee, besides being an occasion for showing and inculcating generosity, may have been in the mind of Jesus himself (though perhaps not clearly so to others) a similar anticipation.[1]

(10) After Peter's epoch-making acknowledgement of Jesus' Messiahship at Cæsarea-Philippi,[2] we note the following tacit allusions to the fact.

(a) The story of the Transfiguration (Mk. ix. 2–10 = Lk. ix. 28–36 = Mt. xvii. 1–9).[3]

(b) The continuance of the authoritative teaching, with more frequent demands for service, self-sacrifice, etc., " for my sake ", or " for my name's sake " (see below, p. 77). We must, however, note that two phrases of this general type—Mk. ix. 41 (" . . . on the ground " [lit. " in name "] " that ye belong to Christ "), and Mt. xxiii. 10 M (" one is your leader—

---

[1] Cf. Schweitzer, *L.J.F.* 421f., 424–426 = *Quest*, 374f., 377–380, 387, *Mystery*, 168–174, 262, 264 ; McNeile, *St. Matthew*, 216 ; Rawlinson, *St. Mark*, 106 ; Dodd in *Myst. Christi*, 60 ; V. Taylor, *Sacrifice*, 185, 243.

[2] See Manson, *Teaching*, 201–211, for the changes in Jesus' way of speech inaugurated by this Confession.

[3] Cf. Otto, *Kingdom*, 223. It is one of the many weaknesses in Schweitzer's interpretation of Jesus' career that he has to put the Transfiguration *before* the Confession at Cæsarea-Philippi (*L.J.F.* 428f. = *Quest*, 381f., *Mystery*, 180f.).

the Christ ")—cannot be regarded as actually spoken by Jesus, for he never referred to himself (as the early Church referred to him) in this way.

(c) Blind Bartimæus' use of the phrase " Son of David " in appealing to Jesus (Mk. x. 47f. = Lk. xviii. 38f. = Mt. xx. 30f. [cf. ix. 27 m]). Bartimæus probably meant the words as a complimentary recognition of Jesus' Messiahship (see below, p. 82) : and the fact that Jesus did not rebuke him or repudiate his form of address is significant.

(d) The story of the Triumphal Entry into Jerusalem (Mk. xi. 1–11 = Lk. xix. 28–38 [xix. 37f. probably coming from L] = Mt. xxi. 1–10). The quasi-Messianic character of this formal entry is seen in (i) the peaceful riding on the royal animal, strongly recalling the words of Zech. ix. 9 (which Mt. xxi. 4f. M or m explicitly quotes), and (ii) the words shouted by the cheering crowd, " Hosanna ! Blessed be he who comes in the name of the Lord ! Blessed be the coming kingdom of our father David ! Hosanna in the highest ! " (Mk. xi. 9f. = Mt. xxi. 9 [m here omits the blessing on the kingdom, and begins with " Hosanna to the Son of David ! ", thus glossing inaccurately]). In Lk. xix. 38 (probably L), the cry runs, " Blessed be he who comes—the king—in the name of the Lord ! Peace on earth, and glory in the highest ! " [1]

(e) The introduction of the Owner's Son in the Parable of the Wicked Vinedressers, and the cryptic allusion to the Cornerstone which immediately follows the Parable (Mk. xii. 1–12 = Lk. xx. 9–19 = Mt. xxi. 33–46 : see above, p. 30). The general tone, in fact, of the incidents that followed upon the Triumphal Entry (especially the cleansing of the Temple-courts, unless we prefer the Johannine dating) suggests continuous tension between Jesus and the religious leaders on the question of his status and authority. " Throughout these scenes at Jerusalem the Messianic claim of our Lord is steadily maintained and put forward by implication, . . .".[2]

(11) Jesus publicly avowed his Messiahship before the Sanhedrin, in response to the direct challenge of the High Priest (Mk. xiv. 61f. = Mt. xxvi. 63f. ; Lk. xxii. 67–70 L). Questioned by Pilate, he accepted (though apparently with some reluctance) the designation " the King of the Jews " as

---

[1] Scholars differ as to precisely how much Messianic significance Jesus intentionally put into this act : but its general suggestiveness must surely have been unmistakable. Cf., e.g., Bruce in *E.Bi.* 2450f. ; Dobschütz, *Eschatol.* 175–177 ; Weinel, *Theol.* 221f. ; Otto, *Kingdom*, 223f. ; Rawlinson, *St. Mark*, 151f.

[2] Rawlinson, *St. Mark*, 160.

true of himself (Mk. xv. 2 = Mt. xxvii. 11 ; Lk. xxiii. 3 L).[1]
The publicity of his Messianic claim is repeatedly attested in
the Passion-story (Mk. xv. 9 = Mt. xxvii. 17 ; Mk. xv. 12 =
Mt. xxvii. 22 ; Mk. xv. 18 = Mt. xxvii. 29 ; Mk. xv. 26 = Mt.
xxvii. 37, cf. Lk. xxiii. 38 L ; Mk. xv. 29–32 = Mt. xxvii.
39–43, cf. Lk. xxiii. 35–37 L ; Lk. xxiii. 39, 42 L. Lk. xxiv.
26 L is a post-Resurrection designation of himself as " the
Christ ").

[1] It has been doubted whether Jesus' reply (σὺ λέγεις) to Pilate's question
was a reluctant affirmation or a simple refusal either to affirm or deny ; but
Mt. xxvi. 25 m, and Mt. xxvi. 64 m and Lk. xxii. 70 L, compared with Mk.
xiv. 62, make it sufficiently clear that it was the former. Even if the true
reading in Mk. xiv. 62 were σὺ εἶπας ὅτι ἐγώ εἰμι (so Streeder, *Four Gospels,*
322 : cf. Rawlinson, *St. Mark,* 222 n.1), the argument would still hold good,
for the sequel shows in any case that Jesus was understood to have at least
admitted that he was the Messiah. And this conclusion is confirmed by the
story as a whole. It was as " King of the Jews " that Jesus was officially
sentenced to death (Mk. xv. 26 = Mt. xxvii. 37 ; Lk. xxiii. 38 L) : and it
was probably because he had avowed himself to be so that Pilate could not
release him without incurring the risk of imperial suspicion (John xix. 12) :
here we have the real reason why Pilate failed to resist the demand of the
crowd—an indirect confirmation of the historical accuracy of the report of
Jesus' admission to him. Cf. also Otto, *Kingdom,* 224f.

CHAPTER V

THE CONQUEROR OF SATAN

(1) Like his Jewish contemporaries, Jesus believed in the existence of a host of evil demons, led by the arch-fiend Satan (2) and at war with God and man. (3) It was they who misled men into folly and sin, (4) afflicted them with illness and misfortune, (5) and sometimes drove them to madness by actually taking up their abode within them. (6) This view of the cause of evil was of mixed origin and long growth : (7) though not a radical solution of the problem, it served as a relatively-good working hypothesis. (8) Jesus often pictured his enterprise as a strenuous campaign against these malignant foes. (9) In this campaign his own Temptation was a decisive initial victory, not concluding the struggle, but so breaking the enemy's power that progress thenceforth was only a matter of diligent continuance. (10) It was in that light that he regarded his work as healer and exorcist. (11) The conquest of Satan and the demons had been anticipated as one of the achievements of the coming Messianic Age ; (12) and Jesus accordingly viewed his successful exorcisms as a proof that God's Kingdom had already come among men.

(1) The Gospels exhibit Jesus frequently speaking of Satan and the demons as real personal beings with whom he and his hearers constantly had to deal. When modern Christians came to the conclusion that probably neither Satan nor the demons actually existed, some of them endeavoured to harmonize this conclusion with a continued belief in the infallibility of Jesus by treating his references to these beings simply as an ad hominem accommodation to the mental habits of his contemporaries and not as reflecting his own personal view. Such a mode of defending his inerrant authority while tacitly presupposing one's own is increasingly felt to be unsatisfactory. The records plainly show that Jesus believed in the existence of Satan and the demons : and that fact is not affected by any difficulty we may feel to-day in believing in it. As a matter of fact, some Christians have in recent times reverted to an

acceptance of it : but that movement of thought does not directly concern us here.[1]

(2) Being at war with God, Satan and the demons organize themselves for ceaseless hostility against men as the special objects of God's love and care. ' They are the cause of all kinds of evils and misfortunes to men . . . they performed in the ancient world all the tasks which we should now assign to bacilli, complexes, bad luck, or the less reputable ' isms ' ".[2] It is quite possible that the last petition of the Lord's Prayer in its Matthaean form ought to be translated, " And bring us not into testing, but rescue us from the evil (one) " (Mt. vi. 13 M : the parallel in Lk. xi. 4 L has nothing after " testing ") : [3] as such it " asks . . . for deliverance from the arch-enemy of God and man ".[4]

(3) Satan and the demons infect men with blind folly and incite them to sin. The two ideas were not sharply distinguished. When Peter tried to dissuade Jesus from looking forward to execution, the latter exclaimed, " Out of my sight, Satan ! Thou dwellest not on God's interests, but on men's " (Mk. viii. 32f. = Mt. xvi. 22f.). In the probably-unoriginal interpretation of the Parable of the Sower, forgetfulness of the message which Jesus had been heard to preach is described thus : " Satan comes and takes away the word that has been sown in them " (Mk. iv. 15 = Lk. viii. 12 [" the devil "] = Mt. xiii. 19 [" the evil one "]). In the still more probably ungenuine interpretation of the Parable of the Tares, " the tares are the sons of the evil (one), and the enemy who sowed them is the devil " (Mt. xiii. 38f. M or m). Any attempt to guarantee the truth of one's affirmation or denial by means of an oath " is from the evil (one) " (Mt. v. 37 M).[5] Moral weakness is again clearly in mind when Jesus says at the Last

---

[1] Cf. Edersheim, *Life . . . of Jes. . . .* , i. 480 ; C. J. Cadoux, *Cathol. and Christianity*, 212–216 ; Manson, *Teaching*, 165, esp. n.2 ; Cadbury, *Peril*, 76–79. A. T. Cadoux (*Theol. of. Jes.* 59–63) argues from Mk. viii. 33 = Mt. xvi. 23 and other indications that Jesus accepted the personality of Satan and the demons only very loosely, pictorial personification accounting for much of his language about them.

[2] Manson, *Teaching*, 153f. ; cf. 156.

[3] Scholars differ as to whether τοῦ πονηροῦ here is masculine or neuter. It was in defence of the Revisers' substitution of the masculine for the neuter, and of the relegation of the latter to the margin, that Bishop Lightfoot published three articles in *The Guardian* for 1881, which were reprinted as an Appendix to the third edition (1891) of his treatise *On a Fresh Revision of the English New Testament* (269–323).

[4] Manson in *Mission*, etc. 462.

[5] There is the same ambiguity between the masculine and the neuter in the two last-quoted passages as in the Lord's Prayer (see n.3 above). I incline, though indecisively, to the masculine in all three places.

Supper, " Simon, Simon, behold, Satan eagerly claimed you (all) that he might sift (you all) like the wheat. But I have prayed for thee, that thy loyalty may not give way " (Lk. xxii. 31f. L). Finally, it seems clear that actual demon-possession, which we must mention again presently, was often closely associated in Jesus' mind with moral depravity : thus we have his description of the man who after being freed from an unclean spirit is re-entered by it, together with " seven other spirits more evil (πονηρότερα) than itself " (Lk. xi. 26 = Mt. xii. 45 Q).

(4) There is obviously a very real difference between suffering from some physical illness (a condition which, however distressing, is not necessarily incompatible with righteousness of life) and being afflicted with madness (such as renders one incapable of healthy moral relations with God and one's fellows). The distinction between the two is for the most part clearly maintained in the Gospels (see above, p. 47). It did not however prevent people believing that purely-physical illnesses might, at least sometimes, be due to the hostile agency of Satan or the demons.[1] The clearest case is that of the woman suffering from curvature of the spine. Not only does Luke say that she had ' had a spirit of infirmity for eighteen years ' (Lk. xiii. 11 L), but he represents Jesus as calling her " this daughter of Abraham whom Satan has bound for eighteen years " (Lk. xiii. 16 L). Similarly Luke says that, when asked to cure Peter's mother-in-law, Jesus ' rebuked the fever ' (Lk. iv. 39 : contrast Mk. i. 31 = Mt. viii. 15), as if it had been a person. It is not quite clear whether the dumb man from whom a demon was driven out (as narrated in Lk. xi. 14 = Mt. ix. 32f. = Mt. xii. 22, apparently Q) is to be thought of as being mad, besides being dumb, or whether dumbness was the only symptom of his being possessed.

A quasi-personal or demonic cause of disease is presupposed also in the story of the Centurion's servant (Lk. vii. 2–10 = Mt. viii. 5–13 Q) : the Centurion is confident that Jesus can heal the servant by an authoritative word spoken at a distance, and his confidence is based on the analogy between Jesus and himself as being each of them " a man placed under authority ". Just as he (the Centurion), because acting under the authority of Herod Antipas, can be sure of the obedience of his soldiers and servants, so Jesus, because acting under God's authority, can (he believes) be sure of obedience on the part of a demon, if he orders it to desist from causing illness. Jesus approves

[1] Cf. Héring, *Royaume*, 18–23.

the Centurion's faith, thus seeming to endorse the theory behind it.[1]

Incidentally, we may note that accidents, as well as sin and sickness, could be brought about by demons, as is suggested by the statement that Jesus ' rebuked the wind, and said to the sea, " Be muzzled ! " ' (Mk. iv. 39 = Lk. viii. 24 = Mt. viii. 26)—the same word as was used in dealing with a demoniac (see above, p. 31).

(5) This is the familiar condition of demon-possession, to which frequent reference is made in the Gospels. There is no necessity to quote all the passages. Of the instances in which details regarding the symptoms are given, the one just alluded to (see above, p. 63) was a case of dumbness (Mt. xii. 22 [m ?] adds blindness), another a clear case of epilepsy and dumbness (Mk. ix. 17–27 = Lk. ix. 38–43a = Mt. xvii. 14–18) ; others were cases of harmless (Mk. i. 23–27 = Lk. iv. 33–36 ; apparently also Mk. vii. 24–30 = Mt. xv. 21–28) or violent (Mk. v. 1–20 = Lk. viii. 26–39 = Mt. viii. 28–34) insanity.[2]

(6) In the Old Testament Satan is first of all described as an official in the court of heaven, whose duty it was to accuse defaulters as deserving of Divine judgment. Later, this unamiable function degenerates into a habit of positively instigating men to sin ; and Satan thus becomes an inherently evil and hostile being, of whom nonetheless God occasionally makes providential use. In the post-Exilic period, contact with Persia greatly developed and enriched the Jewish imagination ; and Satan was furnished with a vast host of subordinate demons, some of them corresponding to certain minor Semitic deities recognized in pre-Exilic times, and was moreover dignified with a number of new appellatives, to the partial confusion of his own personal identity.[3]

(7) As a solution of the problem of the origin of evil, the demonic theory cannot be regarded as satisfactory, for it hardly does more than push the question one stage further back, leaving on our hands the task of explaining why the demons themselves should have become wicked. Moreover, it offered an account of some factors of human experience for

---

[1] The Centurion's argument is strangely misunderstood by Sir J. R. Seeley (*Ecce Homo*, pref. to fifth ed., xvi) and Dr. Jas. Moffatt (who wrongly translates " *though* I am a man under authority myself ", instead of " I *also* am a man under authority ").

[2] Cf. Stevens, *Theol. of the N.T.* 86–89.

[3] Good accounts of Jewish demonology are available in *J.E.* iv (1903) 514b–521b ; Bousset, *Relig. des Jud.* (1926), 331–342, 469, 514 ; and Strack-Billerbeck iv. 501–535. Manson (*Teaching*, 152–158) gives a useful summary. Cf. also, for Persian connexions, etc., Meyer, *Ursprung*, ii. 106–111, 357–361.

which we to-day undoubtedly possess more accurate and therefore preferable explanations. On the other hand, it would be a mistake to dismiss it off-hand as unadulterated delusion. Without forgetting the difference between the imagination of antiquity and scientific evidence, we may observe that there is nothing inherently incredible or improbable in the existence of discarnate beings, who are able to help or harm us in somewhat the same way as our fellow-men still living in the flesh are able. Further, there are certain phenomena in mental disease for which the hypothesis of spirit-possession provides an easier explanation than any other.[1] And the perversity of human affairs to-day on a large scale has led certain modern thinkers to have recourse to a theory of " demonry " as the only adequate cause of the mad folly which seems to have recently entered into the life of certain great peoples.[2] Be that as it may, there is no doubt that, whether hostile spirits actually exist or not, many human beings behave as those spirits were thought to behave, with consequences to their fellows very similar to those ascribed to demonic malignity. Nor must it be supposed that the demonic theory, by treating Satan and the demons as the instigators to sin, thereby involved any denial of human freedom and responsibility. As with the occasionally-evil influence of one's fellows, so with the temptations of the devil, one was not reduced by it to any necessity to sin : successful resistance is always a possibility.[3] And lastly, the history of exorcism is a proof that even a partially-erroneous diagnosis does not necessarily disqualify a lover of his kind for the ministry of healing them of their sicknesses.

(8) See below, pp. 66f. (10).

(9) When Jesus was accused of casting out evil spirits by the help of Beelzebul their ruler, he observed, after exposing the inherent absurdity of the suggestion, " No one can go into the strong man's house, and plunder his goods, unless he first bind the strong man, and then he will plunder his house " (Mk. iii. 27 = Mt. xii. 29). Lk. (xi. 21f.) has a different version of this saying, which may come from Q or possibly L : " When the strong man, fully armed, guards his palace, his belongings are at peace : but when one stronger than he comes up and conquers him, he takes away his armour whereon he was

[1] See, e.g., evidence cited in *The Review of Reviews*, xxxiv. 294 (Sept. 1906).
[2] Cf. G. Barlow in *Contemp. Review*, xcii. 25–42 (July 1907) ; P. Tillich, *Interp. of Hist.* (1936), 77–122, and in *Kingdom of God and Hist.* 115–117, 132–142 ; H.-D. Wendland in the latter work, 158–162, etc., etc. ; and A. E. Garvie in *Hibbert Journ.* xxxix. 26–32 (Oct. 1940).
[3] Cf. Manson, *Teaching*, 156–158, 165, 167.

relying, and distributes his spoil ". Jesus, that is to say, thinks of himself as able, in expelling demons, to play havoc with Satan's property (see above, pp. 63f.), because he has ·already, in some earlier encounter, scored a decisive victory over him.[1] It is difficult to see what else this victory could have been but his successful resistance to the Temptation that beset him in the wilderness shortly after his baptism.[2] The details concerning that Temptation were recorded in Q (Lk. iv. 1–13 = Mt. iv. 1–11 : cf. Mk. i. 12f.), and—unless they are purely imaginary, which is most unlikely—they must have been given by Jesus to the Disciples more or less in the form in which Q narrated them. We cannot base any objection to the theory that the Temptation-story describes a real experience of Jesus, and that he later viewed this experience as a decisive victory over Satan, on the fact that resisting the devil's spoken suggestions to sin is a very different thing from binding a strong man ; for the Oriental mind, in its liberal use of pictorial speech, is not limited to the use of pictures that are consistent with one another.[3] Thus it is possible that we have another, though a quite differently-framed, allusion to the same decisive conflict in the words which Jesus uttered on hearing from the Disciples that the demons were submissive to them when they used his name—words perhaps suggested by Isa. xiv. 12 : " I was watching Satan fall like lightning from heaven " (Lk. x. 17f. L).

(**10**) and (**8**). There are several indications that, in keeping with his vivid picture of an initial victorious conflict with Satan, Jesus viewed his exorcizing activity, wherein he " expelled the demons by the finger of God " (Lk. xi. 20 = Mt. xii. 28 Q [m substitutes " spirit " for " finger "]) as a strenuous and pro-longed campaign to be carried on by him against the realm of Satan and its demonic representatives in order to complete his victory.[4] We must, of course, beware of supposing that he

[1] Cf. Dodd, *Parables*, 123f. ; Otto, *Kingdom*, 97–103. Otto thinks the Lucan version is the more original form of the saying, and sees in it echoes of Iranian mythology and of Isa. xlix. 24f., but urges that the decisive victory is thought of as having been won by God, not by Jesus (so also, apparently, B. T. D. Smith, *Parables*, 92f.). As explained above, pp. 26, 43, I regard this as a false distinction : moreover the victory-winner is clearly the same as the goods-spoiler, i.e., Jesus himself.
[2] So Swete, *St. Mark*, 67a. For a different view, cf. Menzies, *Earliest Gosp.* 101b, and of course Otto (see last note). Menzies thinks Jesus simply *inferred* the decisive binding of Satan from the fact of the exorcisms.
[3] I refer elsewhere (see, e.g., below, pp. 170f. n.1) to Mr. S. Liberty's special interpretation of the three Temptations in his book, *The Political Relations of Christ's Ministry*.
[4] Cf. Otto, *Kingdom*, 43f., 105f.

consistently portrayed his enterprise under any one figure : yet it is surely not without significance in this connexion that his exorcizing work, and indeed his work generally, is now and then represented as something of a struggle. The plundering of the strong man's goods (see just above) involves a certain amount of further conflict. Jesus evidently knew of cases in which exorcism had been followed by relapse into a still more serious state of madness (Lk. xi. 24–26 = Mt. xii. 43–45 Q : m is almost certainly wrong in taking the description to be a figurative warning to " this evil generation "). He knew of another especially-stubborn " class (of demons) " which " cannot (be made to) come out except by prayer and fasting " on the part of the exorcist (Mk. ix. 29 : in Mt. xvii. 20 m substitutes something quite different).[1] His work is so urgent that he commissions his Disciples to carry it on, and endows them with the authority needful to this end (Mk. iii. 15 ; Mk. vi. 7 = Lk. ix. 1 = Mt. x. 1 ; Mk. vi. 13 [cf. Lk. ix. 6] ; Lk. x. 17–20 L : cf. also Mk. ix. 38–40 = Lk. ix. 49f.). He refuses to allow even the Sabbath to intermit his healing activity, rejecting the Rabbinic rule that only cases in which life was in danger might lawfully be attended to on that day (Mk. iii. 1–6 = Lk. vi. 6–11 = Mt. xii. 9–14 ; Lk. xiii. 10–17 L ; Lk. xiv. 1–6 L or just possibly Q).[2] It has been suggested that the walk through the cornfields, when he had to defend his Disciples for a breach of the technical Sabbath-Law (Mk. ii. 23–28 = Lk. vi. 1–5 = Mt. xii. 1–8), was part of a pressing missionary-journey which would not brook delay.[3] The general impression of urgency is confirmed by Mark's frequent introduction of the adverb ' straightway ' into his narrative. Thus there were clearly features in the ministry of Jesus which rendered not unfitting those striking terms, " a great wrestler ", " a noble combatant ", which certain of the early Fathers applied to him.[4]

[1] As is well known, important textual authorities omit the words " and fasting " in Mk. ix. 29, and many moderns excise them (e.g., Weinel, *Theol.* 80 : the English Revisers relegated them to the margin). Yet, as Wellhausen remarks (*Mc.* 73), " Καὶ νηστείᾳ ist gut bezeugt " : the recently-discovered Chesty-Beatty papyrus includes it. The matter can be argued either way ; but I think Couchoud (in *J.T.S.* xxxv. 18f. [Jan. 1934]) is right in urging that *all* exorcisms might be presumed to require prayer (cf. Mk. vii. 34), and that therefore a specially-difficult exorcism would naturally require something more. The removal of the words καὶ νηστείᾳ by certain early copyists would be due to their apparent inconsistency with Mk. ii. 19.

[2] Cf. Montefiore, *S.G.*[2] I. 81f., II. 501.

[3] This plausible suggestion is made by Dr. T. W. Manson in *Mission*, etc. 481f. : cf. id. in *Judaism and Christianity*, iii (1939) 129–131.

[4] Origen says, with reference to Jesus' temptations and sufferings, that he

(11) In keeping with the expectation that, in the coming Messianic Age, but not before, all the great evils of life would be abolished, it was confidently anticipated that with its inauguration the power of Satan and his hosts would be definitely brought to an end.[1]

(12) That being so, Jesus regards his power over evil spirits, not only as a witness to a decisive victory won against Satan in the past, but as a proof that God's Kingdom was already actually present. " If (it is) by the finger of God (that) I expel the demons, then has the Kingdom of God (already) reached you " (Lk. xi. 20 = Mt. xii. 28 Q : see above, p. 66 [10], and below, p. 129 n. 5 and p. 198 n. 4).[2]

---

became a μέγαν ἀγωνιστήν (*Contra Cels.* i. 69) ; and Eusebius compares him, in connexion with the Passion, to a γενναῖος ἀθλητής (*Demonstr. Evang.* X. ii. 473b : in X. viii. 503b he is compared to a μέγας ἀθλητής). We may remember that, in the Pauline Epistles and the Fourth Gospel, the death of Jesus is occasionally thought of as a contest with the demons : see 1 Cor. ii. 6–8 (as often interpreted) ; Col. ii. 15 ; John xii. 31, xiv. 30, xvi. 11.

[1] Strack-Billerbeck ii. 2, iv. 521 bott., 527 *l.* Cf. Manson, *Teaching*, 156, 165f. ; Otto, *Kingdom*, 43.

[2] Cf. H.-D. Wendland, *Eschatologie*, 222–240 ; Otto, *Kingdom*, 102f. : the latter conjectures that Jesus spoke thus more often than the Gospels record, but that this piece of teaching tended later to fall into the background, and was therefore only seldom mentioned.

CHAPTER VI

THE RIGHTFUL LORD OF MEN

(1) Enjoying so unique an experience of closeness to God, (2) and invested with so supreme an office at His hands, (3) Jesus acted as one endowed by Him with the special authority necessary for the fulfilment of his vocation. (4) He claimed therefore that he represented something greater than the great ones of the Old Testament and even than the holy Temple at Jerusalem. (5) He assumed the functions of Teacher (6) and Prophet, (7) and discharged them with an independence and self-confidence which struck his hearers as unprecedented. (8) His personality was apparently possessed of a numinous magnetism, and consequently made the profoundest impression on others. (9) From time to time he issued commands to individuals, and was usually obeyed. (10) He wielded power over the demons and over disease. (11) He claimed the right to declare sins forgiven, (12) to decide what was lawful on the Sabbath, (13) to rebuke the religious leaders of the people, (14) to lay down what it was vital for men to learn and do, (15) and to raise a Temple worthier even than the one at Jerusalem. (16) He asked men to make decisions involving immense sacrifices for his sake. (17) He thought of himself as present in his representatives everywhere, (18) and as destined to have a voice in the future Judgment of mankind. (19) For the sake of his work he imparted a measure of his authority to others. (20) He expected men to judge for themselves whether or not it was from God alone that he derived his competence for all this commanding authority.

(1) The direct dependence of Jesus' authority on his filial consciousness comes out most clearly in the passage, "All things have been handed over to me by my Father ; and no one comes to know the Father except the Son and any one to whom the Son desires to reveal (Him) " (Lk. x. 22 = Mt. xi. 27 Q : see above, pp. 32f., 36.).[1]

---

[1] Cf. Holtzmann, *Theol.* i. 183 (". . . ein erwachtes Bewusstsein um die Ueberlegenheit der eigenen Person . . . dieser Erkenntnis einer durchaus eigentümlichen Stellung zu Gott . . . "), 344 (". . . der Abwesenheit aller auf Gewissensdruck und entsprechende Furcht vor Gott weisenden Züge ; . . . ") ; A. T. Cadoux in *The Lord of Life*, 68 (" Thus the other side of His

(2) The Messiah is ipso facto "the Lord" par excellence (Psa. cx. i). Since Jesus alone is the true Messiah (Mk. xiii. 21f. [cf. 6] = Mt. xxiv. 23f. [cf. 5 ; Lk. xxi. 8]), he alone is entitled to be "teacher" and "leader" (Mt. xxiii. 8, 10 M : the passage is almost certainly an early Christian construction, but the assumption underlying it is rooted in fact). In the Parable of the Vineyard, the "son" and "heir", who clearly represents the Messiah, is expected to be received with due deference (Mk. xii. 6f. = Lk. xx. 13f. = Mt. xxi. 37f.).[1] Yet he wants no salutations as "Lord! Lord!", which are unaccompanied by obedience to his teaching (Lk. vi. 46 Q ? : Mt. vii. 21 M ?).

(3) Inasmuch then as Jesus has been "sent" by God (Mk. ix. 37 = Lk. ix. 48 = Mt. x. 40 ; Lk. x. 16 L or possibly Q : cf. Lk. iv. 43 l [contrast Mk. i. 38]), he acts—as the Centurion at Kapharnaum realized—with the "authority" of Him who has commissioned him (Lk. vii. 2-10 = Mt. viii. 5-13 Q : see above, pp. 63f.). And since the errand is one of such supreme moment, "all things" had "been handed over to" him by his Father (Lk. x. 22 = Mt. xi. 27 Q : Mt. xxviii. 18 M or m ["All authority in heaven and on earth has been given unto me"] is probably an early Christian confession based on the Q-passage). It has been observed that, when once his Messiahship had been definitely acknowledged by the Disciples at Cæsarea-Philippi, Jesus began to use the solemn form of asseveration, "Amen" (i.e., "truly") "I say unto you", more frequently than before, and to import into his speech a new and more terrible emphasis, corresponding to his fixed determination to carry out his Messianic rôle to the bitter end.[2]

(4) When contrasting the discernment shown by the Queen of Sheba and the men of Nineveh with the insensitiveness of his own generation, Jesus said, "Behold, (something) more than Solomon is here ! . . . Behold, (something) more than Jonah is here !" (Lk. xi. 31f. = Mt. xii. 42, 41 Q). The neuter adjectives do not forbid us to translate "one greater" (cf., e.g., Mk. x. 9 = Mt. xix. 6b ; Lk. xix. 10 L ; John vi. 37, 39,

---

inward triumph was His ascendancy over men . . . ") ; Manson, *Teaching*. 106f. (". . . the source of his authority is to be sought in the experience at Jordan which initiates his public activity . . . "), 112 (". . . he claims to make the Father real to men in the same sense that the Father is real to him . . . "). On Jesus' claim to authority generally, cf. Gloege, *Reich Gottes*, 132–137.

[1] Cf. Manson, *Teaching*, 112.
[2] Manson, *Teaching*, 207–211.

xvii. 2, 24 ; 1 John v. 4 [1]) : but it is perhaps safer to assume that the reference is in the first place to Jesus' cause or work rather than to his person, though the two naturally go together.[2] Similarly, in a dispute (it would seem) with the Pharisees, he says, " I tell you, (something) greater than the Temple is here " (Mt. xii. 6 M). John the Baptist's words about " the coming one " who would be stronger and more exalted than himself (Mk. i. 7f. : Lk. iii. 16f. = Mt. iii. 11 Q : see above, pp. 56f.) were in the first place spoken as a characterization of the coming Messiah, not as a direct personal tribute to Jesus : but the Evangelists mean them nonetheless to be a characterization of him, and it is quite possible that Jesus also took them as such.

(5) Jesus was recognized by all and sundry as a teacher. The Greek word $\delta\iota\delta\acute{a}\sigma\kappa\alpha\lambda o\varsigma$, so often used by the Evangelists when recording speeches addressed to him, was the regular equivalent of the technical Hebrew term " Rabbi " (or " Rabbuni "), which actually appears in a few places in the Synoptics (Mk. ix. 5 [Lk. ix. 33 substitutes " Master ", and Mt. xvii. 4 " Lord " (or rather " Sir ")] ; Mk. x. 51 [Lk. xviii. 41 = Mt. xx. 33 and ix. 28 substitute " Lord "] ; Mk. xi. 21 [Mt. xxi. 20 omits] ; Mk. xiv. 45 = Mt. xxvi. 49 [Lk. xxii. 47 omits] ; Mt. xxiii. 7, 8 M ; Mt. xxvi. 25 m [Lk. xxii. 23 L omits]) and frequently in the Fourth Gospel. It was in the manner of a Jewish Rabbi that Jesus *sat* as he taught (Lk. iv. 20 L ; Lk. v. 3 L ; Mt. v. 1 m ; Mk. iv. 1 = Mt. xiii. 1f. ; Mt. xxvi. 55 m [contrast Mk. xiv. 49 = Lk. xxii. 53] ; John viii. 2 : cf. Mt. xxiii. 2 M) ; and he referred to the relations between teacher and pupil as if they applied to himself and his circle (Lk. vi. 40 [Q] = Mt. x. 24f. [Q + M]). It is to be noted that Jewish Rabbis (as teachers of higher rank) received authorization from their seniors by means of a formal ordination.[3]

(6) Jesus was frequently described by his contemporaries as a Prophet (Mk. vi. 15 = Lk. ix. 8 ; Mk. viii. 28 = Lk. ix. 19 = Mt. xvi. 14 ; Lk. vii. 16 L ; Lk. vii. 39 L ; Lk. xxiv. 19 L ; Mt. xxi. 10f. M ; Mt. xxi. 46 m [contrast Mk. xii. 12 = Lk. xx.

---

[1] Cf. also Tennyson, *In Memoriam*, xviii : " And come, whatever loves to weep, | And hear the ritual of the dead ". The neuter singular is used of men by Vergil in *Æneid*, v. 716, the neuter *plural* by Xenophon in *Exped. Cyri*, VII. iii. 11.

[2] Otto, *Kingdom*, 163 (he ignores the distinction between the masc. and the neut.).

[3] Cf. Schürer, *G.J.V.* ii. 375–378 ; Moore, *Judaism*, i. 43f., 105, 320, iii. 105 ; Strack-Billerbeck ii. 647–661 ; D. Daube in *J.T.S.* xxxix. 45–59 (Jan. 1938).

19] ; John iv. 19, vi. 14, vii. 40, 52, ix. 17), and he himself used that word as a correct designation of himself (Mk. vi. 4 = Mt. xiii. 57 ; Lk. iv. 24 L [unless from Mk. ?] ; Lk. xiii. 33 L [cf. Lk. xiii. 34 = Mt. xxiii. 37 Q] ; John iv. 44 : cf. also Lk. xi. 30, probably Q [contrast Mt. xii. 40 m], Mt. x. 41 M, and Mt. vii. 22 m). The least that could be said of a genuine prophet was that he spoke in the name and with the authority of God.[1]

(7) Accustomed to hear the Scribes, as expounders of the Law, base their opinions and decisions on the authority either of tradition or of earlier revered teachers, those who heard Jesus were struck by the contrast which his tone and method presented to the scribal custom. When he had been speaking in the synagogue, ' they were amazed at his teaching, for he was teaching them like one who possessed authority, not like the Scribes ' (Mk. i. 22 = Lk. iv. 32 = Mt. vii. 29).[2] Again and again in the Sermon on the Mount he quoted some precept from the Law, sometimes along with a traditional expansion of it, and immediately added on his own authority some correction, modification, or intensification of it, usually with the formula, " Ye have heard that it was said to the ancients, ' . . . ' ; but I say unto you, ' . . . ' " (Mt. v. 21f., 27f., 31f., 33f., 38f. [cf. Lk. vi. 27 Q ?], 43f.—all M).[3] On another occasion he declared the Mosaic permission of divorce to be an infringement of God's original purpose in creating the sexes (Mk. x. 3–9 = Mt. xix. 4–8) ; and on yet another he was understood to have spoken about defilement in a way which implicitly abolished all legal food-taboos (Mk. vii. 17–19). The Rabbis were indeed accustomed to allude to the differing opinions of learned authorities ; the prophets of old had begun their oracles by saying, " Thus says Yahweh ". But for a prophet to introduce into his declarations the formula, " . . . but *I* say unto you ", was at the very least a startling innovation.[4] *The Messiah* was expected to expound a new Law, but only he.[5]

(8) Frequent reference is made by the Synoptics to the

---

[1] See the valuable essay by Dr. C. H. Dodd in *Myst. Christi*, 51–66, on ' Jesus as Teacher and Prophet ' : also below, p. 99 (13).

[2] Cf. Strack-Billerbeck i. 470.

[3] Cf. Bartlet and Carlyle, *Christianity in Hist.* 1, 35f. ; Windisch, *Bergpredigt*, 92–112.

[4] Cf. Dalman, *Jesus–Jeshua* (1929), 73f. Possibly we ought to consider the words quoted in Lk. xi. 49 (perhaps Q : cf. Mt. xxiii. 34), " Therefore the Wisdom of God said ", as a reverent imitation of the prophetic formula, " Thus says Yahweh ", rather than (with some) a quotation from a lost Wisdom-Book : cf. Strack-Billerbeck ii. 189 ; Dodd in *Myst. Christi*, 57f. ; and the commentaries.

[5] Strack-Billerbeck iv. 1–3.

amazement, often not unmixed with fear, felt by men in Jesus' presence. Some of these allusions are connected with stories of Nature-miracles, the historical reality of which (and therefore the surprise at which) we may feel justified in doubting (Mk. iv. 41 = Lk. viii. 25 = Mt. viii. 27 ; Mk. vi. 51 = Mk. xiv. 33). Others naturally have to do with his works of healing (Mk. ii. 12 = Lk. v. 26 ['. . . they were filled with fear . . .' l] = Mt. ix. 8 ['. . . they were afraid, and glorified God, Who had given such authority to men '—mostly m] ; Mk. v. 17 = Lk. viii. 37 = Mt. viii. 34 [Gerasenes in fear beg him to depart] ; Mk. v. 20 ; Mk. v. 42 = Lk. viii. 56 = Mt. ix. 26 ; Mk. vii. 37 ; Mt. xv. 31 m ; Lk. ix. 43 l ; Lk. xiii. 17 L), or with his teaching (see above, p. 72 [7] ; cf. also Mk. xi. 18 = Lk. xix. 48). The healings were of themselves sufficiently startling : but the impression they made must have been enhanced by Jesus' evident possession of a healing power which sometimes worked without his prior knowledge (Mk. v. 25–34 = Lk. viii. 43–48 = Mt. ix. 20–22 : cf. Mk. vi. 56 = Mt. xiv. 36, also Lk. v. 17 l [' the Lord's power was (with him) so that he should heal '], Lk. vi. 19 l), and also by his telepathic or clairvoyant awareness of what was going on in the minds of others (Mk. ii. 8 = Lk. v. 22 = Mt. ix. 4) and what was happening at a distance (Mk. v. 39 = Lk. viii. 52 = Mt. ix. 23f. ; Mk. vii. 29 = Mt. xv. 28)—an awareness which he possessed on other occasions besides healings (Lk. xix. 5 L ; Mk. xi. 1–6 = Lk. xix. 29–34 = Mt. xxi. 1–6 ; Mk. xiv. 12–16 = Lk. xxii. 7–13 = Mt. xxvi. 17–19). At times he was heard foretelling future events (Mk. xiv. 18–21 = Lk. xxii. 21–23 = Mt. xxvi. 21–25 ; Mk. xiv. 27–30 = Mt. xxvi. 31–35, cf. Lk. xxii. 31–34 L : cf. also the several prophecies of the Passion, the Fall of Jerusalem, etc.). He was frequently treated with profoundly-deferential homage or with enthusiastic salutations ; and he excused those who so honoured him on the ground that they were doing only what was fitting (Lk. vii. 36–50 L ; Mk. xi. 7–10 = Lk. xix. 35f. = Mt. xxi. 7–9 ; Lk. xix. 37f. L ; Lk. xix. 39f. L ; Mt. xxi. 15f. M ; Mk. xiv. 3–9 = Mt. xxvi. 6–13). There are therefore grounds for believing that he was possessed, not only of great winsomeness and attractive power, but of a certain awe-inspiring quality which evoked in those with whom he met unusually-strong feelings either of regard or of opposition.[1]

---

[1] Cf. Abrahams in Montefiore, *S.G.*[2] II. 661, 668 ; Otto, *The Idea of the Holy*, 159–165, *Kingdom*, 164f. (". . . the nimbus of the numinous surrounded Jesus . . ."), 344f. (Jesus as a " charismatic ").

(9) Jesus meets with instant obedience when he calls on Simon, Andrew, Jacob, John, and Levi to follow him (Mk. i. 16–20 = Mt. iv. 18–22 ; cf. Lk. v. 1–11 L ; Mk. ii. 14 = Lk. v. 27f. = Mt. ix. 9), though the same exacting demand did not in every case evoke such ready compliance (Mk. x. 21f. = Lk. xviii. 22f. = Mt. xix. 21f. : the upshot of the cases mentioned in Lk. ix. 57–60 = Mt. viii. 19–22 Q and Lk. ix. 61f. Q ? is not stated). He requisitions an ass whereon to ride into Jerusalem (Mk. xi. 1–6 = Lk. xix. 29–34 = Mt. xxi. 1–6), and an upper room wherein to celebrate the Passover (Mk. xiv. 12–16 = Lk. xxii. 7–13 = Mt. xxvi. 17–19). He walks out unharmed through a crowd of angry Nazarenes (Lk. iv. 28–30 L) ; and with masterful word and gesture he clears the traders out of the Temple-courts (Mk. xi. 15–17 = Lk. xix. 45–47 = Mt. xxi. 12f.). We note, however, that he refused to be made " a judge and divider " in a case of disputed inheritance (Lk. xii. 13f. L).

(10) Passages referring to the power, which Jesus and others were convinced that he possessed, of expelling demons by an authoritative word of dismissal, and of curing illnesses (often by addressing a commanding rebuke to the quasi-personal authors of them), have already been quoted in connexion with Peter's mother-in-law (see above, p. 63), the paralytic (Mk. ii. 11f. = Lk. v. 24f. = Mt. ix. 6f. : see above, p. 73), the Centurion's servant (see above, pp. 63f., 70 [3]), and others (see above, p. 64 [5]). The only passage which it is desirable to quote explicitly here is that which describes how the crowd in the synagogue at Kapharnaum exclaimed, after Jesus had exorcized a demon, " What means this ? (It is) a new teaching—with authority ! He gives orders even to the unclean spirits, and they obey him ! " (Mk. i. 27 = Lk. iv. 36).[1] It was usual for the exorcist to order out the demons in the name of someone greater than himself : Jesus, however, ordered them out on his own authority, without appealing to any more august name (Mk. v. 8 = Lk. viii. 29a ; Mk. ix. 25 = Lk. ix. 42 = Mt. xvii. 18). Moreover, the Disciples and others ordered them out in Jesus' name (Mk. ix. 38 = Lk. ix. 49 ; Lk. x. 17 L ; Mt. vii. 22 M or m : cf. Acts xix. 13).[2] On the other hand, we may reasonably doubt whether Jesus seriously believed that God would send " twelve legions of angels "—if he asked for them—to rescue him in Gethsemane, as M states (Mt. xxvi. 53).

---

[1] On the connexion of teaching with exorcism, cf. D. Daube in *J.T.S.* xxxix. 57–59 (Jan. 1938).
[2] Cf. Schürer, *G.J.V.* iii. 409f.

(11) There is no doubt that the Synoptists believed that Jesus possessed the right of forgiving sins on God's behalf, and that they represent his contemporaries as understanding him on occasions to claim that right. But an examination of the two episodes concerned makes it fairly clear that all he claimed was the right to assure penitent sinners that they were forgiven by God. Here is what we are told about the prostitute who wept over his feet : ' And he said to her, " Thy sins have been forgiven ". And those who were reclining with him began to say within themselves, " Who is this who even forgives sins ? " But he said to the woman, " Thy faith has saved thee ; go in peace " ' (Lk. vii. 48–50 L). The other case is that of the paralytic (Mk. ii. 3–12 = Lk. v. 18–26 = Mt. ix. 2–8). Here the unevenness of the narrative and the early use of the phrase " the Son of Man " (see below, pp. 95–97) suggest that the original narrative has been enlarged by the addition of Mk. ii. 5b–10, and that in its earliest form it told only how the paralytic was healed.[1] This possibility, taken in conjunction with the analogy of Lk. vii. 48–50, and the remarkable absence of any other reference to so daring a claim on Jesus' part, renders it likely that he did not assume more than the right of assuring penitents that God had forgiven them.[2] It is probably in general conformity with this sense that we are to understand his words to the adulteress, " Neither do I condemn thee " (John viii. 11 ; cf. 10).

(12) Several episodes make it clear that Jesus felt himself fully entitled to disregard the Mosaïc rule that no work should be done on the Sabbath, when it was a question of " doing good ", i.e., ministering to human need (Mk. ii. 23–iii. 6 = Lk. vi. 1–11 = Mt. xii. 1–14 ; Lk. xiii. 10–17 L ; Lk. xiv. 1–6 [cf. Mt. xii. 11f.] Q or L). After the incident of the ears of corn, Jesus is reported to have said, " The Sabbath was made for man, and not man for the Sabbath : so that the Son of Man is master even over the Sabbath " (Mk. ii. 27f. : the latter sentence alone is taken over in the parallels, Lk. vi. 5 = Mt. xii. 8). Here again the Synoptists probably understand by " the Son of Man " simply Jesus himself. But the form of the argument and the early date of the incident make it likely that " the Son of Man " originally meant here, not Jesus himself, but (what linguistically the term could easily mean) man as such (in distinction from God).[3] All the

---

[1] So Rawlinson, *St. Mark*, 24–26 : and cf. V. Taylor, *Tradition*, 66–68.

[2] Cf. Menzies, *Earliest Gospel*, 82ab ; Major in *Mission*, etc. 51. Per contra, Otto, *Kingdom*, 165–108. See also below, pp. 95f.

[3] Cf. Manson, *Teaching*, 24, 213f ; and see below, p. 95.

same, he did himself exercise the right of being " master of the Sabbath ".

(13) Detailed references are needless. It may, however, be observed that the greater severity of Jesus' denunciation as recorded by Mt. may be due to some special anti-Pharisaïc bias on the part of M (or m), despite the reverence of M for the Mosaïc Law.[1]

(14) The most impressive piece of evidence under this heading is the passage which stands at the end of both the Lucan and the Matthæan versions of the Sermon on the Mount, and likens the man who listens to Jesus' words and who acts accordingly to a sensible man who, in building a house, builds it on a foundation of rock, so that it is able to withstand the destructive force of storms and torrents, while he who listens and does not comply is like one who provides no solid foundation for his house, so that, when smitten with wind and flooded stream, it comes down with a crash (Lk. vi. 47–49 = Mt. vii. 24–27 Q). This stress on the vital importance of his teaching for those who heard it comes out in the words, " Heaven and earth will pass away ; but my words will not pass away " (Mk. xiii. 31 = Lk. xxi. 33 = Mt. xxiv. 35),[2] and is further confirmed by his justification of Mary of Bethany for listening to him while Martha was busy about the house (Lk. x. 39–42 L), and by his pronunciation of a beatitude over those " who listen to the word of God " (i.e., Jesus' own teaching) " and keep it " (Lk. xi. 28 L).

(15) When Jesus was being tried before the Sanhedrin, certain witnesses gave evidence that they had heard him say, " I will demolish this Temple which has been made with hands, and in three days I will raise up another made without hands " (Mk. xiv. 58 = Mt. xxvi. 61). Mark states that their evidence was false and inconsistent. When he hung on the Cross, the passers-by mocked him, saying, " Ah ! thou who demolishest the Temple and buildest (it) in three days, . . ." (Mk. xv. 29 = Mt. xxvii. 40). In the Johannine account of Jesus' cleansing of the Temple, he is made to say, " Demolish this Temple, and in three days I will raise it up " (John ii. 19). It is not easy with this evidence before us to make up our minds as to

---

[1] Cf. Manson in *Mission*, etc. 313–318. Scholars differ as to what exactly Jesus meant by " the leaven " of the Pharisees, the Sadducees, and Herod, against which he warned the Disciples (Mk. viii. 14–21 = Mt. xvi. 5–12 : Lk. xii. 1 L or l).

[2] " We have here the most striking example of that ' authority ' in Jesus which so amazed His hearers, an authority which rests on His assurance of knowing the Father and the Father's will " (Manson in *Mission*, etc. 626).

exactly what he did say : but it seems clear that he spoke of his cause as a sort of equivalent of the Temple at Jerusalem, and intimated that, even if this latter should be demolished, his cause would replace and supplant it in a surprisingly short time.[1]

(16) He called upon men to be prepared for his sake or " on account of his name " to forfeit the esteem of their kith and kin and therewith their domestic peace (Lk. xii. 51–53 = Mt. x. 34–36 Q), to abandon their homes and families (Mk. x. 29 = Lk. xviii. 29 = Mt. xix. 29), to set aside their love for their parents (Lk. xiv. 26 = Mt. x. 37 Q), to incur the hatred and abuse of men generally (Mk. xiii. 13 = Lk. xxi. 17 = Mt. xxiv. 9 = Mt. x. 22 ; Lk. vi. 22 = Mt. v. 11 Q), to get themselves arraigned before governors and kings (Mk. xiii. 9 = Lk. xxi. 12 = Mt. x. 18), and to deny themselves, carry the cross after him (Lk. xiv. 27 = Mt. x. 38 Q ; Mk. viii. 34 = Lk. ix. 23 = Mt. xvi. 24), and forfeit their lives (Mk. viii. 35 = Lk. ix. 24 = Mt. xvi. 25 ; Lk. xvii. 33 = Mt. x. 39 Q [but only m has " for my sake "]). His parabolic descriptions of the tower-builder and the belligerent king, who both needed to calculate in advance the cost of what they proposed to undertake (Lk. xiv. 28–33 L, or just possibly Q), illustrate unmistakably the exacting character of the demands he made on his followers. Moreover, his call must be either accepted or rejected—" he who is not with me is against me . . ." (Lk. xi. 23 = Mt. xii. 30 Q) : a really neutral attitude is impossible. No monarch with invincible armies at his beck and call could have asked of his subjects more unstinted sacrifices in his service.[2]

(17) Jesus ascribed to himself—on the strength of the supreme significance of his person and claims—a quasi-ubiquity, in the sense that he was himself present in the persons of those who, by believing on him and working for him, were his real representatives, however humble their rank. " He who listens to you listens to me ; and he who rejects you rejects me : but he who rejects me rejects Him Who sent me " (Lk. x. 16 L or possibly Q). " Whoever receives one of such little children in my name receives me ; and whoever receives me receives not me, but Him Who sent me " (Mk. ix. 37 = Lk. ix. 48 = Mt. xviii. 5 : Mt. x. 40 looks like a conflation of a part of both passages [" He who receives you receives me ; and he who receives me receives Him Who sent me "]). There

---

[1] See F. P. Cheetham in *J. T. S.* xxiv. 315–317 (Apl. 1923)
[2] Cf. Moody, *Purpose of Jes.* 54ff., 66, 70f., 132ff.

are two other Matthæan passages with weaker documentary authority, which must however be quoted here. In the description of the Last Judgment, kind actions are reckoned to have been done, or not done, to Jesus himself, according as they had or had not been done " to one of the least " of his " brothers " (Mt. xxv. 40, 45 M : this teaching is quite in line with that just quoted) ; and in a passage and context which bear strong marks of adaptation to early Church-usage, Jesus is represented as saying, " There are not two or three assembled together in my name, with whom I am not—in the midst of them " (Mt. xviii. 20 M or m).[1]

(18) John the Baptist foretold of the Messiah that he would " baptize with fire " (Mk. i. 8 : cf. Lk. iii. 16 fin. = Mt. iii. 11 fin. Q ; see above, p. 56 [a]), winnowing the nation, storing the wheat, " but the chaff he will burn up with fire unquenchable " (Lk. iii. 17 = Mt. iii. 12 Q). We shall be dealing in detail later with Jesus' teaching concerning the future judgment : in order, however, to illustrate his conviction regarding his own part (direct or indirect) in it, it will be sufficient to quote Mk. viii. 38 = Lk. ix. 26 = Mt. xvi. 27 : " Whoever is ashamed of me and of my (follower)s in this adulterous and sinful generation, of him will the Son of Man in his turn be ashamed, whensoever he comes in the glory of his Father with the holy angels " (m adds the gloss : " and then will he repay each man according to his conduct "). The closely-parallel Q-passage in Lk. xii. 8 = Mt. x. 32 may be compared. In Mk. ix. 41 = Mt. x. 42, Jesus declares that any one who gives a cup of water to one of his disciples " will certainly not lose his reward " (but see above, pp. 58f. [b]). On the other hand, " Alas for that man through whom the Son of Man is handed over (to death) ! Good were it for him if that man had not been born ! " (Mk. xiv. 21 = Mt. xxvi. 24 : cf. Lk. xxii. 22 L). And in the great Matthæan picture of the Last Judgment (Mt. xxv. 31–46 M), " the King ", i.e., presumably Jesus, himself sits as judge.[2]

(19) The power which Jesus wields as the authorized representative of God he imparts to others, in order to enable them to extend his work.[3] He appointed ' the Twelve, in order that they might be with him, and that he might send them out to preach, and (might enable them) to have authority to cast out

---

[1] For the text, cf. Wellhausen, *Mt.* 93 ; Manson in *Mission*, etc. 503. See also below, pp. 315–317.
[2] Cf. Manson, *Teaching*, 269 ; Otto, *Kingdom*, 163f. See, however, below, pp. 228f., 321–323.
[3] Manson, *Teaching*, 168–170.

the demons ' (Mk. iii. 14f.). ' He gave them authority over the unclean spirits ' (Mk. vi. 7 = Lk. ix. 1 = Mt. x. 1 [l and m add authority ' to cure diseases ']). This delegated authority is perhaps hinted at in the Parable of the Servants entrusted with Money (Lk. xix. 17, 19 L : Mt. xxv. 21, 23 M differs). The immunity from danger which Jesus promises to confer on his Apostles in Lk. x. 19 L (cf. Lk. xxi. 18 l, and the pseudo-Marcan passage—Mk. xvi. 17f.) probably referred in the first place figuratively to moral and spiritual success.

(20) When Jesus was challenged by the Chief Priests, Scribes, and Elders at Jerusalem to say by what authority he was acting, he evaded the necessity of giving a direct reply by asking the challengers whether they thought " John's baptism was from Heaven or from men "—a question which they were afraid to answer (Mk. xi. 27–33 = Lk. xx. 1–8 = Mt. xxi. 23–27). His question was, however, not a mere " poser ", nor was his putting of it a mere evasion. As he taught that his own work was a continuation of John's, and as he might fairly presume that his questioners would know their own minds about John, his words were a quite reasonable suggestion that they could really answer their question of themselves, if they wanted to.[1] And it is important to note that in Jesus' repeated exhortation, " Let him that has ears to listen with, listen " (see Mk. iv. 9 = Lk. viii. 8 = Mt. xiii. 9 ; Mk. iv. 23 ; Mk. vii. 16 ; Mk. viii. 18 ; Lk. xiv. 35 L or Q ; Mt. xi. 15 M or Q ; Mt. xiii. 43 M), there is a similar appeal to the listener to think the matter over and judge for himself. Despite his authoritative expression, " But I say unto you " (see above, p. 72), Jesus did not mean that the mere fact that an utterance was his was to be taken as the really-final ground for the acceptance of it. In the last analysis, he speaks, not on his own authority, but on God's. Hence he meets a flattering benediction pronounced on his mother, with a superior benediction on " those who listen to the Word of God and keep it " (Lk. xi. 27f. L). Those to whom he speaks, since they possess some means of recognizing, if they will, what comes from God, possess also the means of seeing for themselves that what he is saying and doing truly reflects the mind and will of God.[2]

---

[1] Cf. Wellhausen, *Mc.* 92 ; McNeile, *St. Matthew*, 305a ; F. H. Colson in *J.T.S.* xxv. 71f. (Oct. 1923).
[2] Cf. Rashdall, *Conscience*, 33–36, 77f. ; Bartlet and Carlyle, *Christianity in Hist.* 13 ; Bartlet, *St. Mark*, 160, 244 ; C. J. Cadoux, *Cathol. and Christianity*, 188f. (where other lit. is quoted) ; Manson in *Mission*, etc. 47of. (" . . . His appeal is to the insight of His hearers "), 487f. (" . . . He means : ' What I

say to you is God's truth. If you will face it honestly, you will see that it is . . . ' "), 636 ; Cadbury, *Peril*, 159f. ; A. T. Cadoux, *Theol. of Jes.* 128–130, 215f., 227f.

It was surely because he felt that he possessed and could use, and that others also possessed and could use, this direct awareness of what was true and good, that Jesus took the liberty of freely setting aside one injunction of Scripture in favour of another, and even of appealing from the Mosaic Law itself to ultimate principles grasped intuitively (see above, p. 72). This independent attitude towards the Law did not prevent him quoting as Divine and authoritative those parts of it which he felt to be eternally valid. Yet forasmuch as he did not theorize, after the manner of a modern philosopher, concerning the seat of authority in religion, he did not on such occasions explain—nor indeed was he in all probability conscious—that he was *selecting* on subjective grounds between one part of the Law and another (cf. Weinel, *Theol.* 90f.) : like any other Jew, he then quoted Moses as if the word of Moses were ipso facto the word of God. It is this unanalysed duality in his attitude to the Law which gives it that appearance of inconsistency which evoked so frequently the perplexed criticisms of Montefiore (*S.G.*[2] I. 146, 156–160, 165, 232, II. 48, 53, 223f., 298, 535f. : cf. also Rashdall, *Conscience*, 94–101, and Cadbury, *Peril*, 145–147, 168–174). For the exercise of a similar selective power by the Jewish Rabbis, see Moore, *Judaism*, i. 358f.

THE SON OF DAVID

(1) It was very generally assumed in Jesus' day that the Messiah would have to be a descendant of David. (2) Jesus was accordingly greeted and acclaimed as " Son of David " by certain persons who wished to honour him with a Messianic title. (3) The belief that he actually was a descendant of David was accepted in the Christian Church at an early date, (4) and soon became firmly established. (5) On the other hand, the necessity for the Davidic descent of the Messiah was not universally admitted. (6) Jesus himself never referred, so far as we know, to his personal pedigree ; and he made it clear that, in his view, Davidic descent was neither necessary, nor even easily applicable, to the Messiah. (7) Mark was apparently little interested in the ascription of it to Jesus ; (8) the Didache is ambiguous, (9) the Fourth Gospel so ambiguous as to suggest disbelief, (10) and the Epistle of Barnabas definitely unfavourable. (11) It is therefore arguable that the belief in Jesus' physical descent from David began simply as an inference from the acceptance of Him as Messiah. (12) Yet there is nothing inherently improbable in the hypothesis that his family knew itself to belong to the Davidic line ; (13) and perhaps the least-difficult explanation of all the data is to suppose that it really was so, though Jesus himself, possibly not too sure of the validity of the claim, chose to lay no stress whatever on it.

(1) Old-Testament passages like 2 Sam. vii. 12f., Isa. xi. 10, Jer. xxiii. 5, xxx. 9, Ezek. xxxiv. 23f., Psa. lxxxix. 3f., cxxxii. 11, seemed to make it clear that the coming Messiah would be a prince of the house of David. This view is definitely stated in ' the Psalms of Solomon ' (xvii. 4, 21–46), Pharisaïc compositions of 63–45 B.C., and was generally accepted by the Jewish Scribes in Jesus' time (Mk. xii. 35 = Lk. xx. 41 = Mt. xxii. 41f.). It is commonly assumed in the Rabbinic writings.[1] When, therefore, m represents the crowds as asking, after Jesus had cured a blind and dumb demoniac, " Is this man (possibly) the Son of David ? " (Mt. xii. 23), the

[1] Dalman, *W.J.* 316–318 ; Schürer, *G.J.V.* ii. 615 ; Strack-Billerbeck i. 7–13, 525 ; Moore, *Judaism*, ii. 328–330, iii. 200.

reference is primarily not to Jesus' family-origin, but to his conjectured Messiahship.

(2) The reported cases of Jesus' being greeted with the title "Son of David" by virtue of his supposed Messiahship are neither numerous nor in every case strongly attested. The most reliable instance is that of blind Bartimæus of Jericho (Mk. x. 47f. = Lk. xviii. 38f. = Mt. xx. 30f.).[1] The two blind men of Mt. ix. 27 m are probably fictitious duplicates of the two whom m has created out of Bartimæus. In the Matthæan account of the appeal made to Jesus by the Syro-Phœnician woman, she cries out, "Have mercy on me, Lord, Son of David!" (Mt. xv. 22). The words do not occur in the Marcan story (Mk. vii. 26), and look like another of m's numerous decorations of the narrative, though it is indeed possible that Mt. is here conflating Mk. with a second non-Marcan source. But in any case it is difficult to see what a Gentile woman (for "Gentile" is what Ἑλληνὶς in Mk. vii. 26 means) could have known about Jesus' Messiahship, not to mention his family-descent. Again, in the account of the Triumphal Entry, m introduces the cry, "Hosanna to the Son of David" (Mt. xxi. 9), whereas Mk. has, "Blessed be the coming kingdom of our father David" (Mk. xi. 10). The historically-questionable introduction of children shouting to Jesus in the Temple, "Hosanna to the Son of David" (Mt. xxi. 15), is perhaps the work of M, if not m.[2] The only instance we can feel sure about is therefore that of Bartimæus; and the circumstances of the case (considered in the light of Mt. xii. 23 m) render it almost certain that he meant by his salutation to refer to Jesus' Messiahship, not to his Davidic ancestry, of which latter he probably knew nothing.[3]

(3) The earliest unquestionable, unambiguous, and datable allusion to the physical descent of Jesus from David is Paul's reference to him in the opening verses of his Epistle to the Romans : "who was born of David's seed according to the flesh" (Rom. i. 3). This was written about 56/57 A.D. : but the cast of the passage makes it likely that Paul is here quoting or at least re-echoing a piece of early Christian tradition, so that this testimony may really date from some time indefinitely

---

[1] Cf. Bacon, *Beginnings*, 144, 150; Cadman, *Last Journey*, 110–112 (on Jesus' non-committal reaction to the salutation) ; Major in *Mission*, etc. 136f.
[2] On the historical improbability of the incident, cf. McNeile, *St. Matthew*, 301a.
[3] The Rev. E. F. F. Bishop, in *E.T.* xlvii. 21–25 (Oct. 1935), suggests that Jesus was hailed as "Son of David" by persons needing his help, because, as healer and exorcizer, he reminded the lower classes of the wizard *Solomon*.

earlier than that of the composition of the letter. At all events
it agrees with the statement made by Paul in the speech which
Luke declares him to have made at Antioch in Pisidia (about
48/49 A.D.), to the effect that according to His promise God
had brought forth for Israel a Saviour from the seed of David,
namely Jesus (Acts xiii. 22f.). The speeches in Acts, except
those uttered on occasions when Luke himself was present,
cannot be relied on as verbatim reports, so that a little doubt
must needs attend our acceptance of its evidence here—as also
in ii. 29–36 (where Peter on the day of Pentecost assumes the
Davidic ancestry of Jesus as a fact) and in xv. 16 (where Jacob,
Jesus' brother, speaking about 49 A.D., may be hinting at the
same assumption). But it is in any case clear,that the belief
that Jesus was duly descended from David formed part of the
general creed of the primitive Church. The Lucan genealógy
of Jesus, which affirms his Davidic ancestry (Lk. iii. 23–38),
if a part of Proto-Luke, is probably as early as 57–59 A.D. :
but of this more in a moment.

(4) In post-Pauline times, the belief in question was frequently alluded to. The author of ' Hebrews ', who wrote
perhaps about 67/68 A.D., and presumably " would have been
attracted by the idea of a Messiah of the tribe of Levi ",[1] says,
" It is perfectly clear ($\pi\rho\delta\delta\eta\lambda o\nu$) that our Lord arose from
Judah, in connexion with which tribe Moses said nothing about
priests " (Heb. vii. 14). Luke and the author of Mt. (80–85
A.D.), though willing to incorporate in their Gospels the
puzzling Marcan episode which (as we shall see) seemed to call
the Davidic descent of Jesus in question (Mk. xii. 35–37 =
Lk. xx. 41–44 = Mt. xxii. 41–46), opened their narratives with
detailed birth-stories, in the earliest forms of which the descent
from David was a prominent feature (Lk. i. 27, 32, 69, ii. 4, 11 ;
Mt. i. 20, ii. 5f.). They also included genealogies of Jesus,
tracing his descent through his father Joseph to David and on
beyond him to Abraham—Luke prolonging his line still further
to " Adam the (son) of God " (Lk. iii. 23–38 ; Mt. i. 1–17).
Both genealogies, giving the ancestry of *Joseph*, would be
nugatory if Jesus, being virgin-born, were not his real son ;
and they were therefore clearly drawn up by persons who
believed that Joseph was physically Jesus' father.[2] They
prove at least, then, that belief in Jesus' Davidic descent
ante-dated belief in his miraculous birth. The Emperor

[1] So Dodd, *Hist. and the Gosp.* 68 n.1.
[2] Cf. C. J. Cadoux, *Cathol. and Christianity*, 348–356, where the question is
argued in detail.

Domitian (81–96 A.D.), suspecting the Christians as politically dangerous, threatened all surviving descendants of David with death ; and in that connexion there were brought before him two grandsons of Jesus' brother Judas, who acknowledged that they were of David's line, but were eventually released as harmless peasants.[1] Further evidence of Christian belief in Jesus' actual descent from David appears in the Apocalypse (iii. 7, v. 5, xxii. 16), the letters of Ignatius (Eph. xviii. 2, Trall. ix. 1, Rom. vii. 3, Smyrn. i. 1), and the Pastoral Epistles (2 Tim. ii. 8).

(5) General as was the Jewish view that the Messiah must be a prince of the house of David, the absolute necessity of such an origin was not universally upheld. Those, for instance, who expected a superhuman Messiah descending from the clouds could not have thought of him at the same time as a Davidic king. In the reign of Hadrian, the rebel Barkochba claimed to be the Messiah, and was recognized as such by the distinguished Rabbi Akiba ; yet neither he nor his supporters pretended that he was of Davidic descent. Moreover, the words of Jesus on the subject (Mk. xii. 35–37 = Lk. xx. 41–44 = Mt. xxii. 41–46) show that it was at least possible to suggest plausibly that the prevalent view was mistaken.[2]

(6) We have now to ask what view of the matter is really implied by these words of Jesus, already more than once referred to in this chapter : ' And Jesus, while teaching in the Temple, said in reply, " Why do the Scribes say that the Messiah is son of David ? David himself said by the Holy Spirit, ' The Lord said to my Lord, " Sit down on My right hand, until I make thine enemies a footstool for thy feet " '. David himself calls him ' Lord '. Whence (comes it) then (that) he is his son ? " . . .' (Mk. xii. 35–37 = Lk. xx. 41–44 = Mt. xxii. 41–46). Commentators continue to differ as to whether, in putting this question, Jesus did or did not imply that he was not himself descended from David. Almost all

---

[1] Eusebius, *Church-Hist.* III. xixf., xxxii. 5f.

[2] Cf. Abrahams, *Studies*, i. 136f.; Strack-Billerbeck i. 12 (" Zwar wird man nicht sagen können, dass für das jüdische Empfinden zu allen Zeiten u. unter allen Umständen die d a v i d i s c h e Herkunft eines Mannes die unerlässliche Voraussetzung seiner Anerkennung als Messias gebildet habe . . . "). Schweitzer is surely wrong in urging (*Quest*, 393—omitted in *L.J.F.*) that in Mk. xii. 35–37 Jesus could not have dissociated the Davidic Sonship from the Messiahship, on the ground that such a heresy would have been brought up against him as a charge sufficient to secure his condemnation. There is no evidence to show that doubt as to the Davidic origin of the Messiah was a punishable offence : and even if we accept Schweitzer's own view as to Jesus' real meaning, at least his *apparent* dissociation of Messiahship from Davidic descent remains.

however agree that the passage at least shows him to have laid no stress on the Messiah's Davidic descent, i.e., that he did not regard Davidic descent as an indispensable condition of Messiahship. Such an attitude would be explained by the fact that his whole view of the Messiahship was loftier and more spiritual than that of most Jews. One may, perhaps, go even further, and say that he felt that it was at least a little difficult to harmonize the two conceptions.[1]

(7) Apart from the last-discussed passage, which points rather away from than towards Jesus' descent from David, the only allusions Mark has to the matter are Bartimæus' salutation (see above, p. 82) and the crowd's cry about " the coming kingdom of our father David " (Mk. xi. 10). It is indeed possible that the original beginning of Mk. is, like the original ending, lost,[2] and that, if we possessed it, we might find that it recognized Jesus' descent from David : but even if that precarious conjecture were justified, the general paucity of Mark's allusions to the matter is significant.[3]

(8) The ' Didache ' is at best ambiguous on the Davidic descent. The prayer prescribed therein for use over the cup at the Eucharist runs, " We thank Thee, our Father, for the holy vine of David Thy Servant, which Thou hast made known to us by means of Jesus Thy Servant. To Thee be the glory for ever " (Did. ix. 2). And in the course of the prayer to be offered after the eucharistic meal occur the words, " Let grace come, and let this world pass away ! Hosanna to the God of David ! . . ." (Did. x. 6).[4]

(9) In John vii. 41f. it is stated that, in reply to the suggestion of some in the crowd that Jesus was the Messiah, others said, " (No), for surely the Messiah does not come from Galilee, (does he) ? Has not the Scripture said that the Messiah comes from the seed of David, and from Bethlehem, the village where David was ? " It has been treated as obvious that, since the Fourth Evangelist was presumably, like his readers, familiar with the Synoptic stories, he must have accepted both the Davidic descent of Jesus and his birth at

---

[1] Cf. Bartlet, *St. Mark*, 341f. ; Rawlinson, *St. Mark*, 174 (admits that " this particular passage, taken by itself, might be read in that sense ", viz., as a denial by Jesus that he was descended from David) ; Manson, *Teaching*, 266f. n. 2 ; V. Taylor, *Tradition*, 78 ; Otto, *Kingdom*, 244–246 ; A. T. Cadoux, *Theol. of Jes.* 167f., 195f.

[2] So W. A. Craigie in *Expos.* VIII. xxiv. 303–305 (Oct. 1922).

[3] Cf. Bacon, *Story of Jesus* (1928), 68–72, 79.

[4] Menzies (*Earliest Gospel*, 228 n. 1) regards this last-quoted sentence as implicitly denying the lineal descent of Jesus from David. See also Bigg, as quoted below, p. 87 n. 1.

Bethlehem as historical facts, and that he is therefore in this passage being subtly ironical, making the Jews bring forward against the Messiahship of Jesus objections which, had they only known the truth, they would have seen were really confirmations of it.[1] But, notwithstanding the confidence with which this interpretation has been urged, it may equally well be argued that, with his theory of the Logos, the Fourth Evangelist needed neither virgin-birth, nor birth at Bethlehem, nor Davidic descent, as credentials for Jesus' Saviourhood or Messiahship, and that that is the real reason why he passes over all three in silence, and alludes only indirectly even to the endowment with the Spirit at baptism (John i. 32–34).[2] On this view, John vii. 41f. (cf. 27f.) would be a gentle rejection of both Christian theories—that of the birth at Bethlehem and that of the Davidic descent.[3] If disbelief in the birth at Bethlehem seems unlikely at this early date, let it be borne in mind that the first form of the Lucan birth-stories (80 A.D.?) found no place for the virgin-birth.[4] That a certain view of the matter might be prevalent in the Church did not therefore necessarily mean that it was held unanimously. There are strong reasons for believing that the idea that Jesus was born at Bethlehem was, like the belief that he was virgin-born, simply an inference from an Old-Testament prophecy (Mic. v. 2 ; cf. Isa. vii. 14 in the Septuagint), not a real fact of history.[5] As therefore, on the view under consideration, the Fourth Evangelist was in all probability historically right in assuming that Jesus had not been born at Bethlehem, so too he was possibly right in not believing in his Davidic descent.[6]

(10) The author of the writing long mis-called ' The Epistle of Barnabas ' writes, " Again, behold Jesus, not son of a man, but Son of God, made manifest however in the flesh as a figure ($\tau\acute{\upsilon}\pi\dot{\omega}$). Since therefore they (i.e., the Jews) were bound ($\mu\acute{\epsilon}\lambda\lambda o\upsilon\sigma\iota\nu$) to say that the Messiah was son of David, David himself prophesies (as follows), fearing and understanding the deceitfulness of the sinners, ' The Lord said to my Lord, " Sit

---

[1] So W. M. Ramsay, *Was Christ born at Bethlehem ?* (1898), 95–98.

[2] It is indeed true that, up to a point, he assumes his readers to be familiar with the Synoptic story : but that this must not be over-pressed is shown by his repetition in detail of the narratives of the Crowd-feeding and the Passion ; and that he by no means regarded the Synoptic story as inerrant is abundantly proved by the numerous corrections he tacitly makes in it.

[3] Cf. Meyer, *Ursprung*, i. 63.

[4] Cf. C. J. Cadoux, *Cathol. and Christianity*, 350f.

[5] Cf. C. J. Cadoux, *Cathol. and Christianity*, 352f., 354f.

[6] Cf. Holtzmann, *Theol.* i. 313 ; Oscar Holtzmann, *Life of Jesus* (1904), 82–84, 450 ; Goguel, *Life of Jes.* 256–258.

on My right hand until I make thine enemies a footstool for thy feet " ' . . . " (Ep. Barn. xii. 10f.). The author of this composition wrote either about 75 A.D. or about 97 A.D. or about 130 A.D. He has a very definite axe to grind : he wants to prove that the Old-Testament Law and Prophecies had never been meant to refer to the Jews at all, but were all figurative foreshadowings of the Christian dispensation. His authority therefore as a sober witness cannot be rated very highly. At the same time it is significant that he felt free to assume that Jesus was not in point of fact physically descended from David.[1]

(11) In support of the conclusion that Jesus did not believe that he was descended from David one might plead (a) that on any other view it is hard to explain why any Christians should have doubted it, as we see some at least did ; (b) that the most natural view of Mk. xii. 35–38 = Lk. xx. 41–44 = Mt. xxii. 41–46 is to suppose that Jesus is arguing that one like himself, though not of David's line, might yet be Messiah (possibly in reply to the complaint that he had no right to allow himself to be saluted as " Son of David ") ; [2] (c) that the current view that the Messiah would be of David's line is amply sufficient to account for the belief that Jesus was of that line, just as Mic. v. 2 adequately accounts for the belief that he was born at Bethlehem, and Isa. vii. 14 in the Septuagint-version for the belief that he was born of a virgin.[3]

(12) On the other hand, there is no inherent difficulty in supposing that a family at Nazareth in the first century A.D. may have had good ground for believing that it belonged to the Davidic house. It is true that we are told that King Herod, jealous on account of his own humble origin, " burnt the registers of their (i.e., the Israelites') families " [4]—also that it was mainly the priestly and Levitical houses that were careful over their pedigrees. But this would not mean that no non-Levitical and non-priestly families prided themselves on their descent, or that no genealogical records survived Herod's act of destruction : besides, it would be perfectly possible for a family to retain the knowledge that it was descended from

---

[1] Cf. C. Bigg, *Origins of Christianity* (1909), 58 : " David, says Barnabas, tells us himself that Christ was not his Son. Tatian reproduced the same opinion in the second century, and it may be discovered even in the . . . *Didache* ". On Tatian, cf. J. M. Fuller in Smith's *Dict. of Christ. Biog.* iv (1887) 802f. : he omitted the genealogies in his harmony of the Gospels, and seems to have written treatises to disprove Jesus' Davidic descent.

[2] Montefiore, *S.G.*[2] II. 3 ; Goguel, *Life of Jes.* 257f.

[3] Cf., e.g., the Holtzmanns, as quoted above, p. 86 n. 6.

[4] Julius Africanus, quoted in Eusebius, *Church-Hist.* I. vii. 13.

so-and-so, without being in a position to produce documentary evidence showing that it actually was so. " The family of the house of David " is mentioned, as a still-distinguishable entity, in Zech. xii. 12—a passage written in the third or second century B.C. Other first-century Jews believed themselves to be descended from David, e.g., the Rabbi Hillel. The Davidic relatives of Jesus brought before Domitian (see above, p. 84 top) might indeed have inferred their Davidic origin simply from their kinship with Jesus : but there is no such likelihood in the case of the descendants of David whom Vespasian, after the fall of Jerusalem in 70 A.D., endeavoured to seek out and destroy.[1] Paul knew that he came from the tribe of Benjamin (Phil. iii. 5) ; and from Lk. ii. 36 we learn that Anna the prophetess belonged to the inconspicuous tribe of Asher. In the same way the name " Cohen " borne by many obscure Jews to-day testifies to their priestly origin ; a modern Swabian family claims descent from Charlemagne ; numerous poor Arabs wear the green turban which testifies to their belief that they are descendants of Muhammad, while descendants of Abu Bakr, Muhammad's father-in-law, are still to be found in Syria. Nor is the existence of *two* discrepant genealogies of Jesus in the Gospels a proof that neither of them is genuine ; for, supposing the Lucan list to be substantially accurate, we may well believe that the author of the later Matthæan list was quite equal to improving upon the true genealogy by connecting Jesus more directly with the royal dynasty of the kings of Judah. We must therefore recognize that there is no a priori bar to a claim on the part of Jesus' father that ' he was of the house and family of David ' (Lk. ii. 4).[2]

(13) A definite decision either way is difficult : but perhaps on the whole the assumption that Jesus' family did believe themselves, even before any question of his Messiahship arose, to be descendants of David is the less difficult of the two. It is surely significant that Paul, for whose Christology the Davidic descent of the Messiah was not very vital, and who was writing when several of Jesus' own brothers were still alive, should have so unquestioningly accepted and repeated the earlier Christian belief (see above, pp. 82f [3]). There is, moreover, some little force at least in the plea that, had Jesus not believed himself to be a scion of David's house, he is not very likely to have formed the idea, at the outset of his ministry, that he was

---

[1] Eusebius, *Church-Hist.* III. xii.

[2] Cf. Dalman, *W.J.* 319-324 ; Holtzmann, *Synopt.* 38-40, *Theol.* i. 309-313 ; Strack-Billerbeck i. 4-6 ; G. Kuhn in *Z.N.W.* xxii (1923) 206-228.

THE SON OF DAVID

the Messiah. If he did believe himself to be descended from
David, we should have to interpret Mk. xii. 35–37 = Lk. xx.
41–44 = Mt. xxii. 41–46 as meaning that he had by then come
to see that his Messiahship was not *dependent* on his Davidic
descent, though it was not *necessarily incompatible* with it.
The lukewarm or negative attitude of Mark, the Fourth Gospel,
the Didache, and the Epistle of Barnabas, would then be
explicable as arising from a desire to show Christianity to be
completely independent of Judaism. If, finally, we are satisfied
that Jesus and his family did believe themselves to be descended
from David, the most natural and probable conclusion to draw
is that in point of fact they were so.

CHAPTER VIII

THE SON OF MAN

(1) This is the most problematic of all the titles assigned to Jesus. (2) In the Old Testament generally the term meant " Man " in his creaturely aspect : (3) in Daniel it stood for an ideal individualization of redeemed Israel ; (4) and in the Book of Enoch it was used to describe a personal heavenly Messianic world-judge. (5) In current Aramaïc it would mean simply " the man ", and as such might have served as a modest and indirect self-designation. (6) Jesus certainly used it several times with reference to himself, but in what precise sense ? (7) After setting aside those passages in which the report of his use of it with reference to himself seems to be erroneous, (8) including three in which it apparently first meant " man " in general, (9) and also a few non-eschatological sayings in which it appears simply as an indirect self-designation, we are left with a large group of references to the saving work, the suffering and dying, the resurrection and coming, of the Son of Man. (10) The key to the explanation of these is to be found, not in the notion of an ideal or representative humanity, (11) nor in a simple synonymity between " Son of Man " and " Messiah ", (12) nor in the figure of the Son of Man in Enoch, (13) but in Ezekiel and in the vision described in Daniel vii. (14) This means that, in Jesus' eschatological passages, " the Son of Man " stands primarily for the saved and saving Remnant of Israel, with himself as its head. (15) Jesus, however, enriched the Danielic figure with characteristics drawn from the Servant-passages in Deutero-Isaiah. (16) This combination gives us a suitable interpretation of the passages in question. (17) His use of the phrase in this eschatological sense did not begin until after Peter's Confession at Cæsarea-Philippi, and it was for the most part confined to the circle of the Disciples. (18) The circumstances under which the phrase was used necessarily gave rise to some ambiguity and confusion.

(1) The question as to what precisely Jesus meant by the phrase " the Son of Man " which he so often used is one of the standing problems of Gospel-study. The literature dealing with it is bewilderingly extensive ; and no all-round solution

of it has yet obtained general recognition. The obscurity of the title should warn us not to approach the discussion of it until we have considered the clearer and less problematic designations of Jesus which were used or accepted by himself, and are thus able to examine the harder problem in the light of the solutions of the easier. It is inherently likely that the meaning he gave to the term was striking and original ; and we must therefore be on our guard against hastily adopting false clues, especially those that give results irreconcilable with what we know on less ambiguous evidence.

(2) Philologically the term means, both in Hebrew and Aramaïc, simply " man ", and can be used both in the singular (individually or collectively) and in the plural, and both with and without the sign of determination. It draws attention to the humanity and human characteristics, both lofty (in distinction from the animals) and lowly (in contrast to God), of the person or persons in mind. So we find it used in the Old Testament (chiefly in the later and poetical books), e.g., Num. xxiii. 19 ; Ezek. ii. 1, 3, etc., etc. ; Job xvi. 21, xxv. 6 ; Psa. viii. 4ff. (" What is man, that Thou art mindful of him ? and the son of man, that Thou visitest him ? . . .") ; Dan. viii. 17.[1]

(3) The vision which Daniel is said to have seen is so important for the purpose of our inquiry, that a full summary, with quotation of certain passages, is necessary. The book of Daniel was written in the midst of the Maccabæan rising against Antiochus Epiphanes, king of Syria (about 165 B.C.), but the scene of the story is laid in the times of Nebuchadrezzar and Belshazzar, kings of Babylon in the sixth century. Its prophecies are therefore reflections on the circumstances and destiny of the Israel of 165 B.C., put in the form of the predictions and visions of a sixth-century prophet. Daniel dreams that he sees in succession four dissimilar beasts arise (which, as it appears, represent respectively the Babylonian, Median, Persian, and Alexandrian [more specifically, the Seleucid] empires) : of these the fourth is the most terrible and destructive (Dan. vii. 1–8). Then came a vision of God, aged and white-haired, clad in white and seated on His fiery throne, ready to pronounce judgment and with countless attendants before Him (vii. 9f.). Under His judgment the fourth beast is killed and burned, and the other three deposed (vii. 11f.).

The vision continues thus (I translate direct from the Aramaïc) : " I was looking in the visions of the night, and lo ! with the clouds of heaven there came one like a son of man ;

---

[1] Fullest list in Dalman, *W.J.* 234–236.

and he came up to the One advanced in days, and they brought him near before Him. And there was given to him rule and honour and a kingdom, that all peoples, nations, and tongues should do him reverence : his rule is an age-long rule which will not pass away, and his kingdom one that will not be destroyed" (vii. 13f.). Daniel, on asking in alarm for an explanation, is told by a bystander that the four beasts are four future kings (vii. 15–17), " and the saints of the Most High will receive the kingdom and will possess the kingdom for ages and ages " (vii. 18). He asks further about the fourth beast, recalling specific details and in particular its horn (representing Antiochus Epiphanes) : " I looked, and that horn was making war on the saints, and prevailing against them, until there came the One advanced in days ; and the judgment [sat, and rule] was given to the saints of the Most High, and the time arrived, and the saints took possession of the kingdom " (vii. 19f., 21f.). It is explained to him that this horn is an iniquitous king, who will be for a season allowed to transgress against the regular (Jewish) festivals and the Law (vii. 23–25). " But the judgment will sit ; and his rule will they take away, to ruin and destroy it finally. And the kingdom and the rule and the greatness of the kingdoms under all the heavens will be given to the people of the saints of the Most High : its (i.e., the people's) kingdom will be an age-long kingdom, and all rulers will do reverence to it and obey it " (vii. 26f.). The chapter concludes by describing Daniel's alarm, and his preservation of the whole matter in secrecy (vii. 28).

The points to be observed here are that " Son of Man " simply means a *human* being, in contrast to the four *beasts*, and is introduced in order to bring out Israel's superiority to the heathen kingdoms, and that the " one like a son of man " simply represents collectively, under the figure of an individual quasi-human being, " the people (consisting) of the saints of the Most High ", i.e., the redeemed and restored Israel. This Israel, the prophet anticipates, will—on the downfall of the iniquitous Seleucid power—enter, by God's decree and gift, on a world-wide and everlasting dominion.[1] Such a representation of a whole group by a single individual, though unusual in modern thought and apt to appear bizarre, was a not-infrequent conception among the ancient Hebrews.[2]

[1] Cf. the parallel picture in Dan. ii. 44f., where God's final dominion is inaugurated by " a stone cut without hands ", etc. See also Dalman, *W.J.* 241f. ; Driver, *Daniel (Camb. Bible)*, 94–110 ; Héring, *Royaume*, 75–77.

[2] See Dr. H. Wheeler Robinson's interesting article on ' The Hebrew Conception of Corporate Personality ' in *Beihefte zur Z.A.W.* lxvi (1936) 49–62.

(4) Although the meaning of the phrase " Son of Man " in this passage in Daniel is thus quite clear, it came later on to be carelessly misunderstood as if it designated an individual Messiah. Thus in the ' Similitudes ' of Enoch, xxxvii–lxxi (written probably in the first century B.C.), " the " (or " that ") " Son of Man " figures as a heavenly individual, who judges the world from God's glorious throne, and inaugurates and heads God's universal reign.[1] The idea and the title are both doubtless derived from Daniel ; but it is probable that they owe much to Iranian or Zoroastrian influence (which indeed is thought to have affected Daniel also).[2] In Iranian mythology an important part is played by the notion of a celestial, archetypal, primeval, or ancestral " Man " ;[3] and several of the features characterizing this figure are strikingly paralleled in the Enochic description of the Son of Man.[4] The Fourth Book of Esdras, in its allusions to the Messiah (xiii), echoes in somewhat the same way the language of Dan. vii.[5]

(5) The philological questions connected with the use of the phrase " Son of Man " in Aramaïc, and with its meaning apart from any technical eschatological context, are very complicated, partly because we have no literary records in the language dating actually from the time of Jesus. There seems, however, good reason to believe that the term could have been used in special circumstances as a modest and indirect designation of oneself. Analogous expressions in other languages are plentiful —we may recall Paul's allusion to himself as " a man in Christ " (2 Cor. xii. 2), or (to take modern examples from quite different quarters) Uncle Remus's as " de ole nigger ", or the Chinaman's " p'i jen ", i.e., " (this) unworthy man ". It would sound like " that man—you know whom I mean ", or " I could name someone who . . ."[6] It is certain that such ways of expressing oneself were familiar in Aramaïc ; and it is altogether probable that " the Son of Man " may have been, if not actually one of the phrases commonly so used, sufficiently like them to be easily employed on occasion as one of them.[7]

---

[1] Cf. Dalman, *W.J.* 242–244 ; Schürer, *G.J.V.* ii. 614f. ; Goguel, *Life of Jes.* 575f. ; V. Taylor, *Sacrifice*, 22–26.

[2] Cf. Meyer, *Ursprung*, ii. 189–199 ; Von Gall, Βασιλεία, 412.

[3] Cf. Meyer, *Ursprung*, ii. 345–352 ; Creed in *J.T.S.* xxvi. 113–136 (Jan. 1925) ; Burkitt in *J.T.S.* xxxiii. 307–311 (Apl. 1932).

[4] Cf. Creed, as in last n., 129f. ; Otto, *Kingdom*, 176–218, 388–392, 396–398 ; Héring, *Royaume*, 77–79.

[5] Cf. Dalman, *W.J.* 244f. ; Creed, as in n. 3, 130f.

[6] Cf. Burkitt in *H.C.L.M.K.* 231 = *Jesus Christ*, etc. 35.

[7] Dalman, *W.J.* 235–241, 249f., 256f., *Gramm. des . . . Aram.* (ed. 1905), 108 ; Weinel, *Theol.* 208–210 ; Manson, *Teaching*, 217f.

(**6**) The mysteries attending the development and vogue of the phrase in question led some of the earlier inquirers to deny that Jesus could ever have actually used it with reference to himself.[1] The fact, however, that the Synoptic Gospels put the words into his mouth on about forty different occasions, that the Fourth Gospel, which has no particular theological use to make of them, represents Jesus as using them of himself eleven times, and that—apart from an utterance of Stephen (Acts vii. 56), a couple of allusions in the Apocalypse (i. 13 and xiv. 14), and one perhaps in Hebrews (ii. 6)—they do not occur elsewhere in the New Testament (showing that they were not a *customary* early Christian name for the Lord [cf. Ep. Barn. xii. 10]), suffice to outweigh completely any purely-linguistic objections, and to justify the conclusion that Jesus certainly used them on several occasions, and frequently with reference to himself, though in what precise sense we have still to determine.[2]

(**7**) The next step in the investigation is to set aside those passages in which the occurrence of the words " the Son of Man " with reference to Jesus himself seems to be historically unjustified. That such passages do actually occur can readily be proved by three instances which, as being the most unmistakable, we will take first. In Mt. xvi. 13 (cf. Mk. viii. 27 = Lk. ix. 18), Mt. xvi. 28 (cf. Mk. ix. 1 = Lk. ix. 27), and Mt. xxvi. 2 (cf. Mk. xiv. 1 = Lk.xxii. 1f.), it is clear from the parallels that m has arbitrarily introduced the phrase " the Son of Man " without any authority for it in his Marcan source. It is almost equally clear that Mt. xii. 40 is a fictitious substitute by M or m for the original saying about Jonah reported by Q and preserved in Lk. xi. 30.[3] The interpretation of the Parable of the Tares is on independent grounds adjudged by most modern critics to be a secondary production, and thus necessitates the addition of two more ungenuine occurrences of " the Son of Man " (Mt. xiii. 37 and 41) to our preliminary list.[4]

The interesting fact that all these well-nigh unmistakably erroneous insertions of the term occur in Mt. (i.e., in M or m) makes it unlikely that that Gospel would have omitted it in

---

[1] E.g., Lietzmann, *Der Menschensohn* (1896) ; N. Schmidt in *E. Bi.* 4705–4740.

[2] Cf. Dalman, *W.J.* 250–253, 256, 259 ; Driver in H.*D.B.* iv. 581–583 ; Weinel, *Theol.* 214f. ; Peake in *B.J.R.L.* VIII. i. 71–74 (Jan. 1924) ; Dodd, *Parables*, 89f. ; Héring, *Royaume*, 89f.

[3] Mt. xviii. 11, probably does not belong to the original text of the Gospel.

[4] Cf. Manson, *Teaching*, 222f., and in *Mission*, etc. 486.

any place where the source justified its inclusion. In Lk. vi. 22, therefore, in what looks like an extract from Q, we seem entitled to draw from the fact that the parallel in Mt. v. 11 makes no mention of " the Son of Man " the inference that in Luke it is an editorial intrusion (l).

One more highly-dubious passage remains—Mt. x. 23 : " . . . truly I tell you, ye will by no means finish the cities of Israel until the Son of Man comes ". It clearly belongs to M, a document compiled from a definitely-Judaïstic point of view, and therefore likely to be unsympathetic to Paul's enthusiasm for the Gentile mission (cf. Mt. x. 5). Taken (as Schweitzer and others have taken it) [1] for a genuine saying of Jesus, it is bewilderingly inconsistent with much else in his teaching that is by no means obscure : but understood as a late version of some now-lost saying of Jesus, garbled under the stress of the anti-Pauline conviction of the Jerusalem-church that there would barely be time to evangelize all Israel before the Lord returned, it is perfectly intelligible. That being the case, the authority of M is by no means sufficient to warrant its acceptance.[2]

There are one or two other sayings which, on account either of exclusively-Matthæan attestation, or of the strong suggestion they make of the early Christian mentality, we may reasonably suspect of being secondary—namely, Lk. xviii. 8b L, Mt. xix. 28 M (contrast Lk. xxii. 29f. L), and Mt. xxv. 31 M. But as the case against their genuineness is less strong, it is perhaps best to retain them for the present.

(8) We have, however, to take into consideration three cases in which some confusion seems to have arisen between " the Son of Man " as a self-designation of Jesus and " the Son of Man " as a designation of man as such. Clearly such confusion would be likely sometimes to arise. Some sayings in which the words were used in the latter sense would come to be misunderstood as references made by Jesus to himself. I have already argued that this has happened in Mk. ii. 28 = Lk. vi. 5 = Mt. xii. 8, " so that the Son of Man is master even over the Sabbath " (see above, pp. 75f. [12]).

In regard to Mk. ii. 10 = Lk. v. 24 = Mt. ix. 6 also, reasons have been given for regarding the section in which it occurs as a later addition to the story of the paralytic (see above, p. 75 [11]).

---

[1] E.g., Schweitzer, *L.J.F.* 256, 373, 405, 407f. = *Quest*, 264, 333, 357-359.
[2] Cf. Stanton, *G.H.D.* ii. 330 ; Streeter, *Four Gospels*, 255f., 263, 520, *Primitive Church* (1929), 34f. ; Montefiore, *S.G.*[2] II. 147, 150f. ; Manson, *Teaching*, 221f., and in *Mission*, etc. 474, 476.

In view of the documentary obscurity and dubiousness of the passage, we must, I think, choose between treating the words as a misunderstood expression of an early Christian preacher's belief that Jesus could and did forgive sins, and treating them as a misunderstood assertion made by Jesus himself to the effect that to declare sins forgiven by God was not beyond the competence of man as man. If it be said that neither of these views is quite satisfactory, I would reply that they are somewhat less unsatisfactory than their various alternatives. The latter of the two receives some faint support from the concluding observation of m, to the effect that ' the crowds . . . glorified God, Who had given such authority *to men*' (Mt. ix. 8). If accepted, it implies that " the Son of Man " in Mk. ii. 10 means, not specifically Jesus himself, but man generally.[1]

Finally, in Q's version of the saying about the unpardonable sin (Lk. xii. 10 = Mt. xii. 32), we read, " Whoever says a word against the Son of Man, he will be forgiven : . . . ", whereas in the Marcan version the words occur, " All sins and blasphemies . . . will be forgiven to *the sons of men*; but . . ." (Mk. iii. 28f. [τοῖς υἱοῖς τῶν ἀνθρώπων] = Mt. xii. 31 [τοῖς ἀνθρώποις]). Both forms of the saying can hardly be equally original ; and of the two the one which refers the phrase " the Son of Man " to Jesus is perhaps the less likely to be so, the tendency clearly being to multiply such references rather than to reduce them. Despite the high authority of Q, therefore, I venture to think that in this case it is less reliable than Mk., and to relegate Lk. xii. 10 = Mt. xii. 32 accordingly to the group of probably erroneous reports.[2]

(9) After having thus set aside, on one good ground or another, these eleven occurrences of the term as either certainly unhistorical or at least unreliable, we are left with some twenty-eight passages on our hands, in which the use of it by Jesus with reference to himself is reported on the strength of what seems to be at least fairly-good tradition. Now it is surely very significant that, with one exception (Lk. vii. 34 = Mt. xi. 19 Q), every one of these twenty-eight sayings was, according to our sources, spoken *after* Peter's Confession of Jesus' Messiahship at

---

[1] Cf., in addition to the authorities quoted above, p. 75 nn. 1 and 2, and Dalman, *W.J.* 254, 261f.

[2] Dalman, *W.J.* 254f. ; Driver in *H.D.B.* iv. 587f. I disagree with Schmiedel's argument (ap. Driver) that the pardonability of blasphemy against Jesus could never have been *invented* by a Christian evangelist : to doubt or deny such pardonability would have hampered the Church's appeal for penitent conversion.

Cæsarea-Philippi (on which occasion Jesus first told the Disciples unmistakably about his coming passion) ; all of them but two (which two include the one that preceded Cæsarea-Philippi) have reference to his redemptive mission, his homelessness, his betrayal and death, his resurrection, and his future coming, i.e., they are all, in a broad sense of the word, eschatological ; and all of them but five (which five include the two non-eschatological sayings) were apparently spoken, not to the public, but privately to the Disciples.[1] The two public non-eschatological instances are Lk. vii. 34 = Mt. xi. 19 Q (" The Son of Man has come eating and drinking, and ye say, ' Look ! a glutton and a tippler, a friend of tax-collectors and sinners ! ' . . .") and Lk. xi. 30 (" For as Jonah was a sign to the Ninevites, so will the Son of Man also be to this generation "—for the parallel in Mt. xii. 40, see above, p. 94). These seem to be cases in which Jesus may have originally used the indeterminate form " a son of man ", as a modest and indirect designation of himself (see above, p. 93 [5]), and in which his words were later misunderstood as if they had been " *the* Son of Man " and had been intended in a technical eschatological sense.[2] If we accordingly eliminate these sayings also, the position of the remainder, their contents, and the circumstances under which they were spoken, suggests a clue to their interpretation : they seem to be esoteric allusions to Jesus' self-sacrifice for the sake of men and his final triumph, uttered by him after he had divulged to his Disciples the prospect of his death.[3]

(10) But what is the key to Jesus' use of the particular phrase " the Son of Man " in such a connexion ? Some have thought that he chose a phrase setting forth the idea of humanity as such, because he wished to present himself suggestively to those to whom he so spoke as the representative man, standing for the race as a whole, and, by his unique fulfilment of God's ideal for man, exhibiting in his example what man as such ought to be. Others suppose that he had in mind the lowliness and humiliation of his lot, wherein human weakness and suffering were by a providential paradox to be

---

[1] Cf. Dalman, *W.J.* 259–264 ; Holtzmann, *Theol.* i. 320–322, 326, 330–333 ; Manson, *Teaching*, 214f., 220, 223f.

[2] So Manson, *Teaching*, 217–219.

[3] The exceptions to the general privacy are Lk. ix. 58 = Mt. viii. 20 Q (spoken to a prospective disciple), Lk. xix. 10 L (though its precise occasion is dubious—Manson, *Teaching*, 224f.), and Mk. xiv. 62 = Mt. xxvi. 64 : cf. Lk. xxii. 69 L (spoken to the Sanhedrin). Mt. xxv. 31 M comes in a long set of discourses, whereof the *first* is said to have been addressed to the Disciples : the circumstances of the later ones must be considered doubtful. Lk. xviii. 8b is similarly uncertain.

made the means of a great Divine redemptive act. It is impossible to deny that such ideas might occur to Jesus : but they are somewhat remote from the Palestinian-Jewish habits of thought ; and in any case they hardly suffice to account for the special use Jesus made of this particular term, especially when we bear in mind the fact that he seems to have spoken as if he expected his hearers to be able to discern without explanation what he meant by it. If these ideas played any part in determining the connotation he gave to the term, it must have been quite secondary to some other more dominating motif.[1]

(11) The theory has also been tried out that " the Son of Man " must, in view of the Books of Daniel and Enoch, have been a fairly well-recognized technical term for the Messiah. Against this it used to be urged that, whereas Jesus never openly called himself " Messiah ", he did openly call himself " the Son of Man ". If we are right in conjecturing that his use of the phrase " the Son of Man " was esoteric, this objection loses part of its force. But not all : for if by " the Son of Man " he meant simply " the Messiah ", how is it that, in his private talks with the Disciples after Cæsarea-Philippi, no other and more direct references to the Messiahship (under that name) also appear ? There is, in fact, a fair measure of agreement among scholars to-day on the view that, whatever the special and even Messianic meaning with which the phrase might be deliberately charged, it was not a commonly-understood equivalent for " Messiah " among Jesus' contemporaries.[2]

(12) Was Jesus then perchance shaping his thoughts on the lines suggested by the ' Similitudes ' of Enoch ? Perhaps the strongest support for such a view is to be found in the descriptions in Mt. xix. 28b M (cf. Lk. xxii. 29f. L) and in Mt. xxv. 31 M of " the Son of Man sitting on the throne of his glory " (i.e., on his glorious throne)—a phrase which can be paralleled only in Enoch (xlv. 3, lxi. 8, lxii. 2, 5, lxix. 27). There are other points of contact, e.g., the Father reveals him, he is invested with heavenly glory, administers judgment, is surrounded by faithful followers, and so on.[3] Yet it must be

---

[1] Cf. Dalman, *W.J.* 256f. ; Driver in H.*D.B.* iv. 580f., 585, and esp. 586f. ; Sanday, *Life of Christ in Recent Research* (1907), 127f. ; Holtzmann, *Theol.* i. 323f., 326 ; Bartlet and Carlyle, *Christianity in Hist.* 20–26.

[2] Cf. Dalman, *W.J.* 241–249, 254f., 260.

[3] See above, p. 93 (4). Otto (*Kingdom,* 176–218, 382–387) goes very fully into the Enoch-picture, endeavouring to show striking parallels between it and the Gospels. Cf. also Von Gall, Βασιλεία, 409–412 ; Héring, *Royaume,* 25f. n., 96–98.

maintained that the likelihood of Jesus having drawn from the Book of Enoch is very slight. While we know that, as a pious Jew, he was familiar with the Old Testament, we have absolutely no evidence (beyond the occurrence of the dubious phrases just quoted, which are found only in M) to show that he had ever read Enoch, or that it was known among those with whom he mixed.[1] It is not only that the book itself reveals an elementary standard of intelligence : [2] the point is that, when we have deducted the features which Enoch may have itself drawn from Daniel, there is not sufficient similarity left between Enoch and the Gospels to make any direct dependence of Jesus on the contents of Enoch at all probable, though we may more readily admit the possibility that its language to some extent affected the Gospels, particularly Mt. Furthermore, the somewhat-elaborate Iranian conceptions which pervade Enoch would have made little appeal to one so rooted in the religion of the Old-Testament prophets as Jesus was.[3]

(13) It is otherwise with Ezekiel and Daniel. The phrase " Son of Man " occurs over ninety times in Ezekiel ; and there are numerous points of contact between Jesus' sayings and Daniel. As books of Scripture Ezekiel and Daniel would be as familiar to Jesus' Jewish hearers as they were to himself ; and his use of the phrase " the Son of Man " therefore would not be devoid of meaning for them. Their recollection of Ezekiel would tell them that Jesus also was claiming to speak as a prophet, while their recollection of Daniel vii would suggest to them, if only in a vague way, that he was speaking eschatologically.[4]

---

[1] Cf. Moore, *Judaism*, i. 131, 186.

[2] The late Dr. H. L. Goudge once expressed himself strongly on this matter : " Now the Book of Enoch may surely claim a place among the world's hundred worst books ; it was too much even for the Jewish Rabbis ; and I would as soon take my theology from Zadkiel's Almanac. Moreover, there seems to be no evidence that our Lord had ever seen it, though it imposed upon a good many of the early Christians. But suppose that He had. Does the fact that the Book of Enoch—misunderstanding the passage in Daniel—speaks of a pre-existent Son of Man, and elaborates the picture of him on Messianic lines, in the least suggest that the Lord derived from this stupid book the title that He used of Himself and the belief in His pre-existence ? . . . " (*Oxford Society of Historical Theology : Abstract of Proceedings* . . . 1930–1931, 19).

[3] Cf. Manson, *Teaching*, 228f.

[4] Cf. Dalman, *W.J.* 256–258, 264–266 ; Holtzmann, *Theol.* i. 314, 319f. ; A. T. Cadoux in *Interpreter*, xviii. 202ff. (Apl. 1922) ; Klausner, *Jes. of Naz.* 257. The use of Daniel vii for the purpose of interpreting Jesus' use of the phrase " the Son of Man " is conspicuous by its virtual absence in Otto, *Kingdom* (185 only). I cannot but think that this omission detracts very seriously from the value of Otto's interpretation.

(**14**) It has been made plain above (p. 92) that the " one like a son of man " in Daniel vii is not really an individual person at all, but is the personification of a *community*. However strange it may seem to us at first sight that a Gospel-term which we have hitherto been accustomed to take as an obvious, if mysterious, self-designation of Jesus, often really refers to a community, namely, the saved and saving Remnant of Israel, such is nonetheless the conclusion to which we are driven. The fact that Jesus always thinks of himself as the head of that community still enables us to accept and allow for that reference to himself which his use of the phrase seems so often to imply. At the same time, the fact that the term is more than a mere self-designation enables us to explain what would otherwise be inexplicable—I mean, the differentiation made in certain sayings of Jesus between " the Son of Man " and himself as speaker. These are Mk. viii. 38 = Lk. ix. 26 (cf. Mt. xvi. 27) ; Lk. xii. 8 = Mt. x. 32 Q (Mt. here has " I " instead of Lk's. " the Son of Man " ; but the differentiation between the two and the analogy of Mk. viii. 38 makes the Lucan version the more probable here, despite what is said above on pp. 94f. about Lk. vi. 22) ; Mt. xix. 28 M (cf. Lk. xxii. 28–30 L) ; and Mk. xiv. 62 = Mt. xxvi. 64 (cf. Lk. xxii. 69 L) : in Mt. xxv. 31–46 the distinction is between " the Son of Man " and " the King ", who is apparently Jesus himself.[1] As we shall be investigating these passages later in another connexion, there is no need to discuss them in detail here : but the differentiation in question is worth noting at this point as sufficiently attested and as very hard to explain if the words " the Son of Man " on Jesus' lips always refer to him and to him only.[2]

(**15**) But " the one like a son of man " in Daniel vii was by no means the only Old-Testament figure which Jesus regarded as realized and fulfilled in himself. " The Servant of the Lord " in Deutero-Isaiah also was, as we have seen (pp. 37f.), a foreshadowing of him. As, however, he could not well have thought of himself as filling two radically-different rôles, he

---

[1] Cf. Holtzmann, *Theol.* i. 393–395 ; Manson, *Teaching*, 264f., 270, and in *Mission*, etc. 541–543.

[2] The earlier advocates of this " corporate " interpretation are noticed by N. Schmidt in *E. Bi.* 4720. Cf. also Holtzmann, *Theol.* i. 314 ; J. R. Coates, *The Christ of Revolution* (1920), 76–83 ; A. T. Cadoux in *Interpreter* xviii. 202–214 (Apl. 1922 : cf. his *Theol. of Jes.* 179–213) ; H. Bulcock in *Congreg. Quart.* xvii. 44–55 (Jan. 1939) ; and especially Manson, *Teaching*, 227–236, 269f. Per contra, V. Taylor, *Sacrifice*, 29 ; Flew, *Church*, 75 (disagrees with Manson about the Son of Man, though strongly emphasizing the community-interest of Jesus' work [72–80, and esp. 116 (" . . . Jesus is identifying Himself with His followers . . . ")]).

must have combined the features of both these Scriptural figures in a single picture when visualizing the ideal he was to embody.[1] Different as the two figures were at first sight, they have important characteristics in common. Corresponding to the humiliation and suffering of the Servant is the war which the Fourth Beast makes upon " the saints ", i.e., upon the " Son of Man " (Dan. vii. 7f., 11a, 19–21, 23–25) ; corresponding to the everlasting kingdom given by God to the " Son of Man " is the Servant's final victory and vindication (Isa. xlii. 1, 4, xlix. 6b, l. 7–9, liii. 10–12). And it is interesting to remember that one of the most ancient as well as most modern methods of interpreting the Servant-passages is to understand them as portraying in some sense an idealized Israel. This corporate interpretation would harmonize well with the similar treatment which it would be only natural to apply to the figure in Daniel. Jesus is to be the spokesman and representative of a redeemed and redemptively-active community.

(16) If now, with this clue in our hands, we go back to those twenty-six passages (see above, pp. 96f.) in which Jesus seems to have used the phrase " the Son of Man " eschatologically with reference to himself, we shall find that they all lend themselves fairly readily to a corporate, as well as to a personal, interpretation. They will all come up for detailed consideration later ; but we may well observe here that in the notions of being sent to save the lost, of undergoing privation, betrayal, persecution, and martyrdom, and of rising again from death and reappearing in glory, we have nothing which Jesus may not have applied to the lot of the loyal community he gathered round him, as well as to himself personally as its head.[2] The reader may here be reminded that, in arriving at our set of twenty-six passages, we followed an inclusive rather than a severe process of censorship ; and it is consequently quite possible that some of the twenty-six may, on closer investigation, prove to be assignable to one or other of the eliminated groups. At the moment we only need to note the general fact that the term " the Son of Man ", when used in the connexions just mentioned, at least very often has reference to the community of followers which Jesus collects round him as well as to him in his capacity of their leader.

[1] Cf. Moffatt, *Theol. of the Gospels*, 159f.
[2] It is interesting to note in passing that, whereas of the sources Q, L, M, and Mk., all have allusions to the future coming of the Son of Man, only L and Mk. refer to his mission to serve and save men, only Mk. to his suffering (except for one allusion in Q to his homelessness, and one in L to his betrayal), and only Mk. to his resurrection. Cf. Manson, *Teaching*, 225–227.

(17) See above, pp. 96f. (9).

(18) In closing this investigation, I would not claim that the exegesis advocated here suffices to remove all obscurity from the use of this to us so strange phrase. Perhaps in the circumstances, at this distance of time, and with only such documents as we have, a fairly-considerable margin of uncertainty is bound to remain, whatever line of explanation be adopted. Admittedly the whole problem is very complicated and difficult. It is rendered so partly by the fact that the term itself was fluid and ambiguous in meaning rather than precise and clear. It could have two or three quite distinct denotations : it suggested what was in the speaker's mind, rather than expressed it unmistakably. Possibly Jesus was himself aware that the term was ambiguous, and purposely used it partly for that reason.[1] It is curious that, in the circumstances, none of the Evangelists should have felt the need of making clear to his readers what exactly the words meant. The probability is that they were themselves sometimes uncertain and astray with regard to it, and, writing for an uncritical and mostly unliterary circle of readers, treated the term simply as a self-designation chosen by the Lord, and therefore as sacrosanct and in need of no further exact definition.[2]

[1] Cf. Dalman, *W.J.* 255, 258–260, 264 ; Driver in H.*D.B.* iv. 585f. (19) ; Holtzmann, *Theol.* i. 331, 334f. ; Klausner, *Jes. of Naz.* 257 ; Creed in *J.T.S.* xxvi. 136 (Jan. 1925) ; C. A. Scott in *H.C.L.M.K.* 349 ; Héring, *Royaume,* 105.
[2] Cf. Dalman, *W.J.* 253 ; Bacon, *Mark,* 226 ; Klausner, *Jes. of Naz.* 257.

SUMMARY OF PART ONE

Jesus knows himself to be in closest filial intimacy with God as his Father, so that, while all righteous men are sons of God, he occupies a special place of his own as " the Son " over against " the Father ". He accordingly makes the concerns of God his own, and takes on the rôle of the self-sacrificing Servant of God portrayed in Deutero-Isaiah. This function commits him to a life-effort on behalf of men, the aim of which is to save them from sin, ignorance, illness, and sorrow, and to lead them into the same enjoyment of God's love as he himself possessed. As early as his baptism, he felt himself anointed by God as the predicted and anticipated Messiah of Israel : but as he understood Messiahship in so different a sense from the Jewish public in general, he made no open claim to it. By acted and spoken hint, however, he prompted men to see it in his redemptive mission. At his Temptation he arrived at such critical decisions regarding himself and his future methods that he viewed the occasion as a decisive victory over Satan, by virtue of which he was able thereafter to conquer Satan's underlings and undo their works in the form of demon-possession, illness, and human folly and sin.

In view of his commission, he assumed an authority over men superior to that of any other authority they knew ; yet this authority was not in the last analysis arbitrary and despotic, since he referred men to their own powers of insight for the verification of his pronouncements. He attached the utmost importance, such as involved even their eternal destiny, to their compliance with his teaching. Of his probable descent from King David he made no use, though it may have facilitated for many around him the belief that he was actually the Messiah. Finally, he combined the picture of the Suffering Servant of the Lord with that of the Son of Man, who in Daniel vii personifies the redeemed saints of God. " The Son of Man " is not only his occasional designation of himself, but a name for the holy community which he desires to gather round him —a community which, like its leader, is prepared to suffer in serving man for God's sake, and looks forward to everlasting sovereignty as its promised reward.

PART TWO

THE NATURE AND PRESENCE OF THE KINGDOM OF GOD

CHAPTER I

THE MEANING OF "THE KINGDOM OF GOD"

(1) The great theme of Jesus' teaching was the Kingdom of God. (2) From the fact that this Kingdom was in his time an object of eager expectancy to the Jews generally, (3) and that he must have wished his words to be intelligible to them, we may infer that, however different in some ways his view of it might have been from theirs, there must have been much in common between the two views. (4) In calling it sometimes " the Kingdom of the Heavens ", he was simply using a customary reverent synonym for " God ". (5) The word " Kingdom " in the Gospels means primarily kingship, or royal sovereignty. (6) The meaning of the Kingdom of God for men is therefore in the first place their submission to Him as King : (7) in this intensive sense the term was used both by the Rabbis and by Jesus. (8) But inasmuch as the King is in this case also the Father, His " Kingdom " involves a personal and filial relation to Him. (9) Furthermore, the word can also be used extensively to denote the realm, i.e., the group of those subject to the King. (10) It is thus a social entity, as well as an individual condition ; and, inasmuch as the realization of this social ideal is a matter of growth, (11) the Kingdom often figures as an eschatological concept.

(1) A rough count shows that Q reports sixteen references on the part of Jesus to the Kingdom of God, L seven, Mk. thirteen, and M twenty-six. According to Mk. i. 15 = Mt. iv. 17 he began his public work with a declaration concerning it ; and in his numerous allusions to it in the course of his teaching, it usually stands in the forefront of the argument. In Lk. xvi. 16 (Q or l ? : cf. Mt. xi. 12) he himself indirectly depicts it as the main theme on which he—and apparently John the Baptist also—had preached. Therefore m and l were not misrepresenting the facts when, referring to Jesus in the third person, they spoke as if the Kingdom was his normal topic (l :—Lk. iv. 43, viii. 1 [unless L], ix. 11—cf. Acts i. 3 ; m :—Mt. iv. 23, ix. 35, xiii. 19). Q informs us that its nearness was the main burden of the missionary-addresses of the Disciples (Lk. x. 9 = Mt. x. 7) ; and here again the later editors furnish supplementary notices to the same general effect (Lk. ix. 2 l ; Lk. ix. 60 l

[unless Q [1]]; Lk. x. 11 l; Mt. xxiv. 14a m). There can, therefore, be no doubt as to its central importance in Jesus' whole world-view.[2]

(2) However rare may be the occurrence of the actual phrase " the Kingdom of God " in Jewish literature, there is abundant evidence to show that the idea of it dominated the minds of the people generally, particularly those large sections of it for whom eschatology was of prime importance.[3] While all agreed that in some sense God was King already, and while the thought of His Kingdom as a purely-religious concept survived, as we shall see, among certain of the Rabbis, it was as a glorious future state for the nation, a state soon to be miraculously and catastrophically brought in by God, that the rank and file of the people (including not only the Apocalyptists, but also many of the Pharisees) mostly pictured it. Less than a century before Jesus' ministry, the author of the seventeenth ' Psalm of Solomon ' had written, " But we will rest our hope on God our saviour, because the power of our God (is) for ever with mercy, and the Kingdom of our God (will hold sway) forever over the nations in judgment " (Psa. Sol. xvii. 3) ; and in the sequel he gives a full picture of the hoped-for Messiah of the seed of David.[4] The gospels indicate how much the notion of the coming Kingdom was in the air. John the Baptist may have proclaimed its nearness as part of his announcement of the terrible judgment and winnowing which the one stronger than he was shortly to undertake (Mt. iii. 2 Q or m).[5] Godly men like Joseph of Arimathaia were " on the look-out for the Kingdom of God " (Mk. xv. 43 = Lk. xxiii. 51), in the same way that Symeon was " on the look-out for the consolation of Israel " (Lk. ii. 25), and others " for the redemption of Jerusalem " (Lk. ii. 38). A man who had been listening to Jesus talking at table volunteered the remark, " Happy is he who shall eat bread in the Kingdom of God " (Lk. xiv. 15 L). The Pharisees once asked Jesus to tell them when it was coming (Lk. xvii. 20 L). As he approached Jerusalem, people ' thought that the Kingdom of God was on the point of appearing ' (Lk. xix. 11 l or L). When he rode in triumph into the city,

---

[1] Cf. Manson, *Teaching*, 122.

[2] Cf. K. L. Schmidt in *T.W.N.T.* i. 584f.

[3] Cf. Schürer, *G.J.V.* ii. 628f. ; Bousset, *Relig. des Jud.* (1926), 213–218 ; Moore, *Judaism*, i. 401, 423 ; Von Rad in *T.W.N.T.* i. 565–569.

[4] On the predominantly eschatological idea of the Kingdom, cf. Wellhausen, *Einleitung*, 86–98 : also Major in *Mission*, etc. 35.

[5] Streeter argues that, as the Matthæan account of John's coming was drawn from Q as well as from Mk., Mt. iii. 2 may well come from Q (in *J.T.S.* xiv. 550f. [July 1913], and *Four Gospels*, 205f.). But see below, pp. 240f.

the crowds shouted with enthusiastic expectancy, " Blessed (be) the coming Kingdom of our father David ! " (Mk. xi. 10 : cf. Lk. xix. 38 L and Mt. xxi. 9). Luke pictures the Disciples asking their risen Master, " Lord, is it at this time that thou dost restore the Kingdom to Israel ? " (Acts i. 6), the crucifixion having temporarily quenched their " hope that it was he who was destined to redeem Israel " (Lk. xxiv. 21 L). All this serves to show that, when Jesus spoke in public about the Kingdom of God, he was using a phrase that was already familiar to his hearers as a name for the great hope of the nation.

(3) Mindful of the radical differences between Jesus' conception of the Messiahship and the ideas of it entertained by the people generally (see above, p. 55), many modern scholars have confidently assumed and emphatically asserted that a similar gulf was fixed between his own view of God's Kingdom and that of his fellow-countrymen. As compared with the often grotesque beliefs of the apocalyptic writers, the ideas of Jesus doubtless were very unusual.[1] Caution, however, is necessary at this point. We observe, for instance, that, while the novelty of Jesus' views necessitated great reticence on his part in speaking about his Messiahship, he clearly felt no corresponding need for secrecy as regards the Kingdom of God. On that subject he was apparently quite prepared to run any risks of misunderstanding in which publicity of speech might involve him. May we not infer that his beliefs regarding the Kingdom were sufficiently close to those of his hearers to render it possible for him to convey his meaning to them without difficulty by means of the normal method of his teaching ?

(4) The Kingdom is God's.[2] In Mk. Jesus is always represented as speaking of the Kingdom " of God ". The usage in Lk. is the same, except that we get " Thy Kingdom " in Lk. xi. 2 L (if the reading is correct), " His Kingdom " in Lk. xii. 31 = Mt. vi. 33 Q, " the Kingdom " in Lk. xii. 32 L or l and (parabolically) in Lk. xix. 15 L, and " a Kingdom " in Lk. xxii. 29 L and (parabolically) in Lk. xix. 12 L. In Mt., on the contrary, we find Jesus' normal phrase is " the Kingdom of the Heavens " : but the Marco-Lucan form, " the Kingdom of

---

[1] Cf. Salmond in H.D.B. i. 751a ; Stevens, Theol. of the N.T. 33 ; Dobschütz, Eschatol. 18, 183 ; Charles, Crit. Hist. (1913), 376 ; Weinel, Theol. 61–66 ; A. T. Cadoux, Parables, 129f., 175 ; Manson, Teaching, 37, 273f. ; Dodd, Parables, 22, 38n., 50, 105ff. See also above, pp. 16–18.

[2] We shall note in a moment the occasional assignment of the Kingdom to Jesus himself.

God ", appears in Mt. xii. 28 = Lk. xi. 20 Q, Mt. xix. 24 = Lk. xviii. 25 = Mk. x. 25 (the readings in Mk. and Mt. are doubtful ; but Mt. and Lk. may be based on Mk. x. 23), Mt. xxi. 31 M, and Mt. xxi. 43 M : " Thy Kingdom " appears in Mt. vi. 10 M ; " His Kingdom " in Mt. vi. 33 = Lk. xii. 31 Q ; " the Kingdom of their Father " in Mt. xiii. 43 M or m ; " the Kingdom of my Father " in Mt. xxvi. 29 m (contrast Mk. xiv. 25).

Much has been written on this variation between " the Kingdom of God " and " the Kingdom of the Heavens ". Some have thought that Jesus used only one of them, and that the occurrence of the other was due to the preference of one or other of the Evangelists. It is certain in any case, from the occasional occurrence of " the Kingdom of God " even in Mt., that that formula at least goes back to the most primitive tradition. But it is not likely that the appearance of " the Kingdom of the Heavens " is solely due to the proclivities of M or m : it is more likely that Jesus occasionally used it, and that the proclivities of M or m account rather for its relative frequency in Mt. In regard to its meaning, it is not easy to give a precise explanation of the genitive $\tau\hat{\omega}\nu$ $o\dot{\upsilon}\rho\alpha\nu\hat{\omega}\nu$, namely, as to whether it expresses origin or quality or possession, etc. The probability is that " the Heavens " is here nothing more or less than one of those numerous Jewish equivalents for the Divine Name which saved a speaker from a too-frequent or too-familiar use of this latter (cf. Mk. xi. 30f. = Lk. xx. 4f. = Mt. xxi. 25 ; Lk. xv. 18, 21 L). The genitive $\tau o\hat{\upsilon}$ $\theta\epsilon o\hat{\upsilon}$ seems to be in the first place a possessive genitive, but precisely what it signifies we can ascertain only by a comprehensive study of Jesus' whole teaching on the subject.[1]

We may here take note parenthetically of the occasional description of the Kingdom as belonging to Jesus himself, or to the Son of Man. The usage is rare, and the authorities for it mostly inferior. m introduces it gratuitously in Mt. xvi. 28 (cf. Mk. ix. 1 = Lk. ix. 27) and in Mt. xx. 21 (cf. Mk. x. 37) : and m or possibly M is responsible for it in the probably ungenuine interpretation of the Parable of the Tares (Mt. xiii. 41). L has the idea in the Parable of the Nobleman (Lk. xix. 12, 15, 27) and on the lips of the crucified brigand (Lk. xxiii. 42) ;

[1] Cf., generally, Beyschlag, *Theol.* i. 41–43, 84f. ; Stevens, *Theol. of the N.T.* 27f. ; Dalman, *W.J.* 91–94, 217–219 ; Schürer, *G.J.V.* ii. 628f. (references to the lit. on the subject) ; Holtzmann, *Theol.* i. 249–252; Moffatt, *Theol. of the Gospels*, 63f. ; Gloege, *Reich Gottes*, 49–51 ; Manson, *Teaching*, 118 n.1 ; K. L. Schmidt in *T.W.N.T.* i. 582f.

only once does it occur in a non-parabolic saying of Jesus (Lk. xxii. 29f.). It is an early Christian conception, rather than a thought of Jesus himself (see 1 Cor. xv. 24 ; Col. i. 13 ; Eph. v. 5 ; Lk. i. 33 ; John xviii. 36 ; etc.).[1]

(5) God is frequently depicted and referred to in the Scriptures as " King ", and the appellation remained in use down to New-Testament times, although the only Gospel-document to represent Jesus as using it is M (Mt. v. 35, xviii. 23, xxii. 2, 7, 11, 13). The Aramaïc word מלכו, represented by βασιλεία in the Greek of the Gospels and by " Kingdom " in English, meant primarily, not " realm " or " royal domain ", but " kingship " or " royal sovereignty ". It is therefore a simple abstract noun designating the state and dignity of God considered as the King.[2] " Kingdom ", therefore, which normally means in English " realm " or " royal domain ", is not a very good word to use in translating the Gospel-term βασιλεία ; if, for lack of any obviously-suitable alternative, we continue to use it, we must bear in mind that it represents in the first place " royalty " rather than " realm ".

(6) Such being then the etymological significance of the word, we may next ask what are the ideas so inseparable from that of royal sovereignty that we may safely say of them that no one—ancient oriental or modern westerner—could naturally speak of royal sovereignty without implying them. Surely it would be meaningless to speak of a " King " or a " Kingdom " unless one implied the existence, beside the King, of subjects, of laws laid down by him for their guidance, and of rewards and punishments bestowed by him for obedience and disobedience respectively. For those who had no doubt that both God and men existed, the reality of God's Kingdom would mean in the first place the obedient submission of men to His Law.[3]

---

[1] Cf. Moffatt, *Theol. of the Gospels*, 64f. ; Weinel, *Theol.* 50 ; K. L. Schmidt in *T.W.N.T.* i. 581f.

[2] Cf. Dalman, *W.J.* 94 ; Moffatt, *Theol. of the Gospels*, 62 ; Strack-Billerbeck i. 183 ; Weinel, *Theol.* 53 ; H.-D. Wendland, *Eschatologie*, 15–19 ; K. L. Schmidt in *T.W.N.T.* i. 579f. ; Dodd, *Parables*, 34 with n., 38 n. ; V. Taylor, *Sacrifice*, 8. Gloege (*Reich Gottes*, 51–65, 72, 84, 154–159) lays stress on the idea that God's rule is event (" Geschehen ") and activity.

[3] Cf. Holtzmann, *Theol.* i. 293 n.2 ; Strack-Billerbeck i. 172f. (" . . . Auf Grund vorstehender Gedankenreihe wird man den rabbin. Begriff der מלכות שמים zu definieren haben als die Herrschergewalt, die Gott durch die Offenbarung seines Namens u. sei es Willens über seine Bekenner ausübt.— Dass es sich bei der מלכות שמים in der Tat zunächst um Bindung der Gewissen im Gehorsam gegen Gott handelt, mit andren Worten, dass die מלכות שמים zu allererst ihre Stätte in den Herzen der Menschen hat, zeigen auch folgende Sätze. . . . Die Gottesherrschaft realisiert sich eben

(7) Rabbinic literature contains a number of allusions to the Kingdom of God as a Divine discipline, the yoke of which a man may take upon himself by confessing belief in and love for the One God, and submitting whole-heartedly to the Mosaïc Law.[1] In the teaching of Jesus there is at least one saying which appears to demand a similar interpretation of the idea of the Divine Kingdom : " Every scribe who has been made a disciple to the Kingdom of the Heavens is like a householder ", etc. (Mt. xiii. 52 M). The passage looks original : and it renders the same interpretation probable in the case of some other passages where it is perhaps less obligatory. Thus, " no one who has put his hand to the plough, and looks back, is fit for the Kingdom of God " (Lk. ix. 62 Q or L), and, " Whoever does not receive the Kingdom of God as a little child will certainly not enter into it " (Mk. x. 15 = Lk. xviii. 17 = Mt. xviii. 3b) : on one interpretation of Lk. xvii. 21 L ($\dot{\eta}$ $\beta\alpha\sigma\iota\lambda\epsilon\acute{\iota}\alpha$ $\tau o\hat{\upsilon}$ $\theta\epsilon o\hat{\upsilon}$ $\dot{\epsilon}\nu\tau\grave{o}\varsigma$ $\dot{\upsilon}\mu\hat{\omega}\nu$ $\dot{\epsilon}\sigma\tau\iota\nu$), that saying also ought to be added here.

(8) Just as the Danielic idea of Messiahship was for Jesus fused with, and thus profoundly affected by, the Deutero-Isaianic idea of the Servant of the Lord, so his picture of God as King was fused with and profoundly affected by his thought of Him as Father. It is, of course, true that the Jews of his time were familiar with the doctrine of the Fatherhood of God : but it is clear that with Jesus the doctrine was far more determinative of his whole outlook than it was of theirs, and this partly because of his more sensitive estimate of the human parental relation, and because of his own personal self-consciousness of being God's " Son " in some unique sense (see above, pp. 27–33). Needless to say, he betrays no consciousness of any inconsistency or tension between the two concepts of Fatherhood and Kingship : but the fact that the former was so living a reality to him meant that the Kingdom of God, when viewed in the intensive aspect just described, was seen to involve a personal relationship of confidence and affection between God and man, and not simply a submission on man's

---

überall da, wo sich ein Mensch bewussterweise dem Willen Gottes im Gehorsam unterstellt "), 173–178 (quotations in evidence of the foregoing) ; Manson, *Teaching*, 130f.

[1] Cf. Dalman, *W.J.* 96–98 ; Strack-Billerbeck i. 173 (" Der Mensch kann das Joch der Gottesherrschaft auf sich nehmen, er kann es aber auch von sich werfen. Man nimmt es auf sich, indem man sich zum Monotheismus u. zur Tora bekennt . . . "), 176–178, 608–610 (to recite the Sh'maʿ is to take on the yoke of the Kingdom of Heaven, etc.) ; Otto, *Kingdom*, 37f. ; Kuhn in *T.W.N.T.* i. 570–573

part, however willing, to God's authority. When, therefore, he spoke about " entering the Kingdom of God ", he must have had in mind, among other things, the adoption by the individual disciple of an attitude of warm filial love towards God, involving of course complete and implicit obedience to Him, such as he had himself all through his life adopted. It seems that this aspect of his teaching belonged for the most part to the closing months of the Ministry and to the conversations he then had with the Disciples.[1]

(9) Our authorities tell us that, in Jewish literature at least, the phrase " the Kingdom of God " is always used in an intensive sense, never extensively of the group, realm, or territory over which God reigns.[2] However that may be, it is palpable that in the teaching of Jesus the term often has an extensive connotation. Sayings in which mention is made of " entering " the Kingdom, being " greatest " or " least " in it, seeing the Patriarchs in it (Lk. xiii. 28 = Mt. viii. 11 Q), shining out in it (Mt. xiii. 43 M), being gathered out of it (Mt. xiii. 41 M), or having it closed against one by others (Mt. xxiii. 13 [m or Q: cf. Lk. xi. 52]), cannot be naturally interpreted if " the Kingdom " must always mean only the royal sovereignty of God.[3] The mention of such sovereignty often brings to mind at once the thought of those over whom it is exercised. In passages in which that thought is to the fore, " the Kingdom " will be quite a good English equivalent of the Greek $\acute{\eta}$ $\beta a\sigma\iota\lambda\epsilon\acute{\iota}a$ and the Aramaïc מלכותא behind it.

(10) The Kingdom of God is thus for Jesus, in certain of its aspects, necessarily a society of human beings, and a growing society at that. Whatever else the Marcan Parables of the Seed (Mk. iv. 26–29) and the Mustard (Mk. iv. 30–32) and the Q-Parables of the Mustard and the Leaven (Lk. xiii. 18–21 = Mt. xiii. 31–33) may mean, they at least mean that the Kingdom increases in size, clearly by the multiplication of its members.[4] And forasmuch as these members are living on this earth, the

---

[1] Manson, *Teaching*, 37, 118–136, 161–164 : after an elaborate analysis of all the relevant passages in the four Gospel-sources, Dr. Manson finds that, with the exception of Q, they all represent allusions to entering the Kingdom as late and esoteric.

[2] Dalman, *W.J.* 94 : Strack-Billerbeck i. 183 (" Im Rabbin. findet sich keine Stelle, in der ש׳ מ׳ oder מ׳ יהוח mit ' Reich (= Herrschafts g e b i e t) Gottes ' übersetzt werden m ü s s t e. Die Übersetzung ' Gottes h e r r - s c h a f t ' oder ' Königtum ' Gottes trifft überall, wie die oben beige-brachten Zitate zeigen, den richtigen Sinn . . . ").

[3] Cf. Otto, *Kingdom*, 53f. ; Flew, *Church*, 28–40, 120f. Per contra, cf. Gloege, *Reich Gottes*, 52–54, 67f., 84f.

[4] Cf. Manson, *Teaching*, 133f.

Kingdom also is on earth ; and as its numbers grow, it too will necessarily grow (see below, p. 131 [5]). In spite, therefore, of all that has recently been written against the attempt to interpret the Kingdom of God as a social ideal or as an ideal society (see above, pp. 42f.), it clearly did approximate to some such thing. If we may trust two of the Parables in M, those namely of the Tares (Mt. xiii. 24–30) and the Drag-net (Mt. xiii. 47f.), the Kingdom on earth is sufficiently like a society to have worthy and unworthy members within it, though questions concerning reliability and exegesis would warn us to go cautiously at this point.

((11) But the growth of the Kingdom is not only a present fact : it has a future ; and it is with regard to expectations of its future that the idea of the Kingdom differs most widely from the modern idea of evolutionary progress. / Even with the Rabbis, the intensive idea of the Kingdom did not exclude eschatological hopes : [1] and with Jesus the triumphant climax of the Kingdom's growth was a subject of such keen and many-sided interest that the study of it necessitates special inquiry along several lines.

[1] Dalman, *W.J.* 98–101 ; Otto, *Kingdom*, 38 ; and Strack-Billerbeck, as quoted above, p. 16 n. 2.

CHAPTER II

THE NEW WAY OF LIFE

(1) The Kingdom of God clearly involved a certain Way of Life for men. This Way Jesus expounded along the lines of the best Jewish thought of his time, (2) but made it largely a new Way by exalting ethics over ceremony, re-emphasizing the importance of motive, enlarging the scope of brotherly love, (3) and immensely re-inforcing verbal inculcation by the ascendancy of his own Person. (4) While emphasizing right motive, he described concretely the kind of conduct it ought to prompt, seriously intending his injunctions to be complied with, (5) yet not " legislating " in the sense of prescribing how all the manifold dilemmas of life were to be solved. (6) His guidance was meant to be applicable corporately as well as individually. (7) He proclaimed love for God and love for man to be the two supreme requirements. (8) Without discarding ceremonial observances as negligible, (9) he definitely subordinated them to the purely-spiritual relationship with God and to the righteous treatment of one's fellows : (10) on this last he laid the greatest stress, (11) applying it specifically to the relations of the sexes, (12) the treatment of wrongdoers, the practice of war, (13) and the use of property. (14) His eschatology, whatever it was, did not determine his conception of the Way of Life implied by the Kingdom of God : this he framed independently with an eye to inherent spiritual and moral values.

(1) From the fact that the Kingdom of God meant man's compliance with God's Will it obviously followed that the establishment of the Kingdom necessitated for men a certain Way of Life. A very large proportion of Jesus' recorded sayings is devoted to a description and inculcation of this Way.[1] In describing and inculcating it, he may—with certain qualifications—be said to have followed the lines of the best Jewish thought of his time, as represented by the doctrine of God taught in the prophetical writings of the Old Testament and by the personal piety and the ethical standards of late Judaism. He did indeed steer clear of the extravagances of the Apocalyptists and the hair-splitting tendencies of the Rabbis : but it is not easy to find many specific items of his

---

[1] On the phrase, cf. Flew, *Church*, 72, 148, 156–159, 186.

teaching which, taken by themselves, cannot be paralleled in the Old Testament or in later Jewish literature. Some of the analogies discoverable in this latter field may be in point of date later than the lifetime of Jesus ; but that does not prove that they were drawn from Christian sources. In particular, it must not be supposed that Jewish teaching laid no stress on the rightness of the inward motive as distinct from the rightness of the outward act, or on the duty of forgiving offences and returning good for evil. The closing commandment of the ancient Decalogue itself forbade covetousness, a sin of the heart rather than the hands ; the Book of Proverbs enjoined generosity to an enemy ; and later Jewish books contain teachings of a similar character.[1]

(2) In what, then, it may be asked, does the originality of Jesus and the uniqueness of his teaching consist ? This is a question on which a good deal has been written. It has been claimed by some that Jesus, though not the first to emphasize the duty of loving God and the duty of loving one's neighbour, was the first to select and couple these two duties as the two supreme demands of the Law. That contention is broadly true, in that he was the first to emphasize and popularize the combination, and apply it widely ; but it had, as a matter of fact, been already made in the Testaments of the Twelve Patriarchs.[2] Another instance of novelty is his prohibition of divorce (see below, pp. 124f. [11]), though here again something depends on precisely how we are to understand his words.

What is really new in the teaching of Jesus is rather, in large part, what we may call his peculiar distribution of the stress. He virtually deposed "the Law", as a well-nigh undifferentiated whole consisting of several hundred rules, many of them ceremonial and all considered as the direct commands of God, from the supreme position which the Rabbis had come to give it. In insisting on approaching it only through the highest prophetical teaching and through the dictates of an awakened and sensitive conscience, he implicitly relegated it to a subordinate place (see above, p. 72, and pp. 79f. n. 2). He made the

---

[1] Cf., e.g., Ben Sirach xxxiv. 18f., 25f., and *The Testaments of the Twelve Patriarchs* (i/B.C.) as quoted by Charles, *Crit. Hist.* (1913), 226–233 ; Holtzmann, *Theol.* i. 243 ; Strack-Billerbeck i. 282, 298–302, 470–474 ; Abrahams, *Studies*, ii. 205f. ; Bousset, *Relig. des Jud.* (1926), 138.

[2] *Test. of Issach.* v. 2, vii. 6, *Test. of Dan*, v. 3 : cf. Holtzmann, *Theol.* i. 197, 229 ; Abrahams, *Studies*, i. 18–29 ; Montefiore, *S.G.*[2] I. 285f., II. 464f., and in *Hibbert Journ.* xxviii. 108 (Oct. 1929), 254 (Jan. 1930) ; Moore, *Judaism*, ii. 85–88 ; Major in *Mission*, etc. xxx ; Manson in *Mission*, etc. 552f. On Jesus' new stress on God's Fatherhood, and what it involved in ethics, see above, pp. 112f.

realization of the fundamental and determinative importance of motive much more explicit than it had yet been, thus protecting the law of the Kingdom from the danger of a pettifogging externalism such as was ever threatening to sterilize the system of the Rabbis. By making the duty of love the really-supreme consideration both in religion and in ethics, he provided a norm by the use of which a due sense of balance and proportion could be developed, and he opened up the way for an enormous extension of the exercise of human large-heartedness. His respect for women and children, and his eager self-sacrificing quest for the redemption of sinners and enemies, which were a direct outcome of the decision to love one's neighbour as oneself, were admittedly without close parallels in Jewish ethics.[1]

(3) But these manifestations of originality visible in the content and emphasis of Jesus' teaching were themselves but the outward signs of an inward and more deeply-seated originality. It is to the ultimately-unanalysable quality of his personal life that we have to look if we desire to discover wherein his uniqueness as a teacher really lay. To explain verbally to men the right way of life is to do them a real and positive service ; to set them a good example by following that way oneself is a greater service still : but to be one of such moral and spiritual quality as to bring right home to others the conviction of God's goodness, to impart to them thereby the impulse to love and serve Him, and to kindle in their hearts a passionate longing for His Kingdom—this is the greatest service of all ; and it was being and doing this that constituted the really-unique originality of Jesus, and made possible the marvellous freshness and power of his teaching.[2]

(4) It has been observed above that Jesus laid an unprecedented stress on inward character and motive as distinct from the outward acts of which motive and character are the roots. " There is no such thing as a good tree that produces bad fruit, or a bad tree that produces good fruit : for each tree is known by its own fruit. For men do not gather figs from

[1] Cf. P. Wendland, *Hellenistisch-römische Kultur* (1907), 130f. ; Holtzmann, *Theol.* i. 198, 409 ; W. J. Ferrar in *Contemp. Rev.* cxxiii. 85–92 (Jan. 1923) ; Montefiore, *S.G.*[2] I. cxii, 201, 218, 253, 389, II. 126f., 213f., 275, 468, 520f., 553f., in *Hibbert Journ.* iii. 649–667 (July 1905), xx. 435–446 (Apl. 1922), and xxviii. 98–111 (Oct. 1929), and in *Contemp. Rev.* cxxiii. 615–622 (May 1923).
[2] Cf. Harnack, *What is Christianity ?* (Eng. tr. 1901), 46–49, 51 ; Bousset, *Jesus*, 62f. (Eng. tr. 136–138) ; Holtzmann, *Theol.* i. 418–420 ; Rashdall, *Conscience*, 116f. ; Bartlet and Carlyle, *Christianity in Hist.* 49f. ; Abrahams in Montefiore, *S.G.*[2] II. 661, 668 ; Montefiore in *Hibbert Journ.* xxviii. 110 (Oct. 1929). See above, pp. 72f. (8).

thorn-bushes, nor do they eat grapes off a bramble. The good man out of the good store of his heart brings out what is good, and the evil man from his evil store brings out what is evil. For out of what his heart is full of his mouth speaks " (Lk. vi. 43–45 = Mt. vii. 16–20 = Mt. xii. 33–35 Q). He called men's attention back from the guilt of murder to the guilt of the anger and contempt from which it sprang (Mt. v. 21f. M), and from adultery to the lustful gaze which prompted the impulse to it (Mt. v. 27f. M). The somewhat-obscure saying about the single eye (Lk. xi. 34–36 = Mt. vi. 22f. Q), which by its warning against " the evil eye " inculcates generosity, is also meant to emphasize the inwardness of the real basis of conduct. Some of the words of denunciation which Jesus hurled at the Scribes and Pharisees turn on the same issue (Lk. xi. 37–44 = Mt. xxiii. 23–28 Q + M ; Lk. xvi. 14f. L).[1]

Under the influence of the traditional Lutheran and Protestant version of Paul's teaching against " salvation by works ", many modern scholars have interpreted this stress laid by Jesus on the determinative importance of the state of a man's heart into a depreciation of all rules for outward conduct as negligible in comparison with the one really-fundamental question of character, and they find here the great outstanding contrast between Jesus and the Rabbis. The classic expression of their view is Augustine's alleged formula, " Love God, and do as you please ".[2]

But this is gravely to misconstrue Jesus' meaning, and is not free from injustice to the Rabbis. The Rabbis were indeed in continual danger of losing their sense of proportion, of laying needless emphasis on petty externals, and of rendering their casuistry futile by over-refinement : such errors were incidental to their serious acceptance of the whole Mosaïc Law as Divinely ordained in every detail—an acceptance, from which only the most abnormal insight and originality could in the circumstances have protected them. But they were perfectly well aware of the vital importance of the clean heart and the healthy motive (see above, p. 116), and they even recognized some difference between the lighter and the weightier matters of the Law.[3] And Jesus on his part, while insisting that everything turned

---

[1] Cf. N. Schmidt, *Prophet of Naz.* 300 ; Holtzmann, *Theol.* i. 246–248.

[2] Bousset, *Jesus,* 63 (Eng. tr. 138f.) ; Manson, *Teaching,* 295–308, and in *Judaism and Christianity,* iii (1939) 125–131 (the best modern statements of this, as it seems to me, one-sided and therefore erroneous view).

[3] Strack-Billerbeck i. 249, 901–905 ; Abrahams, *Studies,* ii. 205f. ; Montefiore, *S.G.*[2] I. 63, II. 60, 63, 185f. : and also Manson in *Mission,* etc. 447–449, 454–457, 462.

on the quality of the inward man, did not confine himself (as on the theory under discussion we should have expected him to confine himself) to urging men to love God and their neighbours, and then to do as they pleased. He did urge them to love God and their neighbours ; and we may observe in passing that to do this is just as much a piece of ethical *legislation* as is the prohibition of adultery or theft. But further, knowing as he did that the purified heart is dependent on a wisely-guided judgment if it is to eventuate in a righteous life, he devoted a fair proportion of his time as a teacher to specifying the kind of conduct which the children of God ought to exhibit. We may, if we will, call these detailed injunctions of his simply *illustrations* of the all-important inward spirit ; but that is not to deny that they are at the same time definite laws, not indeed imposed in any arbitrary or external way (see above, p. 79), nor capable of being coercively enforced, but worded—like the laws of the Old Testament—as definite imperatives, addressed to the free and responsible wills of men, and seriously intended by Jesus, not simply as suggestions, still less as impossible demands beyond the power of men to obey,[1] but as requirements which they can and ought to fulfil. The tremendous stress which, at the end of the Sermon on the Mount, he laid on the momentous consequences of obedience or disobedience to his words (see above, p. 76 [**14**]) rules out any understanding of his ethical teaching which denies that he meant it as a law to be obeyed.[2]

(**5**) There are few theses concerning Jesus upon which modern scholars seem to be so unanimous as upon the denial that he was a " legislator ". I have just explained my reasons for believing that in a certain very important sense such a denial is untrue. Yet there *are* meanings we can give to the word " legislation " which would disqualify it as a proper designation of his teaching. He was, of course, no legislator in the sense of one who elaborates a code of rules which are to be enforced on individuals by himself or by some governing authority like the community at large or its officers—not even if we interpret that coercion as effected without physical means, as in the early Christian Church. Traces of an effort to

---

[1] Cf. R. Niebuhr, *An Interp. of Christ. Ethics* (1937), sæpissime ; Dodd, *Hist. and the Gosp.* 127f. : also Moody, *Purpose of Jes.* 58, 64, 73f., 124–126 ; Flew in *E.T.* xlvi. 217a (Feb. 1935).
[2] See the full discussions in Rashdall, *Conscience*, 119–138, 165f., 195–198, in Windisch, *Bergpredigt*, 22–91, esp. 69ff., and in H.-D. Wendland, *Eschatologie*, 122–134 : cf. also Dibelius, *Geschichtliche und übergeschichtliche Religion im Christentum* (1925), 59f., and see below, p. 352 n.1.

construct such items in a Church-code out of certain of his precepts are visible in Mt., and are as a rule clearly recognizable.[1] But in framing his ethical injunctions, Jesus digressed only rarely into the province of the casuist, i.e., of the legislator in the strict sense of the term, whose business it is to explain how cases in which two or more moral principles conflict are to be solved. The only dilemma of this kind upon which he explicitly pronounced was the possible conflict between family-affection and loyalty to himself (Lk. xii. 51–53 = Mt. x. 34–36 Q ; Lk. xiv. 26 = Mt. x. 37 Q ; Mk. x. 28–30 = Lk. xviii. 28–30 = Mt. xix. 27–29 ; Mk. xiii. 12 = Lk. xxi. 16 = Mt. x. 21). For the most part, he seems to have limited himself—in conformity with the special demands of his work—to enunciating the rules of righteousness in general terms, and leaving to the Disciple's own insight the task of dealing with the problems raised by the application of them to the tangled situations of an individual life.[2] But to recognize this self-limitation on Jesus' part is not to say that the task of casuistry (though often badly done) is inherently needless and wrong, or that Jesus did not mean his precepts to be seriously complied with. Such recognition is fully consistent with the contention that he was —in a very important sense of the word—a legislator.

(6) See above, pp. 41–43 (4).

(7) The classical passage is Mk. xii. 28–34a = Mt. xxii. 34–40, the Lucan parallel to which (Lk. x. 25–28) is probably from L, as its sequel—the Parable of the Good Samaritan (Lk. x. 29–37)—undoubtedly is. On the question of the originality of the combination of these two particular injunctions of the Mosaïc Law, see above, p. 116.

(8) In regard to what we may call the ceremonial observances of religion, we find Jesus both practising and enjoining a large measure of compliance with the Law's demands. This attitude was doubtless the result mainly of his upbringing (Lk. ii. 21–24, 39, 41f.). According to the Fourth Gospel, which is certainly trustworthy on this point, he attended several of the annual national religious festivals at Jerusalem. Even if, as is probable, the Synoptists are wrong in representing the Last Supper as a Passover-meal, we at least know from them (Lk. xxii. 15 L) that he had eagerly desired to celebrate that

---

[1] The fact that only in Mt. does Jesus speak of δικαιοσύνη (" righteousness ") is perhaps significant in this connexion. Cf. Weinel, *Theol.* 93 ; Heiler, *Der Katholizismus* (1923), 64.

[2] Cf. Wendt, *Teaching*, i. 129–135 ; McNeile, *St. Matthew*, 66b, 67b, 69ab, 70b, 90a.

Passover-festival with his Disciples. He insisted on lepers
whom he had cured offering the prescribed sacrifices and
carrying out the stipulated procedure before resuming their
normal life in society (Mk. i. 44 = Lk. v. 14 = Mt. viii. 4 ;
Lk. xvii. 14 L). He wore on the corners of his outer cloak the
violet tassels which the Law (Deut. xxii. 12 ; Numb. xv. 37–41
H) commanded every Israelite to wear as a reminder that he
owed unswerving loyalty to Yahweh (Mk. vi. 56 = Mt. xiv. 36 ;
Mt. ix. 20 m [the tassel does not appear in Mk. v. 27 : in Lk.
viii. 44 it was probably not mentioned in the true text] : cf.
Mt. xxiii. 5 M), though we are not told that he ever wore phy-
lacteries. He contemplates his Disciples fasting (Mt. vi. 16–
18 M : cf. Mk. ix. 29 [see above, p. 67 n.1]). While he clearly
sat loose to the sacrificial system associated with the Temple
at Jerusalem, he cannot be shown to have taken up an attitude
of positive antagonism to it on principle : on one occasion he
definitely pictures a disciple (or, let us say, a respectful listener)
bringing his gift to the altar (Mt. v. 23f. M).[1]

There are, however, certain passages often adduced in this
connexion, which need to be treated with great caution. Thus
the saying, " No one, after drinking old (wine), wishes for
new ; for he says, ' The old is nice(st) ' " (Lk. v. 39 L), is
almost certainly in its wrong place, and nobody really knows
what it means : it may be a melancholy comment on the
inherent conservatism of good religious people ; just possibly
it expresses a preference for the Old Testament over and above
either apocalypticism or scribism : it is therefore precarious
to take it as a semi-patronizing appreciation of ceremonial
strictness. The saying, " The Scribes and the Pharisees sit on
Moses' seat : all things therefore, whatsoever they tell you, do
and observe " (Mt. xxiii. 2, 3a), and the insistence on the least
of the commandments (Mt. v. 19), both come from M, and run
so counter to the attitude of Jesus as attested elsewhere that
there is strong reason to believe that they reflect the over-
Judaïstic and anti-Pauline view of the Jerusalem-church
rather than Jesus' own view (see above, p. 21). The same
applies to the words of Mt. xxiii. 23b, " These things " (the

---

[1] For Jesus' attitude to the sacrificial system, see Oesterley in H. D. C. G.
ii. 712f. ; F. W. Lewis in J.T.S. xxi. 173 (Jan. 1920) ; Cheetham in J.T.S.
xxiv. 315–317 (Apl. 1923) ; Caldecott in J.T.S. xxiv. 382–386 (July 1923) ;
Burkitt in J.T.S. xxv. 386–390 (July 1924) ; V. J. K. Brook in The Bible and
Modern Religious Thought, II. iii. 23f., 27–31, 35 (Mar. 1928) ; Burkitt in
H.C.L.M.K. 239–242 = Jesus Christ, etc. 43–46 ; Plooij in E.T. xlii. 36–39
(Oct. 1930) ; Oesterley, Sacrifices in Ancient Israel (1937), 274–281 ; V.
Taylor, Sacrifice, 67–74.

weightier matters of the Law) " ye ought to have done, and not to have left the other " (i.e., tithing herbs) " undone " : this saying is absent from the Bezan text of Lk. xi. 42, and is therefore probably an assimilation of the text of Lk. to that of Mt. ; in that case it would be, not an historical extract from Q, but a legalistic gloss from M or m. And again, obscurity of meaning prevents our appealing to the words about the jot or tittle of the Law not passing away (Lk. xvi. 17 Q ? : cf. Mt. v. 17f. Q + M ?) as evidence of a desire to follow in detail the ceremonies which it prescribed (see below, p. 138).

(9) Jesus was however very ready to set aside the demands of the Law as regards religious observances as soon as ever they came into conflict with, or were given preference over, purely spiritual and moral interests. There is a great body of teaching consisting of passages scattered up and down the Gospels, dealing with the relationship between man and God, and describing this or that phase of it as it ought to be—love, repentance and forgiveness, reverence and worship, imitation and obedience, prayer and trust. It does not fall within the scope of the present work to discuss these in detail : moreover, they are sufficiently well known, and for the most part not difficult of interpretation.[1]

One comment only may perhaps be offered in regard to the duty of obedience. Certain recent writers with Barthian sympathies have urged that the duty of obeying the sovereign commands of God was the one dominant motive beside which in Jesus' view all other goods disappeared into insignificance.[2] Now it is doubtless true that Jesus often envisaged the supreme business of life under the form of obedience to the Will of God ; and, not philosophizing on the ultimate nature of the ethical good, he may often give to our analytic minds the impression that according to him nothing else mattered (e.g., Mk. iii. 31–35 = Lk. viii. 19–21 = Mt. xii. 46–50 ; Lk. xvii. 7–10 L). Nor in a sense, if we think of God comprehensively enough, does anything else matter. Only we must not infer from the dominance of this concept of obedience that Jesus set no store on other vital goods (the ultimate happiness of mankind, for instance) which were not inconsistent with it.

Our immediate point, however, is to observe that he would allow no interference with the fundamentally-important matters of a man's personal relations with God and of his

---

[1] Cf. H.-D. Wendland, *Eschatologie*, 57–98.
[2] E.g., Bultmann, *Jesus*, 103–106, 119–121, 180f. ; cf also K. L. Schmidt in *R.G.G.* iii (1929) 138.

righteous treatment of his fellows, on the plea that he was under obligation to fulfil this or that ceremonial requirement. The evidence is abundant and does not need to be detailed here : [1] several of the instances concern the right use of the Sabbath (see above, pp. 75f.). For the rest, let it suffice to refer to Lk. xi. 42 = Mt. xxiii. 23 Q (" Alas for you, Pharisees, for ye pay tithe on mint and rue and every herb, but ye pass by justice and love for God "—see above, pp. 121f.), Mt. ix. 13 M and xii. 7 M (where Jesus quotes Hos. vi. 6, " I desire mercy, and not sacrifice "), and Mk. vii. 1–23 = Mt. xv. 1–20 (where he condemns closefistedness towards aged parents on the plea of " Korban ", and implicitly denies the distinction between clean and unclean food). See also above, pp. 117f. (4).

(10) Some of the most emphatic utterances of Jesus are concerned with the exercise of love towards one's fellows as the supreme and normative principle governing relations with them. After pronouncing love for God to be the first and greatest commandment in the Law, he continued, " The second is this, ' Thou shalt love thy neighbour as thyself '. There is no other commandment greater than these " (Mk. xii. 31 = Mt. xxii. 39f. [where m has instead of the last clause, " On these two commandments hangs the whole Law and the Prophets "] : cf. Lk. x. 27 L). He told the Scribe who heartily concurred in this pronouncement, " Thou art not far from the Kingdom of God " (Mk. xii. 32–34 : cf. Lk. x. 28 L). It looks as if he were formulating a simple explication of this duty of love when he says, " Just as ye wish that men should act towards you, so act towards them " (Lk. vi. 31 = Mt. vii. 12 Q ; M or m here adds, " for this is the Law and the Prophets ").[2] Reconciliation with one we have wronged is to be effected without delay, even if that means leaving our gift for the time being unoffered before the altar (Mt. v. 23f. M). Knowing how imperfect we ourselves are, we must not condemn other persons (Lk. vi. 37f., 41f. = Mt. vii. 1–5 Q), though this prohibition does not preclude the duty of distinguishing good actions from bad ones (Mt. vii. 16a Q ? [cf. Lk. vi. 44a] ; Mt. vii. 20 m). The Parable of the Good Samaritan is given as an example of neighbourly love shown towards one in need (Lk. x. 29–37 L). Jesus' main object in training his Disciples was to make them " fishers of men " (Mk. i. 17 = Mt. iv. 19 :

[1] The precise significance of Mk. ii. 21f. = Lk. v. 36–38 = Mt. ix. 16f. in this connexion is not quite clear.
[2] Dr. A. M. Hunter in E.T. xlix. 428f. (June 1938) plausibly argues that the grouping of faith, hope, and love as a Christian triad 1 Cor. xiii. 13, etc.) probably goes back to Jesus himself.

cf. Lk. v. 10 L) ; and he himself invited sinners and doubtful characters to partake of his hospitality in order that he might heal them (see above, pp. 48f. [**11**]).

It is important to observe that Jesus enjoins love for others just as if, like any other practice inculcated by an ethical imperative, it were capable of being exercised by any one willing to exercise it. This fact should suffice to teach us that the love in question is something other than that emotional fondness which parents and children, lovers and sweethearts, cannot help feeling for one another. The Christian's love depends, not primarily on the instinctive emotions, but on the will which manipulates and controls them. That being so, and seeing that the words of Jesus about love are ethical imperatives, conformity with them is rightly regarded as a matter of duty, with which the emotions are to be made to conform. How mistaken, therefore, are those who, misconstruing the meaning of the word " love " as Jesus used it, speak of the Christian ethic as if it were an involuntary yielding to an overpowering emotion, with which the sense of duty has little or nothing to do.

(**11**) The passages in the Gospels dealing with sex-relations are Mt. v. 27f., 31f. M ; Lk. xvi. 18 Q ? (or L) ; Mk. vii. 20–23 = Mt. xv. 18–20 ; Mk. x. 1–12 = Mt. xix. 1–9 ; Mt. xix. 10–12 M ; John vii. 53–viii. 11 : cf. 1 Cor. vii. 10f., 39f. Perhaps we should add Mk. ix. 43–48 = Mt. v. 29f. = Mt. xviii. 8f. With the enormous literature handling the interpretation of this teaching we are not here directly concerned. It is, however, pertinent to our immediate interest to note the following points. Jesus seems to have taken for granted the ideal of monogamy at which Jewish ethical feeling had by this time arrived, though without the guidance of any specific Old-Testament law on the matter. A consummated marriage he regards as " that which God has joined together ", on the ground of God's purpose in the creation of the sexes (Mk. x. 6–9 = Mt. xix. 4–6, 8b), or—as we moderns perhaps would put it—because sex-union sets up a mysterious and profound relation between the parties, such as brings permanent mutual responsibilities with it. Seeing that his words here were spoken with special reference to marriages which one or other of the parties might wish to dissolve, the popular limitation of the words "what God has joined together " to ideally-happy marriages is clearly a complete misunderstanding of his meaning. It seems certain that he intended to discountenance explicitly any such separation of married persons as should be followed by the re-marriage of either : the Matthæan exceptions for the case of marital infidelity (Mt. v. 32 M or m, xix. 9 m) are now widely recognized as a later concession to the practical demands of Christian frailty.

(12) The familiar teaching of Jesus about love for enemies, forgiveness of wrongs, and non-resistance, contained primarily in Lk. vi. 27–36 Q = Mt. v. 38–48 Q + M has also been very extensively discussed. There is no occasion to set it forth in detail here : but we do need to note in passing the stress Jesus laid on it, and the originality with which he framed it. The specific application of it to the matter of war will come up for consideration in a later connexion (see below, pp. 171–174).

(13) Similarly with his teaching on property. Without passing any general condemnation on the acquisition and possession of private property, Jesus issues a general warning in the terms, " Ye cannot serve God and Mammon " (Lk. xvi. 13 = Mt. vi. 24 Q) ; but beyond forbidding anxiety regarding the future provision for our bodily welfare (Lk. xii. 22–34= Mt. vi. 25–34, 19–21 Q [+ M ?]), and encouraging generosity to those in need, he gives little in the way of specific guidance. Something will have to be said in the next section regarding certain of his words on this theme (see below, pp. 126f.).

(14) From Jesus' apparent belief that, in a comparatively-short space of time, God's Kingdom would be miraculously and cataclysmically set up, and would bring all normal conditions of human life on earth to a sudden end, many scholars have drawn the inference that the whole of his ethical teaching was fashioned with an eye to that approaching event, and consequently owed its most characteristic features to his expectation that social conditions, as men then knew them, were to last only for a very little while longer. It is that condition, they suggest, and that alone, which explains Jesus' indifference to the security of possessions and to the punishment of wrongdoers : if society is not to last, there is no need to take measures for its stability. And now that we know that this forecast was mistaken, we need have no hesitation—so it is suggested—in refusing to apply to ourselves to-day teaching giving under conditions so totally different from our own.[1]

Now how far Jesus did really believe in an early end of human history, or how early (if he did so believe) he expected the end to come, we have yet to consider. But provisionally

---

[1] Cf., e.g., Herrmann, *The Social Gospel* (1907), 154–225 ; Burkitt in *H.C.L.M.K.* 216f. = *Jesus Christ*, etc. 20f.

granting that he did look forward to an early climax, ought we to infer that the form of his ethical teaching was determined by that expectation ? Was that teaching, in a word, simply an interim-ethic ?

The question must in the main be answered with an emphatic negative. The great majority of the passages quoted in this chapter contain no reference whatever to any coming climax. A few of them indeed refer to the Kingdom, but not specifically to its future aspect. Apart from the allusion to " those who have made themselves eunuchs for the sake of the Kingdom of the Heavens " (Mt. xix. 12 M), what suggestion of eschatology is there, for instance, in Jesus' teaching on sex-questions ? None whatever ; the teaching on marriage and divorce is directly based on God's original purpose in creation. Similarly, when he is speaking about non-retaliation, the ground he explicitly gives for his precepts is not—what on the interim-ethic theory we should expect— that the restraint of wrongdoing is unnecessary because present social conditions are shortly to disappear, but that his disciples must try to imitate the Divine character (Lk. vi. 35 [Q] = Mt. v. 45 [Q + M] ; Mt. v. 9 M)—an altogether-different story.[1] To thrust an eschatological interpretation on Jesus' words about prayer, forgiveness, trust in God, humility, generosity to the poor, overcoming evil with good, truthfulness in speech, and so on, is to read into the Gospel-record of them what is simply not there.[2]

A partial exception to the general rule that Jesus' ethics are independent of his eschatology may possibly be found in some of his more-specific utterances about property (not however in his general principles bearing on that subject). The question has been asked, with what consistency can pacifists maintain their right to follow Jesus' non-resistance teaching literally, while they allow a much more elastic exegesis to the command " Sell whatever thou hast and give to the poor ".[3] The answer is that the two precepts obviously belong to two radically-distinct categories. The former is enunciated generally, and is based on the duty of imitating the ways of God ; the latter was a demand made on a particular individual at what was apparently a very special juncture in the Ministry (cf. Lk. xiv. 25-33 Q [+ L ?]). The various conditions under which

[1] Windisch, *Bergpredigt*, 6-9, 12-15.
[2] Cf. Dobschütz, *Eschatol.* 17, 155-159 ; Sanday in *Hibbert Journ.* x. 103 (Oct. 1911) ; Moffatt, *Theol. of the Gospels*, 59-61 ; Montefiore, *S.G.*[2] I. cxxx, 25f. ; Flew, *Church*, 60-63.
[3] Cf. *The Review of the Churches*, v. 146 (Jan. 1928).

Jesus' teaching and example in the matter of property were framed—the universal practice of hospitality, the elementary economics, the moderate physical needs of life, the entire dependence of the destitute on private charity, the special demands of Jesus' mission, the personal situation of individuals (like the Rich Ruler), and so on—all contributed to make that teaching and that example what they were. It is possible (though not certain) that an expectation of only a comparatively-short span of future human history may also have been one of the contributing factors.[1] But that possibility does not really affect either Jesus' general principles about property or his ethical teaching as a whole. These he based on his own inspired insight into the nature of God and His Will for man ; and he framed them accordingly with an eye to inherently spiritual and moral values, independently of any forecast, long or short, of the length of time during which human society would continue to exist.[2]

[1] Cf. Holtzmann, *Theol.* i. 243f. ; Rashdall, *Conscience*, 63f., 71f., 151.

[2] Cf. Wellhausen, *Einleitung*, 97 (". . . Sicherlich galt ihm die Moral, die er aufstellte, nicht für eine provisorische und nur bis zum nahen Ende der Welt giltige Forderung, sondern für den ewigen Willen Gottes im Himmel wie auf Erden ; . . . ") ; Holtzmann, *Theol.* i. 241–248 ; Bultmann, *Jesus*, 113f., 119–122 ; Dodd, *Parables*, 104f., 108f. ; Cadbury in *H.T.R.* xv. 11f. (Jan. 1922), and *Peril*, 87f. ; Otto, *Kingdom*, 59–62 ; Manson in *Mission*, etc. 637.

Dr. C. H. Dodd, in *Apost. Preaching*, 120–125, 164f., thinks that the increased attention to ethics in Lk. and Mt. as compared with Mk. is due to Christian eschatology having by their time become " futurist " instead of remaining wholly " realized " (as it was with Jesus himself) : he therefore regards these two Gospels as side-tracking the main line of the Christian kerygma, which was continued after Mk. by the Fourth Gospel. I shall discuss later Dr. Dodd's theory of " realized eschatology " (see below, pp. 194–203, 296 n 3 , 311–315) : but I cannot agree that " futurist eschatology " naturally involves more stress on ethics than " realized eschatology " does. Moreover, to give the word " Gospel " a meaning which makes the ethical teaching of Jesus no essential part of it is surely to mistake radically the mind and purpose of Jesus himself.

CHAPTER III

THE KINGDOM ALREADY PRESENT

(1) Since the essence of the Kingdom of God is man's filial submission to His Will, the Kingdom as a reality is not something postponed to a later day, but exists whenever and wherever man so submits. (2) As the obedient Son par excellence, Jesus embodies the Kingdom in his own person ; and in him and his work it is present and active among men. (3) There are at least three sayings in which this fact is unmistakably declared. (4) Other words of Jesus, describing in the present tense the characteristics of those to whom the Kingdom belongs, may on this ground be reasonably held to imply that it is already present, (5) as also may the Parables of Growth. (6) A number of passages, which do not explicitly mention the Kingdom, may be taken to presuppose its presence by their allusions to certain significant events which have already occurred. (7) There are some other probable, but not quite certain, references to the Kingdom as already existing. (8) At the same time, seeing that its growth is far from complete, it is also thought and spoken of as future : (9) and caution must therefore be used in quoting as allusions to the present Kingdom passages which may with equal or greater probability be references to the Kingdom as yet to come.

(1) The original Old-Testament idea of God's sovereignty had pictured it as a present reality embodied in the prosperous Jewish monarchy. Only with the coming of successive national calamities was it transferred to the future and thus became a predominantly-eschatological concept. With the Rabbinic idea of loyalty to the one God and submission to His Law as an acceptance of the yoke of the Kingdom, the idea of the Kingdom as present was brought back into Jewish thought (without however the eschatological hope being abandoned). Since furthermore the intensive meaning of the word " Kingdom " as " royal sovereignty " was primary, it followed that the essential condition of the existence of the Kingdom, namely, man's loving and obedient acceptance of God as Father, was really timeless. The Kingdom, there-

fore, is certainly not exclusively future, but must exist whenever and wherever man so accepts God.[1]

(2) Seeing that Jesus took up, as the Son and Servant of God par excellence and the predicted Messiah, a position of unique significance among men, he must necessarily have assumed also a uniquely-significant function as regards God's Kingdom. If that Kingdom be wherever man yields filial obedience to God, it must be in him, and in him in a specially real and powerful way. Whether or no we can call him, as Origen did, αὐτοβασιλεία (" ideal royalty "),[2] we can say that in him and in his work among men the Kingdom of God was already present and active.[3] It used to be customary among scholars to realize the truth of this so thoroughly that they forgot that there was (as we shall see presently) another side to it ; and their whole interpretation was rejected by thorough-going eschatologists like Johannes Weiss and Albert Schweitzer. More recently still a reaction has set in ; and the presence and activity of the Kingdom in Jesus' own ministry is being increasingly recognized.[4]

(3) The best-attested, as also the clearest, of Jesus' asser- - tions of the presence and power of the Kingdom in his own work is one that formed a part of his reply to the charge of expelling demons by the help of Beelzebul : " If (it is) by the finger of God (that) I expel the demons, then has the Kingdom of God (already) reached you " (Lk. xi. 20 = Mt. xii. 28 Q).[5] In Lk. xvi. 16 = Mt. xi. 12f. Q, we have a saying recorded, the original wording and precise meaning of which are very hard to determine. The Lucan version runs, " The Law and the Prophets (lasted) until John : since then the Kingdom of God is being preached-as-good-news, and everyone forces his

[1] See above, pp. 111f. (5–7) : also Bartlet in H.D.C.G. ii. 701a (small print) ; Moffatt, Theol. of the Gospels, 50f., 68 ; Strack-Billerbeck i. 181f. ; Manson, Teaching, 135 ; Otto, Kingdom, 34–36.
[2] Orig. Comm. in Matth. xiv. 7 (ed. Lommatzsch, iii. 283). Cf. H.-D. Wendland, Eschatologie, 14f.; K. L. Schmidt in T.W.N.T. i. 590–592 ; Manson in Mission, etc. 636f.
[3] The close connexion in Jesus' mind between the Kingdom of God and his own person is largely the theme of W. G. Kümmel's book, Die Eschatologie der Evangelien (e.g., 16f.). Cf. also Gloege, Reich Gottes, 112–126.
[4] Cf. Holtzmann, Theol. i. 284–288, 290f., 294; Moffatt, Theol. of the Gospels, 53f., 57, 68, 71, 77, 83f. ; Charles, Crit. Hist. (1913), 371–378 ; Manson Teaching, 135f., 198, and in Mission, etc. 636f. ; Dodd, Parables, 48–51, 197–199, and in Kingdom of God and Hist. 24f., 32–36 ; Kümmel, Eschatologie, 1–3, 11–13 ; Otto, Kingdom, 67f., 72–75, 80f., 88–93, 102–104, 150–155.
[5] Cf. Gloege, Reich Gottes, 123–126, 142–145 ; Dodd, Parables, 43f., Apost. Preaching, 66, 212 ; Otto, Kingdom, 102f. On the meaning of ἔφθασεν (" reached ", not simply " approached "), see below, p. 198 n.4. Von Gall (Βασιλεία, 473f.) argues that the saying was created by the early Church.

way into it ". The Matthæan version runs, " From the days of John the Baptist until now the Kingdom of the Heavens is being subjected-to-force and men-of-force seize it. For all the Prophets and the Law prophesied until John ". The original saying may have meant either that the Kingdom has, since the Baptist's time, been forging ahead and becoming the possession of enthusiasts, or that the Kingdom has been subjected to the violence of those who wished to establish it by force of arms : perhaps the former interpretation is the more probable of the two, but in either case the existence of the Kingdom in the present is clearly implied : if it did not exist, it could not be subjected to force, either friendly or hostile.[1] In the third place, we have the saying, " The Kingdom of God does not come (in a way discernible) with watching : nor will men say, ' Behold ! here (it is) ! ' or ' there (it is) ! ' For behold ! the Kingdom of God is (already) in your midst ! " (Lk. xvii. 20f. L). Here again, though in this case there is no second version of the saying to confuse or help us, the meaning of it is disputed. The closing words ἐντὸς ὑμῶν ἐστιν are frequently taken to mean " is within you ", i.e., " in your hearts " : but I am disposed to agree with those who hold that they simply mean " in your midst ", i.e., " in the persons and work of me and my disciples ".[2] In either case the words as before presuppose that the Kingdom already exists.

(4) Sayings characterizing in the present tense the possessors of the Kingdom are, " Happy are ye poor, for yours is the Kingdom of God " (Lk. vi. 20 = Mt. v. 3 Q) ; " Happy are they who have been persecuted for righteousness' sake, for theirs is the Kingdom of the Heavens " (Mt. v. 10 M) ; " Let the little children come to me ; do not stop them : for the Kingdom of God belongs to such as they " (τῶν γὰρ τοιούτων ἐστὶν . . . : Mk. x. 14 = Lk. xviii. 16 = Mt. xix. 14) ; " Every scribe who has been made a disciple to the Kingdom of the Heavens is like a householder . . ." (Mt. xiii. 52 M) ; " The tax-collectors and prostitutes are preceding you into the Kingdom of God " (Mt. xxi. 31 M) ; " Ye shut the Kingdom of the Heavens in front of men : for ye enter not in yourselves, nor do ye allow those entering to enter " (Mt. xxiii. 13 M [or Q + m ?] : contrast Lk. xi. 52). While in all these cases,

[1] See below, pp. 171 (9), 232 bott., and cf. Gloege, *Reich Gottes*, 132 ; Dodd, *Parables*, 48.
[2] Cf. Gloege, *Reich Gottes*, 130–132 ; Dodd, *Parables*, 84f. n. 1 ; Manson in *Mission*, etc. 595–597 ; Otto, *Kingdom*, 131–137. Von Gall (Βασιλεία, 474f.) holds that ἰδού, and the tense of ἐστιν, are meant to indicate that the Kingdom will come suddenly with a flash, not that it has already come.

especially in view of the passages adduced above, pp. 129f. **(3)**, it may reasonably be argued that the Kingdom is thought of as present, one must be careful not to overpress the argument : for the tenses in Aramaïc, if the verb was used at all (which is doubtful), did not sharply distinguish present from future time, and even in the Greek of the New Testament the present tense is sometimes used proleptically as equivalent to a future : in the case of both languages, it was often left to the context to make it clear whether present or future time was meant ; [1] and we shall need to note later certain passages which might perhaps have been taken here, but which it is on the whole safer to regard as ambiguous (see below, pp. 134f. [**9**]).

(5) Four of the twelve parables commencing " The Kingdom of God is like . . . " describe processes of growth, all of which processes take a certain amount of time. These are the Parables of the Seed growing mysteriously (Mk. iv. 26–29), the Tares (Mt. xiii. 24–30, 36–43 M, especially 38, 41, 43—a parable which some suppose to be a secondary and less trustworthy version of Mk. iv. 26–29), the Mustard-Seed (Mk. iv. 30–32 ; Lk. xiii. 18f. = Mt. xiii. 31f. Q), and the Leaven (Lk. xiii. 20f. = Mt. xiii. 33 Q). The Parable of the Sower (Mk. iv. 3–9 = Lk. viii. 5–8 = Mt. xiii. 3–9) is not explicitly said to refer to the Kingdom ; but its content and context mark it as belonging to the same group, and in the probably-ungenuine interpretation of it m rightly describes " the Word " alluded to in the Parable as " the Word of the Kingdom " (Mt. xiii. 19 : contrast Mk. iv. 14f. = Lk. viii. 11f.). Now we are not at the moment concerned to determine what precisely Jesus intended by the climax which is reached in each case, or how precisely he thought of the rate of growth or the time during which it would continue : the point is that the growth which is to lead up to the climax has already begun, and the Kingdom itself is likened, not to the climax only, but in two cases to the sowing and in the others to the mustard-seed and the leaven respectively. That is to say, the Kingdom, having already started to grow, must needs be a present reality. [2]

[1] Wellhausen, *Mt.* 14 ; Montefiore, *S.G.* [2] II. 33 ; Héring, *Royaume*, 39–42.
[2] Cf. Holtzmann, *Theol.* i. 287–290 ; Manson, *Teaching*, 133f. ; Dodd, *Parables*, 180–183 ; Héring, *Royaume*, 44–46 ; Otto, *Kingdom*, 123–125. See also Rev. R. W. Stewart's anti-Barthian defence of ' The Idea of " Growth " in the Teaching of Jesus ' in *E.T.* xlvii. 390–394 (June 1936). Schweitzer (*L.J.F.* 402f. = *Quest*, 354) thinks the point is the miraculous character of the production of vast results from minute beginnings.
I cannot follow Dr. B. T. D. Smith (*Parables*, 120, 130) when he says, à propos of the Mustard-seed and the Leaven, " The Kingdom . . . does not grow—it comes " (cf. also Gloege, *Reich Gottes*, 68–72, 75). I should contend that according to Jesus' teaching it does both.

(6) The Kingdom is often present in thought, even when not explicitly named in words, as the Parable of the Sower which we have just been considering indicates. Hence we may without exaggeration or unreality include as testimonies to its presence and activity certain allusions made by Jesus to the obvious magnitude and success of the work he was actually carrying on. Thus his answer to the inquiry sent to him by John the Baptist (see above, pp. 57f. [f]), if it hinted at his Messiahship in only an ambiguous and non-commital way, suggested somewhat less-ambiguously the arrival of the Kingdom.[1] In the synagogue at Nazareth, after reading Isa. lxi. 1, 2a (Lk. iv. 17–19 L : see above, p. 48 [10]), he adds, " To-day has this scripture been fulfilled in your hearing " (Lk. iv. 21 L). He tells the Disciples that he has seen Satan fall from heaven, and that their names have already been written in the heavens (Lk. x. 18, 20 L).[2] Again, " Happy are the eyes that see what ye see ; for I tell you that many prophets and kings wished to behold the things which ye see, and (yet) did not behold them, and to hear the things which ye hear, and (yet) did not hear them ! " (Lk. x. 23f. = Mt. xiii. 16f. Q).[3] What else could the " (something) more " than Solomon, Jonah, or the Temple, something which he declared to be present (see above, pp. 70f [4]), have been but the Kingdom of God present in himself and his work ?

(7) There are one or two explicit allusions to the Kingdom which might reasonably be regarded as implying its present existence, though they cannot be claimed as certainly doing so. Thus the Disciples are told, " To you has the mystery of the Kingdom of God been given : . . . " (Mk. iv. 11 = Lk. viii. 10 = Mt. xiii. 11 : the two latter insert " to know " after " given ").[4] To the scribe who cordially agreed with Jesus' pronouncement about the two greatest commandments, he said, " Thou art not far from the Kingdom of God " (Mk. xii. 34).[5] After warning the Disciples against anxiety over material needs, Jesus added, " But seek ye His Kingdom, and these things will be given you in addition " (Lk. xii. 31 = Mt. vi. 33 Q). The Lucan version of this saying continues, " Fear not, thou little flock ; for the Father is pleased to give you the Kingdom " (Lk. xii. 32 Q or l). The word here translated " is pleased " is $εὐδόκησεν$; but we cannot press the past sense of the aorist ; it is probably simply the normal Greek equivalent

---

[1] Cf. Dodd, *Parables*, 47.
[2] Cf. Streeter in *Stud. in the Syn. Prob.* 433 ; A. T. Cadoux, *Parables*, 120.
[3] Cf. Moffatt, *Theol. of the Gospels*, 71 ; Box, *St. Matthew*, 35f.
[4] W. Manson, *Christ's View*, 95f.
[5] Cf. the grudging concession in Montefiore, *S.G.*[2] I. 286.

of the Hebrew stative perfect, which is quoted in other passages where εὐδόκησ- occurs (Mk. i. 11 = Mt. iii. 17 [= Lk. iii. 22 ?]; Mt. xii. 18 M ; Mt. xvii. 5 m), and means no more than that God's good pleasure is a certainty, without defining its time. Yet the passage may still imply that the Kingdom already exists. Jesus' words to Peter after the latter's Confession at Cæsarea-Philippi, " I will give thee the keys of the Kingdom of the Heavens, . . . " (Mt. xvi. 19 M or m), may possibly presuppose a present Kingdom : but they are of such questionable authenticity and so doubtful in meaning that no weight can be placed on them in this connexion (see above, p. 54 n. 3, and below, pp. 307–309).

(8) The certainty that Jesus thought and spoke of the Kingdom as already present in his Person and Ministry must not be taken to imply that he did not also look forward to its future and cataclysmic coming. The evidence for this latter expectation will be presented in detail later. All that it is necessary to note here is that, in the nature of things, the two ideas are mutually complementary, not mutually exclusive. To that which is already growing, there comes at length a condition of full attainment. It is true that the constitutive principle of the Kingdom—man's acceptance of God's gracious sovereignty—is essentially timeless : hence the Kingdom cannot be *limited* to the future. On the other hand, in the special sense in which Jesus himself was its representative, it had only just begun to grow ; and the idea of its further growth is, as the Parables have shown us, integral to his thought of it. The mind is thus carried forward to the triumphant completion of that process of growth ; and since the modern idea of a purely-continuous evolution was almost certainly remote from Jesus' thoughts, it was only natural that the expectation of a climax should play an important part in his whole idea of the Kingdom, and even that the Kingdom itself should at times have been identified by him rather with the final climax than with the present process of growth.[1]

[1] See above, pp. 113f. (10 and 11). Cf. also Sharman, *Future*, 311–315 ; Holtzmann, *Theol.* i. 284f., 291f., 294 ; Moffatt, *Theol. of the Gospels*, 57, 70f., 76, 78, 82f. ; Charles, *Crit. Hist.* (1913), 374–378 ; Strack-Billerbeck i. 181 ; Von Gall, Βασιλεία, 472–477 ; Montefiore, *S.G.*² II. 34 ; H.-D. Wendland, *Eschatologie*, 27–53 ; Otto, *Kingdom*, 147–149. Dr. C. H. Dodd writes, " This declaration that the Kingdom of God has already come necessarily dislocates the whole eschatological scheme in which its expected coming closes the long vista of the future. The *eschaton* has moved from the future to the present, from the sphere of expectation into that of realized experience . . . ' (*Parables*, 49f., cf. 78f.). This way of putting it seems to me unduly onesided. I shall deal later with what I regard as certain erroneous conclusions based upon it : see below, pp. 194–203, 296 n. 3, 311–315.

(9) The considerations advanced in the last paragraph should serve to warn us against rushing to the conclusion that the present reality of the Kingdom is referred to in every passage which, if taken by itself, might possibly be construed in that sense. Such a warning is needed, for instance, in the case of some sayings couched in the present tense, the occasional ambiguity of which has already been mentioned (see above, pp. 130f. [4]). A crying instance is the utterance about the Baptist : " Among those that have been born of women there has not arisen a greater than John : but he that is least in the Kingdom of God is (even) greater than he " (Mt. xi. 11 = Lk. vii. 28 Q : the text in Lk. is uncertain, D transferring the first clause to the end of 26, and perhaps representing Lk's. original wording, which was later assimilated, as so often happened, to Mt. ; but the differences do not affect the present argument). One sees this passage unquestionably quoted on all hands as an allusion to the present Kingdom, presumably because of the present tense $\dot{\epsilon}\sigma\tau\iota\nu$ at its close and of the purport of what precedes it (Lk. vii. 22f. = Mt. xi.'4–6 Q).[1] It is not usually observed that, if the tense of $\dot{\epsilon}\sigma\tau\iota\nu$ is to be pressed, the saying becomes self-contradictory ; for then the second clause would render the first untrue, since certain persons greater than John *had* arisen. I do not deny that the tacit exception of the present members of the Kingdom *may possibly* be presupposed in the first clause, in which case the second clause may refer to the Kingdom as present : this supposition, moreover, is strengthened by the reply given to John, if we may assume that Q's setting of our passage is historical. What I do deny is that the saying can be confidently taken without discussion as a reference to the present, in distinction from the future, Kingdom. The obvious need of caution with this passage should put us on our guard in dealing with another reference to greatness in the Kingdom : " Whoever therefore shall humble ($\tau\alpha\pi\epsilon\iota\nu\omega\sigma\epsilon\iota$) himself like this little child, he is ($\dot{\epsilon}\sigma\tau\iota\nu$) the greatest in the Kingdom of the Heavens " (Mt. xviii. 4 M or m ; observe also that m introduces the Kingdom into the question about greatness which had arisen [Mt. xviii. 1 ; contrast Mk. ix. 34 = Lk. ix. 46]). Here again it has been taken for granted that the Kingdom is present : [2]

[1] E.g., Wellhausen, *Mt.* 54 ; Moffatt, *Theol. of the Gospels*, 50f., 53 ; Charles, *Crit. Hist.* (1913), 374 ; Strack-Billerbeck i. 598 ; Box, *St. Matthew*, 36 ; Dodd, *Parables*, 47 ; Manson in *Mission*, etc. 362. Wendt (*Teaching*, ii. 29) realizes the need for special explanation : cf. also Montefiore, *S.G.*[2] II. 161 ; Héring, *Royaume*, 42 n.1.

[2] Moffatt, *Theol. of the Gospels*, 52.

but we may observe that the first part of the sentence puts the self-humbling in the future, and that the preceding verse speaks of entering the Kingdom in the future. Other passages sometimes over-hastily claimed as allusions to the Kingdom as present are :—Mt. xiii. 44–46 M (the Parables of the Treasure and the Pearl) ; [1] Mt. xviii. 23 M ; [2] Mk. x. 15 = Lk. xviii. 17 = Mt. xviii. 3b (" Whoever does not receive the Kingdom of God as a little child, will certainly not enter into it ") ; [3] Lk. xiii. 24 Q (cf. Mt. vii. 13f.).[4] With a recent suggestion to the effect that ἤγγικεν in Mk. i. 15 = Mt. iv. 17 and similar passages means " has arrived " rather than " has drawn near " [5] I shall deal later (see below, pp. 198f. n. 4).

[1] Dodd, *Parables*, 47 n.1.
[2] So " some ", mentioned by Montefiore, *S.G.*[2] II. 256, on the ground of the aorist ὡμοιώθη ! The same argument would have to be applied to Mt. xiii. 24 M and Mt. xxii. 2 m (or M).
[3] Streeter in *Stud. in the Syn. Prob.* 432 (*f*) ; Dodd, *Parables*, 47 n.1.
[4] Dr. Moffatt (*Theol. of the Gospels*, 72), by charging Mt. with eschatologizing the saying, implies that in Lk. it is not eschatological. The Kingdom however is not explicitly mentioned.
[5] Dodd in *Myst. Christi*, 66 n., and *Parables*, 44f.

CHAPTER IV

THE KINGDOM FOR THE JEWS

(1) Throughout his life Jesus frequently thought and spoke of the Kingdom as if it were, mainly at least, the concern of the people of Israel. (2) As a Jew born and bred, he was naturally to some extent imbued with the strong particularism characteristic of his race. He had a Jew's veneration for the nation's Scriptures, Law, Temple, and Holy City. (3) The rôle for which his Messianic claim marked him out was a definitely-national one. (4) He therefore confined himself mostly to Jewish territory, (5) addressed himself to the Jewish public as such, (6) tacitly assumed that the Kingdom was to be theirs, (7) drew contrasts between the right way of life for its members on the one hand and Gentile practices on the other, (8) and refrained from any direct appeal to the Gentile populations. (9) He fixed the number of his personal Disciples at twelve, with evident reference to the Twelve Tribes of Israel ; (10) and he depicted the Future Life and the Last Judgment on a Jewish pattern. (11) Of the Gentiles he often spoke as of offenders and outsiders. (12) When Israel as a whole proved unreceptive of his message, he resorted to the Old-Testament concept of a faithful Remnant of the People.

(1) The detailed evidence to be adduced in support of this first statement will be presented in later paragraphs (see below, pp. 139–143 [4–8]). It is for the most part cumulative. The statement tself merely summarizes the general fact which is made clear by several different lines of argument—the fact, namely, that Jesus regarded the whole Jewish people as the prospective recipients of his good news of the Kingdom, and endeavoured to induce them as a people to accept it. His special desire to win the capital city as the heart of the nation, and therefore as likely to settle the line to be taken by Israel as a whole, comes out in his sorrowful words, " O Jerusalem, Jerusalem ! . . . How often have I wished to gather thy children together, as a mother-bird gathers her brood of nestlings under her wings, . . . " (Lk. xiii. 34 = Mt. xxiii. 37 Q).[1]

[1] Cf. Wellhausen, *Mc.* 7 (" Wie die Propheten, so haben auch Johannes und Jesus eine Umkehr d e s V o l k e s im Auge, nicht bloss einzelner Individuen, am wenigsten auch solcher, die nicht zum jüdischen Volk gehören

There is, of course, as we shall see, much evidence of a broader sympathy in Jesus : it is, moreover, true that much of the particularistic teaching in the Gospels comes from M, a somewhat untrustworthy informant on this issue (see above, pp. 21f.). It is however in my judgment going beyond what the evidence warrants to say that " Jesus paid scant respect to distinctions of race " and " attached no value to pride of race ".[1]

(2) A great mass of available information shows that the dominant attitude of Palestinian Jews to the non-Jewish world was one of fear, aloofness, disapproval, and hatred. It was not altogether-unnatural that this should be so. Their national history had acquainted them at first hand with the cruelty and vice of the Gentile powers. Their own holy land, which had been traditionally regarded as Yahweh's special preserve, was dotted over, to its defilement, by Gentile settlements. Their political independence had been taken away. Their peculiar habits and beliefs evoked the contempt of non-Jews generally ; and the more passionately they clung to their national faith and their national religious observances, the more they disliked the uncircumcised heathen who ignored or flouted them. They thought of them en masse as meriting God's wrath, and as destined shortly to have it poured out upon them. There were indeed universalistic passages in the Old Testament which could not have been wholly forgotten ; and individual Rabbis now and then gave expression to a charitable and broadminded sympathy with non-Jews. These facts should warn us against speaking too sweepingly : but there can be no doubt that the normal and prevalent attitude of the Palestinian Jews, even the godly and kind-hearted ones amongst them, was of the kind that has been described.[2]

. . . ") ; Holtzmann, *Theol.* i. 276, 299 ; Montefiore, *S.G.*[2] I. 16 (". . . we have no clear evidence that Jesus thought of the Kingdom . . . upon *deliberately unnational* lines. There is no clear evidence that he rejected the primacy of Israel, or its continuance as a nation, in the new order and in the Kingdom . . ."). Cf. also Meyer, *Ursprung*, i. 300f.

[1] So Rev. Alan Richardson in *The Student Movement*, xxxix (1937) 147b. Cf. Kümmel, *Eschatologie*, 8 (". . . Jesus verbindet keinerlei nationale Hoffnungen mit der Gottesherrschaft, . . .").

[2] The evidence is abundant. I select a few witnesses only :—*Wisdom of Sol.* xii. 22a ; Psa. of Sol. xvii. 28b, 45b ; *Fourth Ezra*, vi. 56, 59 ; Gal. ii. 15 (ἐξ ἐθνῶν ἁμαρτωλοί) ; E. G. Hirsch in *J.E.* v (1903) 616–619, x (1905), 223b ; J. D. Eisenstein in *J.E.* v (1903) 619–624 ; Schürer, *G.J.V.* ii. 89–94, iii. 163, 55of. ; Strack-Billerbeck i. 182, 353–363, 373f., ii. 139 (on Lk. ii. 32), iv. 32, 35–37, 353–414 ; Bousset, *Relig. des Jud.* (1926), 82–85 ; Montefiore, *S.G.*[2] II. 80, 85 ; Moore, *Judaism*, i. 19–23, 54, 56, 197f., 219–226, iii. 4 ; D. C. Simpson in *H.C.L.M.K.* 152f., 163 ; Manson, *Teaching*, 254, 256–259.

We are not of course obliged to infer that Jesus shared the narrow-minded antipathy of his fellow-countrymen towards the Gentiles. But having been born and bred in a purely-Jewish atmosphere, he must in the nature of things have been to some extent affected by its prevalent tone. Certain it is at all events that Jewish self-centredness to some extent colours not only the Gospel of 'Matthew', but even the more universal-istic Gospel of Luke, especially in their birth- and infancy-narratives (Mt. i. 21, ii. 6; Lk. i. 33, 54, 68–79, ii. 10. 32). Jesus himself evinces all the veneration felt by the pious Jew for his nation's Scriptures, for the Mosaic Law, for the Holy City (Mt. iv. 5 Q or m?; Mt. v. 35 M) and the Temple.[1] His respect for the Law is amply attested, even if we have to exclude from consideration certain doubtful passages. Mt. v. 19 M and Mt. xxiii. 2, 3a M, for example, probably represent the anti-Pauline view of the Jerusalem-church rather than the mind of Jesus himself (see above, pp. 121f.). Possibly Mt. vii. 15 M ("Beware of the false prophets, . . .") is another anti-Pauline thrust. The obscure saying in Lk. xvi. 17 ("It is easier for heaven and earth to pass away than for a single tittle of the Law to fall") is probably from Q, for it has a parallel in Mt. v. 18 : it must therefore be reckoned with as a probable saying of Jesus ; and possibly the same claim might be made for Mt. v. 17 M, with which Mt. has conflated it : "Do not think that I have come to overthrow the Law. . . . I have not come to overthrow, but to fulfil". The saying about the tittle of the Law is so inconsistent with the free attitude which Jesus elsewhere takes up that its authenticity has naturally been doubted. The latest suggestion is that it was meant ironically by Jesus, as a tart comment "on the obstinate conservatism of the Scribes".[2] This may well be right ; but it is a precarious theory, and the possibility must be left open that, perhaps at the beginning of his ministry, Jesus ascribed to the Law a sanctity with which his later criticisms were not fully consistent, and that he did seriously regard himself as loyally fulfilling it. The ascription to him of extreme passages like Mt. v. 19 M and Mt. xxiii. 2, 3a M becomes on this theory somewhat more easily intelligible.

(3) There are no solid reasons for doubting the plain evidence of the Gospels to the effect that Jesus regarded himself as the Messiah of Israel (see above, pp. 51f.). Apart

---

[1] See above, pp. 120–122, and cf. Heiler, *Der Katholizismus* (1923), 30f., and C. J. Cadoux in *E.T.* xxxviii. 58b, 59b (Nov. 1926).
[2] So Manson in *Mission*, etc. 316f., 427, 446.

from other passages, the statements repeated by all four Gospels that he acknowledged himself to Pilate to be " the King of the Jews " (Mk. xv. 2 = Mt. xxvii. 11 ; Lk. xxiii. 3 L ; John xviii. 33–37) [1] and that he was officially sentenced to crucifixion as such (Mk. xv. 9, 12, 18, 26, 32 = Mt. xxvii. 17, 22, 29, 37, 42 ; Lk. xxiii. 37, 38 L ; John xix. 19) are explicable on no other view. There is no real reason for questioning the historicity of the Evangelists' report of his reply to Pilate : the words were uttered in public ; they are not likely to have been invented by the early Church ; and they help to explain Pilate's subsequent proceedings. Now it is doubtless true that Messiahship meant for Jesus something very different from what it meant for the average Jew : but there was one feature about Messiahship without which the term—almost the very idea—would have been meaningless ; and that feature was the national character of the office. Jesus must then have thought of himself as charged with a distinctively-national task. [2]

(4) On only one occasion, so far as our information goes, did Jesus visit wholly non-Jewish territory ; and that was when, for purposes of privacy, or possibly in order to escape the clutches of Herod Antipas, he went for a season to Phœnicia (Mk. vii. 24–31 = Mt. xv. 21–29 : we note that m here, in order to avoid obtruding the statement that Jesus actually entered Gentile territory, says that the Canaanite woman " came out from those territories [ὁρίων] " to see him, though he had already withdrawn " to the parts of Tyre and Sidon "). [3] There were, of course, plenty of Gentiles to be met with in the mainly-Jewish parts of Palestine to which he normally confined himself ; and he occasionally came into contact with them : the statement in Mt. xv. 31 m (or M ?) that the crowd, after seeing his healings, " glorified the God of Israel " seems to imply that it was a Gentile crowd ; but the documentary authority for the statement is not very high (see below, p. 154 n. 3). It is in any case clear that Jesus never set himself seriously to evangelize the Gentile territory. Even at the end

---

[1] On the meaning of " Thou sayest (it) ", see above, p. 60 n.1.

[2] A. T. Cadoux aptly suggests (*Theol. of Jes.* 252) that this *national* reference explains why Jesus began his main ministry only after John's work was over, and why he did not baptize. John baptized because he wished to " separate individuals from the mass ". It was only after Israel *as a nation* had rejected Jesus that his Disciples resumed John's method. See also below, pp. 309f,

[3] The visit of Jesus to the tetrarchy of Philip (Mk. viii. 27ff. = Mt. xvi. 13ff.) is not really an exception to the above statement, notwithstanding the fact that the population was predominantly Gentile : considerable numbers of Jews were settled there (Schürer, *G.J.V.* i. 425–429).

he journeyed to Jerusalem to die, when he could easily have saved his life by withdrawing to some Gentile country.

(5) Several pieces of evidence unite to show that Jesus directly devoted his ministry of healing and teaching, not to men in general, nor to a select body of " Disciples ", but to the Jewish people of Palestine as such.[1] He pictures his followers fasting and sacrificing (see above, p. 121), just as pious Jews normally did. One of the clearest of the indications referred to is his use of the term " brothers " as a designation of those to whom he is speaking. Years afterwards, Christian readers of the Gospels understood this word to refer to " fellow-disciples ", in contradistinction to non-Christian Jews and pagans. But in Jesus' time, the word could to his hearers mean only " fellow-Jews " (considered especially in their capacity as co-religionists).[2] Lk. vi. 41f. = Mt. vii. 3–5 Q (about the mote and the beam) and Lk. xvii. 3b, 4 = Mt. xviii. 15, 21 Q (about forgiving a repentant offender) are proofs that he used the word when uttering general ethical injunctions. There is no reason, therefore, to doubt the reports of M to the same effect (Mt. v. 22 ; Mt. v. 23f. ; Mt. xviii. 35), or to give the word in all these passages any other sense than that of " fellow-Jew ". In Mt. v. 46f. an explicit contrast is drawn between " your brothers " and (a) " the tax-collectors " and (b) " the Gentiles " ; and it is probable that this represents the original wording of Q, rather than the parallels in Lk. vi. 32–34 (where the contrast is with " the sinners "). The Sermon on the Mount, therefore, and Jesus' public teaching generally, must be regarded as addressed to the Jewish people as such, just like the message of John or any of the ancient prophets.[3] There are, indeed, a few passages in which we seem to trace the later meaning of the word as designating " fellow-Christians " (e.g., Mt. xviii. 15–17 M [forgiving a fellow-

[1] Cf. Liberty, *Political Relations*, 78–81, 87 ; Flew, *Church*, 105, 121.
[2] Cf. Exod. ii. 11, iv. 18 ; Numb. xxxii. 6 ; Deut. x. 9, xv. 2f., xvii. 15, 20, xviii. 2, xxiii. 19f., xxiv. 7 ; Jer. xxxiv. 14 ; Acts ii. 29, 37, iii. 17, vii. 2, xiii. 26, xxii. 5, xxviii. 21 ; Rom. ix. 3 : Hatch, *Organization of the Early Christian Churches* (1881), 44 ; Strack-Billerbeck i. 276.
[3] I believe that Dr. H. Marriott is quite mistaken in holding that the Sermon on the Mount was " mainly addressed to the Twelve " and in calling it " a Sermon addressed to newly-ordained men in the presence of their relatives and friends and of a large congregation " (*Sermon on the Mount* [1925], 50, 225 : cf. Moody, *Purpose of Jes.* 64–66 ; Windisch, *Bergpredigt*, 44f., 107 ; Flew, *Church*, 58f., 63 top.), and that the late Dr. B. W. Bacon was similarly in error in holding that it implies that the " disciples are already a separate body " (*Matthew*, 340), though this latter view may be true as regards the few sayings in the Sermon (uttered when ?) about persecution. Cf. Gore, *The Holy Spirit and the Church* (1924), 42–47 ; Dodd, *Hist. and the Gosp.* 131–134.

member of " the Church "],[1] Mt. xxiii. 8 M ["All ye are brothers "] ; Mt. xxv. 40 M [" one of the least of these my brothers "]). Nay more, Jesus himself, when it had become clear to him that Israel as a whole would not follow him, doubtless occasionally used the term to designate the small circle of those who would (e.g., Lk. xxii. 32 L : " strengthen thy brothers "). But this was only at the end of his ministry, and does not hold good for his earlier public teaching.

In line with the view here taken of the implication of Jesus' use of the word " brothers " is his way of defending himself for healing the woman with curvature of the spine on the Sabbath and for accepting the hospitality of Zacchæus : the former was " a daughter of Abraham " (Lk. xiii. 16 L), and even the latter ($\kappa\alpha\theta\delta\tau\iota$ $\kappa\alpha\iota$ $\alpha\dot{\upsilon}\tau\delta$s) " a son of Abraham " (Lk. xix. 9 L). He used a similar expression, if we may trust the Gospel according to the Hebrews, in addressing the Rich Ruler : he reproaches him with having been stingy to the poor, " many of thy brothers, sons of Abraham ".[2] The reference in Jer. xvi. 16 to the scattered Israelites being fished and hunted for, and restored by God to their land, suggests that Jesus' wish to make his Disciples " fishers of men " *may* likewise have been an allusion primarily to his work for Israel.[3] But not much weight can be placed on this, nor on the words of Mt. xxiv. 20, " Pray that your flight happen not . . . on a Sabbath " (for the reference to the Sabbath is from m [contrast Mk. xiii. 18], and in any case the passage belongs to " the Little Apocalypse " [see above, pp. 11f.]).

(6) That Jesus at first took it for granted that the Kingdom would belong to Israel follows from the evidence presented at the close of this section and elsewhere in the chapter : but we must take note here of a few sayings of doubtful historicity in which it is assumed that his Jewish contemporaries are either already in possession of the Kingdom or, as " sons of the Kingdom " might reasonably be expected to be so. Thus in Mt. xxi. 43 M Jesus tells the Jews round him that " the Kingdom of God will be taken away from " them. In Mt. viii. 12 the expulsion of " the sons of the Kingdom " into outer darkness is foretold ; but the different wording in Lk. xiii. 28f. makes it impossible to say whether the expression in Mt. is that of Q

---

[1] Cf. Heiler, *Der Katholizismus* (1923), 42f. ; C. J. Cadoux, *Cathol. and Christianity*, 377–379, 386f. ; Manson in *Mission*, etc. 502.

[2] Preuschen, *Antilegomena*, 6 (11) ; James, *Apocr. N.T.* 6.

[3] Cf. Bacon, *Beginnings*, xxxvi. Dr. R. N. Flew (*Church*, 96–99) thinks Jesus went up to Jerusalem to die, because only there could he appeal to *the nation*.

or m. We hear of " the sons of the Kingdom " again in the probably-ungenuine interpretation of the Parable of the Tares (Mt. xiii. 38 M) : here, indeed, they are the righteous who later shine forth in it (Mt. xiii. 43 M) ; yet the evil have to be collected " out of " the Kingdom (Mt. xiii. 41 M). The Parable's of the Vineyard (Mk. xii. 1–12 = Lk. xx. 9–19 = Mt. xxi. 33–46) and of the Great Feast (Lk. xiv. 16–24 = Mt. xxii.1–9 Q ?) and the passionate denunciation recorded in Lk. xi. 49–51 = Mt. xxiii. 34–36 Q also probably presuppose the belief that Israel as such had been primarily destined for the Kingdom.[1]

(7) When Jesus contrasted what he wanted his hearers and disciples to do, with what was customary among " the Gentiles ", his contrast tacitly presupposed that these hearers and disciples were Jews quâ Jews, not simply some small section of Jews. One such contrast at least is recorded by Q : " Be not therefore anxious . . . for after all these things do the Gentiles seek : . . . " (Lk. xii. 29f. = Mt. vi. 31f. Q). A possible second from Q runs, " If ye salute your brothers only, what extra (thing) do ye do ? Do not even the Gentiles do the same ? " (Mt. v. 47 : see above, p. 140). Mk. has one, based on the normal behaviour of Gentile rulers : " . . . those who aspire to rule over the Gentiles lord it over them, . . . But it is not so among you . . . " (Mk. x. 42f. = Mt. xx. 25f.) ; and a close parallel to this evidently stood in L (Lk. xxii. 25f.). M has one concerning the method of praying : " When ye pray, do not babble on, as the Gentiles do ; . . . Do not therefore get like them ; . . . " (Mt. vi. 7f.).

(8) In spite of the orders attributed to Jesus after the Resurrection for the evangelization of the world, and his supposed earlier allusions to this evangelization (which we shall have to consider later : see below, pp. 158, 176, 300f.), it seems clear that, in point of fact, Jesus himself never did explicitly enjoin on his Disciples such a world-wide mission. Only by supposing that there was no injunction to this effect can we account for the difficulty which arose between Paul and the Jerusalem-leaders over the Gentile mission, and of which we read in Acts xv and the Epistle to the Galatians. Had either Paul or the Jerusalem-" pillars " known of any such words as are ascribed in Lk. and Mt. to the risen Lord, they could hardly have acted and spoken as they did.[2]

---

[1] Cf. W. B. Selbie in *E.T.* xxxvii. 267f. (Mar. 1926) ; C. H. Dodd in *Myst. Christi*, 64 ; K. L. Schmidt in *T.W.N.T.* i. 587. Per contra, Weinel, *Theol.* 65f. (6).

[2] Harnack, *Mission*, etc. i. 38–41 ; Holtzmann, *Theol.* i. 283 ; Meyer, *Ursprung*, ii. 426f.

Our supposition is to some slight degree confirmed by Jesus' own limitation of his efforts to Israel. Of special significance here is the Marcan report of his hesitation to exorcize the demon from the Phœnician woman's daughter. "Let the children first be satisfied", he said, "for it is not right to take the children's bread and throw it to the dogs" (Mk. vii. 27 = Mt. xv. 26). However the hesitation is to be explained, we have—in view of other evidence regarding Jesus' practice—no right to doubt its reality. There is therefore something to be said for the historicity of the parallel in Mt. xv. 24 (where, as elsewhere in this story, the Evangelist seems to be conflating Mk. with some non-Marcan source) : " I was not sent to any but the lost sheep of the house of Israel ".[1]

We come next to the particularistic sayings in the Matthæan version of the mission-charge to the Twelve. " Do not depart along any road to the Gentiles, and do not enter into any city of the Samaritans ; but make your way rather to the lost sheep of the house of Israel" (Mt. x. 5f. M). "When they persecute you in this city, flee to another : for truly I tell you, ye will by no means finish the cities of Israel until the Son of Man comes " (Mt. x. 23 M). It is inherently likely that the form in which the Lord's mission-instructions were recorded would reflect the convictions of the early Church in regard to her propaganda-work : and it has already been argued (see above, p. 95) that Mt. x. 23 was fashioned under the stress of the Jerusalem-controversy with Paul. Possibly the same applies to Mt. x. 5f. : but it is not easy to understand the presence of such words in the record if Jesus had in point of fact practised or definitely enjoined the evangelization of the Gentile lands.[2]

(9) Whatever doubts may exist, owing to the discrepancies in our records, as to the names of one or two of the less prominent members of the circle of Jesus' intimate Disciples, there is no question that he himself fixed their number at twelve (Mk. iii. 14 = Lk. vi. 13 = Mt. x. 2 ; etc., etc.). It seems a safe conjecture (and virtually all scholars concur in it) [3] that this number had direct reference to that of the Tribes of Israel ; and the conjecture is amply confirmed by an obscure saying which appears in different forms in L and M, in which Jesus

---

[1] It is with reference to these and similar words that Heiler says, " Auch in Jesu Seele liess dieser grosse Gedanke des Gottesvolkes tiefe Spuren zurück ; auch in seinem Wirken offenbart sich diese jüdische Exklusivität . . ." (Der Katholizismus [1923], 32f.).

[2] Cf. Holtzmann, Theol. i. 276.

[3] Dr. M. Goguel (Life of Jes. 34of., 497) is an exception.

promises them that in the coming Kingdom they shall " sit on thrones, judging the twelve Tribes of Israel " (Lk. xxii. 30 ; Mt. xix. 28b).[1] It is clear therefore that the relevance of his work to the Jews as a people was a very prominent element in his whole world-view.

(10) We shall be examining in detail later the teaching of Jesus about the Last Judgment and the Future Life : all we need to note here is the strongly-Jewish colour which pervades that teaching. Not only does it contain numerous allusions to the Messianic Feast, one of the most frequent and characteristic items of Jewish eschatology, but it depicts Abraham, Isaac, Jacob, and the Prophets as reclining at table in the future Kingdom (Lk. xiii. 28f. = Mt. viii. 11f. Q), and describes the poor beggar Lazarus as carried by the angels at his death to Abraham's bosom and Abraham as conversing thereafter with the Rich Man in Hades across a great gulf (Lk. xvi. 22–31 L). In the Lucan version of the passage quoted above in connexion with the Twelve, Jesus promises them that they shall " eat and drink at my table in my Kingdom ; and ye shall sit on thrones, judging the twelve Tribes of Israel " (Lk. xxii. 30 L : cf. Mt. xix. 28b M). In the great picture of the Judgment given in Mt. xxv. 31–46 M, while " the King " represents Jesus himself, and " the Son of Man " the redeemed and triumphant community of his " brethren ", with him at its head (see above, p. 100 [14]), " all the nations " ($\pi\acute{a}\nu\tau a \ \tau\grave{a} \ \check{\epsilon}\theta\nu\eta$) gathered before him for judgment are clearly the Gentiles : the redeemed community stands for idealized Israel, the de facto and partially-unresponsive Israel being for the sake of simplicity ignored.

(11) We have already taken note of a number of well-attested sayings of Jesus, wherein he contrasted the customs of the Gentiles with the better ways of conduct which he desired his own disciples to follow (see above, p. 142 [7]). In Mk. x. 33f. = Lk. xviii. 32f. = Mt. xx. 19 is recorded his prediction of his being handed over to the Gentiles, and put to a cruel and shameful death. Other characterizations of the Gentiles rest on less solid authority. " The Little Apocalypse " foretells their internecine wars (Mk. xiii. 8 = Lk. xxi. 10 = Mt. xxiv. 7), and the Lucan parallel to it mentions also their capture and destruction of Jerusalem and the dispersal of its enslaved inhabitants among them " until the seasons of the Gentiles are fulfilled " (Lk. xxi. 24 L or l). m is certainly

---

[1] Cf., e.g., Creed, *St. Luke*, 86f.

glossing, but is probably glossing correctly, in depicting the Gentiles as hating and persecuting the disciples of Jesus (Mt. x. 18 [contrast Lk. xxi. 13 = Mk. xiii. 9] ; Mt. xxiv. 9 fin. [contrast Mk. xiii. 13 = Lk. xxi. 17 = Mt. x. 22a]). The Gentile, like the unpatriotic Jewish tax-collector, figures as a typical outsider from the point of view of the community of disciples, when advice is given to treat an irreconcilable offending fellow-disciple " like the Gentile and the tax-collector " (Mt. xviii. 15–17 M) : but the accuracy of the report and its precise meaning are dubious (see above, p. 141 n. 1).

It is with the foregoing evidence before us that we must now approach the question as to how far, if at all, Jesus participated in the custom of the more vehement and outspoken Jews of at least occasionally referring to the Gentiles as " dogs " and " swine ". It is difficult to know precisely how prevalent the custom was ; possibly one ought not to speak of " custom " at all in this connexion. But without wishing to exaggerate, we must at least observe that several instances of the use of both terms by Jews are on record, of course with reference to the supposed habitual vices of the Gentile world ; [1] and certainly these two words are not at all too severe to be consistent with the dislike and disapproval with which the stricter Jews normally regarded those outside the Jewish pale (see above, p. 137). Now when the Phœnician woman begged Jesus to cure her daughter, he justified his hesitation with the words, " Let the children first be satisfied ; for it is not right to take the children's bread and throw it to the dogs " (Mk. vii. 27 = Mt. xv. 26). It is true that the word for " dogs " in the Greek is a diminutive, that the reference is probably to house-dogs, not to dogs who roamed wild, and that it is just possible to interpret Jesus' words as spoken in a kindly spirit.[2] Still the fact remains that Jesus certainly did make use on this occasion of the uncomplimentary name in question.

M preserves a still more striking saying : " Give not your ear-rings to the dogs, nor throw your pearls before the swine, lest they trample them with their feet, and then turn and tear you " (Mt. vii. 6).[3] Modern Christians usually evade the unwelcome conclusion that Jesus spoke thus of the Gentiles, either by rejecting the record as here unhistorical,[4] or by

[1] Cf. Cheyne in *E. Bi.* 1125 ; Kohler in *J.E.* iv (1903) 632 ; Strack-Billerbeck i. 449f., 724f. ; Abrahams, *Studies*, ii. 195f. ; Montefiore, *S.G.*[2] I. 167f.
[2] Cf. Bartlet, *St. Mark*, 234 ; Rawlinson, *St. Mark*, 99.
[3] For the rendering, cf. McNeile, *St. Matthew*, 91ab ; Perles in *Z.N.W.* xxv (1926) 163f., 319.
[4] So Martineau, *Seat of Authority* (ed. 1898), 596f.

145

referring the words, not to the Gentiles, but simply to the spiritually-unresponsive (cf. Mk. vi. 11 = Lk. ix. 5, x. 10f. = Mt. x. 14). It is not clear that either expedient is historically justifiable. It may be quite true that the Evangelist would never have included the words among those of Jesus, if he had understood them to be a direct reference to Gentiles. But he may have given them a meaning which differed from that intended by the speaker. Certainty is, of course, impossible ; but our natural wish to believe that Jesus said nothing but what we can without difficulty approve of, and what was consistent with all that he said at other times, is not a sufficient warrant for positively denying the accuracy of the record at this point, especially in face of the rest of the evidence which bears on his general attitude to the Gentiles.[1]

(12) Finally, when bitter experience of the unresponsiveness of Israel gradually but irreparably broke up his treasured hope that he might gather the whole nation to himself, he reacted to the disappointment, not (as we might have expected) by throwing Judaïsm and its claims to the four winds and turning for a more promising reception to the Gentile world, but by resorting to the old Prophetic idea of a faithful Remnant of Israel which, even through suffering and martyrdom (like the Deutero-Isaianic Servant of the Lord), should do in the world the work God had originally intended Israel to do. This " Son of Man ", this " people of the Saints of the Most High ", to whom after grievous oppression the everlasting Kingdom should be given, would remain, even though the bulk of those who were Jews by race should apostatize ; and of that Remnant he would himself be the representative and the head, bound to it by the bond of a New Covenant, and destined after all to see the Lord's purpose prosper in his hands.[2]

[1] Cf. Menzies, *Earliest Gospel*, 157a (" . . . We must not wonder if Jesus expressed his loyalty and devotion to his own people in the language of his day ") ; Holtzmann, *Theol.* i. 281f. ; Burkitt in *H.C.L.M.K.* 201 = *Jesus Christ*, etc. 4.

[2] Cf. Dodd in *Myst. Christi*, 64 ; A. T. Cadoux, *Parables*, 146–151, *Theol. of Jes.* 262f. ; Kümmel, *Eschatologie*, 13f. ; and particularly, Manson, *Teaching*, 175–196, 229–236.

CHAPTER V

THE KINGDOM FOR THE GENTILES

(1) Jewish monotheism logically implied a positive concern on God's part with all the nations ; and the later writers of the Old Testament had frequently pictured Israel (or a Remnant thereof) as commissioned to spread the light of true religion to the Gentiles. (2) The Jews of the Dispersion had carried on an active religious and ethical propaganda ; in Palestine, however, a very exclusive spirit prevailed. (3) Jesus was led to feel and express the duty of Israel to the Gentile world, firstly, by the universalistic passages in the Old Testament, (4) secondly, by the traditional claim of the Messiah to worldwide dominion, (5) and thirdly, by the broadly-human character of his teaching. (6) Several of his well-attested sayings mention or clearly imply the participation of Gentiles in the full blessings of the Kingdom : (7) others may be plausibly claimed as implying it, though the claim must be pronounced rather dubious ; (8) while yet others must be considered as at best quite ambiguous. (9) The universalism of the Synoptists themselves is readily visible, and should warn us against exaggerating the universalistic teaching they report. (10) Jesus perhaps never completely synthetized his Jewish and Gentile sympathies : (11) but he clearly recognized that the Gentiles had a place in the Kingdom of God. His concentration on the Jews is explicable as an attempt to fit them for the task of enlightening the Gentiles ; (12) and his comparative reticence regarding the latter is explicable as a necessary condition of securing a hearing with his own people.

(1) In the early stages of Hebrew religion, Yahweh, the God of Israel, was thought of simply as a tribal deity, alongside of whom there existed many other deities worshipped by and caring for other tribes and nations (see, e.g., Judg. xi. 23f., 1 Sam. xxvi. 19 fin.). He was naturally regarded as the best of all gods, and certainly as the only one whom Israel ought to worship, but by no means as the only god that existed. In process of time, however, the thought dawned on the Hebrew mind that Yahweh was the sole deity in heaven and earth, and that " all the gods of the nations are idols " (Psa. xcvi. 5).

Now this great monotheistic conviction clearly implied that, whatever Israel's privileges might be, not Israel only, but all the nations of the earth, must be the objects of God's providential care. It took time indeed for this implication to be seen and accepted ; and we can trace dimly the successive stages of the process. Amos, in the eighth century B.C., made a beginning by telling his fellow-countrymen that Israel's special relation to Yahweh meant severer discipline rather than greater indulgence (Amos iii. 2), and that Yahweh was just as much responsible for the migrations of the Ethiopians, the Philistines, and the Syrians, as He was for those of the Hebrews (Amos ix. 7).

In the Exilic period, the author of the Servant-poems early incorporated by Deutero-Isaiah in his own work (see above, pp. 37f.) depicts the Servant as extending the knowledge of God's Law to the eagerly-awaiting Gentiles (Isa. xlii. 1, 4). " It is too light a thing ", so he pictures Yahweh saying, " that thou shouldest by My Servant (in order) to raise up the tribes of Jacob (only) and to restore the dispersed of Israel (only). I will also set thee as a light for the Gentiles, that My salvation may extend to the end of the earth " (Isa. xlix. 6). Deutero-Isaiah himself, writing about 540 B.C., repeats this forecast on his own account (Isa. xlii. 6, li. 4f.).

The prophetical books of the Old Testament contain numerous allusions to the coming participation of the Gentile peoples of the world in the pure religion of Israel. It is possible that one or two of these utterances were written before the Exile : but the bulk of them belong in all probability to the post-Exilic period. The more important of them are to be found in the following passages :—Isa. ii. 3f., xix. 18–25, xxv. 6–8, lvi. 6f. (" . . . My house shall be called a house of prayer for all the peoples "), Jer. iii. 17, xvi. 19–21, Mic. iv. 1–5, Hab. ii. 14, Zeph. iii. 9, Zech. ii. 11, viii. 22f., xiv. 16–19, Mal. i. 11.

The two beautiful books of Ruth and Jonah were probably written as indirect protests against the narrow Jewish nationalism generated by the difficulties of the struggling little community and greatly encouraged by the policies of Nehemiah and Ezra. Universalistic expressions frequently occur in the late Jewish writings, e.g., Sibyll. Orac. iii. 732–795 ; Tobit xiii. 11, xiv. 6f. ; etc.

(2) The best Jewish minds in the late pre-Christian period hoped therefore for something better than the forcible subjection of the Gentile nations to the resurgent empire of Israel :

they looked and worked for a conversion of these peoples to a saving belief in God and for their full participation in His coming kingdom. A patent corollary of this hope was the conviction that to the Jew fell the task of disseminating the true faith throughout the world. The religious propaganda thus necessitated was particularly vigorous and successful in the Diaspora. The freer and more liberal atmosphere breathed by the Greek-speaking Jews who were settled up and down the Mediterranean lands outside Palestine was highly favourable to this missionary work. In the less-ritualistic and more-ethical monotheistic teaching of the synagogues of the Dispersion there was much to interest and attract the serious-minded pagans of the vicinity. The earnest claims on the strength of which this propaganda was carried on are ironically quoted by Paul, when in his Epistle to the Romans (ii.17–20) he is demonstrating the Jews' own need of salvation : " Thou bearest the name of a Jew, and reliest upon the Law, and boastest of God, and knowest His will, and approvest what is excellent, being instructed from the Law ; and thou art confident that thou thyself art a guide of the blind, a light to them that are in darkness, a corrector of the foolish, a teacher of babes, having in the Law the form of knowledge and of truth ". Probably almost every synagogue had its penumbra of Gentile hangers-on, who came to hear the Jewish Scriptures read, to follow the prayers, and listen to the preacher's exhortations : these were " the devout " (οἱ σεβόμενοι) of whom we read in Acts (xiii. 50, xvi. 14, xvii. 4 [note that here Ἕλληνες means simply " Gentiles "], 17, xviii. 7) as present at Antioch in Pisidia, at Thessalonica, and elsewhere. But in addition to these there were also the proselytes, i.e., Gentiles who felt prepared to identify themselves wholly with Israel as a religious community and who were admitted, after baptism, circumcision, and other formalities, to what was virtually full membership in it. Apart from the personal work done in and around the synagogues, much of the literature produced by the Jews of the Dispersion in the late pre-Christian period was intended as a religious appeal to Gentiles generally to accept the Divine revelation granted to Israel.

It must, of course, be borne in mind that a desire to make proselytes, while it may arise from a genuine concern for the welfare of others, can also go along with a very narrow-minded exclusiveness, a mere desire to gain adherents to support one's party : and there is some reason to believe that the propaganda maintained by the conservative Judaïsm of

Palestine tended more and more to be of this latter type. In Jesus' day, the Palestinian Scribes and Pharisees were apparently keen proselytizers : " Ye compass sea and land to make one proselyte ", Jesus says to them (Mt. xxiii. 15 M). It is indeed only reasonable to believe that with some of the leaders the motives behind their enthusiasm were broad and charitable. Thus Hillel, the great Rabbi of the times immediately before Jesus' ministry, wrote, " Be ye of the disciples of Aaron, . . . loving mankind, and bringing them nigh to the Law ".[1] The same was probably true of the sagacious Gamaliel, who was the teacher of the Pharisee Paul, and of whose good sense we read in Acts v. 34–40. But from the growingly narrow and bitter attitude taken up by Palestinian Jews generally towards Gentiles (see above, p. 137), one is forced to infer that such proselytism as they engaged in arose in the main from a jealous party-spirit. Certain it is that this main line of Jewish life represented by Rabbinism paid very little regard to the universalistic ideals represented in the Old Testament, and became eventually so self-centred that even the zeal for proselytism faded away.[2]

(3) Before investigating in detail the evidence which goes to show that Jesus recognized and emphasized the duty of Israel to the Gentile world and the Divine intention that the Gentiles should participate in the blessings of the Kingdom, we shall do well to take account of three inherent conditions which favourably affected the working of his mind in this connexion.

The first of these is the universalism of the Old Testament. We cannot be at all sure that he knew anything of the late Jewish non-canonical literature produced in the Diaspora for the purpose of reconciling the Gentile world to Judaïsm, or

---

[1] *Pirke Aboth*, i. 12 (in Danby, *Mishnah*, 447).

[2] On the whole question of Jewish universalism, the universal mission, and the proselytes, see Hirsch in *J.E.* x (1905) 220–224 ; P. Wendland, *Hellenistisch-römische Kultur* (1907), 118 ; Schürer, *G.J.V.* ii. 593–596, 629–632, iii. 3, 150–188 (esp. 162ff.), 422f., 573 ; Harnack, *Mission*, etc. i. 16–18 ; Meyer, *Ursprung*, ii. 17–28, 34, 353–357 ; Strack-Billerbeck i. 182, 368–371, 924–931, ii. 538f., 703–705, 728, iii. 98–105, 144, 150–152, iv. 883 ; A. Causse, *Israël et la Vision de l'Humanité* (1924), passim ; Merrill, *Essays in Early Christ. Hist.* (1924), 41 n. 2 (a plea for caution in estimating the extent of Jewish propagandism) ; Bousset, *Relig. des Jud.* (1926), 53–56, 60f., 72–96 ; C. J. Cadoux in *E.T.* xxxviii. 55f. (Nov. 1926) ; Montefiore, *S.G.*[2] I. cxiv, II. 36, 481 ; Moore, *Judaism*, i. 226–231, 323–353, 399f., 528f., iii. 107–114 ; Georg Rosen, *Juden und Phönizier. Das antike Judentum als Missionsreligion und die Erstehung der jüdischen Diaspora* (Tübingen, 1929) ; D. C. Simpson in *H.C.L.M.K.* 143f., 152f., 162f. ; A. Causse in *Rev. d'Hist. et de Phil. religieuses*, 1935, 495–529 ; and most recently H. H. Rowley, *Israel's Mission to the World* (1939), 1–86.

(despite Mt. xxiii. 15 M) that he was very familiar with the propaganda-work being done by the synagogues of the Diaspora generally. But he did know the Old Testament ; and—what is more—he was accustomed to pick and choose among its contents with sovereign freedom, to set passage against passage, to choose one dictum and reject another, with an independence which must have scandalized the conservative Biblicists of his day (see above, pp. 72 [**7**], 79f.). Nor are we without direct evidence of the strong appeal which the universalistic teaching of certain parts of the Old Testament made to him. One section of the Scriptures in which this teaching bulks most largely and is expressed most unmistakably is Deutero-Isaiah, including the Servant-poems (see above, p. 148) ; and it has been already shown that these passages had special significance for him as foreshadowing his own career (see above, pp. 37f.).[1] It is inconceivable that he could have quoted and re-echoed these passages as he did, had he not been deeply impressed by the universalism that animates them. Not only so : but, as we shall see when we come to consider his own sayings in detail, several of them, including some of the least ambiguous, include a fairly-direct appeal to some universalistic passage in the Old Testament.[2]

(**4**) A second condition prompting in Jesus' mind the thought that the Gentiles lay within his province was the traditional belief that to the Messiah of Israel worldwide dominion had been promised by God. Jesus knows himself to be the Messiah of Israel ; and one of the Temptations which as Messiah he has at the outset of his Ministry to face is the temptation to seize lordship over all the kingdoms of the world by military conquest (Lk. iv. 5–8 = Mt. iv. 8–10 Q). If the interpretation of this episode which I have given below (pp. 169f. [**9**]) be true, it follows that Jesus regarded worldwide dominion, acquired somehow, but not by force of arms, as his rightful lot. Such a belief of course involved the peaceful inclusion of the Gentile peoples in his plan.

(**5**) A third condition telling in the same direction was the broad general principles on which, as he made it clear, his teaching was based. In this he had been anticipated by John the Baptist. " Do not ", John had said to the crowds, " begin

---

[1] Cf. Manson, *Teaching*, 178–181, 256–260 (Jesus adopts the idea of the *saving* Remnant of the Servant-poems and Deutero-Isaiah, rather than that of the *saved* Remnant of Ezekiel, the choice of Rabbinism being on the whole the other way round).

[2] See below, pp. 153f., and cf., generally, Holtzmann, *Theol.* i. 277, 282 ; Moffatt, *Theol. of the Gospels*, 144 ; and Rowley, as in last n. but one, 76ff.

to say within yourselves, ' We have (got) Abraham (for) our father, (and therefore are safe) '. For I tell you that from these stones God can raise up children for Abraham. Moreover, the axe is already lying at the root of the trees : so every tree that does not produce good fruit will be cut down, and thrown into the fire " (Lk. iii. 8f. = Mt. iii. 9f. Q). It is only natural to suppose that these convictions that mere Jewish nationality would not suffice to secure salvation, and that God's judgment would be based rather on broad ethical considerations, must have been shared by Jesus also.[1] Jesus addresses God in prayer as " Lord of the heaven and of the earth " (Lk. x. 21 = Mt. xi. 25 Q)—an expression clearly inconsistent with any limitation of the Divine interest to Israel. The prayer, " May Thy Will be done, as in heaven, so also on earth " (Mt. vi. 10 M), might be similarly characterized. So too might the phrase, " the field is the world " (Mt. xiii. 38 M) ; only it is almost certainly ungenuine. Jesus' most general ethical injunctions regarding love for one's fellows are couched, not in Jewish, but in broadly human terms. Thus, " As ye wish that *men* should do to you, do ye likewise to them " (Lk. vi. 31 = Mt. vii. 12 Q : Mt. has some insignificant variations). In commenting on the Jewish principle, " Thou shalt love thy neighbour as thyself ", he makes it more than once unmistakably plain that he does not limit the duty of love to relations between fellow-Jews (Lk. vi. 27–36 [Q] = Mt. v. 38–48 [Q + M] ; Lk. x. 25–37 L ; Lk. xxiii. 34 L).[2] His independent attitude to the Law seems to be always determined by general, not by Jewish principles : thus, " The Sabbath was made for man, not man for the Sabbath ; . . " (Mk. ii. 27 : cf. also Mk. ii. 28 = Lk. vi. 5 = Mt. xii. 8, and see above, pp. 75f. [12] and 95 [8]). His twice-recorded quotation of Hosea's words, " I desire mercy, and not sacrifice " (Mt. ix. 13a M ; Mt. xii. 7 M : Hosea vi. 6), even if we understand them to mean—as we probably should, in accordance with the Biblical idiom (see below, p. 202 n. 2)—" I desire mercy *more than* sacrifice ", advocates a simple ethical, rather than a Jewish ritualistic, basis for the service of God. It must not, of course, be hastily assumed that, because Jesus enunciated principles which presupposed universalism, he consciously and explicitly drew all the practical inferences which they logically

---

[1] Cf. Holtzmann, *Theol.* i. 277–280 ; Manson, *Teaching,* 272–275.
[2] The fact that some Rabbis maintained that love should be shown to the resident foreigner (the גר : Moore, *Judaism*, i. 116) does not obliterate the broad distinction between " brother " or " neighbour " and " Gentile ", which dominates the paragraph Mt. v. 43–48 (see esp. verse 47).

implied. But when, as in his case, the logical implication has not one basis but three, and when it is accompanied by a certain amount of evidence to the effect that it *was* realized and implemented, then the significance of it becomes unmistakable.

(**6**) In collecting the best-attested universalistic utterances of Jesus, it may be convenient to take first those which include some appeal to the universalistic element in the Old Testament. It so happens that there is one of these in each of our three best sources, Q, Mk, and L.

Q reports Jesus' offer of " the sign of Jonah " as the only concession he would make to the Scribes' and Pharisees' request for a sign (Lk. xi. 16, 29 = Mt. xii. 38f. = Mt. xvi. 1, 2a, 4 : curiously enough, Mk. [viii. 11–13] has the request, and Jesus' refusal of it, unqualified by any mention of Jonah). But what *was* the sign of Jonah ? Clearly not what is given in the next verse in Mt. (xii. 40), which draws a very unreal parallel between Jonah's three days in the belly of the whale and the Son of Man's three days in the tomb—a clearly-unhistorical Christian fancy provided by M or m. The parallel in Lk. (xi. 30), however, looks original, and probably gives us the real wording of Q : " For as Jonah became a sign to the Ninevites, so will the Son of Man also be a sign to this generation ". The repentance of the Ninevites at Jonah's preaching (like the Queen of Sheba's interest in Solomon's wisdom) is in the immediate sequel held up as a reproach to Jesus' unresponsive contemporaries, seeing that he brings them something that is more than Solomon or Jonah (Lk. xi. 31f. = Mt. xii. 41f. Q). Now Jonah is the only prophet of the Old Testament who is said to have been sent with a warning and saving message to Gentiles : and the choice of him as a sign is therefore indicative of the inclusive range of Jesus' appeal, just as the allusions to the Ninevites' repentance and the Queen of Sheba's docility are indicative of his hopes for the Gentile world.[1]

Mark reports that, when Jesus had driven the traders out of the Temple-courts, he ' began to teach and to say, " Has it not been written, ' My house shall be called a house of prayer for all the nations ' ? But ye have made it a cave of robbers ! " ' (Mk. xi. 17 : the words quoted are the post-Exilic passage, Isa. lvi. 7). The fact that the Lucan and Matthæan parallels

---

[1] Cf. Liberty, *Political Relations*, 88–90 (strangely accepts the genuineness of Mt. xii. 40) ; Rawlinson, *St. Mark*, 257 (misses the point) ; A. T. Cadoux, *Parables*, 113–115.

(Lk. xix. 46 = Mt. xxi. 13) omit the words " for all the nations " does not tell against their originality in Mk. or against the probability that Jesus used them. The Marcan passage shows that he had in mind the late Old-Testament idea of the Temple at Jerusalem being the religious centre of the world (see above, p. 148).[1]

L records that, when preaching in the synagogue at Nazareth, Jesus provoked his audience into expelling him in anger, by saying to them, " Truly I tell you, there were many widows in the days of Elijah in Israel, when the heaven was closed for three years and six months, when a great famine came over the whole land ; and (yet) to none of them was Elijah sent, but to Zarephath in the (land) of Sidon to a widow. And there were many lepers in Israel in (the time of) Elisha the prophet ; and (yet) none of them was cleansed, but only Naaman the Syrian " (Lk. iv. 25–27 L). The precise interpretation of this utterance is not free from difficulty, for the immediately-preceding context does not allude to the antithesis between Jews and Gentiles, but to the difficulty felt by the Jews of Nazareth in honouring their fellow-townsman as a prophet, particularly as he was not doing in Nazareth the great works he had done in Kapharnaum, presumably among the Jewish inhabitants there. The quasi-parallels in Mk. vi. 1–6 = Mt. xiii. 53–58 do not help us.[2] Still, Jesus would not have alluded in this pointed way to the Phœnician widow and the Syrian captain, had he not felt that his redemptive work (Lk. iv. 18f., 21 L) had some direct relation to Gentile need.

Turning now to well-attested universalistic sayings of Jesus, in which no reference to the Old Testament is made, we may note first the reassuring words he addressed, after hesitation, to the Syro-Phœnician women, who had begged him to cure her daughter—" For saying this, go thy way : the demon has gone out of thy daughter " (Mk. vii. 29), or " O woman, great is thy faith. May it happen to thee as thou wishest ! " (Mt. xv. 28 M ?).[3]

---

[1] Cf. Major in *Mission*, etc. 142.

[2] Cf. Wellhausen, *Lc.* 10 ; Montefiore, *S.G.*[2] II. 398f. ; Lightfoot, *Hist. and Interp.* 203f.

[3] We never hear of Jesus preaching directly to Gentiles : on the contrary, much of his public speaking rather clearly implies their absence (see above, pp. 140–142). On the other hand, there were clearly many of them about in Galilee and elsewhere in Palestine ; and when Jesus was speaking, not in the synagogues, but in the open air, it is natural to suppose that Gentiles were sometimes among his hearers. Mt. xv. 31 m (or M ?) even implies that his healings (of Gentile sufferers ?) on one occasion caused a Gentile crowd to " glorify the God of Israel " ; but the trustworthiness of the statement is doubtful (see above, p. 139 bott.).

Next come a couple of utterances contained in Q. When Jesus was on his way to cure the Gentile Centurion's servant at Kapharnaum, and had received his deprecating message (see above, pp. 63f.), he exclaimed, " I tell you, not even in Israel have I found such great faith " (Lk. vii. 9 = Mt. viii. 10 Q). It is true that the Centurion was friendly to Judaïsm, and had built the Jews of Kapharnaum a synagogue, and that on this account he has been thought to have been a proselyte of some grade : on the other hand, the narrative is silent as to any such status, and the words " not even in Israel " are against it.[1]

The second Q-passage runs as follows in Lk. : " There there will be weeping and gnashing of teeth, when ye see Abraham and Isaac and Jacob and all the Prophets in the Kingdom of God and yourselves thrown outside. And men will come from east and west and from north and south, and will recline at table in the Kingdom of God. And behold ! there are (some) last who will (then) be first, and there are (some) first who will (then) be last " (Lk. xiii. 28–30). The Matthæan version of all but the last sentence of this passage (Mt. viii. 11f.) appears immediately after the Matthæan account of the Centurion's faith ; this was probably not its original place in Q, but the choice of it shows that the compiler of Mt. saw the common significance of both passages. The wording and the sequence of clauses in Mt. differ a little from those in Lk. ; but the differences are not important, except for the phrase " the sons of the Kingdom " used in Mt. instead of Lk's. " you " (or " yourselves "). Mt's. parallel to Lk's. last clause is found in Mt. xix. 30, based on Mk. x. 31 and repeated by m in Mt. xx. 16. But there is little doubt that Lk's. grouping is right. The saying is unambiguously universalistic. Those (in Mt. " many ") who come from east and west, etc., are clearly Gentiles : they cannot be Jews of the Dispersion, for these, as Jews, are already included among " the sons of the Kingdom ", some at least of whom are to be expelled (see above, pp. 141f. [6]). Similarly with those whose positions as respectively first and last are to be reversed.[2]

The two passages from Q are followed by two from M. The first of these—Mt. v. 13–16—is of great importance. It runs as follows : (13) " Ye are the salt of the earth ! But if the salt gets spoilt, with what can it be salted ? It is no longer fit for

---

[1] Cf. Flew, *Church*, 86 with note.

[2] Cf. Harnack, *Mission*, etc. i. 40 ; Easton, *The Gospel before the Gospels* (1928), 103 ; Montefiore, *S.G.*[2] II. 358 ; Creed, *St. Luke*, 186a.

anything, except to be cast out and trodden down by men. (14) Ye are the light of the world ! A city placed on a mountain(-top) cannot be hidden : (15) nor do men light a lamp and put it under the two-gallon measure ; but (they put it) on the lampstand, and it shines on all who are in the house. (16) Let your light so shine before men, that they may see your good works, and glorify your Father in the heavens ". The precise documentary origin and character of this Matthæan passage are very puzzling. It is clearly, as it stands, a unity ; but is its unity original ? Mt. v. 13 has a fairly-close parallel in Lk. xiv. 34 (which lacks however the opening phrase, " Ye are the salt of the earth ") and a very rough parallel in Mk. ix. 50. Mt. v. 14 has no canonical parallel, and reappears only as part of one of the Oxyrhynchus Sayings of Jesus.[1] Mt. v. 15 has a fairly-close parallel in Lk. xi. 33, and another in Mk. iv. 21 = Lk. viii. 16. Finally, Mt. v. 16 is unparalleled. One may well hesitate, therefore, to acclaim the whole passage, Mt. v. 13–16, as a well-attested version of a single piece of Jesus' teaching : it might be argued that it was a cento of detached sentences from Q and Mk. combined, unified, and embroidered by the editor of M.[2] On the other hand, when we take account of the undoubted fact (here illustrated) that independent versions of the same saying did exist in different sources, and of the probability that Jesus at times repeated portions of his teaching, it can be plausibly argued that Mt. v. 13–16 is a reliable version of a single piece of teaching. That view is supported also by the fitness of the contents to the conditions under which his teaching was given. For while the final compiler of the Gospel probably thought, as most Christians think to-day, that the words were addressed to some little group of faithful disciples Jesus had gathered round him, and so to the Christian community as such, there can be little doubt that they were originally directed to Israel as a people (see pp. 140f., esp. n. 3). " The earth " of which Israel is to be the salt is the earth inhabited mainly by Gentiles ; " the world " of which it is to be the light is the Gentile world (cf. Isa. xlix. 6) ; the " men " before whom its works are to shine are the as-yet unconverted Gentiles. So understood, the words harmonize admirably with the rest of Jesus' early message, and express his sympathetic grasp of the universalism found in the Old Testament.[3]

[1] See Preuschen, *Antilegomena*, 23 (6) ; James, *Apocr. N.T.* 27 (xii).
[2] So B. T. D. Smith, *Parables*, 45.
[3] Cf. Simkhovitch, *Understanding of Jes.* 51 ; A. T. Cadoux, *Parables*, 80–83, 111 ; Dodd, *Parables*, 139–146.

The second passage from M is the description of the Last Judgment in Mt. xxv. 31–46, wherein " all the Gentiles " (lit. " nations ", xxv. 32) are judged. Those of them who have shown kindness to Jesus' followers are admitted to the Kingdom ; those who have not are dismissed into eternal punishment. This does not tell us much, for nothing is said about Jews who did not follow Jesus, or about Gentiles who never came in contact with his followers : nor, indeed, does the trustworthiness of the passage itself, as a transcript of something that Jesus actually said, rank very high. Still it may stand as another, though minor, indication that Jesus anticipated for the Gentiles a share in the blessings of the future Kingdom.

Of only indirect and slight significance as disproving any consistently-narrow Judaïsm in Jesus are his appreciative references to Samaritans, namely, in the Parable of the Good Samaritan (Lk. x. 29–37 L) (unless we accept the view of some that, in the original form of the Parable, the merciful passer-by was just a lay Israelite), and in his allusion to the gratitude of the cured Samaritan leper (Lk. xvii. 15–18 L).[1]

(7) When once the main fact of Jesus' interest in the Gentiles is established, it is natural to suspect that it is expressed or hinted at in passages which do not refer to it quite explicitly. This interpretation, for instance, has been put upon the Parables of the Mustard-Seed (Lk. xiii. 18f. = Mt. xiii. 31f. Q : also Mk. iv. 30–32),[2] of the Leaven (Lk. xiii. 20 = Mt. xiii. 33 Q),[3] of the Great Feast (Lk. xiv. 16–24 Q ? : cf. Mt. xxii. 1–10 Q + m ?),[4] of the Lost Sheep and the Lost Coin (Lk. xv. 4–10 Q or L : Mt. xviii. 12–14 Q or M),[5] and of the Labourers hired to work in the Vineyard (Mt. xx. 1–16 M).[6] These are all well-attested sayings : but that Jesus really did intend them to be hints in the interests of what we are calling universalism —although that interpretation is possible and even in some cases quite probable—must remain uncertain. The same applies to the cryptic saying about the Temple being destroyed, and rebuilt in three days (see above, pp. 76f. [15]), and even to the echoes of Isa. liii. 11f. in " the many " of Mk. x. 45 = Mt.

---

[1] Cf. Holtzmann, *Synopt.* 392f. ; Harnack, *Mission*, etc. i. 41f. n. 5 ; Montefiore, *S.G.*[2] II. 465–468, 545 (" The tenth typifies the conversion and salvation of the Gentiles ").

[2] Cf. Manson, *Teaching*, 133 n. 1 ; B. T. D. Smith, *Parables*, 28f. n. 3, 120f.

[3] Cf. A. T. Cadoux, *Parables*, 104f.

[4] Cf., e.g., Manson, in *Mission*, etc. 422.

[5] Dodd, *Parables*, 120 n. 1.

[6] See below, pp. 177f.

xx. 28 and Mk. xiv. 24 = Mt. xxvi. 28,[1] for, although Isa. lii. 13—liii. 12 is probably (like others of the Servant-poems) universalistic in interest, it cannot be regarded as quite certain that " the many " of Isa. liii. 11f. are meant to be the Gentiles. A possible view would be that in the foregoing passages Jesus was subconsciously implying, but not deliberately expressing, the universalism of his scheme.

The Mission of the Seventy-two recorded in Lk. x. 1–20 L (+ M) is often treated as a hint at the universal range of Jesus' interest, seventy-two (or seventy—the readings vary) being the traditional Jewish number of the Gentile races of the world.[2] But there are serious reasons for believing that the narrative is an unhistorical duplicate of the story of the Mission of the Twelve ; and in any case the *number* is the only hint given, the Missionaries are not sent to the Gentiles, nor do their instructions contain any suggestion that these latter are to be appealed to.

In Mk. xiii. 10 = Mt. xxiv. 14a (not a part of " the Little Apocalypse ") Jesus is stated to have said that " the Gospel " will (presumably in the fairly-near future) " be proclaimed to all the nations " ; and in Mk. xiv. 9 = Mt. xxvi. 13, he is made to refer to " the Gospel " being " proclaimed throughout the world ". In view, however, of the facts adduced above, pp. 142f., we have no option but to infer that these Marcan reports are, at least in their present form, historically dubious, on the same grounds as we must so adjudge the explicit injunction of a world-mission ascribed to the Risen Jesus in Lk. (xxiv. 47 L) and Mt. (xxviii. 19 M or m).[3] m's allusion to Gentiles in Mt. x. 18, as those to whom persecuted Christians will bear testimony, is an obvious gloss (contrast Mk. xiii. 9 fin. = Lk. xxi. 13) : true, the " governors and kings " of the context are doubtless thought of mainly as Gentiles, only they are persecutors, not converts.

(8) We may conclude our presentation of the evidence for Jesus' universalism by referring to a group of passages in which any real reference to Gentiles is not more than a bare possibility (see, however, below, p. 162). These are :—Mk. i. 17 =

---

[1] Mr. M. Kiddle has argued in *J.T.S.* xxxv. 45–50 (Jan. 1934) that Mark intended to set forth Jesus' death as the great condition for the admission of Gentiles to the Kingdom.

[2] Cf. Schürer, *G.J.V.* ii. 406 n. 42 ; Montefiore, *S.G.*[2] II. 460 : per contra, Manson in *Mission*, etc. 549.

[3] Cf. Harnack, *Mission*, etc. i. 36–43 : per contra, J. B. Mayor in *Expos*, VII. viii. 385–399 (Nov. 1909) ; W. Hobhouse, *The Church and the World* (1910), 348–350, and Max Meinertz, *Jesus und die Heidenmission* (1908, 1925).

Mt. iv. 19, cf. Lk. v. 10 L (" fishers of men ") ; Lk. vii. 31f. =
Mt. xi. 16f. Q (children in the market-place, etc.) ; Lk. vii. 35
= Mt. xi. 19 fin. Q (Wisdom vindicated) ; [1] Lk. xii. 47f. L
(slave who knew not his master's will, etc.) ; Lk. xiv. 7–10 L
+ Lk. xiv. 11 = Mt. xxiii. 12 Q (against self-advancement at
a feast) ; [2] Lk. xv. 11–32 L (Prodigal Son and his Elder
Brother) ; Lk. xvii. 32 L or Q ? (" Remember Lot's wife ") ; [3]
Lk. xix. 20–26 L, cf. Mt. xxv. 18, 24–30 M (Parable of a
Servant who hid his master's money instead of getting interest
on it) ; [4] and Mt. xvii. 24–27 M (the Temple-tax).[5]

(9) It must, of course, not be forgotten that all this material
incorporated in the Synoptic Gospels was incorporated in them
at a time when there had long ceased to exist—in the circles in
which they were written and read—any question as to the
worldwide scope of the Christian Gospel. The Synoptists,
that is to say, all believed that the Gospel proclaimed by
Christ was intended by him for Gentile and Jew alike. The
universalism of Mk.—a gospel written at Rome about 66/67
A.D.—is revealed by its apparent lack of interest in Jesus'
Davidic descent (see above, p. 85 [7]) and in his fulfilment
of prophecy : the author doubtless intends the cry of the
Gentile centurion at Jesus' death, " Truly this man was God's
Son ! " (Mk. xv. 39), to be understood as a full acknowledgement of Jesus' Divine Lordship, and to suggest and typify
the conversion of the Gentiles to Christianity.[6] The universalism of Luke comes out, not only in the broad humanism of
his narrative, (e.g., his characteristic interest in Samaritans,
women, the poor, etc.),[7] but in certain touches in his birth-
stories—Lk. ii. 1 (the story related to world-history : cf. Lk.
iii. 1f. l), ii. 14 (εἰρήνη ἐν ἀνθρώποις εὐδοκίας, i.e., Christians

---

[1] A. T. Cadoux, *Parables*, 30–32, 109–111 (the sitting children = Jews, who
laid down unfairly-hard conditions of conversion for the Gentiles : Lk. vii. 35
= Mt. xi. 19 fin. [i.e., the Gentiles to be won by Jewish example, not words]
forms the true continuation and explanation of the parable about the
children).

[2] A. T. Cadoux, *Parables*, 95f. (individual application unethical and therefore improbable : the " parable " [Lk. xiv. 7] refers to Israel's sense of
deserving primacy of honour among the nations).

[3] A. T. Cadoux, *Parables*, 112f. (a detached saying, in its wrong place,
warning Jews against gloating over the Divine judgment on Gentiles).

[4] A. T. [Cadoux, *Parables*, 105–109 (Jewish defence of narrowness on
plea of purity not sincere, for Jews do not do what they might to help
Gentiles).

[5] A. T. Cadoux, *Parables*, 167f. (Jesus' comment a protest against Jewish
religious nationalism). But cf. McNeile, *St. Matthew*, 258b (Jesus' comment
so anti-Jewish that the genuineness of the report is dubious).

[6] Cf. Rawlinson, *St. Mark*, 238.

[7] Cf. Meyer, *Ursprung*, i. 301f.

[?]), ii. 32 (" a light for a revelation to the Gentiles " : cf. Lk. iii. 6 l)—and in his carrying-back of Jesus' genealogy to Adam (Lk. iii. 38 L) : he too has been thought to have purposely inserted in his Passion-narrative a hint at the conversion of the Gentiles in the story of the penitent brigand (Lk. xxiii. 39–43 L). The universalism of the markedly-Jewish Mt. appears in the genealogy of Jesus with which this gospel opens, explicitly mentioning as it does the Gentile women Rahab and Ruth (Mt. i. 5 M or m), in its account of the visit of the astrologers from the east (Mt. ii. 1–12 M or m), in its specification of the scene of Jesus' early ministry as " Galilee of the Gentiles " (Mt. iv. 15 m, quoting Isa. ix. 1), in its quotation of certain phrases about the Gentiles from one of the Servant-poems as fulfilled by Jesus (Mt. xii. 18, 21 m, quoting Isa. xlii. 1, 4—see also above, p. 154 n. 3), and, of course, its ascription to the Risen Lord of an injunction to " make disciples of all the nations " (Mt. xxviii. 19 M or m).

We should therefore expect the Synoptists to admit to their records of Jesus' teaching as much as they could find that was universalistic in tone, especially as they have included on the whole a good deal which (at least at first sight) seems hard to reconcile with it. It would, however, be a mistake to infer that the whole of the universalism ascribed to him was the creation of the early Church : inherent probability and the character of the documentary sources warrant us in treating both aspects of the recorded teaching as going back to Jesus himself, though doubtless caution is necessary in view of the natural tendency of later hands to emphasize the universalistic elements.

(10) What then are we to make of this strange two-sidedness in Jesus' outlook ? There is, I believe, no single formula which will completely harmonize both sides, and show his attitude throughout to have been uniform and fully self-consistent. In particular, we moderns must resist the temptation to set the Judaïsm of Jesus aside as in some way unreal. His particularistic feelings are not to be explained away as if they were simply assumed ; his hesitation over the request of the Syro-Phœnician woman for his help (Mk. vii. 26–29 = Mt. xv. 23–28) is much better explained as due to a genuine if temporary tension in his mind, than as a pose assumed in order to try the good woman's faith. Nor can it be proved that he abandoned all his particularistic leanings before the end of his ministry (see, e.g., Lk. xxii. 30 L : cf. Mt. xix. 28b M). Even to the last, he probably never anticipated that the great distinction

between Israel and the other nations was to be abolished.[1] It is even arguable that—just as he apparently never arrived at a fully-consistent theory of the authority of Scripture (see above, p. 80)—so he never arrived at a complete logical synthesis between his Jewish loyalties and his worldwide sympathies. He was clearly aware at times—for instance, when he was appealed to by the Syro-Phœnician woman—of the tension between the two; and his hesitation at that juncture indicates that, at least in the matter of practical application, he was not prepared with a thought-out means of solving the tension. How far, if at all, was the same unpreparedness present in his theoretical attitude to the antithesis?

(11) Although no synthesis is made explicit and clear in the Gospel-reports of what Jesus said, we do not need to look very far for a partial solution, which—being clearly set forth in certain parts of the Old Testament, particularly in those parts which we know him to have applied to himself (see above, pp. 37f., 148, 150f.)—can never have been very far below the surface of consciousness in his own mind. I refer, of course, to the hope and desire that Israel should bring the knowledge of the true God to the Gentile peoples, and should prevail upon them to serve Him aright. With no intention of reading into the Gospels what is not there, we are yet surely warranted in supposing that this great ideal did not escape his notice when he pondered the words of Scripture. The supposition enables us to understand (what is otherwise inexplicable) the juxtaposition of strongly - Judaïstic and strongly - universalistic sentiments in his speech. We shall never know the precise extent to which he consciously pre-figured to himself the actual process of the conversion of the Gentiles, or consciously thought-out the inter-relations between that conversion and the primacy of Israel : but the evidence we have studied in this chapter puts it beyond reasonable doubt that the ideal of Israel as God's instrument for the salvation of the whole world was an integral part of his faith, and that plans for its realization formed an integral part of his own enterprise. Not only so, but this supposition is the only hypothesis which accounts for the striking fact that, notwithstanding all the Jewish limits within which he worked, the movement which he started developed rapidly into a world-religion, and gave him—for

[1] I think Holtzmann exaggerates in contending that Jesus' religious individualism " schliesst jeden Partikularismus grundsätzlich aus ", and that his beginning with the Jews was " nur eine geographische Beschränkung " (*Theol.* i. 278).

every serious student of the past—a place of greater significance in the history of mankind than is held by any other of whom human record tells.

(12) Such being the case, we may perhaps venture a step further, and offer a conjectural explanation for the comparative unobtrusiveness of Jesus' universalistic teaching. Assuming it to be made out that such teaching was an essential part of what he was concerned to convey, we should probably be right in supposing that, had he been noticeably indifferent to the nationalistic way in which Jews looked at things, he would probably have forfeited his power to impress individual Jews, whereas, had he openly and explicitly proclaimed his full mind in his public addresses, he would probably have roused such violent antipathy among his fellow-countrymen as would have lost him all further chance of getting a hearing (see Acts xxii. 21–23). He therefore confined himself to purely-occasional thrusts and to that parabolic teaching which was his peculiar method of controversy—a method which evoked the consent of the listeners before they fully realized what was involved in their consent. If that be a reasonable supposition, it would add to the probability that several of Jesus' ambiguous parables and parabolic sayings may contain universalistic teaching under a more or less subtle disguise.[1] It is significant that, until towards the end of his life (see below, p. 252), Jesus never seems to have so far offended the particularistic prejudices of his fellow-countrymen as to make the matter a cause of controversy between himself and them.[2]

[1] Cf. Winstanley, *Future*, 72–76 ; A. T. Cadoux, *Parables*, 89–91 ; and see above, pp. 157–159 (7 and 8).

[2] Further, regarding the universalism of Jesus, cf. Friedrich Spitta, *Jesus und die Heidenmission* (Giessen, 1909) ; J. B. Mayor in *Expos.* VII. viii. 385–399 (Nov. 1909) ; Holtzmann, *Theol.* i. 274–283 ; C. J. Cadoux in *E.T.* xxxviii. 136–140 (Dec. 1926) ; Easton, *The Gospel before the Gospels* (1928), 102–109 ; H.-D. Wendland, *Eschatologie*, 54–57 ; Goguel in *Rev. d'Hist. et de Phil. religieuses*, 1932, 193–211 (' Jésus et les origines de l'universalisme chrétien ').

CHAPTER VI

THE POLITICAL SIGNIFICANCE OF THE KINGDOM

(1) It is inherently probable that Jesus concerned himself with the political condition of the Israel of his time ; (2) for, as Messiah, his rôle was a distinctly-national one, (3) and— since he hoped at first to be accepted by the nation, (4) and thought of God's Kingdom as destined to come *on earth*— (5) he could hardly have ignored the grave political plight of his people, namely, their subjection to a foreign power. (6) He must have taken up some definite attitude, positive or negative, to the general expectation that the Messiah would crush the Gentile oppressors ; (7) and the universalistic element in his teaching makes it most unlikely that he shared that expectation. (8) It is against such a background that we have to consider (9) his refusal at the Temptation to snatch at world-empire, (10) his injunctions about love for enemies, (11) and his advice about paying tribute to Cæsar. (12) We may conclude, therefore, that he wished Israel, not to seek vengeance on Rome, but through humility and reconciliation to become the spiritual and moral guide of the Gentile world generally. (13) This conclusion receives abundant confirmation from the terms in which he spoke of the dire consequences of Israel's rejection of his leadership.

(1) It would be possible to fill a fair-sized note-book with quotations from exegetes of every period and type to the effect that Jesus entirely excluded political affairs from his orbit. The general idea is that he was so wrapt up in expounding purely moral and spiritual truth and in attending to the moral and spiritual needs of the individuals who craved his help that he regarded political matters as of secondary importance, and did not undertake to deal with them in any way. All he would say about the rights or wrongs of Cæsar's rule in Palestine was to bid men give to Cæsar what belonged to Cæsar, and to God what belonged to God. He framed no political programme, enunciated no political principles, and gave no ruling on the legitimacy or otherwise of war.[1]

---

[1] The following are selected from a larger number :—Wendt, *Teaching*, ii. 395f. ; Schweitzer, *Mystery*, 119f. ; Sanday in *Economic Review*, xvi. 390–395

It is perhaps not difficult to account for the prevalence of this negative view.

It has at least a partial justification in the palpable fact that, so far as we know, Jesus never took any personal part in governmental activities, whether local or national, and that it is hard to find any of his recorded sayings (apart from that about tribute to Cæsar) which bears directly on any specific political practice.

It also owes something to men's proneness to think of Jesus only in the light of his worldwide and eternal significance. What should one who came to speak to men " the words of eternal life " have to do with petty political questions of presumably only temporary and local importance ? The unwillingness to believe that Jesus enunciated any specific ethical laws (see above, pp. 118f.) is another expression of the same attitude.

Furthermore, it has become increasingly customary among Protestant Christians since 1660 to regard political questions (except in so far as these affected religious liberty) as no concern of the Christian Church. The principle behind the cry, " No politics in the pulpit ! ", reflects this widespread feeling ; and the Church, concentrating on the conversion and edification of individuals, got into the habit of letting politics take their own course. That is not so much the case to-day : but it was sufficiently part of the atmosphere in which most Gospel-students of the past did their work to render them predisposed to attribute to Jesus the same limitation of interest.

Reasons will be given in the remaining parts of this chapter for believing that, despite his apparent detachment from practical political activity, Jesus was very far from being unconcerned with certain larger political questions which radically affected the life of the nation of Israel. At the moment it is sufficient to observe that the cleavage which Protestantism learnt to make between religion and politics is largely a modern device—Luther would doubtless have approved of it up to a point, but Calvin would have scouted it, while it would have been simply unintelligible to an Old-

(Oct. 1906) ; Holtzmann, *Theol.* i. 275f. ; Meyer, *Ursprung*, ii. 445 ; Easton, *Christ in the Gospels*, 132 ; Troeltsch, *Social Teaching of the Christian Churches* (1931), i. 59, ii. 803, 817 ; Goguel, *Life of Jes.* 377, 402f., 569 ; Mackinnon, *Historic Jesus*, 49, 57, 105f., 110, 176, 183f., 321f. ; Cadbury, *Peril*, 129f. ; B. T. D. Smith, *Parables*, 77 ; R. Niebuhr, *An Interp. of Christ. Ethics* (1937), 49 ; Hempel, *Politische Absicht und politische Wirkung im biblischen Schrifttum* (1938), 7, 45f. Sharman (*Future*, 103–106, 109) draws attention to the ' Absence of Political Background from the Gospels ' (in distinction, that is, from the actual thought and words of Jesus).

Testament prophet.[1] That is not to say, of course, that Jesus could not have made such a cleavage, but it creates a presumption against the idea that he did so. And this presumption is strengthened by the fact, more and more being recognized by scholars, that the universal and eternal significance of his Ministry was attained by way of, not by the exclusion of, his interest in and attention to the special and concrete concerns of his contemporaries (see above, pp. 15f.).

There is therefore a very good primâ-facie case for asking whether the prevalent assumption may not be incorrect, and whether there may not have been after all some real political significance in Jesus' Gospel of the Kingdom.[2]

(2) See above, pp. 138f. (3).

(3) See below, pp. 183–193.

(4) If Jesus then, a national Messiah expecting Israel to accept him as such, had any political views or plans at all, they must have been in some way integrally related to his views and plans regarding the Kingdom of God. Such relation becomes even more certain and more intelligible when we remember, not only that he believed (as we have seen above, pp. 128–133) the Kingdom to be already present on earth in his own person and work, but also that he expected the future "coming" of it to which he looked forward (see above, pp. 133f., and below, pp. 194ff.) to be brought about on earth also. The latter statement is in the first place strongly suggested by the former : the natural arena for the completion of a process is the arena of its inception and its continuance. But we are not limited to such presumption. When Jesus said, "Truly I tell you that there are some here of those standing (round me) who will certainly not taste death until they see that the Kingdom of God has come with power " (Mk. ix. 1 = Lk. ix. 27 = Mt. xvi. 28), by far the most natural interpretation

[1] Cf. Hempel, as in last note, passim.
[2] Several writers have made contributions of a positive kind to this problem. See, e.g., D. S. Cairns in *Contemp. Review*, lxxix. 195–211 (Feb. 1901) ; H. Weinel, *Die Stellung des Urchristentums zum Staat* (1908) ; Sharman, *Future* (1909), 106–109, 114 (7) ; S. Liberty, *The Political Relations of Christ's Ministry* (1916), e.g., 44f. ; J. R. Coates, *The Christ of Revolution* (1920), 9–16 ; Lily Dougall in *Hibbert Journ.* xx. 113–123 ('The Salvation of the Nations' : Oct. 1921), and in *The Lord of Thought* (1922), 120–122, 136–153, 177 ; V. G. Simkhovitch, *Towards the Understanding of Jesus* (1923) ; E. Grubb in *E.T.* xxxiv. 214–217 (Feb. 1923) ; S. Dickey, *The Constructive Revolution of Jesus* (1923), 13–38, 85–114 ; Bacon, *Matthew* (1930), 422–425 ; Montefiore in *Hibbert Journ.* xxx. 301–306, 312f., 318 (Jan. 1932) ; C. J. Cadoux in *Congreg. Quart.* xiv. 58–67 (Jan. 1936) ; L. Curtis, *Civitas Dei*, i (1934), 138–142, 157–182 ; H. P. Kingdon in *Hibbert Journ.* xxxv. 556–567 ('Had the Crucifixion a political significance ? ' : July 1937).

of his words is that the event to be seen will be one occurring on earth. Such, furthermore, is the unmistakable meaning of the prayer he enjoined, " May Thy Kingdom come, may Thy Will be done—as in heaven, (so) also on earth " (Mt. vi. 10 M). True, these last words (" as in heaven " etc.) are not found in the Lucan version of the Lord's Prayer (Lk. xi. 2 L), which (because it is shorter) is usually supposed to be its more primitive form ; but they may nonetheless be genuine, for (a) in the petition for forgiveness the Matthæan form is more primitive than the Lucan ; (b) the parallelisms and generally-rhythmical structure of the Matthæan prayer are in favour of its high antiquity ; and (c), if the original text of Lk. xi. 2 fin. was, as some believe, " May Thy holy Spirit come upon us and cleanse us ",[1] then the Matthæan text has undoubtedly stronger claims to give the more primitive form of the prayer. Taking these several items of evidence together, we seem warranted in inferring that Jesus thought of the future " coming " of the Kingdom (just as he thought of its inception and growth) as taking place *on earth*. Now had he had in mind a successful plan for Israel on earth, it must almost certainly have included some practical solution of Israel's great political difficulty.[2]

(5) We must be careful not to exaggerate the political discontent felt by the Jews of Palestine because they were under the rule of Herodian princes and Roman governors. The Sadducees, for instance, had apparently no complaints to make : they dreaded and opposed any manifestation of ill-will towards the ruling powers as dangerous to the settled order of things (cf. John xi. 47–50). For very different reasons, the Essenes (as essentially quietists) would be equally averse from any overt enmity. In regard to the Romans, indeed, the Jews as a people had in 4 B.C. actually sent a deputation to Augustus, begging that they might be placed under an imperial governor, rather than under the sons of Herod the Great.[3] There were also large numbers of Jews who held that in any case it was Israel's duty not to revolt against the government, but to await redress at the hands of God. Some Pharisees there were who even appreciated the political suzerainty of the

---

[1] Cf. Streeter, *Four Gospels*, 277 : per contra, Burkitt in *J.T.S.* xxvi. 288–290 (Apl. 1925), and Creed, *St. Luke*, 156 ab.

[2] Cf. Holtzmann, *Theol.* i. 249f. ; Shailer Mathews, *Social Teaching of Jes.* (ed. 1910), 70, 73 ; H. T. Andrews in *Congreg. Quart.* v. 266 (July 1927) ; Manson, *Teaching*, 129 (against the genuineness of " Thy Kingdom come . . . ") ; C. C. McCown in *J.R.* xvi (1936) 36, 39, 45f.

[3] Josephus, *Wars*, II. vi, *Antiq.* XVII. xi.

foreigners because it left them the freer for the study of the Law.[1]

But when allowance has been made for all these qualifications, we cannot mistake the strong impression which the Jewish history of the period makes upon us, that the national mind was on the whole in a state of the most profound disquiet at the condition of things as they were. We have already seen with what strong disfavour the Gentiles as such were regarded by Jews, especially in Palestine (see above, p. 137). Yet these Palestinian Jews saw their own holy land defiled by the presence of innumerable Gentile settlements. More than that —politically, Israel was in chains. Instead of having a Jewish monarch of Davidic or even Hasmonæan blood righteously and mightily reigning over them at Jerusalem, they saw one half of the country (Judæa and Samaria) being administered by a Roman Procurator, and the other half (Galilee, Peræa, and the lands north and east of the Sea of Galilee) governed under Roman protection by two sons of the hated Herod. The Romans might attempt to humour Jewish prejudice and administer justice evenhandedly; but the Roman Governors were mostly avaricious, Roman judicial penalties brutally cruel, and the Roman method of suppressing disorder ferocious (e.g., Lk. xiii. 1 L).[2] The Herodian princes might, like their father, make efforts to conciliate Jewish feeling—Philip, in fact, was a really high-principled ruler : but his territory was only sparsely peopled with Jews, and both he and Antipas (tetrarch of Galilee and Peræa) were scions of the " half-Jew " Herod, and freely followed heathen and even idolatrous practices (temple-building, public games, etc.) in order to curry favour with the Roman Emperor and their Gentile subjects, friends, and patrons. Herod Antipas was a despotic voluptuary, who executed John the Baptist to satisfy his step-daughter.

No serious-minded Jew, unless he were a Sadducee or an Essene, could do other than regard the whole situation with profound disgust[3]. He might resignedly submit to it, or—like

[1] Bousset, *Relig. des Jud.* (1926), 58, cf. 431 ; Moore, *Judaism*, i. 77.

[2] Josephus tells us (*Antiq.* XVIII. vi. 5) that Tiberius purposely left his provincial governors in office a long time, out of regard for their subjects, who would otherwise have been fleeced more frequently : he compared them to a wounded man who, to spare himself repeated torment, preferred to let the flies remain on his sores rather than have them driven away. Cf. Strack-Billerbeck i. 153 : " Ferner ist daran zu erinnern, dass alle Völker nach jüdischer Anschauung unter der Leitung von mehr oder weniger gottfeindlichen Engelfürsten stehen, *insonderheit die damalige römische Weltmacht unter der Leitung Sammaëls* (= *Satans*) *selbst* " (italics mine).

[3] Cf. Liberty, *Political Relations*, 11f., 17 ; Simkhovitch, *Understanding of Jes.* 12–19, 25, 49.

the Zealot—he might revolt against it : but in either case, he loathed it, and looked forward longingly to the day when God, in fulfilment of His promises, would break the heathen yoke from off His people's neck, and visit these idolaters with condign and terrible vengeance. There is no need to quote specific pieces of evidence : the pages of Josephus are full of it ; and his picture is amply confirmed by all other trust-worthy witnesses. The sad story reaches its tragic conclusion in the war of 66–71 A.D., which involved the destruction of Jerusalem and its Temple.[1]

Now it is idle to suppose that any person, Messiah or other, who felt charged with a mission to contemporary Israel, a mission to be wrought out on earth, could have blandly ignored this terrible obsession with which the mind of virtually the whole nation in Palestine was seething. To come forward as a national leader, to call as such for national acceptance and obedience, and yet to have no word to say or course to suggest with regard to the biggest practical problem with which the nation was agog, would surely have meant such trifling as we could not, without the strongest evidence, reasonably ascribe to any serious prophet, least of all to such a prophet as Jesus.[2]

(6) There was one further circumstance which made it more than ever impossible for him to ignore the problem in question —the general belief, namely, that the personal instrument of the Divine overthrow and chastisement of the Gentiles would be none other than the Messiah himself.[3] Such a belief could find ample warrant in the Old Testament and—for those who accepted their authority—in the Jewish post-canonical writings : and what sacred writings foreshadowed, present necessity amply justified ; for, according to all accepted ethical standards, an oppressed and enslaved people is fully warranted in rebelling against the tyrant-power that holds it in sub-jection. Even supposing, therefore, that as a mere prophet Jesus might have ignored the national subjection to the Gentiles, it would have been impossible for him to do so as Messiah. He must either have accepted or rejected the Messiah's provi-dential rôle as conqueror of heathendom.

[1] Cf. Simkhovitch, *Understanding of Jes.* 5–11, 26–28. He ascribes the pre-valence of nervous disorders in Palestine in Jesus' day partly to the political tension of the times (30).
[2] Cf. Weinel, *Stellung des Urchrist. zum Staat* (1908), 9 : " Sein ganzes Leben ist ein Kampf mit der politischen Frage seines Volkes gewesen, . . . "
[3] The belief is echoed in Lk. i. 74–79. Cf. Schürer, *G.J.V.* ii. 622–625 ; Meyer, *Ursprung,* i. 164 ; Simkhovitch, *Understanding of Jes.* 34, 69 ; Bousset, *Relig. des Jud.* (1926), 218–222, 228f., 233–236 ; Moore, *Judaism,* i. 400, ii. 332f., 341, 343.

(7) Now we have already seen (above, pp. 150–154) to what a considerable extent Jesus appreciated and appropriated those universalistic passages in the Old Testament (both in the Servant-poems and elsewhere) in which the saving knowledge of Israel's God was thought of as being imparted to the heathen peoples, and further how much else there is in his teaching (see above, pp. 154–159) to attest his eager desire that the Gentiles should enjoy the benefits and blessings of God's Kingdom. It is inconceivable that, alongside of these hopes and desires, he should have contemplated overthrowing and decimating them in a Messianic war. He must have thought of the idea of such a Messianic war—and have thought of it only to reject it.

(8) So far we have been dealing with presumptions, inherent probabilities, and so forth. None of these, of course, has value as direct evidence of how Jesus thought of the Roman supremacy : they have value only as furnishing the context within which we must read the direct evidence, or the background against which we must view it. As context or background these inherent probabilities have very considerable weight : but it is to the *direct* pieces of evidence which the Gospels furnish that we must now turn.

(9) First, then, let us study the story of how, at his Temptation, Jesus felt invited by Satan to receive at his hand " all the kingdoms of the world and the glory of them " on condition of bowing down and worshipping him. He repels the suggestion with the words of Deut. vi. 13, " Thou shalt worship the Lord thy God, and Him only shalt thou serve " (Lk. iv. 5–8 = Mt. iv. 8–10 Q). The story, which probably goes back to the account of the incident given by Jesus himself to the Disciples, is told with all the vivid imagery customary to an Oriental mind : but it is not really difficult to re-interpret it in modern terms. Bowing down and worshipping Satan is probably a poetical equivalent for doing something which is seen to be morally wrong. What was in this case the morally-wrong deed ? Not the desire to sway the Kingdoms of the world, for that was the predicted right of the Messiah, and nothing less than that would have satisfied Jesus' concern for the complete triumph of God's Kingdom under His appointed representative, i.e., under himself. We are therefore compelled to seek the relevant moral iniquity in military conquest, as the most natural, the speediest, and the most direct method of securing world-supremacy. The idea of using that method was bound to occur at some stage to any claimant to the Messiahship ; and even if we had no Temptation-story, we should be warranted in

surmising that it must at some time have occurred to Jesus'
mind (see below, p. 171 n. fin.). But he speedily discerned that
such a method, however natural, would be a moral transgres-
sion, because it would, (a) by involving bloodshed and cruelty,
infringe the law of love for others, and (b), by involving
coercion, defeat his object of convincing and converting
others. His repudiation of the idea meant that he definitely
turned his back on the current expectation of a Messianic
war for the overthrow and punishment of the Gentiles (see above,
p. 151 [4]).

But we must not make the common mistake of treating
" political " and " military " in this connexion as if they were
synonymous. It is often but very inexactly stated that the
Temptation which Jesus here met was a temptation to found a
" worldly " or " political kingdom ". But if by political we
mean that which concerns men in their corporate, national,
and international, as distinct from their individual, relationships, then a political kingdom was exactly what Jesus did
want. He saw and probably resented the injustice and severity
of the Roman administration. All he repudiated was the use
of coercion in acquiring the political sovereignty he desired.
That, no doubt, made a vast difference, but it did not render
his object non-political. Certainly a political kingdom without
arms or coercion was something no one had ever known ; and
so unfamiliar was the idea of it that, because of the military
associations of the royal title, Jesus long kept his claim to
Messianic royalty a secret, and resisted the attempt of a
Galilæan crowd " to take him by force, to make him king "
(John vi. 15, and see above, p. 56 [8]). Even so, it is probable
that Herod Antipas and other opponents of Jesus feared
political trouble. But that Jesus did not surrender the idea of
political power is proved by his acquiescence in the title, " The
King of the Jews ", when at the end of his life he was asked by
Pilate if that was what he claimed to be ; and that his
acquiescence in it was seen to be significant is proved by the
fact that it was the official ground for Pilate's sentence and
was repeatedly recalled during the crucifixion (Mk. xv. 2 =
Mt. xxvii. 11 ; Lk. xxiii. 3 L ; Mk. xv. 9, 12 = Mt. xxvii. 17, 22 ;
Mk. xv. 18 = Mt. xxvii. 29; Mk. xv. 26 = Mt. xxvii. 37 ;
Mk. xv. 32 = Mt. xxvii. 42 ; Lk. xxiii. 37f. L : cf. John xviii.
33f., 37, 39, xix. 3, 14f., 19-22 ; and see above, pp. 59f. [11],
138f. [3]).[1]

---

[1] On re-reading Mr. S. Liberty's *Political Relations of Christ's Ministry*, I
cannot help feeling that his attempt (72) to relate the three Temptations of

On one of the two possible interpretations of Lk. xvi. 16 =
Mt. xi. 12f. Q (see above, pp. 129f.), the words there recorded
as having been spoken by Jesus contained a disapproving
allusion to the Zealots, the " men of force " who seize upon
the Kingdom, i.e., who endeavour to establish the Kingdom
by deeds of violence.

(10) The important section in the Sermon on the Mount
enjoining non-resistance and love for enemies (Lk. vi. 27–36 =
Mt. v. 38–48 Q [+ M ?]) has usually been taken to refer
exclusively to the conduct of individuals in the private
relationships of life.[1] That view resulted from the tacit
assumption that the Sermon was addressed to a small circle
of Jesus' personal disciples (in contradistinction to the rest of
the world, Jewish and Gentile alike : see above, p. 140), and
that Jesus never by any chance made any pronouncement on
the duties of men in their civic or corporate capacity.

There are, however, several grounds for thinking that such
a view is distinctly erroneous. To begin with, the references to
" brothers " (i.e., fellow-Jews—like " neighbour " in Mt. v. 43)
and to " Gentiles " in Mt. v. 47 (references which Luke, writing
for Gentile Christians, disguises—Lk. vi. 32–34) prove conclusively that the speaker is addressing his words, not to any
small group of his personal disciples, but to pious Jews as such
(see above, pp. 140f.). The word used to describe their enemies
—ἐχθροί—might equally well mean either private adversaries
or public national enemies. The " enemies " of average pious
Jews might, it is true, quite conceivably be other Jews, such as
tax-collectors, slave-owners, landlords, etc. : but it is still
more natural to think in this connexion of Gentiles, renegade
Jews, and in particular Roman and Herodian soldiers and
officials. That these latter are in mind is suggested by the
overbearing type of conduct instanced by Jesus : it can hardly
have been customary for a Jew to be struck in the face by his
fellow-Jew : and even if it were, it must have been still more
customary for him to be so treated by the foreign soldier or
courtier. The suggestion is confirmed to the point of certainty
by the allusion to someone who might " compel " (ἀγγαρεύσει)

Jesus (stones, pinnacle, kingdoms) to the national policies and principles of
the Sadducees (59–61), Pharisees (61–68), and Herodians (57, 68–71) respectively, is too far-fetched, and requires too much to be read into the narrative,
to be probable. In particular, I do not share his feeling (57) that a temptation
to try military conquest cannot reasonably be thought to have assailed Jesus.
I confess I am not clear as to the precise significance of the other two temptations (Lk. iv. 2–4, 9–12 = Mt. iv. 2–7 Q) for the interpretation of his mission.
[1] E.g., Rashdall, *Conscience*, 143f.; yet cf. 108–114.

the ordinary Jew " to go one mile " (Mt. v. 41 [M ?]). Here we find introduced the technical term used for the exaction of forced labour from the rank and file of the population at the hands of the military and civil agents of the government : the same verb is used, for instance, in Mk. xv. 21 = Mt. xxvii. 32 (cf. Lk. xxiii. 26 [L ?]) for the action of the Roman soldiers in " compelling " Simon of Cyrene to carry Jesus' cross. While therefore it would probably be wrong to argue that this section of the Sermon has exclusive reference to any one kind or group of wrongdoers, it is on several counts virtually certain that Jesus is here legislating for the conduct of his hearers in their relations with Gentiles or Herodian Jews, especially those who represented either the Roman or the Herodian government, and in that capacity treated the normal Jewish civilian oppressively. Such teaching implies a deliberate view as to the right Jewish attitude to the non-Jewish or semi-Jewish powers that be.[1]

(11) Much difference of opinion exists as to the precise meaning in Jesus' mind when, on being asked whether the payment of tribute to the Roman Emperor was lawful for Jews, he replied, " Give to Cæsar what belongs to Cæsar, and to God what belongs to God " (Mk. xii. 13–17 = Lk. xx. 20–26 = Mt. xxii. 15–22). The words have sometimes been interpreted as if they meant a half-impatient refusal to pronounce on the rightness of Cæsar's rule as a question in which Jesus refused to be entangled : more commonly they have been understood to extend to that rule a certain justification, even if only of a relative and qualified kind.[2] Some modern ethicists have appealed to it as ordaining obedience to almost anything the State may demand of the individual. For our present purpose, we do not need to determine the difficult question whether any—and if so, what—precise theory of governmental authority was meant to be conveyed by the words : it is sufficient to note that Jesus here shows himself to be in favour of the Jews dutifully paying the taxes demanded by the Roman government, while he takes the opportunity to remind them at the same time that they must be no less careful to comply with the demands made upon them by God. If one

---

[1] Cf. Burkitt in *H.C.L.M.K.* 217 = *Jesus Christ*, etc. 21 (" Do not resist, do not fight against evil : there can be little doubt that the primary meaning of this famous utterance is ' Do not rebel against Rome, against the domination of the Gentiles ', . . . "). Per contra, cf. Montefiore, *S.G.*[2] II. 85, and in *Hibbert Journ.* xxviii. 108 (Oct. 1929).

[2] E.g., Liberty, *Political Relations*, 96–101 ; C. J. Cadoux, *The Early Church and the World* (1925), 39f.

asks, What Divine demands in particular is Jesus here thinking of ?, the problem raised by the question put to him (submission or otherwise to the Romans) perhaps warrants the conjecture that he is thinking of the command to love their enemies and to spread the knowledge of God to the Gentile peoples of the world.

(12) The general conclusion to which all the foregoing arguments and pieces of evidence point is this : that it was an integral part of Jesus' plan—a plan which he expected at first would succeed—to prevail on Israel as a people to give up the old yearning for vengeance on Rome and for the defeat and destruction of the Gentiles generally, to submit meekly for the time being to servitude and injustice, and trusting wholly to deeds of love and words of truth, like the Servant of the Lord in Deutero-Isaiah, to undercut pagan hostility, outmanœuvre political domination, convert enemies to friends,[1] and stand forth in the name and power of God as the heralds and teachers of the one true religion, as " a light to them that are in darkness ", as the guides, philosophers, and friends of mankind.[2] " Happy ", indeed, " are the gentle, for they will inherit the earth (Mt. v. 5 M or m) . . . Happy the peace-makers, for they will be called ' sons of God ' " (Mt. v. 9 M). The coming of God's Kingdom on earth involved such healing ministry as this on Israel's part—a zealous, united, and triumphant execution of that mission to heathendon which had been so sporadically and half-heartedly attempted in the course of the few preceding centuries (see above, pp. 148–150). The presence of a Zealot and a tax-collector within the circle of his chosen Disciples fitly reflects in miniature the reconciliation Jesus hoped to effect between the wrath-kindled peoples of the world.

Nor must such an aspiration be hastily pronounced impracticable and quixotic, and therefore probably nothing more than another imaginary modernization of Jesus' story. We know a good deal about human nature ; but we do not know enough about it to brand as " impossible " the loyal submission of the great mass of Palestinian Jews to the leadership of Jesus and

[1] R. Niebuhr (An Interp. of Christ. Ethics [1937], 51, cf. 56f.) describes this work of turning enemies into friends as merely a " social and prudential possibility " which " has been read into the admonition of Jesus by liberal Christianity ". But why may we not assume that, in giving his admonitions, Jesus normally had the natural and beneficent consequences of obedience to them in mind ? The onus probandi surely rests on those who would contend that he did not.

[2] Cf. Sharman, Future, 119f. (11) ; Liberty, Political Relations, 13f., 17, 93–101.

their consequent achievement of such changes in the religious and moral convictions of the heathen world that the decline and corruption of the Dark Ages would have been to a very large extent circumvented.[1]

(13) If any such hope or purpose was actually entertained by Jesus, he must in the nature of things have considered at the same time what would happen if his counsel were rejected. We now know that his counsel was rejected, with the inevitable result that the breach with Rome was never finally healed, and that the irritation thus kept alive finally blazed out in the Jewish revolt of 66–71 A.D., which was suppressed by the Roman legions with unspeakable bloodshed and cruelty. Such indeed was the logical conclusion of the course which Israel chose to follow in preference to the policy for which Jesus had pleaded. As such, it might easily have been foreseen ; and Jesus certainly foresaw it. The repeated and impassioned warnings which in the latter part of his Ministry he uttered concerning the calamities awaiting his disobedient fellow-countrymen, and the unmistakable terms in which most of these warnings are couched, constitute no small confirmation of the theory framed in the foregoing paragraph (see below, pp. 266ff.).

[1] Cf. Bartlet, *St. Mark*, 63f. (" Had the nation as a whole responded to this ' Gospel ' as Jesus at first anticipated, both it and he, ' the Son of man ', would have realized their Divine vocations at first intention. The Kingdom would have come without the need of vicarious suffering to overcome man's sinful reluctance, and so to achieve salvation by ' redemptive ' Love, that is, Grace not only as Divine gift, but as costly sacrifice on the part of God and His own : the way of the Cross would have been spared both Jesus and his true followers— ' the holy remnant ', at once the nucleus of the Messianic Israel and the body of Messiah, as its personal Head ") ; A. T. Cadoux in *The Lord of Life*, 77–80 ; H. G. Wood, *Christianity and the Nature of Hist.* (1934), 105.

CHAPTER VII

THE PRICELESS VALUE OF THE KINGDOM

(1) Jesus was accustomed to describe his proclamation of the Kingdom of God as " good news ". (2) In his Parables of the Treasure and the Pearl, he represented the Kingdom itself as something of supreme value, for the sake of which it was well worth while to surrender everything else. (3) He also compared it to employment and pay offered to out-of-works, (4) and again to a rich feast, to which the poor were freely invited. (5) In one aspect at least the Kingdom is a gift from God. (6) The yoke and the burden which it imposes are light. (7) Unlike the severe and menacing message of John the Baptist, therefore, the message of Jesus was one of comfort ; and the early months of his Ministry were a time of joy.

(1) The word translated " the Gospel " (i.e., " God's spell ") or, more literally, " the good news " (τὸ εὐαγγέλιον), became the standing Christian designation for the Church's message about Jesus Christ as Saviour of men, and the simple title of the books written describing his life, passion, and rising again.[1] Its correlative verb εὐαγγελίζεσθαι, " to give good news " or " to proclaim . . . as good news ", is used in the New Testament with fair frequency to designate the act of delivering the message.   Concerning the use made of these two words by the early Church there is no doubt : but the evidence that Jesus himself used them, though on the whole sufficient to warrant belief, is not so strong as to put the statement beyond question. It is certainly curious that the noun never occurs in Lk., and the verb never in Mk. and Mt.   Since, however, the two are so closely correlative, perhaps little weight can be put on this distinction.

It is possible, though it cannot be proved, that Q represented Jesus as calling his message " good news ".   In Lk. vii. 22 fin. he concludes his list of activities by saying, " the poor have good news given to them " ; but the similar words in the

---

[1] The oldest titles of our Gospels seem to have been εὐαγγέλιον κατὰ Ματθαῖον, κατὰ Λουκᾶν, etc.; but I believe Mk. i. 1 to be an improvised scribal heading to a document of which the original commencement had been lost (see above, p. 85 n.2).

parallel in Mt. xi. 5 are probably no part of the original text : [1] it is possible therefore that in Lk., instead of being drawn from Q, they are the work of l. Again, in Lk. xvi. 16, Jesus is made to say, " The Kingdom of God is proclaimed-as-good-news " ; but the Matthæan parallel (Mt. xi. 12), though it mentions the Kingdom, has nothing about εὐαγγελίζεται, which may therefore belong to l instead of being drawn from Q. L, however, records that at Nazareth, Jesus applied to himself the words of Isaiah lxi. 1, ".The Lord . . . has sent me to give good news to the afflicted " (Lk. iv. 18 L) ; and Mark's version of the opening proclamation of Jesus' Galilæan ministry concludes with the words, " Repent, and believe in the good news " (Mk. i. 15).[2] In four other places in Mk. he is represented as referring to the good news : but two of these we have already had on historical grounds to ascribe in their present form to the early Church rather than to him—Mk. xiii. 10 = Mt. xxiv. 14a, and Mk. xiv. 9 = Mt. xxvi. 13 (see above, pp. 142, 158, and below, pp. 300f.) ; while in the other two places (Mk. viii. 35 = Lk. ix. 24 = Mt. xvi. 25, and Mk. x. 29 = Lk. xviii. 29 = Mt. xix. 29) the reference to "the good news" is rather strangely omitted by the parallels. No authority attaches to the introduction of the verb εὐαγγελίσασθαι by l in Lk. iv. 43 (contrast Mk. i. 38).

The Synoptists themselves speak often enough of the good news being given by Jesus (Mk. i. 14 ; Lk. viii. 1 L ; Lk. xx. 1 l ; Mt. iv. 23 m ; Mt. ix. 35 m)—also by John the Baptist (Lk. iii. 18 l) and by the Disciples (Lk. ix. 6 l) : [3] but this tells us nothing as to Jesus' own use of the term.

The evidence therefore on this latter point cannot be said to be overwhelming ; and the possibility must be left open that the ascription of these terms to Jesus may be due to the language of the Church being tacitly carried back to him by the Evangelists. On the other hand, Mk. and L, witnessing independently, make a fairly strong combination ; and it is perhaps easier to understand the early vogue of the expression if Jesus himself had used it than if he had not used it.[4]

(2) " The Kingdom of the Heavens is like a treasure hidden in the field, which a man found and hid (again) ; and in his joy he goes away, and sells whatever he possesses, and buys

---

[1] A point missed by Kümmel (*Eschatologie*, 10).

[2] The construction of πιστεύω with ἐν is unusual, but not unparalleled : see Swete, *St. Mark*, 13f.

[3] The word is also used in the Birth-Stories—Lk. i. 19, ii. 10.

[4] Cf. N. Schmidt, *Prophet of Naz.* 298f. ; Friedrich in *T.W.N.T.* ii. 715f., 724-726 ; Kümmel, *Eschatologie*, 9-11, and the lit. there quoted.

that field " (Mt. xiii. 44 M). " Again, the Kingdom of the Heavens is like a merchant seeking for pearls ; and when he had found a certain very valuable pearl, he went away, and sold all he possessed and bought it " (Mt. xiii. 45f. M). The man who hid the treasure before he bought the field was acting in an ethically-questionable way ; and one cannot help wondering what the pearl-merchant did next after disposing of all his property in order to acquire the one supremely-valuable pearl.[1] Another feature that has attracted attention is that in both cases the discovery of the precious possession is apparently accidental and unforeseen.[2] But such considerations throw no light on the problem as to what Jesus intended to convey when he uttered the Parables. His purpose was simply to bring out—by means of a couple of vivid stories—one point, namely that, in order to possess the Kingdom of God and what it involves, it is worth while to sacrifice anything however valued, which stands in the way of possessing it. Any reluctance to make the needful surrender is submerged by the realization of the infinite blessing to be gained.[3]

(3) Much discussion has taken place as to the meaning of the Parable reported in Mt. xx. 1–16 M, about the householder who hired labourers for his vineyard at different hours of the day, and at evening generously paid those who, because no one else had hired them, had worked for him only one hour the same full and normal daily wage that he had promised to those who had toiled the whole day. The use made of this parable by the Evangelist shows that he totally failed to understand it : for he inserts it between two similar utterances about the last being first and the first last (Mt. xix. 30 [taken from Mk. x. 31] and Mt. xx. 16 m) for the quite insufficient reason that in the story the last men to be hired are the first paid (Mt. xx. 8 M) —an arrangement needed only in order to explain why those

---

[1] Thus A. T. Cadoux (*Parables*, 142f., 146–148) regards both parables as covert explanations of Jesus' strategic self-limitation to Israel with a view to the ultimate inclusion of the Gentiles (see above, p. 162 [12])—the story of the Treasure referring to his reticence concerning the Gentiles, that of the Pearl to his " concentration in the interests of extension ". This exegesis seems to me over-subtle : who of his hearers could have guessed his real meaning, if that had been it ?

[2] Otto (*Kingdom*, 56 f., 129f.) exploits this feature in the interests of his favourite idea that the Kingdom is " a blessing of salvation ; one cannot compute it, know about it of oneself, and personally seek access to it. It must meet one, let one find it, flash forth of itself, not by a human quest ". This again I should regard as far-fetched and forced, especially as the merchant is explicitly described as " *seeking* for pearls ".

[3] Cf. N. Schmidt, *Prophet of Naz.* 298f. ; Manson, *Teaching*, 165f. ; Otto, *Kingdom*, 128f.

who were last paid complained. We are thus thrown back as usual on the internal evidence of the parable itself. It is a mistake to treat it as an allegorical forecast of the Last Judgment,[1] and also to regard the procedure of the householder as quixotic : he knew that a labourer could not properly support himself on less than a denarius a day, and that the shortness of the labour of the last-hired was due to lack of opportunity, not to laziness : so he did the generous thing, and gave the day's wage to all alike. The least then that the Parable teaches is that God's Kingdom means God's generosity—His willingness to bless men on a scale more lavish than the purely-commercial relationship necessitates, one conforming rather to the normal generosity of a parent : He offers in the Kingdom not what men deserve, but what they most urgently need.

Some significance probably attaches to the fact that the men first hired had a definite covenant with their employer, while all hired later trusted him to do what was fair. It is surely not fanciful to see here a suggested contrast between the Jews as the covenant-people, who were serving God all the time, and the Gentiles, who needed true religion just as much as the Jews, but through no fault of their own had never enjoyed the Jews' privileges and opportunities of service.[2]

(4) The Parable of the Feast is given in Lk. xiv. 16–24 and Mt. xxii. 2–10. The similarity between the two versions is sufficient to warrant the conjecture that the Parable stood in Q ; but both of them display secondary features. For example, Mt. xxii. 6f. is clearly m's unwarranted application of the story to the calamity of 70 A.D., whereas in Lk. the duplication of the host's order to the slave to bring in the vagrants looks like a needless complication of an otherwise simple story. The point to be noted here, however, is one not affected by such documentary difficulties as these : it is simply concerned with the comparison of the Kingdom (Mt. xxii. 2 Q ? [cf. Lk. xiv. 15]) to the free invitation of poor and needy men to come and partake of a rich man's banquet.

(5) Among the various aspects in which Jesus describes the Kingdom is the conception of it as a free gift from God. This thought is conveyed, not only by such parables as we have just been considering, but quite explicitly in at least one passage : " Fear not, thou little flock, for the Father is pleased to give you the Kingdom " (Lk. xii. 32 Q or l). The documentary origin of this verse is uncertain ; and we cannot therefore be

---

[1] Cf. B. T. D. Smith, *Parables*, 186f.
[2] So A. T. Cadoux, *Parables*, 98–103.

very confident that Jesus really uttered the words : but the idea they convey is undoubtedly true to his representation of the Kingdom as a whole. So much is indubitable : but it is a mistake on the part of modern scholars to press the idea of a Divine gift so far as to exclude the notion of the need of strenuous efforts on man's part in order to be able to receive the gift. The Rabbis laid hardly more stress on the need for such efforts than Jesus himself did : and to argue—as some do —that Jesus taught that man's part in the Kingdom was merely the passive acceptance of a boon at God's hand is a grave misrepresentation of his meaning.[1]

(6) "Come hither unto me, all ye who are toiling and burdened, and I will give you rest. ᵎTake on yourselves my yoke, and learn from me, for I am gentle and humble in heart, and ye will find rest for your souls, for my yoke is kindly, and my burden light " (Mt. xi. 28–30 M). On the genuineness of this passage, see above, pp. 44f. Here again, although no explicit mention is made of the Kingdom of God, that is nevertheless the reality in the speaker's mind. Jesus has come to confer on men the one really-satisfying boon for which they are craving. Doubtless a very real paradox faces us when we set side by side Jesus' easy yoke and his searching moral demands. We may solve the paradox, not by shutting our eyes to his legislation for fear lest we lapse into Pelagianism, but by noting the immense access of strength imparted (perhaps unconsciously) to the will of man when he realizes the greatness of God's love for him.[2]

(7) It is perhaps sufficient here to quote Mk. ii. 18f. = Lk. v. 33f. = Mt. ix. 14, 15a.[3]

[1] Cf. Strack-Billerbeck i. 180f. ; Manson in *Mission*, etc. 637 ; and see above, pp. 26., 43, 66 n. 1, and below, pp. 188f., 203–207.

[2] Cf. also Otto, *Kingdom*, 56f. (e), 70f. (3, 4).

[3] Cf. Otto, *Kingdom*, 76–81, for an interesting study of the contrast between Jesus and John the Baptist : also Bartlet and Carlyle, *Christianity in Hist.* 8–12.

SUMMARY OF PART TWO

The Kingdom of God meant in essence men's loyal compliance with God's Will. Since, however, God is not only King, but also Father, this compliance involves on man's part a personal and filial relation to Him. Extensively, the Kingdom denotes the persons who stand in such a relationship to God ; and since the number of these increases as time goes on, the term becomes patient of a social and also of an eschatological meaning.

Obedience to God as a new Way of Life is explicated, both in its general and in its particular aspects, in Jesus' teaching based on the principles of love for God and love for man.

Inasmuch as the Kingdom is present whenever and wherever man loyally and lovingly accepts the Will of God as his supreme concern, it follows that the Kingdom already exists in the persons of Jesus himself and his Disciples, and is indeed proved to exist by the work they do.

As a Jewish prophet appealing to the rank and file of the Jewish nation, Jesus often spoke of the Kingdom as mainly, if not exclusively, a Jewish concern. It is probable that his thought and speech in this connexion underwent change from time to time, for we find him also manifesting unmistakable signs of a conviction that God's Kingdom is destined to embrace Gentiles as well, on the lines of the universalistic passages in the Old Testament. This apparent incongruity in his attitude is to be further explained, partly as a temporary strategic postponement of his universalistic message pending the fuller preparation of Israel, and partly as a recognition that Israel, God's instrument for the conversion of the world, needed very special preparation for the task. In any case, his universalism implied his rejection of the idea of a Messianic war as the appointed means of ending the oppressive Gentile power in the world : on the contrary, he laboured to induce Israel to lay aside hatred and vengefulness, and to seek to win heathendom and Rome by love and service, even if that should mean submission to injustice in the immediate future.

Finally, Jesus declared the Kingdom to be so great a blessing to men, that it was better for them to lose all else than to miss it.

PART THREE

THE FUTURE OF THE KINGDOM AS FIRST ENVISAGED

CHAPTER I

JESUS' INITIAL EXPECTATIONS OF SUCCESS

(1) ʿWe have to distinguish between the earlier and later views of Jesus regarding the Future, because at the beginning of his Ministry he did not anticipate the rejection and martyrdom which he later saw would befall him. (2) There is no reason to suppose that any anticipation of it came to him at his Baptism,ʿ(3) despite the fact that on that occasion the words of certain of the Servant-poems were present to his mind. (4) It was alien from all current ideas concerning the lot of the Messiah ; (5) nor was it necessarily involved in his rejection (at the Temptation) of the plan of military conquest, (6) or in the general dissimilarity between his own ideals and those of the nation's rulers. (7) It would have been sheer fatalism to feel certain in advance that Israel would not respond to God's call. (8) The tragic fate of John the Baptist did not necessarily mean that Jesus was fore-doomed to similar treatment. (9) The opening months of the Galilæan Ministry were a time of joy ; (10) and Jesus' allusion to the removal of the Bridegroom cannot be proved to be an early prophecy of the Passion. (11) All the other prophecies of the Passion are represented as having been uttered late in the Ministry. (12) Finally, the bitter disappointment expressed by Jesus, towards the end, over Israel's failure to accept him, is an indubitable proof that he had once hoped for a better reception.

(1) The topics discussed in Chapters III–VII of Part Two pointed forward with varying degrees of directness to the whole question of Jesus' expectations regarding the future course of human history. In studying the evidence for his belief that the Kingdom was already present (Chapter III), we noted by way of anticipation that there was also evidence for his belief that in some sense it had still to come. His description of it as something which had prime significance for the Jews (Chapter IV) inevitably raised the question as to what was in store for them as the Chosen People of God. Still more, if the Kingdom was a blessing destined to reach and embrace the Gentile peoples (Chapter V), the fulfilment of its destiny obviously lay as yet in the womb of the future, especially if a part of that fulfilment was to consist of a Jewish campaign of goodwill towards heathendom in general and Rome in particular

(Chapter VI), while in presenting it as an invaluable treasure and a source of supreme comfort (Chapter VII), Jesus was unmistakably turning men's thoughts to the Kingdom as it was to be in the days to come.

We are thus led on to a study of his thoughts regarding the future course of his mission. A glance at our Table of Contents will show that this question will be dealt with under two chronologically-distinct aspects—the Future as Jesus first envisaged it, and the Future as he last envisaged it. The ground of this distinction lies in the probability that at the beginning of his ministry Jesus seriously expected to secure the acceptance and loyal obedience of the nation at large (even at the cost of strenuous toil and some painful self-denial), and that his ultimate rejection at its hands signified not only the frustration of his efforts, but the disappointment of his expectations (see above, p. 18).

The recognition of this probability does not, of course, imply that we can draw a sharp line at some date or other in the Ministry, clearly marking off the earlier stage from the later, or that we can make a hard and fast classification of all his sayings as belonging unambiguously to one or other of them, and so construct a complete picture of the two separate forecasts. For one thing, the change from the earlier to the later state of mind must itself have been gradual ; and the whole middle part of the Ministry must have been a period of uncertainty, in which hope and despair contended with one another, and now one, now the other, would be uppermost in Jesus' mind. Again, since the final issue was his rejection, the Evangelists were naturally inclined to assume as a matter of course that there had never been a time in the Ministry when any other dénouement was contemplated as possible. In the foreshortening of the story, as they looked back upon it, they would inevitably tend to overlay and obscure the earlier period of hope with the dark shadows of the great Passion-story.[1] And even Jesus himself, in the manner of a devout Jew, would tend, in proportion as the likelihood or certainty of Israel's ultimate rejection of him was borne in upon his mind, to think and speak of that rejection as providentially ordained, but without on that account desisting from his efforts to avert it, just as pious parents might feel and act to-day, in the case of the fatal illness of a beloved child.[2]

---

[1] Cf. Bartlet, *St. Mark*, 47f., 55, 64 with n., 144.
[2] Cf. Holtzmann, *Theol.* i. 358 ; Burkitt, *Earliest Sources*, 70f. ; V. Taylor, *Sacrifice*, 113f., 255f. ; Flew, *Church*, 95.

Yet, while all this is true, the fact remains that, if any such gradual change in Jesus' forecast did take place, it must have very radically affected his whole view of the future. In the nature of the case, the materials for reconstructing his later view are comparatively abundant, and the conclusions to which they point fairly clear, whereas our means of making out his initial expectations are correspondingly meagre and confusing. But this state of affairs does not exempt the student from the necessity of attempting to keep the two distinct, seeing that the dissimilarity between them was so great.

Obviously much will depend on the accuracy or inaccuracy of our initial theory, which is the sole ground for positing the distinction referred to. Our immediate task therefore is to set forth the reasons for holding that, at the outset of his ministry, Jesus seriously hoped to succeed—not indeed without self-denying service, and perhaps not even without some suffering (see below, pp. 186ff., 218, 235 n. 2, 301f.)—in persuading the people of Israel to accept and follow him as their Messiah.[1]

(2) It has been inferred from Jesus' later allusions to his coming death as a " baptism " (Mk. x. 38f. [Mt. xx. 22 omits the phrase] ; Lk. xii. 50 L or Q) and from Paul's words in Rom. vi. 4, that Jesus' baptism was for him " an initiation to his passion and death ".[2] But this is gravely to overstrain the evidence. Baptism stood indeed for initiation into a new religious life, whether for the Gentiles converted to Judaism, for the converts of John the Baptist, or for those who

---

[1] Such is the view of Wendt, *Teaching*, i. 379f., 396–400, ii. 219–222 ; Wellhausen, *Mc.* 62f. ; Holtzmann, *Theol.* i. 356f., 357f., 360 ; Charles, *Crit. Hist.* (1913), 376–378 ; Bartlet, *St. Mark*, 56f., 64 ; C. J. Shebbeare in *The Atonement in History and in Life* (ed. Grensted, 1929), 312 n. 2 ; H. H. Farmer in *Congreg. Quart.* viii (1930) 275 ; Mackinnon, *Historic Jesus*, 196 ; A. D. Martin, *The Holiness of Jesus* (1934), 208f. (quoting R. Mackintosh) ; and Major in *Mission*, etc. 29.   Otto (*Kingdom*, 237 [1]) admits it as a possibility. The contrary view, viz., that Jesus foresaw his Passion from the beginning of his Ministry, is taken by Dobschütz, *Eschatol.* 6f. ; E. F. Scott, *The Kingdom and the Messiah* (1911), 228 ; Relton, *Study in Christol.* 234f. ; Dehn, *Man and Revelation* (1936), 44f. ; Macaulay, *Death of Jes.* 92–97, 110, 118, 128f. ; and others mentioned below, p. 186 n. 1.

This latter view can be, and often is, argued for on fully-critical grounds : but it is shared by many who feel the force of the old dogmatic assertion of Jesus' necessary omniscience.   On a certain widely-held view of Jesus' Person (that shared, e.g., by Fundamentalists and Roman Catholics), no suggestion that he ever anticipated anything which did not actually happen could be admitted.   Such a presupposition is incompatible with the assumptions on which the present investigation is based ; but a full discussion of it in this place would involve too great a digression to be profitable.

[2] So D. Plooij in *Amicitiæ Corolla* (1933), 239–244, 249, 252.

later entered the Christian Church. Jesus' use of the term
" baptism " when alluding to his death was clearly metaphorical, the idea common to the two experiences being that of an
epoch-making ordeal. But apart from the later experience of
Jesus himself, there was nothing in the nature of baptism as
such which would suggest the solemn acceptance of the
prospect of death.

(3) The contention that Jesus foresaw the Passion at latest
from the time of his baptism can be defended with much
greater force by adducing the fact that on this occasion he
called to mind certain passages from the first of the Deutero-
Isaianic Servant-poems and their context, namely, Isa. xlii. 1,
xliv. 2, lxii. 4 (see above, pp. 37f.), and that the second and third
of these poems (Isa. xlix. 1–6, l. 4–9) represent the Servant as
incurring difficulty and opposition, while the fourth (lii. 13–
liii) depicts him as suffering a martyr's death. It is argued,
not without force, that, seeing that Jesus knew, not only one
of these poems, but all of them (as passages in the one roll of
" Isaiah "), if he identified himself with the Servant at all (as
we know that he did), he must have accepted also the picture of
Isa. lii. 13–liii as destined to be fulfilled by himself.[1] The
argument undoubtedly has some weight ; and if it stood by
itself, it might not unreasonably be held to settle the question
against us. Since, however, it is our business to take *all* the
pertinent evidence into account, we must needs ask whether
the argument under discussion is or is not finally decisive. We
have to remember that the Messianic interpretation of the
Servant-passages was apparently not adopted by the Jews
until post-Christian times : it is therefore quite possible that
Jesus' application of them to himself was a gradual and piecemeal process. It was not in that day customary, when
quoting Scripture, to pay much regard to the context, so long

---

[1] Cf. W. Manson, *Christ's View*, 127–129 ; Moffatt, *Theol. of the Gospels*,
140–142 (" . . . The consciousness of this need [his own death], however, in
the light of the Servant-prophecy, was not an after-thought. It must have
been present to His mind more or less definitely from the first "), 149 ; Moody,
Purpose of Jes. 93f. ; Hoskyns in *Myst. Christi*, 86f. (" . . . The death of
Jesus was not primarily effected by the secret and malicious planning of the
Jewish authorities, . . . It was involved from the beginning of His ministry
in His creative definition of the Messiahship as the Son of Man. The initiative
rested wholly with Jesus Himself. He provoked His death consciously and
of set purpose, because its necessity was laid upon Him as the Messiah in
order that the Old Testament Scriptures might be fulfilled . . . ") ; Hoskyns
and Davey, *Riddle*, 84, 98 (" . . . so that He went to His death consciously
in order that the Scripture might be fulfilled, and ordered 'His ministry to
that end ") ; Plooij, as above, p. 185 n. 2. Schweitzer also holds (*Mystery*,
223f.) that " his messianic consciousness was never without the thought of
the Passion . . .".

as the words actually quoted were appropriate.[1] We cannot therefore pronounce it to have been impossible that Jesus should, as early as his baptism, have applied the first of the Servant-sections to himself, and even have noted the idea of difficulty and opposition foreshadowed in the second and third, and yet not have necessarily taken to himself the tragic predictions of the fourth.[2]

(4) Allusion has just been made to the probability that, until post-Christian times, the Jews had formed no idea of a suffering or dying Messiah.[3] It is true that Jesus, in his ideas of the Messiahship, departed widely from the expectations in vogue among his fellow-countrymen (see above, pp. 138f. [3]) : we cannot therefore place any great stress on the fact just referred to. But it does not therefore follow that we can lay on it no stress at all ; for, although Jesus disregarded many current and traditional notions concerning the Messiahship, it is obvious that he did not discard them altogether, since in that case he could never have considered himself as Messiah at all. So far as it goes, therefore, the Jewish belief in a successful Messiah, taken by itself, renders it rather more probable than otherwise that at the outset Jesus' own belief was similar.

(5) It has been argued that, when, at the Temptation, Jesus definitely rejected the idea of attempting to acquire world-dominion by force of arms, he necessarily and consciously sentenced himself to earthly failure and death as the only alternative.[4] But are we justified in insisting on that inference ? The Jewish prophetic mind did not normally take a restricted view of God's power when it was shaping a forecast of what He would do in the future on behalf of His people ; and there is no real need to suppose that, when Jesus repudiated the way of military conquest, he must have immediately and before trial drawn the conclusion that he would himself have to suffer a martyr's death.

(6) It is but an extension of the argument to which we have

---

[1] Thus, the Targum of Jonathan referred Isa. liii to the Messiah, but not those verses of it that spoke of the Servant's *sufferings* ! (Schürer, *G.J.V.* ii. 650f. ; Moore, *Judaism*, i. 229, iii. 63 top, 166 ; Héring, *Royaume*, 67f. n. 2 ; V. Taylor, *Sacrifice*, 46). Cf. Moody, *Purpose of Jes.* 93f.

[2] Cf. Holtzmann, *Theol.* i. 357 ; Bartlet, *St. Mark*, 269f. (see below, p. 189 n. 3) ; Mackinnon, *Historic Jesus*, 196.

[3] Schürer, *G.J.V.* ii. 648–651 : cf. Lk. iii. 16f. = Mt. iii. 11f. Q ; Mk. viii. 32 = Mt. xvi. 22 ; Lk. xviii. 34 l ; Lk. xxiv. 21 L ; John xii. 34.

[4] Cf. Holtzmann, *Synopt.* 48 : " Also entweder, im Bunde mit dem unreinen Geist, mühelos in die Höhe oder, in entsagungsvollem Kampfe mit ihm, in den Tod. Denn Entfaltung einer Messiasfahne, die im Gegensatze zu den nationalen Erwartungen steht, bedeutet bei gleichzeitigem Verzicht auf weltliche Machtmittel, auf die Waffen des Argen, sicheren Untergang . . .''

just replied, to appeal to the general dissimilarity between the
ideals and methods of Jesus on the one hand and those of the
mass of the people and particularly their leaders on the other
hand as proving that from the time of the Temptation onwards
he must have known for a certainty that he was foredoomed
to failure.[1]   But here again the answer is that, in estimating
the possibilities of success, Jesus would be very unlikely to take
a pessimistic or even what we should call a coldly-practical
view.   He was conscious of living at a very critical juncture in
the world's history, and of being charged by his Father with a
very unique and eventful mission ; and in entering upon his
great function he would naturally expect that the God Who
had called him to it would so prepare men's hearts that they
would be capable of unprecedented achievements.   There
would be nothing improbable or unworthy in such a hope.

(7) It was surely a hope which could amply justify itself,
not only by looking at the unlimited power of God, but by
paying regard to the moral responsibilities of man.   The
Jewish mind was indeed strongly inclined to determinism, and
was very prone to express itself in language which tacitly
presupposed the sole causality of God.   But, with a saving
inconsistency, it never drew from that presupposed doctrine
(as some modern interpreters are in the habit of drawing) the
inference that man's initiative and responsibility are ruled
out as either non-existent or non-determinative factors in the
situation.   Different as God's Messiah might be from what
Israel expected, why must Israel necessarily reject him ?   There
was no difficulty in expecting some at least to accept him ;
and if some could freely accept him, why not many—or a
majority—or even all ?   *After* the Divine call had been
disobeyed, then indeed might the prophet or teacher speak of
the issue as Divinely foreseen and even predetermined (Acts ii.
23, iii. 18, iv. 27f., xiii. 27 ; Rom. ix–xi, esp. xi. 8, 25).   But
can it be shown that, *prior* to trial, disobedience was ever
explicitly foretold ?[2]   And even supposing there actually
were cases in which the prophet, speaking under intense
provocation, accompanied his appeal with an open declaration
that it would not be listened to, we can at least say that the
normal teaching of Scripture, like the normal teaching of
experience, is that God gives man the free choice of obedience

---

[1] Plooij in *Amicitiæ Corolla* (1933), 250–252.
[2] Cases like Isa. vi. 9f. (cf. Gray, *Isaiah*, 101, 110), Mk. iv. 11f. = Lk. viii. 10
= Mt. xiii. 11, 13, Mt. xiii. 14f. m, and so on, are probably instances of vaticinia
post eventus (see below, pp. 212f.).

or disobedience, and neither pronounces sentence nor even foretells the outcome until that choice has been exercised.[1]

(8) Some have seen an anticipation of trouble on Jesus' part in the fact that he postponed the commencement of his distinctive work until John the Baptist was thrown into prison. Whether that conjecture be well-founded or not, the synchronism is an historical fact—Jesus began his work when John, whom he regarded as more than a prophet (Lk. vii. 26 =Mt. xi. 9 Q), was actually in prison ; and he had not carried it on for long when John was beheaded. Certainly John's fate must have thrown an ominous shadow across Jesus' path : and that Jesus realized this is clear from the obscure words which he spoke immediately after the Transfiguration (Mk. ix. 11–13 =Mt. xvii. 10–13). In answer to this it must be observed (a) that, if (as may plausibly be argued) the Johannine chronology is to be trusted,[2] the baptism of Jesus preceded the commencement of his Galilæan ministry by nearly twelve months ; (b) that the imprisonment of John was not due to the enmity of the Jewish leaders (who, although they were hostile to him, were afraid so much as to speak openly against him [Mk. xi. 32 = Lk. xx. 6 = Mt. xxi. 26 : cf. Lk. vii. 29f. L ; Mt. xxi. 32 M]), but to the rancour and suspicion of Herod Antipas ; (c) that John's imprisonment could not have appeared a *fatal* set-back until his death ; and it may be conceded without detriment to our thesis that by that time Jesus may well have become less confident about his own success ; and (d) that similarly the late date of the speech in Mk. ix. 11–13 = Mt. xvii. 10–13 renders it of little or no value as evidence of what Jesus might be expecting at the time of the Baptism and Temptation.[3]

(9) In Mk. ii. 19 = Lk. v. 34 = Mt. ix. 15a Jesus defends his Disciples for not fasting by saying, " Can the sons of the wedding-chamber observe a fast, while the Bridegroom is with them ? As long as they have the Bridegroom with them, they cannot observe a fast ". If we consider these words by themselves, apart from their immediate sequel, which we must

---

[1] Jesus' prediction of Peter's denial (Mk. xiv. 29–31 = Lk. xxii. 33f. = Mt. xxvi. 33–35) seems at first sight a glaring exception : but perhaps it is best understood as a grave warning couched in Oriental terms. At all events, its exceptional character is patent. Cf. A. T. Cadoux in *The Lord of Life*, 62, 78.

[2] Cf. C. J. Cadoux in *J.T.S.* xx. 316–320 (July 1919).

[3] Dr. Bartlet makes the interesting and not-impossible suggestion (*St. Mark*, 269f.) that Jesus at first saw, in the fate of John, a sample-fulfilment of Isa. liii—an interpretation which allowed him for a time to cherish the hope that the Messiah himself would meet with a worthier reception.

discuss in a moment, they depict the early ministry in Galilee as a joyous and triumphant episode—a picture not easily harmonized with the certainty of approaching tragedy. Nor can we suppose that it resembled marriage-festivities for the Disciples only, while Jesus kept his sorrow hidden in his heart ; for that would imply a strong lack of a sense of reality on his part—either he (the Bridegroom) was himself rejoicing, or there could have been no rejoicing at all. Other direct if less significant traces of his hopes of success appear from time to time —his tacit assumption that Jews as such will listen to and follow his teaching (see above, pp. 140f.), the Parable of the Sower with its vindication of the sower's confidence that he will reap an abundant crop (see above, p. 48 [10]), and his claim to have bound the Strong Man and be plundering his goods and to have seen Satan fall like lightning from heaven (see above, pp. 65f. [9]).

This argument has been rebutted by the plea that the references to Satan mean only that Jesus is sure of the *final* triumph of his cause, despite the nation's refusal of him, that even the Parable of the Sower contains allusions to several sources of loss,[1] and that his addressing himself to Jews as such was simply due to his self-limitation to them as his chosen field, while as for the reference to the wedding-festivities, it is followed immediately (so we are reminded) by an unmistakable prediction of the Passion : " But there will come days when the Bridegroom will be taken away from them ; and then they will observe a fast on that day " (Mk. ii. 20 = Lk. v. 35 = Mt. ix. 15b).[2]

These replies, however, do not suffice to undo the force of the comparison of the Galilæan Ministry to a wedding-feast, or to disprove what that comparison implies. The allusion, for instance, to the binding of Satan is not really compatible with an expectation of death at the hands of men instigated by him. The Parable of the Sower, though it contemplates a *margin* of waste, suggests that at least the bulk of the seed sown will be fruitful. As for the tacit contrast Jesus draws between Jews as his hearers and Gentiles, that way of speech could never have commended itself to him, had he known from the first that the nation as a whole would end by repudiating him.

(10) The allusion to the removal of the Bridegroom is a more serious objection ; but it is far from fatal. Some are disposed to deny that it comes from Jesus at all, and to treat

---

[1] Cf. Bartlet, *St. Mark*, 60f.
[2] Cf. Dehn, *Man and Revelation* (1936), 44f. ; V. Taylor, *Sacrifice*, 82–85, 90.

it as an early Christian gloss inserted in order to complete the preceding words in the light of subsequent events, and in order to represent the Church's practice of fasting as having the Lord's authority.[1] Others admit it as a genuine saying of Jesus, but do not understand it to refer to a violent death.[2] Most however admit that it is a real reference to the Passion, but hold that the loose Marcan chronology is here outweighed by the probability that the words, if genuine, belong to a later stage in the Ministry than that to which Mark has assigned them.[3]

(11) Apart from the echoes of the Servant-poems at the Baptism and in the synagogue at Nazareth, and the allusion to the removal of the Bridegroom, all the references made by Jesus to his coming Passion are placed by the Synoptists after Peter's acknowledgement of his Messiaship at Cæsarea-Philippi.[4] Assuming the Marco-Lucan chronology to be trustworthy on this point, it does not, of course, necessarily follow that the thought of the Passion could not have occurred to him earlier : it may have done so, and Jesus may for certain reasons have said nothing to his Disciples about it for some time.[5] Yet it is surely more natural, seeing that Cæsarea-Philippi evidently constituted an important landmark in the development of his thought and teaching,[6] to suppose that the virtual conviction that he must suffer death had come home to him recently, rather than that he had been silently nursing it throughout the whole earlier period of the Ministry. We ought not to forget that, even as late as the agony in Gethsemane, Jesus hoped that possibly the Father might be able to remove the cup from him (Mk. xiv. 35f. = Lk. xxii. 41f. = Mt. xxvi. 39). Is it not therefore probable that, long before that stage had been reached, his belief in the possibility of his being spared the cup would have been much stronger ?

(12) Jesus' lamentation over those Galilæan towns which did not repent (Lk. x. 13–15 = Mt. xi. 20–24 Q : see above, pp. 41f.) suggests very strongly that he was disappointed with them. Still less mistakable is the tone of disappointment in

---

[1] This view is discussed in McNeile, *St. Matthew*, 121b ; Rashdall, *Conscience*, 161f. ; Dibelius, *Die Formgeschichte des Evangeliums* (1919), 33f. ; V. Taylor, *Tradition*, 34f. ; B. T. D. Smith, *Parables*, 95.

[2] See McNeile, as in last note ; A. T. Cadoux, *Parables*, 72–74 ; Dodd, *Parables*, 116f. n. 2.

[3] See above, p. 57 (d) : cf. also Menzies, *Earliest Gospel*, 87b ; Bartlet, *St. Mark*, 136f., 144, 251 ; Montefiore, *S.G.*[2] I, 58.

[4] Mt. x. 37f. (= Lk. xiv. 26f. Q) is an exception : but the Matthæan chronology is notoriously erratic.

[5] Cf. Wendt, *Teaching*, i. 388 ; Bartlet, *St. Mark*, 64, 136, 249.

[6] See Manson, *Teaching*, 201–211.

his address to Jerusalem: " O Jerusalem, Jerusalem ! . . . How often have I wished to gather thy children together, as a mother-bird gathers her brood of nestlings under her wings, and ye would not come ! . . . " (Lk. xiii. 34 = Mt. xxiii. 37 Q). There is no good reason for doubting the accuracy of the record of these words. The multiplicity of the visits to Jerusalem presupposed by them is warranted, not only by the Fourth Gospel, but by a number of indirect allusions in the Synoptics.[1] The words stand in the oldest and best Gospel-document we know. There is nothing unlikely in them as a report of what Jesus said—in particular, there is no need to suppose that they are a quotation drawn from some lost Jewish book on the Divine Wisdom (for Lk. xi. 49 [Q ?] comes from quite a different Lucan context : see above, p. 72 n. 4), or that for this or any other reason they represent the lamentation of God only and not that of Jesus himself. The Gospels do not enable us to say precisely when this lamentation was uttered, but its terms suffice to show that it must have come late in the Ministry.

Side by side with these well-attested words, and in confirmation of them, we may set the somewhat less-strongly attested, but very credible, account of what happened as Jesus approached Jerusalem for the last time. ' And as he drew near, having caught sight of the city, he wept over it, saying, " O if only thou hadst come to know, even at this (late) day, the things (needful) for thy peace ! But now, they have been hidden from thine eyes ! . . . thou knewest not the season of thy visitation (from God) ! " ' (Lk. xix. 41–44 L).

Now if Jesus spoke in this way, and meant what he said, and was not simply indulging in meaningless stage-play or unintelligent fatalism, he was expressing real and passionate disappointment. No feasible alternative view is possible. If these utterances do not evince a most poignant sense of frustration, they mean nothing. But to say that is to say also that Jesus had formerly and for some considerable time expected confidently that the children of Jerusalem *would* flock together under him, and that the city *would* realize that his ministry was a Divine visitation, and *would* eagerly accept his message as essential for her peace.[2] It is submitted

---

[1] Moffatt, *I.L.N.T.* 542–544 ; C. J. Cadoux in *Expos.* IX. iii. 175–192 (Mar. 1925).

[2] Cf. Manson in *Mission*, etc. 633 : " This short dialogue " (he is referring to Lk. xxii. 35–38) " throws a brilliant light on the tragedy of the Ministry. It goes with the Q lamentation over Jerusalem (Lk. 13[34f.] || Mt. 23[37–39]) ; and, like that elegy, it is full of bitter disillusionment . . . ".

that these passages of themselves are sufficient proof of the thesis here maintained, and amply outweigh any objections to it which can be based on the other items of evidence just examined. As it is, however, their weight is considerably increased by several of the items in question.

CHAPTER II

THE FUTURE COMING OF THE KINGDOM

(1) **Contemporary Jewish thought about the Kingdom of God pictured its full realization as an event in the future. (2) It was inherently natural that Jesus should similarly have thought of a coming climax, (3) as the necessary counterpart of the initial presence of the Kingdom in his own person and work, (4) and as an implication of his Parables of Growth. (5) The evidence is not easily collected because, at this stage, we can use only sayings which contain no reference to his coming death. (6) Yet a sufficient number of such sayings is preserved (7) to justify the belief (despite Luke xvii. 20f.) (8) that, altogether apart from any anticipation of his death, Jesus looked forward to a catastrophic and spectacular Coming of the Kingdom within the lifetime of his own generation. (9) This Future Coming of the Kingdom he regarded as dependent, not only on the Providence of God, but also on the co-operative service and prayers of men.**

(1) While, strictly speaking, the Rabbis would have agreed that God's Kingdom was an already-existing reality, because there already existed faithful Israelites who believed in Him as King and obeyed His royal Law (see above, pp. 128f.), the general conditions under which Israel was actually living were so contrary to what was believed to be God's Will for the nation that for most Jews His Kingdom had come to be thought of as a state of future blessedness, when the wrongs of the existing situation would be put right, and God's royal sway would be established and acknowledged not only in Israel, but throughout the world. The distinction between " this age " (העולם הזה) and " the coming age " (העולם הבא) was one of the commonplaces of Jewish eschatology, though sometimes a distinction was drawn between the latter and the reign of the Messiah preceding it.[1] When this great coming era would begin no one knew : but it was the prayer and the longing and for many the expectation that it would begin very soon. John

---

[1] Schürer, *G.J.V.* ii. 628f., 636f. ; Strack-Billerbeck, i. 178–180 ; Bousset, *Relig. des Jud.* (1926), 213–218 ; Von Gall, Βασιλεία, 470–472 ; Dodd, *Parables*, 36–38.

the Baptist held it to be imminent, and urgently warned his hearers to make ready for it.

(2) The fact that stress was so generally laid on the futurity of the Kingdom renders it initially and inherently likely that Jesus also looked forward to a coming climax. For, though we may by no means take it for granted that he thought as his fellow-countrymen thought, and may still less force the evidence of the Gospels so as to make it support such an assumption, yet we must on the other hand remember that, while Jesus is using the language of the people and (it may be confidently presumed) desiring to be understood by them, it is likely that he gave to the great leading terms he used a connotation at least approximately identical with that which his hearers would naturally assume him to be giving.[1]

(3) In the present instance the presumption is amply confirmed by the evidence of the Gospels. In the first place, we have already noted in detail the grounds for believing that Jesus thought of the Kingdom of God as in a real sense already present in his own person and saving work (see above, pp. 128–135). It has been assumed that this thought of his " dislocates the whole eschatological scheme, in which its expected coming closes the long vista of the future." [2] But so far from the fact that the Kingdom is already present excluding the idea of a final or cataclysmic coming of it in the future, the two ideas are complementary to one another and mutually necessary. For the presence of the Kingdom in the work Jesus was then engaged on was at most only an *initial* presence ; and however successful and hopeful he might be in it, he could not regard it as in any way a *full or sufficient*

---

[1] Cf. Schmidt in *R.G.G.* iii (1929) 130f. On Galilee as a region in which special interest was taken in apocalyptic eschatology, see Charles, *Crit. Hist.* (1913), 193 ; Otto, *Kingdom*, 13–19.

[2] So Dodd, *Parables*, 49f., 78f. (" . . . the declaration that the Kingdom of God has come, breaks up, in any case, the old eschatological scheme, and makes room for a new set of ideas ").

I observe that Dr. Dodd, following the recent example of certain Continental scholars (e.g., Kuhn in *T.W.N.T.* i. 573 ; Otto, *Reich Gottes und Menschensohn* [1934], 39, 81, 127 ; Héring, *Royaume*, 44), frequently uses the term " the *eschaton* ", as if it were a regular and technical designation used by the early Christians for the Divinely-ordained climax of history (*Parables*, 36, 43, 79, 193, *Apost. Preaching*, 66, 71, 97, 198–201, 204f., 207, 210, 217, 232, *Hist. and the Gospel*, 60, 108 ; also in *Kingdom of God and Hist.* 24f., 32). So also H. V. Martin in *E. T.* li. 88–90 (Nov. 1939) and H. Cunliffe-Jones in *E.T.* li. 231b (Feb. 1940). I am not aware of the ancient authority for this technical use of the neuter adjective τὸ ἔσχατον as a noun in this connexion. It is not a New-Testament usage (τὸ τέλος being the term usually employed), nor does it occur in the Apostolic Fathers. I am consequently doubtful as to the legitimacy of the use that is now being made of it.

presence of the Kingdom. It necessarily pointed forward to a future " coming " of the Kingdom " in power ", whenever or by whatever means that " coming " was to be effected (see above, p. 133 [**8**]).

(**4**) These preliminary judgments regarding inherent probabilities are reinforced by evidence of a more direct kind—and, in the first place, by the Parables of Growth (see above, p. 131 [**5**]).[1] To moderns disposed to discover in the teaching of Jesus a doctrine of ethical and spiritual evolution, these parables were specially welcome : and in the recent reaction against all liberal methods of understanding the Gospels, some scholars have been at pains to exclude the notions of gradualness, slowness, and so forth, from their interpretation of them. But after all, growth is growth : and in the case of all these parables, the process culminates in some sort of a climax of completeness. Such is the case with most processes of natural growth : and the onus probandi lies on the shoulders of those who, in the case of the Kingdom of God, would draw from the fact that its growth has already begun the inference that Jesus could not or did not look forward to a special " coming " of it in the future.

(**5**) Before clinching the argument with an array of explicit testimonia, let us refer in passing to the limitations imposed upon us in our collection of such testimonia by the supposition on which we are working, namely, that the views of Jesus touching the future were, in the course of the Ministry, radically altered by an unexpected anticipation of his approaching death. Seeing therefore that we are at present trying to reconstruct his views as they were prior to that tragic realization, we are debarred from appealing to any prediction of the future coming of the Kingdom with which some reference to the Passion is connected.

(**6**) We may introduce our array of testimonia by recalling in the first place a little group of somewhat ambiguous passages which are at times adduced as allusions to the already-present Kingdom, but which, as I have been at pains to show (see above, pp. 134f. [**9**]), can be equally or almost equally well interpreted as presupposing its futurity. Of the passages treated in this group, further reference here is needed only to—

(a) Mt. xiii. 44–46 M. The Parables of the Hidden Treasure and of the Pearl might be taken to envisage the Kingdom either as present or as future : but since the acquisition of the valuable

---

[1] Cf. Dodd in *Theology*, xiv. 260 (May 1927).

object is in both cases the culminating point of a quest, the balance of probability leans towards the future side.

(b) Mk. x. 15 = Lk. xviii. 17 = Mt. xviii. 3b. This is one of a number of sayings in which Jesus speaks of " entering the Kingdom of God ". It is significant that in a majority of these, the entering is explicitly spoken of in the future tense (see below, pp. 231f., where the passages are collected and discussed, and pp. 233f., where Mt. v. 19 M is quoted). The significance of the future tense which is used (or implied) in these passages ought perhaps not to be pressed : for the future time contemplated might lie in the immediate future, and does not necessarily imply a coming climax of any kind. Yet when taken in conjunction with the evidence now to be quoted, most of these passages do seem to bear a distinctly-eschatological meaning.

The prediction in Q of many (Gentiles) coming from all quarters to sit down with the Patriarchs in the Kingdom of God (Lk. xiii. 28-30 = Mt. viii. 11f. : see above, p. 155) quite obviously implies, if not explicitly a future " coming " of the Kingdom, at least a future climax in the story of it as significant for men.[1]

---

[1] Dr. Dodd rightly observes (*Parables*, 55 ; cf. 42) that the saying does not conflict with the teaching of Jesus that the Kingdom had already been revealed on earth. He adds, " It would however be susceptible of the meaning that at some date in the future the present earthly manifestation of the Kingdom of God will yield to a purely transcendent order in which it will be absolute ".

In several passages in his two books, *Parables* (42, 55f., 71-74, 80, 82, 84, 94, 96, 100 n. 2, 102, 105 n., 106-109, 208f.) and *Apost. Preaching* (157, 197-207, 217 : cf. also *Hist. and The Gosp.* 170-172, 181f., and in *Kingdom of God and Hist.* 20, 23, 25), Dr. Dodd broaches the idea that the full completeness of the Kingdom to which Jesus refers is a completeness belonging not to the historical order, but to the transcendent order beyond time and space. (Bultmann [*Jesus*, 53f.] makes a somewhat similar suggestion). Such a sublimation, or at least some tendency towards it, is conceivable in the sphere of early Gentile Christianity under the influence of Platonic and Alexandrian ways of thinking : it is the sort of thing, for instance, which we find in Philo. Traces of it are discernible in the New Testament, in Hebrews and the Fourth Gospel. It has links with the late-Jewish idea of there being a pre-existing-heavenly counterpart to earthly objects of supreme religious value (Gal. iv. 26 ; Heb. viii. 5, ix. 23, etc. : see Oepke's valuable note in his comm. on Galatians [1937], 86f. ; also Strack-Billerbeck iii. 573, 796 ; Moore, *Judaism*, i. 526, iii. 161). But it goes very far beyond such a conception, and was—I should contend—quite foreign to the Palestinian Jewish mind (cf. Flew, *Church*, 45 n.). We may be unable to rationalize to our satisfaction the particulars regarding time and space given in Jesus' teaching on the full completeness of the Kingdom : but it is not legitimate for us to solve the difficulty by imposing on that teaching a platonizing interpretation which must have been utterly alien to his whole way of thinking. For him future time meant future time, and earth and heaven meant respectively earth and heaven, however difficult we may find it to harmonize his expressions with our modern scientific outlook.

Dismissing therefore any idea of a Kingdom beyond space and time, we

The public proclamation with which Jesus opened the Galilæan ministry began " The time has been fulfilled, and the Kingdom of God has drawn near " (ἤγγικεν ἡ βασιλεία τοῦ θεοῦ : Mk. i. 15 = Mt. iv. 17). According to Mt. iii. 2 (m ?) John the Baptist had also said, " The Kingdom of the Heavens has drawn near " : but this is thought by many to be an unhistorical anticipation of Jesus' own announcement.[1] Be that as it may, we find the utterance of a similar announcement enjoined upon the Disciples on their missionary journeys (Lk. x. 9 [ἤγγικεν ἐφ' ὑμᾶς ἡ βασιλεία τοῦ θεοῦ][2] = Mt. x. 7 [ὅτι ἤγγικεν ἡ βασιλεία τῶν οὐρανῶν] Q : cf. Lk. x. 11b [ἤγγικεν ἡ βασιλεία τοῦ θεοῦ] 1 ? ;[3] Lk. ix. 2 1), and the expectation of the immediate appearance of the Kingdom entertained by Jesus' followers (Lk. xvii. 20 L, xix. 11 1: cf. Mk. xv. 43 = Lk. xxiii. 51 [Joseph of Arimathæa " was on the look-out for the Kingdom of God " : Mt. xxvii. 57 omits], and Mk. xii. 34 [οὐ μακρὰν εἶ ἀπὸ τῆς βασιλείας τοῦ θεοῦ]). There can be little doubt that the declaration that the Kingdom had drawn near meant that, in the sense in which the Kingdom was then being spoken of, it was shortly to come, but had not yet done so.[4]

---

may find in the words quoted at the commencement of this note a virtual acknowledgment of that very futurist eschatology which Dr. Dodd elsewhere declines to recognize as a real part of the teaching of Jesus.

[1] E.g., Otto, *Kingdom*, 69 (1) : but see above, p. 108 n. 5.

[2] Creed (*St. Luke*, 146a) considers that the addition of ἐφ' ὑμᾶς suggests that the Kingdom may be thought of as already present.

[3] Cf., however, Manson, *Teaching*, 122 (Lk. x. 11 probably from Q).

[4] Dr. Dodd, in *Theology*, xiv. 259f. (May 1927), in *Myst. Christi*, 66 n., and *Parables*, 43–45, argues on linguistic grounds and on the analogy of Lk. xi. 20 = Mt. xii. 28 Q (ἄρα ἔφθασεν ἐφ' ὑμᾶς ἡ βασιλεία τοῦ θεοῦ), that ἤγγικεν ἡ βασιλεία τοῦ θεοῦ means, not " The Kingdom . . . has drawn near ", but " The Kingdom has come ", both sentences being identical in meaning. His view is favourably received by Prof. R. H. Lightfoot (*Hist. and Interp.* 65, 107 n. 1). Cf. also A. T. Cadoux, *Theol. of Jes.* 46 (" . . . ' at hand ' must mean ' within reach ' not soon to become so, for otherwise the time would not be ' fulfilled ' "). But in *E.T.* xlviii. 91b–92b (Nov. 1936), Mr. J. Y. Campbell adduced evidence from the LXX and the N.T. to show that ἤγγικεν almost certainly means " has drawn near ", and further (92b–93a) that even ἔφθασεν in Lk. xi. 20 = Mt. xii. 28 Q may mean the same. Very similarly, Mr. K. W. Clark in *Journ. of Bibl. Lit.* lix. 367–383 (Sept. 1940 : ἤγγικεν *must* mean " has drawn near " : ἔφθασεν cannot mean " has come ", except in the sense " has just reached "or " has come into contact with " you). In *E. T.* xlviii.138b–140a (Dec. 1936), Dr. Dodd successfully showed that ἔφθασεν in this passage can mean only " has come " : in the case of ἤγγικεν (140a–141a), he admitted that he had inaccurately summarized the philological evidence, but advanced other reasons for holding that " has come " was at least a permissible rendering. He assumed, however (138a), that Mr. Campbell agreed with him that the two passages bear the same meaning, which was not the case : nor, in point

There is another important passage referring to the future coming of the Kingdom : " Truly I tell you that there are some here of those standing (round me) who will certainly not taste death until they see that the Kingdom of God has come with power " (Mk. ix. 1 [... τὴν βασιλείαν τοῦ θεοῦ ἐληλυθυῖαν ἐν δυνάμει] = Lk. ix. 27 [... τὴν βασιλείαν τοῦ θεοῦ] = Mt. xvi. 28 [... τὸν υἱὸν τοῦ ἀνθρώπου ἐρχόμενον ἐν τῇ βασιλείᾳ αὐτοῦ]). Since this passage immediately follows a paragraph containing a formal prediction of the Passion and a call for self-denial and courage on the part of the Disciples when persecuted, the question might well be raised whether we are, in view of the rubric we are following (see above, p. 196 [5]), entitled to quote it in this section of our study. It should, however, be observed that Mark introduces it with a special introductory formula, Καὶ ἔλεγεν αὐτοῖς, which is probably an indication that he originally found it in some other setting.[1] It may therefore perhaps be tentatively treated as an independent logion. The Greek perfect participle (which we may assume to be required by the underlying Aramaïc) forbids us to translate, " see the Kingdom of God *coming* with power " : the coming clearly precedes the seeing. At the same time, the coming cannot be thought of as preceding the seeing by a long interval ; otherwise the whole force of the sentence is lost. Still more, to argue that the coming referred to is the coming that took place in Jesus' own ministry reduces the prophecy almost to an absurdity. It would make him say, " The Kingdom has come already, and within the next thirty or forty years some of you will see that it has done so " ! On any reasonable interpretation, and without doing violence to the

---

of fact, do they necessarily mean the same. It seems to me that the balance of probability inclines to the view that in Mk. i. 15 etc. ἤγγικεν means " has drawn near ". (One strong argument used by Mr. Campbell is that in Mt. iii. 2 [see above, p. 108 n. 5] the expression is ascribed to *the Baptist*, who cannot have been thought to mean that the Kingdom had already come). The view here advocated is that adopted by Dr. B. T. D. Smith (*Parables*, 78 n.), and by Mr. H. V. Martin in *E. T.* lii. 271–273 (Apl. 1941). For adverse criticism of Dr. Dodd's attempt to show that Jesus' eschatology was wholly " realized eschatology ", i.e., that the only coming of the Kingdom of which he spoke was the coming already achieved in his own person and work, cf. B. T. D. Smith as just quoted, and W. L. Knox in *J.T.S.* xxxviii. 75f. (Jan. 1937).

Dr. Moffatt (*Theol. of the Gospels*, 54f.) understands Mk. i. 15 = Mt. iv. 17 to refer to a future " glorious consummation ", but not to presuppose any " apocalyptic calculation ". Easton (*Christ in the Gospels*, 160) says that the phrase " meant to everyone who heard it, ' The end of the world is at hand ', and could not possibly have had any other significance ". Cf. Dalman, *W.J.* 106f.

[1] So Holtzmann, *Synopt.* 150.

Greek perfect participle, we must insist that we have here a prediction of a special and spectacular coming of the Kingdom " with power ", sufficiently soon *and sufficiently late* for " some " of the bystanders to live to see that this had happened.[1]

Jesus seems to have been accustomed to take for granted, in his ordinary teaching, the familiar distinction between " this age " and " the coming age ", which implied a special future for the Kingdom, though the documentary evidence on the point is not of the strongest character.[2] His declaration that he who speaks a word against the Holy Spirit will not be forgiven " either in this age or in the coming (age) " rests on the sole authority of Mt. (xii. 32 : contrast Lk. xii. 10) ; and the clause in question may be simply a gloss of m. The contrast between " the sons of this age " who marry and beget offspring, and " those who have been accounted worthy to attain to that age and to the resurrection from the dead " is found only in Lk. (xx. 34f. : contrast Mk. xii. 25 = Mt. xxii. 30) ; and we cannot be sure whether it is drawn from some older source, or is simply constructed by l. The mention of " the sons of this age " in Lk. xvi. 8 is probably due to an explanatory gloss by l. " The age ", meaning " the present age ", is referred to in the probably-ungenuine interpretation of the Parable of the Sower (Mk. iv. 19 = Mt. xiii. 22 : Lk. viii. 14 otherwise), and also occurs in the phrase " the consummation of the age ", which is found five times in Mt. and in no other Gospel (see below, p. 292). Once in Mk. (x. 30 = Lk. xviii. 30 = Mt. xix. 29) Jesus says that he who has made sacrifices for his sake and the Gospel's will receive " in the age that is coming eternal life " ($\zeta\omega\grave{\eta}\nu$ $\alpha\grave{\iota}\acute{\omega}\nu\iota o\nu$). The adjective $\alpha\grave{\iota}\acute{\omega}\nu\iota o\varsigma$ here really means, not " everlasting ", but " characteristic of

---

[1] As against Mr. J. Y. Campbell (*E.T.* xlviii. 93a–94b [Nov. 1936]) and Mr. K. W. Clark (*Journ. of Bibl. Lit.* lix. 372f. [Sept. 1940]), I think Dr. Dodd is right in arguing (*Parables*, 42, 53f., and in *E.T.* xlviii. 141a–142b [Dec. 1936]) that ἐληλυθυῖαν ought not to be treated as if it were just equivalent to ἐρχομένην, and that the sentence therefore ought not to be rendered, " . . . see the Kingdom of God coming with power ". On the other hand, I hold that the absurdity or at least extreme awkwardness mentioned in the text above is quite fatal to his plea (*Parables*, 54, and in *E.T.* xlviii. 142b [Dec. 1936]) that the " coming " in question may be that which took place during Jesus' ministry : even Pentecost is much too early to be described as occurring before " some " of the bystanders should taste death. Prof. J. M. Creed (in *E.T.* xlviii. 184a–185b [Jan. 1937]) insists that the coming of the Kingdom in power is a future coming, almost, if not quite, contemporary with certain survivors seeing it ; but he assumes that the verse is to be closely linked with those that precede it.

[2] Weinel (*Theol.* 54, small print) rejects it. Cf. also Dalman, *W.J.* 147-156 ; Sharman, *Future*, 254–256 ; Sasse in *T.W.N.T.* i. 202–209.

the (coming) age " (see below, pp. 234f.). Jesus' occasional use of this adjective renders it more credible that he used the noun from which it comes, though it so happens that the direct evidence for this latter statement is somewhat weak. What is to happen in, and to characterize, the coming age will need to be considered later under other headings.

Both the Lucan and the Matthæan versions of Jesus' model prayer contain the petition, " May Thy Kingdom come " (Lk. xi. 2 L ; Mt. vi. 10 M). Unless we adopt in Lk. the precarious variant reading, " May Thy Holy Spirit come upon us and cleanse us " (see above, p. 166 n. 1), we have no good reason for doubting that " May Thy Kingdom come " is what Luke wrote.[1] It is difficult to feel sure, one way or another, in regard to the original text of Lk. : but even if it did not contain any mention of the Kingdom, it would not follow that the petitions in Mt., " May Thy Kingdom come, may Thy Will be done—as in heaven, (so) also on earth ", are not primitive (see above, p. 166) ; and if they be accepted as probably a part of what Jesus dictated, then they reveal unambiguously his belief in a future " coming " of the Kingdom, distinguishable from any presence of it already realized, and apparently capable of being hastened on by his followers' prayers.[2]

I close my array of testimonia with a dubious reference, on which I should be disposed to lay no stress : in the interpretation of the Parable of the Tares, Jesus is made to say, " Then will the righteous shine out like the sun in the Kingdom of their Father " (Mt. xiii. 43 M or m). If it were genuine, we could group this saying with Lk. xiii. 28–30 = Mt. viii. 11f. Q (see above, p. 197). One might perhaps quote also Mt. xxv. 34 M, except for the fact that the description, in presupposing the grievous sufferings of Jesus' followers, hardly belongs to the body of evidence we are at present studying.

(7) Before attempting to summarize the import of the passages just discussed, note must be taken of one interesting saying of an apparently-contrary signification. According to Lk. xvii. 20f. L, Jesus, ' having been asked by the Pharisees

---

[1] I take it that Dr. Manson (*Teaching*, 128f.) is inclined to reject " Thy Kingdom come " in favour of the v.l. about the Spirit. He does not give any other convincing reason against it. Dr. Moffatt (*Theol. of the Gospels*, 73 n.) thinks Luke purposely omitted " May Thy Kingdom come," because of its eschatological or semi-political connotation.

[2] Dr. Dodd quotes the prayer for the coming of the Kingdom as echoing " (though, as we shall see, with a difference) " the futurist eschatology of the Jews (*Parables*, 42) : but he nowhere discusses the question as to how he would reconcile it with his contention that Jesus taught only " realized eschatology "

when the Kingdom of God was coming, replied to them and said, " The Kingdom of God does not come (in a way discernible) with watching, nor will men say, " Behold ! here (it is) ! ' or ' There (it is) ! ' For behold ! the Kingdom of God is (already) in your midst ! " ' Now altogether apart from the interesting question as to whether the closing words should be rendered so or " within you " (see above, p. 130 [3]), the preceding phrases certainly seem to deny that spectacular coming which certain other sayings (e.g., Mk. ix. 1 = Lk. ix. 27 = Mt. xvi. 28) seem to predict.[1] It is indeed clear that, however we render ἐντὸς ὑμῶν, Jesus is here speaking of the Kingdom as a present reality, in the way in which (as we have fully recognized) he often spoke and thought of it. Perhaps the true explanation of the passage is that, desiring to emphasize this present aspect, he does so in a manner strange indeed to us, but customary in Bible-times, namely, by rhetorically denying for the moment the contrasted (futuristic) aspect, without however seriously meaning that it ought not to be entertained.[2] Some allowance ought also perhaps to be made for the possibility that, as different topics came successively before him, Jesus's words were not always rigidly and literally consistent with all he had said at other times ; nor can the tendency of the early Church (or of a particular Evangelist) to gloss certain of the Lord's sayings for the sake of interpretation be altogether excluded from our calculations.[3] In this case, one may

---

[1] Unless, with Von Gall (Βασιλεία, 474f.), we can take the words to mean that the Kingdom will come so suddenly that no purpose will be served by watching for it (see above, p. 130 n. 2).

[2] Numerous examples of emphasis obtained by such means may be found in the Bible : see, e.g., 1 Kings xxii. 31 = 2 Chron. xviii. 30, Isa. xi. 3f., Mk. ix. 37, 1 Cor. ii. 4, iv. 20, Eph. vi. 7, John vi. 27, vii. 16, xii. 44, 49, xiv. 24, 1 John iii. 18 : probably also Hos. vi. 6, quoted in Mt. ix. 13a, xii. 7 M (see above, p. 152). A somewhat analogous idiom is seen in passages like Lk. xiv. 14 L, Isa. xii. 1 (Heb.), Rom. vi. 17 (Gk. and A.V.), where English requires a *concessive* sentence : these put us in the way of a true exegesis of Lk. x. 21 = Mt. xi. 25 Q—as McNeile (*St. Matthew*, 161b) says, " Jesus was thankful, not that the σοφοί were ignorant but, that the νήπιοι knew ". A proper recognition of the existence of this custom of securing emphasis by means of some form of overstatement or hyperbole (cf. Mk. xi. 23 = Mt. xvii. 20b = Mt. xxi. 21 [cf. Lk. xvii. 6 Q ?] ; Mk. x. 25 = Lk. xviii. 25 = Mt. xix. 24) will help us to a right understanding of other difficult passages, such as Isa. xxii. 14, Mk. ii. 17b = Lk. v. 32 = Mt. ix. 13b, Mk. iii. 28f. = Mt. xii. 31 and Lk. xii. 10 = Mt. xii. 32 Q (the unpardonable sin—see below, p. 213), and Lk. xv. 7 (Q ?) = Mt. xviii. 13 (Q + m ?) : perhaps also Phil. iii. 7. Rabbinic literature abounds in such instances of hyperbole. Cf. C. J. Cadoux in *E. T.* lii. 378–381 (July 1941).

[3] Apart from Lk. xxii. 30, " the Kingdom is not presented in Proto-Luke as an eschatological idea. It does not come with observation (xvii. 20), and its presence is nowhere associated with the Coming of the Son of Man . . . " (V. Taylor, *Third Gosp.* 256f.).

hesitate to dogmatize ; but it is certainly unsafe to pit this single passage against the combined weight of the other evidence.

(8) That evidence seems to me amply sufficient to show that, from the beginning of the Ministry, and before the tragic end of it was anticipated, Jesus, besides finding in the success of his work a proof that in a real sense God's Kingdom was already present and active, looked forward to some sort of future climax, at which the Kingdom would, in another sense, " come with power ", in a way for all men to see.[1] In regard to the problem as to how soon he expected it to come, there does indeed seem to be a very considerable difference between saying, " The time has been fulfilled, and the Kingdom of God has drawn near ", and saying that some persons of that generation should not die until they should see that the Kingdom had actually come with power ; and the question might not unreasonably be asked, Can these two utterances possibly refer to the same coming event ? Yet we must remember that, while the present and the future manifestations of the Kingdom were usually distinct in Jesus' mind, there may well have come moments when the two could be temporarily fused in a single conception. While I have argued above (pp. 198f. n. 4) that his opening proclamation means rather the near approach than the actual arrival of the Kingdom, yet it is not impossible that he was thinking loosely of it as a coming glory, without differentiating between chronologically nearer and remoter stages of its progress. There is the further possibility that Mk. ix. 1 = Lk. ix. 27 = Mt. xvi. 28 may after all belong to the period subsequent to Jesus' foreknowledge of the Passion, where in fact the Gospels place it (see above, p. 199). On the other hand, if we were right in attributing to Jesus a real wish that Israel should under him convert the Gentile world (see above, pp. 147-162) and become reconciled to the Roman Empire (see above, pp. 163-174)—both of them schemes inconsistent with his own failure to win Israel—then we must infer that he expected some years at least to elapse before the final consummation should occur.

(9) There has been a very marked tendency on the part of modern scholars to lay special stress on those sayings of Jesus which, either by direct statement or by suggestion, refer the

---

[1] Cf. N. Schmidt, *Prophet of Naz.* 298 ; *The Lord of Life*, 61 n. ; Otto, *Kingdom*, 51, 147-149 ; H. V. Martin in *E.T.* li. 88-90 (Nov. 1939 : he attempts to do justice to the data by describing the eschatology of Jesus neither as " realized ", nor as " futurist ", but as " proleptic ").

final and triumphant coming of the Kingdom to the sovereign initiative and agency of God, and to interpret these statements and suggestions as if they were intended to deny implicitly that this coming is to any degree or in any way dependent on the behaviour of men.[1] By some the Kingdom is represented as a kind of irresistible automatic power, which forges its way ahead irrespective of human co-operation or resistance.[2]

Such language is in some measure justified by the well-known Semitic and ancient Jewish habit of speaking of God as the sole cause of all happenings. The language of the Bible is, as all readers of it know, strongly tinged with religious determinism ;[3] and Jesus himself, as was only natural, occasionally used language of a deterministic colour. But far more has been read into these Gospel-allusions to the supreme causality of God than the authors of the words ever intended them to convey ; and the idea has been exaggerated by some almost to the point of absurdity and self-contradiction.[4] The exaggeration is

[1] So Holtzmann, *Synopt.* 132 ("Niemand kann das Kommen des Reiches Gottes durch selbstthätiges Mitanfassen beschleunigen ; es kommt, wenn nach Gottes Willen seine Zeit da ist . . . ") ; Burkitt, *Earliest Sources,* 62 (". . . it is for God, not for man, to bring it in . . . " : see also above, p. 26 n. 2) ; Bultmann, *Jesus,* 35 (". . . Sie ist als eschatologische eine schlechthin übernatürliche Grösse ", not needing man for its realization) ; Rawlinson, *St. Mark,* 56 (". . . our Lord regards the *dénouement* of the Kingdom as in no sense the work of man—nay, not even as His own work— but as the work of God. All that man can do is to prepare and make ready for the great Event "), 58 ; Gloege, *Reich Gottes,* 67–71 (yet cf. 31f.) ; K. L. Schmidt in *R.G.G.* iii (1929) 126 (C. 1), 129f. (C. 2a : ". . . Die Frage ist die, ob wir Menschen, wenn das Reich kommt—und es kommt ohne uns, ohne unser Zutun—, zu ihm gehören oder nicht. Das Reich Gottes herbeizwingen wollen,ist menschlicher Fürwitz, ist verfeinertes Zelotentum, ist selbstgerechtes Pharisäertum . . ."), 134 ; Easton, *Christ in the Gospels,* 160 (". . . the new age is almost anything rather than the result of evolutionary process . . . ") ; K. L. Schmidt in *T.W.N.T.* i. 585f., 588f. ; R. N. Flew in *E.T.* xlvi. 216f. (Feb. 1935) ; Dodd, *Parables,* 45 (". . . the coming of the Kingdom of God is not represented as something dependent on the attitude of men ") ; Kümmel, *Eschatologie,* 12f. (no development of the Kingdom on earth) ; Cadbury, *Peril,* 183 (". . . Jesus' relation with God was not active and eager coöperation but loyal acceptance of what God determined ") ; B. T. D. Smith, *Parables,* 79 (". . . the rule of God is at hand, and nothing that man can do or fail to do will hinder its appearing : . . . ") ; Otto, *Kingdom,* 113, 117–120 ; V. Taylor, *Sacrifice,* 10f. ; Flew, *Church,* 120, 254 ; Dodd, *Hist. and the Gosp.* 123 ("The Kingdom of God . . . is not a programme for human action, but the proclamation of an act of God ").

[2] Cf. Rawlinson, *St. Mark,* 58 ("The bringing in of the Kingdom is God's affair, and His victory is assured, and that soon ") ; Manson, *Teaching,* 166– 170 ("The Kingdom of God must and will triumph : . . . Against the might of the Kingdom of God all the forces of evil are powerless . . . the sovereignty of God is essentially the working out, to a predetermined and inevitable end, of God's holy purpose . . . ") ; Otto, *Kingdom,* 54f., 103–112 ; B. T. D. Smith, *Parables,* 79 (as in last n.).

[3] Cf. Schürer, *G. J. V.* ii. 461–463.

[4] See the excellent art. by Rev. J. Lendrum on 'The Impression from the

partly due (with some authors almost wholly due) to the prevalent passion for showing up the errors of liberalism. The liberals often spoke of " building ", " extending ", or " bringing in ", the Kingdom of God among men : and it is largely under the influence of that strong conservative reaction against liberalism from which we are now suffering that modern theologians are laying all the stress on the impotence of man and the exclusive agency of God.[1]

But, as I have already more than once pointed out (see above, pp. 26, 43, 66 n. 1, 178f. [5], 188f. [7]), this Biblical determinism (if we may call it that) was never in practical life interpreted as excluding the vigorous activity and even the initiative of man. God might be said to harden Pharaoh's heart : but nonetheless Pharaoh was thought of and treated just as if he were personally responsible. The betrayal of the Son of Man might be fore-ordained ; but nonetheless is Judas condemned.[2] And if the Hebrew felt no logical difficulty in thus carrying back even the iniquities of men to the ordinances of Providence, much more ready was he to ascribe to God those human achievements over which he could rejoice. When Jonathan was about to make his desperate assault on the Philistine garrison, what he said to his armour-bearer was, " It may be that Yahweh will act for us " (1 Sam. xiv. 6). No Hebrew soldier ever made his belief that victory and defeat depended upon God an excuse for not fighting himself to the best of his ability (see Joab's words in 2 Sam. x. 12).[3] It is only in the fictitious stories in the Book of Chronicles that the Hebrew host is told, " . . . The battle is not yours, but God's . . . Ye shall not need to fight in this battle, . . . ", and triumphs over a horde of enemies without striking a blow (2 Chron. xx. 1–30). The Hebrew builder did not omit to plan and erect his house because in his devout

---

Gospels that all was fixed Beforehand ', in *E.T.* xlii. 345–350 (May 1931). He is, however, disposed to think that the Evangelists have exaggerated the use of deterministic language by Jesus.

[1] For a typical statement, see Rev. Alan Richardson's art. in *The Student Movement*, xxxix (1937) 122b. Cf. also W. Temple in *Church, Community, and State*, iv (1938) 61f. The Barthians are naturally to the fore in this new trend in Gospel-criticism.

[2] Menzies, *Earliest Gospel*, 251b, 255a ; Bartlet, *St. Mark*, 383.

[3] We get a more modern instance of the same attitude in the custom of the Calvinist William of Orange to ascribe directly to the Will of God all the fortunes of the war the Dutch were strenuously waging against Spain : see Motley, *Dutch Republic* (ed. 1874), 408b, 518b, 522b, 572a, 849b (" ' . . . God has said that he would furnish the ravens with food, and the lions with their prey ', said he ; ' but the birds and the lions do not, therefore, sit in their nests and their lairs, waiting for their food to descend from heaven, but they seek it where it is to be found ' . . . "), 881b.

moods he realized that " Except the Lord build the house, they labour in vain that build it " (Psa. cxxvii. 1 ; cf. also 3, concerning offspring). Nor would it ever have occurred to the Hebrew husbandman to neglect his toilsome ploughing, sowing, and reaping, because forsooth the harvest was God's gift.

So too, surely, in the case of the Kingdom of God. Just as many of the Rabbis held that the time for the Messiah's coming was dependent on Israel's repentance and obedience,[1] so did Jesus make it clear, both by his own strenuous activity and by his urgent teaching and his injunction that men should pray for the coming of the Kingdom (see above, p. 201), that human agency had an indispensable part to play in securing the triumph of God's cause. Some modern expositors have been misled by Jesus' undoubted disapproval of the violence of the Zealots into hastily concluding that he assigned no part at all to human responsibility in the matter.[2] His Parable of the Seed growing secretly (Mk. iv. 26–29) has often been explained as if its purpose was to bring out the insignificance or almost the irrelevance of any human activity in regard to the coming of the Kingdom, and the sole dependence of this latter on the sovereign act of God.[3] But if so, the Parable—with its allusions to the farmer's sowing and reaping, and his dependence on the clock-like succession of the seasons—is singularly ill-adapted to its purpose. It brings out, indeed, the mystery of the Divine workings, and (by implication) the impotence of man without them : but so far from " excluding the thought of human agency ", or emphasizing the incalculability of the time at which God will act, it does the exact opposite. The farmer's strenuous co-operation with God and his confident reliance on a harvest at a particular time are integral parts of the truth which the Parable conveys.[4] Moreover, if, as we have seen (above, pp. 112f.), the Kingdom meant for Jesus, not the victory of God's irresistible royal power, but the willing personal acceptance of his fatherly rule by men, then it is childish and self-contradictory to talk of the Kingdom coming

---

[1] Cohen, *Everyman's Talmud* (1932), 373. Cf. N. Micklem in *Queen's Quarterly* (Kingston, Canada), Spring 1929, 211 (" The advent of the day of blessedness in the teaching of the great prophets . . . is always ethically conditioned and therefore undetermined "), 216.

[2] Cf. Montefiore, *S.G.*[2] I. 105f., and K. L. Schmidt, as quoted above, p. 204 n.1.

[3] Cf. Holtzmann, *Theol.* i. 289f. ; Bultmann, *Jesus*, 35 ; Rawlinson, *St. Mark*, 56 ; Otto, *Kingdom*, 113, 117–122 ; B. T. D. Smith, *Parables*, 120, 130 (" The statement that the earth bears fruit of itself is intended to exclude the thought of human agency. As the harvest is God-given, so is the Kingdom . . . ").

[4] Cf. Moffatt, *Theol. of the Gospels*, 57–59 ; A. T. Cadoux, *Parables*, 163.

irrespective of anything that man can do to oppose or to forward it.[1]

While Jesus therefore occasionally used deterministic language, he is not with strict accuracy to be described as a determinist or predestinarian.[2] In vindicating his teaching against what I hold to be a one-sided and erroneous interpretation of it, I neither ignore the existence of the serious problem of God's causality, nor do I claim to have solved it. All theists must grant that, since God is the Creator of all, He is *in some sense* the cause of all that happens. Moreover, if man's freedom is within its limits absolute, it is hard to see any ground for being sure of God's ultimate triumph. Though guaranteed on the arena of eternity, that triumph may, within the limits of the finite, be necessarily insecure. But whatever be the ultimate solution of this deep problem, we may be sure of the falsity of any proffered solution which refuses to recognize a part of the essential data of the problem—the freedom and consequent responsibility of man.

[1] Cf. A. T. Cadoux, *Theol. of Jes.* 52–55: the injunction to " seek His kingdom " is " quite unintelligible of a catastrophically introduced heavenly kingdom, which might be watched for, but could hardly be sought ".

[2] Cf. Schweitzer, *L.J.F.* 400–405 = *Quest*, 352–356 ; Holtzmann, *Theol.* i. 262–264 ; Cadbury, *Peril*, 184–186.

CHAPTER III

REWARDS AND PUNISHMENTS IN GENERAL

(1) Confining ourselves to the same limits in regard to materials as before, (2) we note that Jesus often spoke quite generally of Rewards (3) and Punishments, (4) special figures used by him for the former being Life (5) and Salvation, (6) and for the latter Loss. (7) His expectations in regard to conditions on earth in the immediate future can be dimly traced, (8) but those concerning the ulterior future of man are complicated by his apparent fusion into a single forecast of ideas concerning the life after death with those concerning the life after the final Coming of the Kingdom.

(1) A very considerable portion of the recorded teaching of Jesus is concerned more or less directly with the rewards and punishments which attend on human conduct. This body of instruction wears at first sight an appearance of great complexity, even of confusion. Possibly the conditions of the records are such that no real clarification or unification of the teaching can now be effected. Even so, however, it is worth our while to follow up such clues as we have, and to disentangle the several items of teaching with a view to seeing how far unity of thought can be discerned in what at first seems so unsystematic. We therefore propose in the first place to refrain as before from using any allusion made by Jesus to reward or punishment which involves a reference to his Passion. Within the field thus narrowed, we shall in this chapter confine ourselves to the more generally-worded allusions, those namely which do not seem to deal specifically with the life after death or with the final crisis considered in the previous chapter. It must, of course, be borne in mind that, even when Jesus spoke apparently in quite general terms, he may yet have had in mind some fairly-definite and concrete form of reward or punishment. Nevertheless, it is useful to set the general utterances by themselves, as these enable us to grasp perhaps more clearly the truths and principles conveyed by the less simple and more pictorial descriptions.

(2) We may well begin with a group of sayings in which Jesus makes use of the very word " reward " ($\mu\iota\sigma\theta\acute{o}\varsigma$). The

Greek word and its Semitic original mean simply " pay ",
" wages ", " recompense " : thus, in the Parable of the Hired
Labourers, the master says to his steward, " Call the labourers,
and pay (them) the(ir) wages " (ἀπόδος τὸν μισθόν : Mt. xx.
8 M) ; and Jesus himself, when authorizing his missionaries to
live on hospitality, says, " For the labourer deserves his wages "
(Lk. x. 7 [ἄξιος . . . τοῦ μισθοῦ αὐτοῦ] = Mt. x. 10b [where
τροφῆς, " food ", appears instead of μισθοῦ] Q). The word
therefore clearly belongs to the sphere of paid industry ; yet
Jesus uses it several times over, not only of the way in which
God requites obedience, but as a definite inducement to
obedience. One may observe in passing that theologians of a
certain school (which I need not characterize further) would
do well to devote a little time to pondering over the sayings
now to be quoted.[1]

To those who suffer for righteousness sake, Jesus says,
" Rejoice on that day, and leap for joy ; for behold ! great is
your reward in the heavens " (Lk. vi. 23 = Mt. v. 12 Q : but
see below, pp. 238f.).

In the teaching about love for enemies (Lk. vi. 32–36 =
Mt. v. 43–48), which certainly goes back to Q, but in Mt. may
depend on conflation with M, both versions contain the word
" reward ", thus proving it to have stood in Q. Lk. has
(vi. 35), " your reward will be great ". Mt. has (v. 46), " For
if ye love (only) those who love you, what reward do ye get ? "
— a clause for which the Lucan equivalent is, " What thanks
(χάρις) do ye get ? " (Lk. vi. 32, 33, 34).

Mk. ix. 41: " Whoever gives you a cup of water to drink,
because ye belong to Christ, I tell you truly, he will certainly
not lose his reward ". Jesus could not have used the second
of these clauses (ἐν ὀνόματι ὅτι χριστοῦ ἐστέ—see above,
pp. 58f. [b]), which is missing from the Matthæan parallel (Mt. x.
42) ; but the rest of the verse may quite well be a genuine
logion. Mt. prefixes to it two similar ones, probably from M :
" He who receives a prophet on the ground of his being a
prophet will receive a prophet's reward ; and he who receives
a righteous man on the ground of his being a righteous man will
receive a righteous man's reward " (Mt. x. 41 M).

Mt. vi. 1 M : " Take heed not to do your (deeds of)
righteousness before men, in order to be seen by them : other-

---

[1] Cf. also Holtzmann, *Theol.* i. 258–262 ; Rashdall, *Conscience*, 290–294 ;
Box, *St. Matthew*, 110 ; Montefiore, *S.G.*[2] II. 40–43, 82 ; Windisch, *Bergpredigt.*,
16f. ; R. Niebuhr, *An Interp. of Christ. Ethics* (1937), 62–66 ; Westermarck,
Christianity and Morals (1939), 60–68.

wise ye get no reward from your Father in the heavens ". In the immediate sequel, it is three times over stated that those who indulge in such self-display " duly receive *their* reward " (ἀπέχουσιν τὸν μισθὸν αὐτῶν : Mt. vi. 2, 5, 16 M), and that God " will duly requite " (ἀποδώσει) those who give alms, pray, and fast in secret (Mt. vi. 4, 6, 18 M). We may note here, not only that the requiting is in one case stated to be done " publicly " (ἐν τῷ φανερῷ, Mt. vi. 4—though the reading is not certain), but—what is still more significant—that the words for " duly receiving " and " duly requiting " (ἀπέχω, ἀποδίδωμι) are, like μισθός, thoroughly commercial terms, which are frequently found in commercial documents, though they are also used in more general senses.[1]

One of the above-quoted passages (Lk. vi. 23 = Mt. v. 12 Q) forms the latter half of a " beatitude "—another formula for alluding to the rewards of the righteous. Most of the beatitudes are immediately followed by a clause stating the ground of the happiness, and are therefore dealt with by us elsewhere ; but there are two which do not do so :—

Lk. vii. 23 = Mt. xi. 6 Q : " And happy is any one who is not made to stumble (by what he sees) in me ".

Lk. xi. 28 L : " Happy are they who listen to the word of God and keep it ".

We may note next a little group of sayings referring to the future exaltation of the humble (Lk. xiv. 11b = Mt. xxiii. 12b Q ; Lk. xviii. 14 fin. L) : the last will be first (Mk. x. 31 = Mt. xix. 30 = Mt. xx. 16 ; Lk. xiii. 30a L) : he and he only who makes himself a servant of others can hope for true greatness (Mk. x. 43f. = Mt. xx. 26f. [+ Mt. xxiii. 11] : cf. Lk. xxii. 26 L)—a lesson enforced on one occasion by the example of a little child (Mk. ix. 35f. = Lk. ix. 47f. = Mt. xviii. 2, 4). Of the many called, only a few are chosen (Mt. xxii. 14 M).

In several passages, the reward takes the form of comfort for those in distress—the mourners will laugh (Lk. vi. 21b = Mt. v. 4 Q) ; the hungry will be filled (Lk. vi. 21a = Mt. v. 6 Q) ; the merciful will be treated with mercy (Mt. v. 7 M) ; those who pray will receive, those who seek will find, those who knock will have the door opened to them (Lk. xi. 9f. = Mt. vii. 7f. Q) ; those who go to Jesus and learn from him will find rest, and be made to bear only an easy yoke (Mt. xi. 28–30 M).

Finally, we have a little collection of miscellaneous utterances, which exhibit great variety of expression, but may

[1] See Moulton and Milligan, *Vocab. of the Gk. N.T.* i (1914) 57f., 61b.

all perhaps be taken as expressing in some way the notion of spiritual achievement or efficiency. Here they are :—

" Happy are the pure in heart, for they will see God " (Mt. v. 8 M).

" Happy are the peacemakers, for they will be called sons of God " (Mt. v. 9 M).[1]

" Whoever does the Will of God—this (person is) my brother and sister and mother " (Mk. iii. 35 = Lk. viii. 21 = Mt. xii. 50).

" Every well-trained (disciple) will be like his teacher " (Lk. vi. 40b = Mt. x. 25a Q [but Mt. probably conflates Q and M]).

" And other (seed)s fell into the sound soil, and yielded fruit, coming up and growing, and bore thirty-fold and sixty-fold and a hundred-fold . . . And those who were sowed on the sound soil are those who listen to the word and accept it, and bear fruit thirty-fold and sixty-fold and a hundred-fold " (Mk. iv. 8, 20 = Lk. viii. 8a, 15 = Mt. xiii. 8, 23) : the second of these two verses belongs to the probably-ungenuine allegorical interpretation of the Parable of the Sower (see above, p. 48) : yet the interpretation is correct enough for our present purpose.

" For he who has—to him will (more) be given " (Mk. iv. 25a = Lk. viii. 18a = Mt. xiii. 12a [m adding " and he will be made to abound "]). Similar words are found at the end of the Parable of the Servants entrusted with Money, both in Lk. (xix. 26a) and Mt. (xxv. 29a, where M again has the additional clause).

" For on-the-strength-of thy words wilt thou be pronounced innocent " (Mt. xii. 37a M : ἐκ γὰρ τῶν λόγων σου δικαιωθήσῃ).

Acquittal at the hands of God depends on our willingness to acquit others. " Judge not, and ye will not be judged ; and condemn not, and ye will not be condemned ; let others off, and ye will be let off (yourselves) : give, and it will be given to you ; good measure, pressed down, shaken (together), overflowing, will men put into your bosom : for on the (same) scale with which ye measure (for others) will (your share) be measured out for you in return " (Lk. vi. 37f. = Mt. vii. 1f. Q : cf. Mk. iv. 24b).[2]

(3) Jesus' general allusions to punishment correspond directly in many cases to his allusions to reward. Thus, when speaking of μισθός, he implicitly affirms that those who love only those who love them will get little or none (Lk. vi. 32–34 = Mt. v. 46 Q : see above, p. 209). Those who perform the

---

[1] Cf. Windisch's art. on this Beatitude in *Z.N.W.* xxiv (1925) 240–260.
[2] Cf. Strack-Billerbeck i. 443.

observances of religion in public in order to be seen by men achieve their object, and that is their only " reward " ; they get no " reward " from God (Mt. vi. 1, 2, 5, 16 M : see above, pp. 209f.). Just as the humble will be exalted, so will those who uplift themselves be humbled (Lk. xiv. 11a = Mt. xxiii. 12a Q ; Lk. xviii. 14 L) : many of the first will be last (Mk. x. 31 = Mt. xix. 30 = Mt. xx. 16 ; Lk. xiii. 30b L). As comfort is promised to those in distress, so woes are pronounced over the fortunate (see above, p. 42 n. 1, on the meaning of οὐαί), for hunger, tears, discomfort, and discredit await them (Lk. vi. 24–26 : just possibly Q, but many would say l and ungenuine). Contrasted with the seed which, falling into good ground, produces a plentiful crop is that which for one reason or another remains unfruitful (Mk. iv. 4–7 = Lk. viii. 5–7 = Mt. xiii. 4–7) : and although the assignment of each lot of unfruitful seed to some particular group of unresponsive or inconstant hearers of Jesus' message (Mk. iv. 15–19 = Lk. viii. 12–14 = Mt. xiii. 19–22) does not in all probability go back to Jesus himself, being a part of the allegorical interpretation of the Parable (see above, p. 48), yet his general allusion in the Parable to his failure to win and hold all who heard him is plain enough. The giving of more to him who has is paralleled by the withdrawal from him who has not of even what he has (Mk. iv. 25b = Lk. viii. 18b = Mt. xiii. 12b ; Lk. xix. 26b L ? =Mt. xxii. 29b M or Q ?)—a paradoxical oriental way of saying that a man's resources increase or dwindle according to the use he makes of them. As acquittal will be pronounced on the strength of a man's words, so also will condemnation (Mt. xii. 37b M).

The notion of inefficiency suggested by Jesus' picture of the unfruitful seed reappears in a few other passages. In Mk. iv. 11f. = Lk. viii. 10 = Mt. xiii. 11, 13, and m's appendage in Mt. xiii. 14f., Jesus is represented as describing " those outside " (in distinction from " those who were about him with the Twelve ") as so incapable of understanding his teaching that he puts all things to them in parables, " in order that " they may not understand them ! Explanation of this extraordinary utterance may be sought, either (a) by taking Mark's word for " in order that " (ἵνα) as a mistaken rendering of the Aramaic relative pronoun, whereby " those outside ", who get the Parables, are simply described as being devoid of understanding ; [1] or (b) by accepting the accuracy of the record and taking Jesus'

---

[1] Manson, *Teaching,* 74–80.

words as an extreme instance of his use of deterministic language, which blurred the distinction between purpose and (even regretted) result, or (c) by regarding the passage as a quasi-Pauline explanation (by means of the notion of " judicial blindness "—cf., e.g., Rom. ix. 18, x. 16, xi. 8, 25, 1 Cor. xiv. 22a) of Jesus' failure to win Israel (see above, pp. 188f.), or (d) possibly as a confession on the part of the Church that she found the Parables hard to explain.[1] But whichever of these alternatives we prefer, if the words are words of Jesus at all, they express his awareness of a condition of insensitiveness to the truth which he could hardly have thought of as undeserved. Other allusions to inefficiency are—the saying about spoilt salt, which can no longer be made use of (Mk. ix. 50a = Lk. xiv. 34f. [Q ?] = Mt. v. 13 [Q + m ?]) ; that about untrustworthiness in regard to real riches (Lk. xvi. 10–12 L) ; that which runs, " Every plant which my heavenly Father did not plant will be rooted out " (Mt. xv. 13 M) ; and the rhetorical question, " Can a blind man guide a blind man ? Will they not both fall into a pit ? " (Lk. vi. 39 = Mt. xv. 14b Q).

Another and very terrible punishment threatened by Jesus is the refusal of Divine forgiveness of sin to those who are unforgiving to their fellow-men (Lk. xi. 4a L ; Mt. vi. 12 M ; Mt. vi. 14f. m ? ; Mk. xi. 25 ; Lk. xvii. 4 = Mt. xviii. 21f. Q ? ; Mt. xviii. 23–35 M) and to those who blaspheme against the Holy Spirit (Mk. iii. 29–30 = Mt. xii. 31 ; Lk. xii. 10 = Mt. xii. 32 Q—m adding " either in this age or in the coming [age] "). Along with these passages, we ought perhaps to take the declarations that it would be better for one who causes others to stumble to be thrown into the sea with a millstone round his neck (Mk. ix. 42 = Mt. xviii. 6 ; Lk. xvii. 1f. = Mt. xviii. 7 Q), and for the betrayer of the Son of Man never to have been born (Mk. xiv. 21 = Lk. xxii. 22 = Mt. xxvi. 24). In the interpretation of these passages, it is necessary to remember what was said a few pages back (p. 202 n. 2) to the effect that the use of strong hyperbole, not intended to be taken literally, as a means of securing emphasis, was a well-understood habit of Jewish speech.[2]

[1] A. T. Cadoux, *Parables*, 24f.

[2] Cf., in addition to the passages quoted above, the qualified use of עד־עולם in 1 Sam. i. 22 and Isa. xxxii. 14 (cf. 15), of לעלם in Exod. xxi. 6, of עולם in Deut. xv. 17, 1 Sam. xxvii. 12, and Job. xl. 28 (Eng. xli. 4), and of נצח (לנצח) in Psa. xiii. 1, lxxix. 5, lxxxix. 46a. " If the Lord spoke as a Jew to Jews, and used a type of expression current in His day, and derived from the O.T., He meant, and would be understood to mean, no more than that blasphemy against the Holy Spirit, by whose power He worked, was a terrible sin,—more

Jesus' account of a demoniac who, after exorcism, suffers a relapse, so that his last state is worse than his first, is rather an observation in pathology than an allusion to punishment, although m takes it as a description of what will happen to " this wicked generation " (Lk. xi. 24–26 = Mt. xii. 43–45 Q).

I conclude this collection of Jesus' references in general terms to punishment by alluding to two passages on which I forbear, because of their obscurity, to enlarge :—

Lk. xx. 18 L : " Everyone who falls upon this stone will be shattered ; but as for him upon whom it falls it will crush him to powder ". The saying probably does not belong to its present context : what it may have meant in its original context, who shall say ? [1]

Mt. v. 21f. M. Several suggestions have been made regarding the original order and precise meaning of the clauses in this passage : but none of them is sufficiently sure to call for further comment at this point.

(4) One important concept used by Jesus in his description of future rewards is that of " life ".[2] The word (usually the cognate verb) is used in the Gospels, and by Jesus himself, in the ordinary sense of human animal existence prior to bodily death (Lk. ii. 36 ; Lk. xvi. 25 L ; Mt. xxvii. 63 M), especially in the sense of such existence when secured in spite of physical danger (Mk. v. 23 = Mt. ix. 18, of Jairus' daughter ; Lk. xxiv. 5 l and 23 L, of Jesus after his resurrection). In Jewish parlance, however, life was especially a characteristic of God (Mt. xvi. 16 m ; Mt. xxvi. 63 m), though Jesus himself does not use it in this connexion. He does however use it of that rightful mode of moral and spiritual existence which God has ordained, provided, and willed for man, thus :—

Lk. iv. 4 = Mt. iv. 4 Q, quoting Deut. viii. 3 : " It has been written, ' Not on bread alone shall man live ' " : m completes the quotation, ' but on every word that issues from the mouth of God '.

Lk. xii. 15 L : " See to it, and guard yourselves against all covetousness, because a man's life does not consist of the things that belong to him when he has abundance ".

Lk. xv. 24 L : " This son of mine was dead, and has come to life again ; he was lost, and has been found ". Almost the

---

terrible than blasphemy against man " (McNeile, *St. Matthew*, 179). Cf. also Leckie, *World to Come*, 149f., 350; C. J. Cadoux in *E.T.* lii. 378–381 (July 1941).
    [1] For suggestions, see A. T. Cadoux, *Parables*, 198f. ; Creed, *St. Luke*, 246f.
    [2] Cf. Gloege, *Reich Gottes*, 162–170 ; H-D. Wendland, *Eschatologie*, 74–89.

same words recur in Lk. xv. 32 L.   The contrast to such true
life in the case of the prodigal was his wanton behaviour in the
far country (Lk. xv. 13 L : ζ ῶ ν ἀσώτως).

(5) Closely allied to the conception of life is the conception
of salvation or safety.   We do not need to linger over the use
made of it by others than Jesus in the Lucan Protevangelion,
where it occasionally recalls the Old-Testament idea of a
national or at least a communal triumph over, or rescue from,
enemies or other dangers (Lk. i. 69, 71), but is also employed
to designate deliverance from sin by forgiveness (Lk. i. 77 :
cf. Mt. i. 21), so that—in the passages in which its specific
character is unnamed—it may be taken to refer generally to
the coming achievements of the newly-born Messiah (Lk. i. 47,
ii. 11, 30).   l, completing a quotation from the Septuagint of
Isa. xl. 3–5, uses it in this sense in connexion with John the
Baptist's message (Lk. iii. 6), just as Symeon had used it in
connexion with the dedication of Jesus in the Temple (ii. 30).

Jesus himself and those who talk with him refer to the
restoration of physical or mental health as " saving " (Mk. iii. 4
=Lk. vi. 9 [withered hand] ; Mk. v. 23 and Lk. viii. 50 l [illness[1]
resembling death] ; Mk. v. 28 = Mt. ix. 21, Mk. v. 34 = Lk.
viii. 48 = Mt. ix. 22a, and Mt. ix. 22b m [issue of blood] ; Mk.
vi. 56 = Mt. xiv. 36 [miscellaneous sickness] ; Mk. x. 52 =
Lk. xviii. 42 [blindness] ; Lk. viii. 36 l [madness] ; Lk. xvii.
19 L [leprosy]), and similarly describe a rescue from drowning
(Mt. viii. 25 m ; Mt. xiv. 30 M or m), from burning (Lk. ix. 56
L, if the reading may be accepted), or from crucifixion (Mk.
xv. 30 = Mt. xxvii. 40 ; Mk. xv. 31 = Lk. xxiii. 35 = Mt.
xxvii. 42 ; Mt. xxvii. 49 m).

He was, however, concerned in a deeper sense with the word
and its derivatives.   " Salvation " of some kind was, as we
have just seen, thought of as being par excellence the work of the
Messiah (Lk. i. 47, ii. 11, 30 ; Lk, iii. 6 l) : and it was doubtless in
this sense that on the cross Jesus was ironically said to have
" saved others " (Mk. xv. 31 = Lk. xxiii. 35 = Mt. xxvii. 42),[2]
and that l, in reproducing Mark's interpretation of the Parable
of the Sower, speaks of men being " saved " by having believed
on his word (Lk. viii. 12).   In an apparently-general way Jesus
declares that the Son of Man had come for the purpose of saving
those in danger of being lost (Lk. ix. 56 L [though the reading is
doubtful] ; Lk. xix. 10 L).   More concrete content is given to
the idea of salvation when it is closely connected with forgive-

---

[1] Cf. Swete, *St. Mark*, 102a.
[2] McNeile, *St. Matthew*, 420a

ness of sins, as is the case in the Lucan and Matthæan birth-stories (Lk. i. 77 and Mt. i. 21) and in Jesus' words to the penitent prostitute (Lk. vii. 48, 50 L) and concerning the reformed Zacchæus (Lk. xix. 9 L).

We shall see in a moment that the idea of salvation is the exact opposite of the idea of loss : another exact opposite of " being lost " is " being found ", which latter term must therefore rank as an exact synonym of " being saved ". We must therefore include here a reference to the Parables of the finding of the Lost Sheep (Lk. xv. 4–7 = Mt. xviii. 12–14 Q), the finding of the Lost Coin (Lk. xv. 8–10 Q or L ?), and the return of the Prodigal Son (Lk. xv. 24, 32 L)—in all of which the finding is bound up with the repentance of the sinner. Another synonym is that of " justification ", used by Jesus of the penitent tax-collector praying in the Temple (Lk. xviii. 14 L).

We shall have to note later—under a more specifically-eschatological heading—other passages in which " finding " appears as a synonym of " saving ". But it may be worth while at this point to consider the root-idea lying beneath this group of words. This is most clearly seen by a comprehensive study of the use of the word "loss" ($\dot{a}\pi\dot{\omega}\lambda\epsilon\iota a$) and its cognates, the results of which study (see below, pp. 217f.) we may now be allowed to anticipate. The one common notion running through all the occurrences of words derived from this latter root, whether used literally or metaphorically, is that of the frustration, accidental or intentional, temporary or permanent, of the will of the owner of the lost object, the non-fulfilment of the purpose for which he intended to use it. If this frustration should (as in the case of the Lost Coin and the Lost Sheep) happen to take the form of ignorance as to the object's where-abouts, then the surmounting of such frustration is the " finding " of what was lost. More generally, however, especially if the frustration arises from some other cause, the surmounting of it is described as " salvation ". As applied to men in their relation to God, " salvation " then must mean the fulfilment by man of God's purpose for him, i.e., man's filial, loving, obedient, and intimate relationship with God. What frustrates that purpose of God is mostly the sin of man, though it may also be something other than sin (ignorance, mental disease, etc.). Hence the close connexion we find between salvation and the forgiveness of sins, and the inclusion of the refusal of Divine forgiveness among the punishments that wait on certain forms of sin (see above, p. 213). It may also be noted that, while these particular forms of reward and punishment are often spoken of in eschatological terms, they are in their essence unattached to any particular time, and are therefore rightly included under our present general heading.

(6) The English verbs " to lose ", " to perish ", " to destroy ", with their several parts and with the nouns and adjectives corresponding to them, all have to be used in our English Bible in order to translate the various parts of a single Greek verb, ἀπόλλυμι, and the abstract noun derived from it, ἀπώλεια. The root-idea behind these Greek words is, as has just been explained, that of the frustration of an owner's purpose. Thus, we find them used in the Gospels of spilt wine and burst wine-skins (Mk. ii. 22 = Lk. v. 37 = Mt. ix. 17), of wrongly-used perfume (Mk. xiv. 4 = Mt. xxvi. 8), of a mis-laid coin (Lk. xv. 8f. Q or L ?), and of straying sheep (Lk. xv. 4, 4, 6 Q [but Mt. (xviii. 12–14) introduces the word only in the moral to the story] ; Mt. x. 6 M ; Mt. xv. 24 M or m[1])—also of failing to win a reward (Mk. ix. 41 = Mt. x. 42). As applied to human life, they can be used of some part of the body that is severed, e.g., hair (Lk. xxi. 18 l), eye (Mt. v. 29 m), or hand (Mt. v. 30 m). The verb ἀπόλλυμι in the active means virtually to kill (Mk. i. 24 = Lk. iv. 34 ; Mk. iii. 6 = Mt. xii. 14 ; Mk. ix. 22 ; Mk. xi. 18 = Lk. xix. 47 ; Mk. xii. 9 = Lk. xx. 16 = Mt. xxi. 41 ; Lk. vi. 9 [Mk. iii. 4 has ἀποκτεῖναι] ; Lk. xvii. 27 Q ? [Mt. xxiv. 39 has ἦρεν] ; Lk. xvii. 29 Q ? ; Mt. ii. 13 ; Mt. xxii. 7 m ; Mt. xxvii. 20 m) : in the middle voice it means to undergo violent or untoward death (Mk. iv. 38 = Lk. viii. 24 = Mt. viii. 25 [drowning] ; Lk. xi. 51 Q ? [= Mt. xxiii. 35 ; assassination] ; Lk. xiii. 33 L [martyrdom] ; Lk. xv. 17 L [starvation] ; Mt. xxvi. 52 M [slaughter]).

In the deeper religious sense the idea of " loss " forms, as has been said, the exact antithesis of " salvation ". It stands for the fate of those who stray from God's purpose for them. This fact comes out most clearly in Mt. xviii. 14 (M or m), " Thus it is not will(ed) before my Father in the heavens that one of these little ones should be lost ". Jesus speaks of " the lost sheep of the House of Israel " (Mt. x. 6 M ; Mt. xv. 24 M or m : see above), and more generally of " that which has been lost " (Lk. xix. 10 L : τὸ ἀπολωλός—on the neuter singular, see above, pp. 70f. [4]). The three Parables of Loss (Lk. xv. 4–7=Mt. xviii. 12–14 Q ; Lk. xv. 8–10 Q ? ; Lk. xv. 11–32 L) pictorially illustrate the condition. The Prodigal Son, for instance, while

---

[1] McNeile (*St. Matthew*, 130a, 134a) prefers in these last two passages the stronger meaning of " perished " or " lying helpless ".

absent from his father's house, was " lost ", and that not simply because his father did not know where he was (Lk. xv. 24, 32 L). In all these instances, Jesus himself is set to reverse the process. He and his Disciples are sent after the lost sheep of the House of Israel ; " that which was lost " was what the Son of Man had come to seek and to save ; for he had come " not to destroy (ἀπολέσαι) men's lives, but to save them " (Lk. ix. 56 L, if genuine : cf. Lk. vi. 9 fin., 10 [Mk. iii. 4 f. otherwise]). The Parables of Loss, with their happy endings, are intended to be illustrations of Jesus' own redemptive work among men.

While " loss " usually refers to the persons concerned, it can also refer quite generally to the missed " reward " (Mk. ix. 41 = Mt. x. 42).

The only passages in which " dead " appears as a synonym for " lost " are Lk. xv. 24, 32 L (the Prodigal Son) and possibly Lk. vii. 22 = Mt. xi. 5 Q (see above, p. 47 n. 4).

(7) It is not possible for us to do more towards reconstructing Jesus' early expectations regarding the immediate future of human history beyond conjecturally and vaguely piecing together what our evidence leads us to infer. The task is made still more difficult by the fact that the evidence on which we have to depend has been so thoroughly overlaid by matter reflecting the darker outlook of the latter part of the Ministry. We can, however, more or less clearly discern a few general ideas concerning the coming times. The Kingdom of God would, through the activity of Jesus himself, his Disciples, and his reawakened fellow-countrymen, extend throughout the earth, until the time was ripe for God to bring about the great climax. All thought of a rebellion against Rome or a war of vengeance to be waged on the Gentiles would vanish away ; and the gentle, the peacemakers, the true sons of God, would, after a preliminary period of suffering, inherit the earth. The Son of Man, " the people of the saints of the Most High ", would become the unofficial leaders and teachers of the race. In the shade of the great tree would the birds of heaven be glad to roost. God's Will would at last be done by all mankind.

(8) All searching human thought regarding the future is apt to be complicated by an irremovable duality of interest which makes it almost impossible to produce a satisfactorily-unified forecast. Man is interested in the future fortunes of his kind on this earth ; man is also interested in the future fortunes of individuals after death. Neither of these spheres

can be ignored : but even supposing an approximate solution of the mystery in each of them is obtainable, how are the two solutions to be brought into harmonious relations with each other ?

This duality of interest had operated as a confusing factor in Jewish apocalyptic ever since Jewish thinkers had come to take seriously the idea of a future life after death. Numerous ways of getting out of the confusion had been attempted : but none had obtained general recognition ; and with such materials as the Apocalyptists employed there was little hope of unity being reached.[1]

It has, I believe, to be recognized that no such unity is discoverable in the Gospels. Jesus speaks at times about the life of men beyond the grave—a life on which they were entering in considerable numbers on every day of his own life-time. He also speaks still more frequently of the approaching cataclysm when, apparently for the whole race at once, an entire set of new conditions would, by the Coming of the Kingdom, be introduced. In speaking of both the two spheres—the conditions for the individual after his bodily death, and the conditions for men generally after the great cataclysm—Jesus uses very largely the same set of technical terms and ideas—life, death, salvation, loss, acquittal, condemnation, heaven, Hades, Paradise, Gehenna. So that it is a matter of no small difficulty to isolate the teaching about the one sphere from that about the other, while any attempt to ascertain how in the thought of Jesus they were related to one another seems quite beyond our power. We have no option but to accept, as one of the conditions of our study, this strange fusion of apparently-disparate topics, and to be prepared to forgo that measure of clarity which we instinctively desire.[2]

[1] Wendt, *Teaching*, i. 70–75 ; Leckie, *World to Come*, 28, 30, 82.

[2] Cf. W. Manson, *Christ's View*, 161 : " the fact that Jesus nowhere co-ordinates the two issues shows it was no part of His purpose to describe the future in exact or literal terms ".

CHAPTER IV

REWARDS AND PUNISHMENTS IN THE LIFE AFTER DEATH

(1) Jesus' general view of the life beyond was apparently similar to that held by his Jewish contemporaries, (2) and included belief in Paradise, an upper realm of life and joy for the righteous, (3) and in Hades or Gehenna, a nether realm of fiery torment for the unrighteous. (4) He did not explicitly express the belief, held by some, in an Intermediate State for the departed between bodily death and the general Resurrection and Judgment.

(1) Along with the vast majority of his fellow-countrymen, Jesus took the reality of the life after death for granted. When challenged by the Sadducees, he defended his belief in it by an appeal to the Old Testament. " But as for the dead being raised, have ye not read in the Book of Moses, . . . how God said to him, ' I am the God of Abraham, and God of Isaac and God of Jacob ' ? He is not a God of dead men, but of living. Ye greatly err " (Mk. xii. 26f. = Lk. xx. 37f. = Mt. xxii. 31f.). Logically and historically, this quotation does not prove the point ; but the heart of Jesus' argument is that the very existence and character of intimate relations between God and man show that God cannot allow man to perish.[1] So far as we can make out, Jesus pictured the life after death much on the same lines as other Jews did. It is, however, worth observing that, as compared with his words about the coming Kingdom, his words about the life beyond the grave are few. It has been maintained that he was particularly reticent on the subject ;[2] and certainly the bulk and number of his sayings on the subject are not great. His extant words are however characterized by extremely vivid and concrete imagery.

(2) His picture reproduces the well-known Jewish dualism. There are only two realms—one above, and one below ; and between them there is a great chasm fixed, so that no one can pass from one to the other (Lk. xvi. 26 L). The upper realm is

[1] Cf. H. T. Andrews in *Congreg. Quart.* v. 268f. (July 1927).
[2] As H. T. Andrews thinks (as in last note).

220

called " Paradise " (Lk. xxiii. 43 L : this saying must surely reflect the life-long belief of Jesus, and not solely his belief at the moment of speaking). The righteous, who by God's power at once rise or are raised into this realm from among the dead (Mk. xii. 23, 25f. = Lk. xx. 33, 35–37 = Mt. xxii. 28, 30f. ; cf. also Lk. xiv. 14 L), or (as is expressly stated in the case of Lazarus) are transported thither by the angels (Lk. xvi. 22 L), recline at table rejoicing (Lk. xvi. 25 fin. L) and feasting with Abraham (such being probably the meaning of the phrase " in Abraham's bosom " in Lk. xvi. 22f. L).[1]   The sphere seems to be once referred to by Jesus as " the Kingdom of God " (Mk. ix. 47) ; but twice in the same context it is called " the life " (Mk. ix. 43 = Mt. xviii. 8 ; Mk. ix. 45), as it is also in the Matthæan parallel to the Marcan reference to it as " the Kingdom " (Mt. xviii. 9).[2]   It is, indeed, the abode of life par excellence, for " God is not God of the dead, but of the living " (Mk. xii. 27 = Lk. xx. 38 [l adding " for all live for Him "] = Mt. xxii. 32) ; hence it is referred to as " the eternal dwellings " (Lk. xvi. 9 L).   Those living there are pictured as possessed of their earthly bodies, for they not only recline and feast, but they retain whatever mutilation or disfigurement they have suffered whilst on earth (Mk. ix. 43, 45, 47 = Mt. xviii. 8f. = Mt. v. 29f.).   On the other hand, since there is no more death (Lk. xx. 36 l : οὐδὲ γὰρ ἀποθανεῖν ἔτι δύνανται), there is no further need for the procreation of offspring : so " they neither marry, nor are married, but they are like the angels who are in the heavens " (Mk. xii. 25 = Lk. xx. 34–36 [l possibly re-writing—but see below, pp. 226 n. 2] = Mt. xxii. 30).

(3) The nether alternative to Paradise (which is visible from it—Lk. xvi. 23 L) is named " Hades ", the Greek equivalent of the old Hebrew " She'ol ", a name which originally designated simply the abode of the dead, whether good or bad, but was more and more appropriated in late Jewish thought to the place of future punishment for the unrighteous.[3]   As such, the rich man of the Parable, leaving all his earthly goods behind him (Lk. xvi. 25 L: cf. Lk. xii. 20 L), goes into it after burial (Lk. xvi. 22f. L), and is tortured by fire (Lk. xvi. 23–25, 28 L).

---

[1] Geden in *H.D.C.G.* i. 8f. ; Lambert, *ibid.* 220ab : per contra, B. T. D. Smith, *Parables*, 136 n.   Cf. John xiii. 23, 25.   On the " rising ", see below, pp. 225–227.

[2] The analogy of these passages with Lk. xii. 4f. = Mt. x. 28 Q (see next page) proves that they refer to the life after death as such, and not especially to any Last Judgment.   On them and on the equivalence of " the life " and " the Kingdom of God ", cf. Manson, *Teaching*, 276, 294 n. 4.

[3] Cf. Strack-Billerbeck iv. 1016–1026 ; Moore, *Judaism*, ii. 289–291, iii. 196.

The mention of the fire establishes the identity of this " Hades" with the region elsewhere designated as " Gehenna " (Mk. ix. 43 [" the unquenchable fire "] = Mt. xviii. 8 [" the eternal fire "] = Mt. v. 30 [" Gehenna "]; Mk. ix. 45 [" the Gehenna "]; Mk. ix. 47 [" Gehenna "] = Mt. xviii. 9 [" the Gehenna of fire "] = Mt. v. 29 [" Gehenna "]), " where their worm dies not, and the fire is not quenched " (Mk. ix. 48, quoting Isa. lxvi. 24).   Jesus was apparently referring to God when he told his followers to fear, not those who could kill only the body, but Him who is able " to destroy both soul and body in Gehenna " (Mt. x. 28 Q [+ m ?]), or " after killing to cast into the Gehenna " (Lk. xii. 5 Q [+ 1 ?]).[1] m's allusion (Mt. v. 29f.) to the extracted eye and severed hand " perishing " ($\dot{a}\pi\acute{o}\lambda\eta\tau\alpha\iota$), as the only alternative to the whole body being cast or departing into Gehenna, implies that " perishing " is also the lot of whatever goes into Gehenna.

Seeing that Paradise is the abode of " the living ", Gehenna ought by rights to be the abode of " the dead " ; but this is not expressly stated.   Whether those in Gehenna would be considered as excluded from the class of the living, who must be living because God is their God (Mk. xii. 27 = Lk. xx. 38 [$\pi\acute{a}\nu\tau\epsilon\varsigma$ $\gamma\grave{a}\rho$ $a\dot{v}\tau\hat{\omega}$ $\zeta\hat{\omega}\sigma\iota\nu$] = Mt. xxii. 32) is not made clear : [2] but they are obviously thought of as being still sensitive to physical pain (Lk. xvi. 23f., 25 fin., 28 L) ; and nothing is said as to whether their sufferings are temporary or permanent, though the presumption is that the latter is intended (cf. Mt. xxv. 46 M).[3]

(4) Some Jewish thinkers, in the effort to establish some intelligible relation between the life after death and the End of the World, introduced the theory of an " Intermediate State ", in which the dead stayed for the yet-remaining period of human history, pending the final settlement of their lot at the Last Judgment.   In these schemes, Paradise was occasionally treated as the purely-temporary dwelling-place of the righteous : and some Christian commentators have supposed that, in the story of the Rich Man and Lazarus, both Abraham's bosom and the place of torment are located in " Hades " (as if Abraham could have been anywhere but in the final abode of the blest), and that the " Paradise " of Lk. xxiii. 43 L is not intended to be the final abode of the blest, but only

---

[1] Cf. Strack-Billerbeck i. 581.   On Gehenna, etc., see also below, pp. 239–242.

[2] Cf. Bartlet, *St. Mark*, 335.

[3] But cf. Leckie, *World to Come*, 140–143.

a temporary waiting-room.[1]   It might indeed be urged that, if one believes at all in a general future resurrection, one necessarily implies the existence of some sort of " intermediate state " between the individual's bodily death and that coming event.   Such a state is clearly presupposed in the Sadducees' question to Jesus about the oft-married woman (Mk. xii. 23 = Lk. xx. 33 = Mt. xxii. 28) : " At the Resurrection, when (men) rise, to which of them will she be(long as) wife ? "   Since Jesus seems to defend the view which the Sadducees were criticizing, it might be plausibly argued that he must himself have believed in the existence of an intermediate state.   At the same time, the very unfixed character of Jewish beliefs on the subject must be borne in mind : and there are no sufficient grounds for applying any of Jesus' recorded words to this state *as distinct from the final lot of mankind.*

[1] Cf. Wendt, *Teaching*, i. 168–170, 222f. ; Schürer, *G.J.V.* ii. 639–643 ; Holtzmann, *Theol.* i. 101f. ; Leckie, *World to Come*, 69–73, 88f., 93f., 101f. ; Weinel, *Theol.* 60f. ; Bousset, *Relig. des Jud.* (1926), 282–289, 293–297, 518f. ; Moore, *Judaism*, i. 282, ii. 301f., 390f. ; Strack-Billerbeck ii. 264–269, iv. 5, 1016–1022, 1043–1075 ; Creed, *St. Luke*, 212a (". . . nor is . . . Paradise ever located in Sheol "), 288a ; B. T. D. Smith, *Parables*, 136f. See also below, pp. 239f.

CHAPTER V

REWARDS AND PUNISHMENTS IN THE COMING AGE

(1) Any reconstruction of Jesus' earlier beliefs regarding the Last Things is bound to be shadowy : yet it is worth while marshalling the evidence. (2) In common with his contemporaries, (3) he believed there would be a Resurrection, but of the righteous only, (4) and also a Divine Judgment, (5) though some of his allusions to the latter are rather general. (6) God would be the Judge, and the Son of Man the witness. (7) There are references (often ambiguous as regards time) to the Kingdom of God as a reward : (8) thus, the Kingdom is God's gift, to be received by men ; (9) but there are conditions to be fulfilled, (10) as is clear from Jesus' allusions to entering into the Kingdom, (11) from his designation of those to whom it actually or potentially belongs, (12) from his words about greatness and littleness in it, (13) and from his miscellaneous utterances about it. (14) He also describes the future reward as " Life " (15) or " Salvation ", the corresponding punishment being (not " death " but) " Loss " or " Destruction " : (16) and again the exacting conditions of salvation are made clear. (17) The reward is also said to be " in the Heavens ". (18) The sphere of punishment is Hades (19) or Gehenna, and its instrument fire. (20) Its severity is marked by the descriptions of ejection " into the outer darkness " and of " weeping and gnashing of teeth ". (21) Yet another form which the final reward takes in Jesus' mind is the Messianic Feast, exclusion from which constitutes the last bitter penalty. (22) The simile of the Two Houses built respectively on the Rock and the Sand also illustrates the gravity of the approaching crisis.

(1) I have collected and discussed above (pp. 194–203) the evidence in favour of the view that Jesus, besides holding that God's Kingdom was already present and active in the world in his own person and work, looked forward to a future climax, when the Kingdom would be seen by all to have " come in power ". We have now to essay the difficult task of ascertaining his thoughts regarding that climax, in respect, not of the certainty of its occurrence or of its date, but of its import of weal or woe for different classes of human beings. The task

is difficult, because the evidence, though fairly plentiful, lies before us in so piecemeal a condition that at every turn we find ourselves asking whether we are entitled to stitch together into a unified picture scraps and hints of so disconnected and occasional a character. When to this condition we add the necessity of allowing for the different degrees of credibility in our sources, and of excluding for the present all passages in which the death of Jesus is presupposed, we must be prepared to find that the outlines of the picture are in many places faint, fragmentary, and doubtful, and that the only reconstruction we can make is a vague and shadowy one. It was probably never clearly or completely defined in Jesus' own thoughts : for while he seems to have shared in a general way the beliefs of his time regarding the Last Things, those beliefs themselves exhibited the greatest variety in detail (see above, pp. 16f.). Only the individual apocalyptist attempted to produce a coherent programme ; and he was often inconsistent with himself in doing so : while Jesus did not even undertake anything of the kind, but spoke his thought, just as he happened to have framed it, and just as the successive occasions seemed to require. In these circumstances, our best plan is to take up in order the principal items in the eschatological scheme, which are common to Jesus' teaching and to Jewish thought, and try to see what each of them meant to him.

(2) We begin with the Resurrection of the Dead. Amid the seething variety of Jewish views on the subject,[1] the general fact stands out clear that belief in a Resurrection, as distinct from a simple belief in a life after death, was necessitated by the urgently-felt desire to ensure, for those who should have died before the great final Day, a real part in the Judgment, the rewards, and the penalties, which that Day would bring. The necessity of some such bridge to connect the life of the individual after death with the unfolding of the world-drama made belief in a coming Resurrection an indispensable item in nearly all Jewish forecasts of the future. Writers differed greatly from one another, however, on the question as to whether all the dead would rise for judgment, or whether only the righteous would rise, the punishment of the unrighteous in that case continuing in the region to which they had already been consigned.

(3) In dealing with Jesus' teaching on the Resurrection, we

---

[1] Schürer, *G.J.V.* ii. 638–644 ; Meyer, *Ursprung,* ii. 174–184 ; Bousset, *Relig. des Jud.* (1926), 269–274 ; Strack-Billerbeck i. 747, 893–897, iv. 1166–1198 ; Moore, *Judaism,* i. 68, 86, 172, ii. 295–318, 338–345, 377–395.

must first set aside, as not pertinent at the moment, his allusions to special risings from the dead *before* the great Day (e.g., Lk. xvi. 30 f. L), and in particular, therefore, to his own Resurrection (which must form the subject of a separate discussion : see below, pp. 28off.). More to our purpose is it to note that he describes the righteous as " rising from the dead " and becoming after bodily death like the angels (Mk. xii. 25-27 = Lk. xx. 35-38 = Mt. xxii. 30-32). The time at which this rising takes place is not clear, for while on the one hand the Sadducees' question on this occasion suggests that it would not occur until the great future Day (see above, p. 223), on the other hand (a) Lk. xvi. 22 L describes Lazarus as being carried by the angels *immediately after death* to Abraham's bosom, from which he could hardly expect to " rise " later on to a yet higher sphere, and (b) the Patriarchs, seeing that ex hypothesi God has long been " the God of Abraham and God of Isaac and God of Jacob ", must already have " risen " (see above, p. 220), although the Resurrection-Day had not yet come.[1] In the Lucan version of the words about the dead rising, the author makes it clear that the reference is to the time following the great future Day. " The sons of this age ", Jesus is made to say, " are begotten and beget, marry and are married. But they that have been accounted worthy to attain to that age and to the Resurrection from (among) the dead, neither marry nor are married ; for they cannot die any more, for they are equal to angels, and are sons of God, being sons of the Resurrection " (Lk. xx. 34-36).[2] However much or little authority there may be for the Lucan interpretation of Mark's words in this passage, it would seem that Jesus did entertain the idea of a single great Resurrection yet to come. He once advised his host to offer his hospitality to the poor, adding, " And thou wilt be happy, because they are unable to repay thee, for repayment will be made to thee at the resurrection of the righteous " (Lk. xiv. 14 L). Here the reference is apparently not to the man's life immediately after death : he is to look forward to the great assize. We note, however, that Jesus adopts the view that the Resurrection is for the righteous only,[3] and

---

[1] But cf. McNeile, *St. Matthew*, 322f. : also Otto, *Kingdom*, 237-240.

[2] Opinions differ as to whether Luke is here simply re-editing what he found in Mk. (Streeter, *Four Gospels*, 215f.), or whether he was making use of an independent source as well as of Mk. (V. Taylor, *Third Gosp.* 99f.).

[3] Charles (*Crit. Hist* [1913], 397f.) regards the words of l in Lk. xx. 38b (πάντες γὰρ αὐτῷ ζῶσιν) as intended to intimate that good and bad alike would be raised : see above, p. 222. Salmond also (in H.D.B. i. 752a). ascribes to Jesus a doctrine of universal resurrection ; but the passages he

further that he does not undertake to explain its precise relation to the life lived immediately after bodily death, when men are described, not explicitly indeed as " rising from the dead ", but as enjoying fully-equivalent privileges (see above, pp. 221, 226).[1]

(4) The natural sequel to the Resurrection was the Judgment ; [2] and Jesus brings the two ideas together in the passage just quoted—Lk. xiv. 14 L. In sending out the Disciples as missionaries, he says with reference to any city that will not receive them, " I tell you that it will be more bearable on that day for Sodom than for that city " (Lk. x. 12 Q) ; but the Matthæan parallel has " on (the) day of Judgment " instead of " on that day " (Mt. x. 15 = xi. 24 Q). Again, he tells Khorazin and Bethsaida, " It will be more bearable for Tyre and Sidon at the Judgment than for you " (Lk. x. 14 Q) ; and once more the Matthæan parallel has " on (the) day of Judgment " (Mt. xi. 22 Q). In somewhat similar vein—" the Queen of the South will rise at the Judgment with this generation, and will condemn it ", for she appreciated Solomon's wisdom ; so too will the Ninevites, for they repented at Jonah's preaching : whereas Jesus' contemporaries do not respond to what is greater than either Solomon or Jonah (Lk. xi. 31f. = Mt. xii. 41f. Q).[3] Thus the idea of a definite future Day of Judgment was certainly present to Jesus' mind, though we cannot affirm

---

quotes in support of this view (Mt. v. 29f., x. 28, Lk. xiv. 14 : cf. John v. 29) do not suffice to establish it.

[1] For Jesus' teaching on the Resurrection and Judgment generally, cf. Sharman, *Future*, 215–254 ; Gloege, *Reich Gottes*, 179–184 ; Oepke in *T.W.N.T.* i. 371f. ; Büchsel in *T.W.N.T.* iii. 936-938.

[2] Schürer, *G.J.V.* ii. 644–648 ; Meyer, *Ursprung*, ii. 199–204 ; Bousset, *Relig. des Jud.* (1926), 257–259 ; Moore, *Judaism*, i. 120, ii. 295–322, 379–389, iii. 197–199, 204–206 ; Strack-Billerbeck i. 605, iv. 1036–1043, 1093–1118, 1199–1212 ; Büchsel in *T.W.N.T.* iii. 935f.

[3] The differences between the two versions are negligible. Some contend that the Aramaïc behind ἐγερθήσεται (ἀναστήσονται) ἐν τῇ κρίσει would mean simply " will accuse " (Wellhausen, *Mt.* 65 ; McNeile, *St. Matthew*, 182b) ; even so the reference must still be to the Last Judgment (cf. Dalman, *W.J.* 64)—otherwise why the future tenses ?

" Will condemn " means " will show to be·wrong ". The idea of judgment being passed on one by comparison with the conduct of another (cf. *Wisdom of Sol.* iv. 16 ; Heb. xi. 7 ; Strack-Billerbeck i. 635, 65of.)—as in the case of " this generation " by comparison with the Queen and the Ninevites—is cursorily expressed in Lk. xi. 19 = Mt. xii. 27 Q, where Jesus says to the Scribes about their " sons " who exorcized demons, " They therefore shall be your judges " ; i.e., in attributing Jesus' exorcisms to Beelzebul, the Scribes implicitly assigned the same evil origin to the exorcisms of their own disciples.

On the idea that the Judgment will be determined on purely ethical grounds, and that no advantage will belong to the Jew as Jew, cf. Schürer, *G.J.V.* ii. 648 ; Holtzmann, *Theol.* i. 395 ; Montefiore, *S.G.*[2] I. cxvii ; Manson, *Teaching*, 274f.

positively that the actual phrase stood in Q. It occurs once more—in M : " But I tell you that every thoughtless speech that men speak, they shall give account for it on (the) day of Judgment . . . " (Mt. xii. 36 M). The declaration in Lk. xii. 48b L, to the effect that the demands to be made on men will vary in proportion to the amounts entrusted to them (see below, p. 325), possibly refers to the Last Judgment as such, apart from any idea of the Parousia.

(5) The other items of evidence about the Judgment are less direct.

The command, " Judge not, and ye will not be judged ; . . . " (Lk. vi. 37f. = Mt. vii. 1f. Q ; cf. Mk. iv. 24b, and see above, p. 211), *may* have reference to the Last Judgment, but may, on the other hand, be simply a general reference to human judgment.

The warning that hypocritical Scribes " will receive an extra heavy judgment " (Mk. xii. 40 = Lk. xx. 47) might perhaps be pleaded as a purely-general threat : yet it may also be a concrete allusion to the great assize—as also may the dubious query addressed, according to m, to the Scribes and Pharisees, " Serpents ! Offspring of vipers ! how are ye to escape from the judgment of Gehenna ? " (Mt. xxiii. 33 m).[1]

The allusion to " the judgment " in Mt. v. 21f. M is so obscure that, beyond surmising that there is here probably some reference to the Last Judgment, we can hardly base any conclusion upon the passage.

The " judgment ", which m (quoting Isa. xlii. 1, 3) says Jesus will proclaim and establish among the Gentiles (Mt. xii. 18, 20 m) probably meant originally the true religion of Yahweh : but m may well have had the Last Judgment in mind.[2]

(6) If the question be asked, Who will conduct the Judgment ?, the answer must surely be, God. That answer is in the first place implied by the silence of the passages hitherto quoted in regard to any other judge. It would, furthermore, be in line with the normal Jewish belief.[3] The utterances of Jesus reported in the Synoptic Gospels, in which he himself is depicted as judge, are all more or less directly connected with his later view of a future coming of himself in glory. (A possible exception is Lk. xiii. 25–27 = Mt. vii. 22f. Q ? [cf. Mt. xxv. 10–12 M], though here the figure is not that of a judge

[1] McNeile, *St. Matthew*, 338f. : but see below, p. 241 top.
[2] McNeile, *St. Matthew*, 172b.
[3] Cf. Holtzmann, *Theol.* i. 96, 392, 395 ; Strack-Billerbeck iv. 1095, 1100, 1104 ; Manson in *Mission*, etc. 541.
[4] Holtzmann, *Theol.* i. 392–395. See also below, pp. 321–323.

pronouncing sentence, but of a host excluding unworthy guests).[1] Now since it seems probable that the idea of a future coming of himself in glory was first suggested to him by the certainty that defeat and death awaited him on earth, the idea that he himself would act as judge was in all probability similarly dependent on the same dark prospect. If we ask, What future rôle then did Jesus assign to himself before the shadow of the Cross darkened his path ?, we must reply that there is little evidence to tell us. That he would be Lord, and would preside at the Messianic Feast (see below, pp. 243–245), we may assume were among his expectations : but the assumption that he would himself conduct the Last Judgment we cannot at this stage ascribe to him. There is, in fact, a passage in Q, in which " the Son of Man " (i.e., the personification of the redeemed community, with Jesus at its head) appears as a witness for or against men at a future Divine Judgment : " But I tell you, every one who acknowledges me before men, the Son of Man in his turn will acknowledge him before the angels of God. But he who has disowned me in the presence of men will be disowned in the presence of the angels of God " (Lk. xii. 8f. = Mt. x. 32f. [Mt. has no reference to " the Son of Man ", but puts " *I* will acknowledge ", and " *I* will disown " : on the differentiation between " the Son of Man " and Jesus himself, see above, p. 100. m also correctly paraphrases " the angels of God " as " my Father in the Heavens "]). A very similar warning appears in Mk. viii. 38 = Lk. ix. 26 (= Mt. xvi. 27), where the Parousia of the Son of Man, and therefore presumably also his Passion, are presupposed. Possibly the same presupposition lies behind Lk. xii. 8f. = Mt. x. 32f. Q : in any case, even the Marcan passage suggests that the Son of Man is, there too, witness and not judge.[2]

(7) Nearly all statements in the Gospels concerning the Kingdom of God as man's supreme blessing and reward (see above, pp. 175–179)[3] are to some extent ambiguous as regards the question we are at present investigating, for the Kingdom is conceived of both as already present (see above, pp. 128–135) and as future (see above, pp. 194–203), and also, qualitatively or intensively, as timeless (see above, pp. 111–113, 133) ; moreover,

[1] Holtzmann, *Theol.* i. 393 ; Strack-Billerbeck i. 467f.

[2] Cf. Manson, *Teaching*, 263. On God as judge rather than Jesus, cf. Bousset, *Jesus*, 86, 89, 92f. (Eng. tr. 189, 194, 203–205) ; Winstanley, *Future*, 149–167, 290, 292 (2), 312f., 375f. ; Rashdall, *Conscience*, 48f. n.2. Per contra, Denney, *Jes. and the Gosp.* (1913), 248–253.

[3] On the Kingdom as a reward, cf. Holtzmann, *Theol.* i. 258, 260.

the distinction between these several senses is not always clearly marked. Future time is sometimes indicated vividly by the present tense : and the Greek future tense (representing an Aramaïc imperfect or participle) may refer perhaps to the immediate as well as the more distant future, and even to what, being true generally or proverbially, is really present. We can hardly then do more than simply classify the sayings of Jesus in which the Kingdom seems referred to as a reward, noting the tenses used, and bearing in mind both the present and the future significance of the term.

(8) In the first place, then, the Kingdom is spoken of as something which God does and will give to men. The contrast has often been drawn between John the Baptist and Jesus in this connexion. Both begin with a call to repentance ; but, whereas with John the call is primarily a solemn warning of approaching trial, with Jesus it is part of a " Gospel ", a consoling invitation.[1] So, " Fear not, thou little flock ; for your Father is pleased to give you the Kingdom " (Lk. xii. 32 Q or l : the verb is aorist, $\epsilon\dot{u}\delta\acute{o}\kappa\eta\sigma\epsilon\nu$, and might be translated "has been pleased ", but even so the actual giving could still lie in the future ; see above, pp. 132f., 178f.).

The Disciples were told, " To you has the mystery of the Kingdom of God been given " (Mk. iv. 11 = Lk. viii. 10 = Mt. xiii. 11), a declaration which—in view of Lk. x. 23f. = Mt. xiii. 16f. Q—looks very much like a reference to the present possession of the Kingdom. In another passage, however, we find the future tense used : " the Kingdom . . . will be given to a nation which produces the fruits thereof " (Mt. xxi. 43 M : possibly an early Christian gloss, in which the Christian Church is referred to as an $\check{\epsilon}\theta\nu\sigma$).

The normal counterpart of giving is receiving : hence the pertinence of the warning, " Truly I tell you, whoever does not receive the Kingdom of God as a little child, will certainly not enter into it " (Mk. x. 15 = Lk. xviii. 17 =Mt. xviii. 3b).[2]

---

[1] Wellhausen, *Mt.* 13 ; Bartlet, *St. Mark*, 82f. ; see also above, p. 179 (6f.).
[2] Much has been written on the question as to precisely what phase of child-likeness Jesus is here demanding. Clearly, certain phases would be excluded. Perhaps we cannot get further than saying that simple and trustful receptive-ness is what he has in mind (cf., e.g., Menzies, *Earliest Gospel*, 190f. ; Burkitt in *H.C.L.M.K.* 235 = *Jesus Christ*, etc. 39). Rashdall (*Conscience*, 125) suggests, with some plausibility, that Jesus has in mind the insignificance of children as engaged in menial service in their homes.

Dr. W. K. L. Clarke (*New Test. Problems* [1929], 37f.) makes the interesting suggestion that $\pi\alpha\iota\delta\acute{\iota}o\nu$ in Mk. x. 15 is not a nominative but an accusative. The Kingdom belongs to such children (Mk. x. 14 = Lk. xviii. 16 = Mt. xix. 14) : in " receiving " *them*, therefore (Mk. ix. 36f. = Lk. ix. 47f. = Mt. xviii.

(9) The last-quoted saying, however it is to be interpreted, reminds us that there are conditions attending the bestowal of the Kingdom as a gift. It is not given to every one. It has to be " sought " (Lk. xii. 31 = Mt. vi. 33 Q),[1] as one might seek to acquire a field in which a rich treasure was hidden, or a valuable pearl (Mt. xiii. 44-46 M). The Parable of the Dishonest Steward (Lk. xvi. 1-7 L + 8 l) points to the need of intelligence in securing it. One has to be " made a disciple to it ", as many " a scribe " has been (Mt. xiii. 52 M). The simple admonition that, in order to remain in the Kingdom, one must fulfil the prescribed conditions is clearly conveyed in the story of the man expelled from the banquet because he had not clad himself in a wedding-garment (Mt. xxii. 2, 11-13 M), even if we can derive from it with confidence nothing more specific than that.

(10) What these conditions are is to some extent indicated in other groups of sayings. Let us take first those in which Jesus speaks of " entering into " the Kingdom.[2] The following are the passages in which this entering is clearly spoken of as future (see above, p. 197) :—

Mk. x. 15 = Lk. xviii. 7 = Mt. xviii. 3b : " Truly I tell you, whoever does not receive the Kingdom of God as a little child, will certainly not enter into it " (Mt. has, " If ye do not turn and become as little children, ye " etc. See previous page).

Mk. x. 23 = Lk. xviii. 24 = Mt. xix. 23 : " With what difficulty will those who have riches enter into the Kingdom of God ! " The future here indicates that the following verses (Mk. x. 24-27 = Lk. xviii. 25-27 = Mt. xix. 24-26), though their tenses are present, must be interpreted in a future sense.

Mt. v. 20 M : " For I tell you, that, unless your righteousness surpasses (that of) the Scribes and Pharisees, ye will certainly not enter into the Kingdom of the Heavens ".

Mt. vii. 21 M ? (cf. Lk. vi. 46 [not mentioning the Kingdom] Q ?) : " Not every one who says to me, ' Lord, Lord ! ' will

---

2, 5), one receives the Kingdom. This interpretation is not only inherently plausible, but it relieves a difficulty. " ' Receiving ' and ' entering ' ", as Dr. Clarke says, " are completely different metaphors ; why should you need to enter what you have already received ? " If this view be accepted, then it is the *present* Kingdom that is received, and the *future* that is entered. Cf., however, Manson, *Teaching*, 135 n.1, and Dodd, *Parables*, 41f. On the general subject of giving and receiving the Kingdom, Dalman, *W.J.* 123-125.

[1] Cf. Dalman, *W.J.* 121-123.

[2] Dr. Manson believes that Jesus so spoke only after Peter's Confession at Cæsarea-Philippi (*Teaching*, 119f., 124-130, 201, 205-207), whereas previously he had spoken mostly of the Kingdom as coming. For Rabbinic parallels to the phrase about " entering ", cf. Dalman, *W.J.* 116-118 ; Strack-Billerbeck i. 252f. See also above, p. 113, and cf. H-D. Wendland, *Eschatologie*, 41-44.

enter into the Kingdom of the Heavens, but he who does the will of my Father who is in the Heavens ".[1]

There are three other allusions in the Gospels to entering into the Kingdom (see above, p. 197) :—

Mk. ix. 47 = Mt. xviii. 9 : " If thine eye be a hindrance to thee, cast it out : it is well that thou (καλόν σέ ἐστιν . . .) shouldst enter into the Kingdom of God one-eyed, rather than that, having two eyes, thou shouldst be cast into Gehenna ". Twice in parallel passages in the same Marcan context, and in the Matthæan parallel to Mk. (Mt. xviii. 8f.), " the life " takes the place of " the Kingdom of God ". In any case, the time referred to is clearly future, and the reference seems to be primarily to the life after death (see above, p. 221 n. 2).[2] The passage as a whole is apparently a figurative injunction of the strenuous curbing of unlawful sex-impulse.

Mt. xxi. 31f. M : " Truly I tell you, the tax-collectors and the prostitutes are preceding you (προάγουσιν ὑμᾶς) into the Kingdom of God : for John came to you in the way of righteousness, and ye did not believe him. But the tax-collectors and the prostitutes believed him : but not even when ye saw this, did ye change your mind later, so as to believe him ". Here the reference (if genuine) may be either to the present or to the future Kingdom.

Mt. xxiii. 13 = Lk. xi. 52 Q : " . . . ye shut the Kingdom of the Heavens in front of men : for ye enter not in yourselves, nor do ye allow those entering to enter ". But here the reference to the Kingdom is found in Mt. only, and is perhaps due to m.[3]

A virtual " entering " into the Kingdom is spoken of in Lk. xiii. 28f. = Mt. viii. 11f., to which we shall refer later in other connexions (see below, pp. 233, 242–245), and probably also in Lk. xvi. 16 = Mt. xi. 12f. (see above, pp. 129f.), if we take the view that, in its original form, it referred to the eager enthusiasm of the first members of the already-present Kingdom.

(11) A second group of sayings is concerned with the question as to who possess the Kingdom, or who might be expected to possess it.[4] The Kingdom is said (in the present tense) to

---

[1] Dobschütz (Eschatol. 80–83) and Manson (Teaching, 121f.) argue for the secondary character of the Matthæan version. It is in connexion with this passage that the latter remarks, " the whole notion of entry into the Kingdom as the reward of merit is Matthæan ".

[2] Cf. Manson, Teaching, 294 n. 4.

[3] Cf. Manson, Teaching, 122f.

[4] Cf. Dalman, W.J. 127f.

belong to "the poor" (Lk. vi. 20 = Mt. v. 3 [m adding "in spirit"]), to the childlike (Mk. x. 14 =Lk. xviii. 16 = Mt. xix. 14), and to "those who have been persecuted for righteousness' sake" (Mt. v. 10 M). Such persons are evidently "the sons of the Kingdom" mentioned in the interpretation of the Parable of the Tares (Mt. xiii. 38 M or m).[1]

But this very phrase—"the sons of the Kingdom"—is used elsewhere of those (presumably, many Jews—see above, pp. 141f.) who forfeit the privilege which might nave been theirs, and will be expelled from the Kingdom in favour of others (Lk. xiii. 28f. = Mt. viii. 11f. Q : Mt. only, however, has the words "the sons of the Kingdom"). The same idea, without the use of this particular phrase, is expressed in Mt. xiii. 41 M or m (the Son of Man's angels will gather out of his Kingdom "all the hindrances and all those who act lawlessly"), in Mt. xxi. 43 M (". . . the Kingdom of God will be taken away from you, . . ."), in Mt. xxii. 2, 11–13 M (the man without the wedding-garment : cf. the reference to the Kingdom in Mt. xxii. 2 M [or Q ?]), in Lk. xiii. 30 L and Mk. x. 31 = Mt. xix. 30 = Mt. xx. 16 Q (last first, and first last : cf. the references to the Kingdom in Lk. xiii. 28 Q and Mt. xx. 1 M), possibly also in Mt. xiii. 47–50 M (the Parable of the Net : cf. the reference to the Kingdom in Mt. xiii. 47 M).

(12) Yet a third group of sayings deals with the question of comparative greatness or littleness in the coming Kingdom.[2] Here again we find the present and future tenses mixed. The most interesting passage is Lk. vii. 28 = Mt. xi. 11 Q : "But I tell you, he who is least in the Kingdom of God is greater than he" (i.e., than John the Baptist). I have discussed above (see p. 134) the question as to whether this saying contemplates the Kingdom as present or future : it may be understood either way.

The other passages are of dubious authenticity. '"Who then is (ἐστίν) greatest in the Kingdom of the Heavens?" . . . "Whosoever therefore who humbles himself like this child, he is (ἐστιν) the greatest in the Kingdom of the Heavens"' (Mt. xviii. 1, 4)—but the parallels (Mk. ix. 34f. = Lk. ix. 46–48) make no mention of the Kingdom here, and the reference to it is clearly due to m.[3] Finally, we have the saying in Mt. v.

---

[1] Cf. Dalman, *W.J.* 115f.

[2] On Jewish views as to differences of rank in the Kingdom, cf. Dalman, *W.J.* 113–115 ; Strack-Billerbeck i. 249f., 773, iv. 1131f., 1139–1143.

[3] Cf. McNeile, *St. Matthew*, 259b : "Mk.'s τίς μείζων . . . , 'who is the greatest', *sc.* at the present time, is interpreted by Mt. of precedence in the coming Kingdom . . .".

19 M : " Whoever therefore relaxes one of these smallest commandments and teaches men accordingly, will be called (the) smallest in the Kingdom of the Heavens: but whoever carries them out, and teaches (others to do so), he will be called great in the Kingdom of the Heavens ". But those scholars are probably right who believe that we have here a fairly-distinct piece of Judæo-Christian anti-Pauline apologetic (see above, pp. 21f. [M and Mt.]).

(**13**) I conclude this survey of allusions to the Kingdom as a reward with four passages not easy to classify :—

Mt. xiii. 43 M or m : " Then will the righteous shine forth like the sun in the Kingdom of their Father ". This concluding sentence of the interpretation of the Parable of the Tares is probably not a genuine saying of Jesus.

Lk. ix. 62 Q or L : " No one who has put his hand to the plough, and looks backward, is ($\dot{\epsilon}\sigma\tau\iota\nu$) fitted for the Kingdom of God "—a clear intimation that tenacity and concentration are requisite qualities.[1]

Mk. xii. 34a (Lk. x. 28 otherwise) : ' And when Jesus saw that he ' (the questioning Scribe) ' had answered sensibly ' (in agreeing that love for God and love for man were far more important than sacrifices), ' he said to him, " Thou art not far from the Kingdom of God " '. Nobody knows for certain what this concluding phrase means : it may mean that the Scribe was well on his way toward entering the Kingdom, just as the tax-collectors and prostitutes were further on their way thither than the Scribes (Mt. xxi. 31 M). Thus if the future Kingdom is in mind, qualitative fitness for it is expressed under a spatial figure.[2]

Mt. xix. 12c M : " There are eunuchs who made themselves eunuchs for the sake of the Kingdom of the Heavens ". The reference here seems to be to stringent celibacy as a special self-denial in the interests of God's service (see above, p. 232). The Kingdom may be thought of either as present or future or vaguely both.

(**14**) We have studied above (pp. 214f.) the general allusions Jesus makes to " life " as one form of the reward for righteous-ness. We are concerned here to collect his references to life in a more definitely eschatological sense—" eternal life " ($\zeta\omega\grave{\eta}$ $a\grave{\iota}\acute{\omega}\nu\iota\sigma$), as it is usually called in that connexion.[3] The

---

[1] Cf. Dalman, *W.J.* 119f.
[2] Wellhausen, *Mc.* 97 ; Rawlinson, *St. Mark*, 172.
[3] Cf. Holtzmann, *Theol.* i. 255f. ; McNeile, *St. Matthew*, 262f. ; Bultmann in *T.W.N.T.* ii. 864–867.

adjective " eternal " does not etymologically mean " never-ending " : it means pertaining to the coming Messianic age ($a\iota\acute{\omega}\nu$) of blessedness, and therefore supremely good and happy. Everlastingness was normally understood to be included, though only in a vague and general way.[1] The words spoken by Jesus to the Disciples when, after the departure of the Rich Ruler, Peter reminded him how much they had given up, furnish us with the clearest allusion to the eternal life as a future reward. Emending the difficult text of Mk. with the help of Clemens of Alexandria's quotation of it, we read that Jesus said, " Truly I tell you, there is no one who has left house or brothers or sisters or mother or children or lands, for my sake and for the sake of the Gospel, but will receive a hundred-fold. To what end (does he expect) to have now in this season houses and brothers and sisters and mothers and children and lands, along with persecutions ? But in the coming age there is eternal life " (Mk. x. 29f. = Lk. xviii. 29 = Mt. xix. 28f.).[2] It is therefore in all probability with reference to the coming age that Jesus twice undertook to answer the question, " What have I to do in order to inherit eternal life ? " (Mk. x. 17 = Lk. xviii. 18 = Mt. xix. 16f. ; Lk. x. 25 L : the Greek is slightly different in the two passages, but the meaning is the same). In the case of the Rich Ruler, the context indicates that the prospect of possessing treasure in heaven is to be identified with the prospect of inheriting eternal life (Mk. x. 21 = Lk. xviii. 22 = Mt. xix. 21) : in the case of the Lawyer, the words, " Do this and thou wilt live ", answers the inquirer's question (Lk. x. 28 L).

The two other eschatological allusions to life are documentarily dubious.

Mt. vii. 14 : " . . . narrow and confined is the road which leads away to the life, and few are they who find it ". The Lucan parallel is quite different (Lk. xiii. 23f.) ; and it is impossible to be sure that the Matthæan words have any higher authority than that of M or m. Yet we may compare the references to " the life " in Mk. ix. 43 = Mt. xviii. 8 ;

[1] Cf. Holtzmann, *Theol.* i. 102f. ; Strack-Billerbeck i. 463f., 829.
[2] For the text, cf. Clem. Alex., *Quis Dives ?* iv. 10, xxii. 1, xxv. 1, 8 ; Wellhausen, *Mc.* 80–82.   But even if the usually-printed text is accepted, the point we are immediately concerned with is not affected. Seeing that the words were spoken towards the end of the Ministry, it is doubtful whether we ought to use them here. Yet they contain no explicit allusion to the Passion ; and from the very first Jesus must have expected *some* measure of hardship for his followers. Mk. iii. 29 = Mt. xii. 31, and Mt. xii. 32 fin. m, seem to show that Jesus' idea of " the coming age " was not dependent on his prevision of death.

Mk. ix. 45 ; Mt. xviii. 9 (see above, p. 221). For the " few ", cf. Mt. xxii. 14 M.

Lk. xvii. 33 = Mt. x. 39 Q (see below, pp. 236f.). Life implies activity ; and activity is occasionally hinted at by Jesus as part of the reward (Lk. xii. 44 = Mt. xxiv. 47 Q ; Lk. xix. 17, 19 L ; Mt. xxv. 21, 23 M).[1]

(15) A frequently-used equivalent of the conceptions of entering the Kingdom and inheriting eternal life is the idea of the " salvation " of one's life ($\psi\nu\chi\acute{\eta}$), the exact opposite of which is its " loss " or " destruction " ($\mathring{a}\pi\acute{\omega}\lambda\epsilon\iota a$). We have already studied the use of these ideas in a general sense (see above, pp. 215–218), and noted the allusion to punishment after death as God's " destruction " of soul ($\psi\nu\chi\acute{\eta}$) and body in Gehenna (see above, pp. 221f.). The two complementary terms are certainly used by Jesus in an eschatological sense, though it is not always easy to delimit the passages with precision. Possibly Lk. iii. 6 l (" All flesh will see the salvation of God ") is a distinct hint at the final climax of redemption.

There is one important saying of Jesus on the subject which we must quote in full, although, as it mentions persecution unto death, it ought possibly to be considered later (see above, p. 235 n. 2). It is preserved independently in Q and Mk. ; and we observe that in the various forms in which it comes to us, " finding ", " preserving alive ", and " acquiring " appear as synonyms of " saving ", and " forfeiting " as a synonym of " losing ". It is needful also to note that the paradoxical form of the pronouncement is apparently due to the fact that the word $\psi\nu\chi\acute{\eta}$ is used in a twofold sense, firstly, of the bodily life which can be destroyed in persecution, and secondly of the personal self which survives bodily death and can receive reward or punishment.[2] Here are the passages :—

Lk. xvii. 33 Q : " Whoever seeks to acquire ($\pi\epsilon\rho\iota\pi o\iota\acute{\eta}\sigma a\sigma\theta a\iota$) his life will lose it ; and whoever loses (his life) will preserve it alive ". The Matthæan form runs (Mt. x. 39 Q) : " He who has found " ($\epsilon\mathring{v}\rho\acute{\omega}\nu$, possibly a " gnomic aorist ", meaning " finds ") " his life will lose it, and he who has lost " (or " loses ") " his life for my sake will find it ". Mk. viii. 35–37 = Lk. ix. 24f. = Mt. xvi. 25f. : " For whoever intends to save his own life will lose it ; but whoever loses his life for my sake and the Gospel's will save it " (Mt. has " will find it "). " For

[1] Cf. Manson, *Teaching*, 277.
[2] Those unfamiliar with the Greek text may be reminded that this word $\psi\nu\chi\acute{\eta}$ (here translated " life ") is not the same as the Greek word ($\zeta\omega\acute{\eta}$) used in such phrases as " eternal life " (cf. Holtzmann, *Theol.* i. 66f. [1f.]).

what advantage is it for a man to gain the whole world and forfeit his life ? " (Lk. has "himself"). " For what is a man to give as an equivalent for his life ? " (Lk. omits).[1]

(16) That this final salvation is won, and the final ἀπώλεια avoided, only with difficulty, is suggested in one or two sayings. In Lk. xiii. 23 L we read that someone asked Jesus, " Lord, are those who are being saved few ? ",[2] and in Lk. xiii. 24 Q ? Jesus answers, " Strive to enter through the narrow door, for many, I tell you, will seek to go in (by it), and will be unable ". Mt. has a parallel to this, which is probably an amalgam of Q and M or m (Mt. vii. 13f.) : " Enter through the narrow gate, because broad is the gate, and spacious the road, which leads away to destruction (ἀπώλειαν), and many there are who enter through it ; because narrow and close is the road which leads away to life, and few are they who find it ". After hearing " how difficult it is to enter into the Kingdom of God ", the Disciples ask, " Who then can be saved ? " ; and Jesus answers, " With men it is impossible, but with God possible " (Mk. x. 24–27 = Lk. xviii. 25–27 = Mt. xix. 24–26). And in Mk. xiii. 13b = Lk. xxi. 18f. = Mt. x. 22b = Mt. xxiv. 13, he is reported as saying, " He that has endured " (or " endures.") " to the end—he will be saved " (the Lucan parallel runs, " And not a hair of your head shall perish. In your endurance will ye gain possession of [κτήσεσθε] your lives ").

(17) " The heaven " or " the heavens " are never explicitly mentioned by Jesus as a place or region where the righteous will dwell after judgment has been passed upon them. He uses the word most frequently as part of his customary title for the Kingdom of God as " the Kingdom of the Heavens ". The phrase is found in Mt. only, and in all probability simply exemplifies the use of the word " the Heavens " as a reverent synonym for God (see above, p. 110). It is not always, however, such a synonym, for Jesus frequently speaks of God as the " Father Who is *in* the Heavens ".[3] Heaven is thus God's special abode or " throne " (Mt. v. 34 M, xxiii. 22 M). Hence the angelic representatives or guardians of Jesus' humble followers are thought of as being there : " I tell you, in (the)

---

[1] Cf. McNeile, *St. Matthew*, 148f.
[2] Cf. Strack-Billerbeck i. 883.
[3] This phrase is almost entirely confined to Mt., as the adj. οὐράνιος, as used to describe God, is entirely. Hence some scholars (e.g., Weinel, *Theol.* 148f.) deny that Jesus spoke of " the Father in the heavens ". But in view of Mk. xi. 25, Lk. xi. 13 Q, xv. 7 (Q ?), so sweeping a negative seems un-warranted. It is likely enough that the instances are artificially multiplied in Mt

Heavens their angels always look on the face of my Father Who is in (the) Heavens " (Mt. xviii. 10 M : the genuineness of the first ἐν οὐρανοῖς is dubious, but its absence would not affect the sense). It is natural for us to ask the question, Did Jesus always think cf Heaven as a spatial region above the level of the earth ? : but it is a question we have no sufficient means of answering. The probability is that, when he transferred his thought from the sky to which he looked up when praying to God, to the spiritual or ideal realm of God's interests and power,[1] he was unconcious of any transition. So different was the ancient Eastern from the modern Western mind. The local and the spiritual meanings are merged together in the opening words of Jesus' model prayer (in its Matthæan form), " Our Father Who art in the Heavens ! May Thy Name be hallowed, Thy Kingdom come, Thy Will be done—as in Heaven, (so) also upon earth ! " (Mt. vi. 9f. M : see above, p. 166). The sayings about Heaven in Mt. xvi. 19, xviii. 18 (M or m) can hardly be considered genuine sayings of Jesus,[2] and in any case are not relevant to our immediate enquiry.

So far as the rewards of men are concerned, the main connexion in which Jesus speaks of Heaven is as the place where the reward or treasures of the righteous are stored—apparently in readiness to be enjoyed on a future day. Thus, " Store not up for yourselves treasures on earth, where moth and corrosion destroy (ἀφανίζει), and where thieves break in and steal " (Mt. vi. 19 M). " But store up for yourselves treasures in heaven, where neither moth nor corrosion destroys, and where no thieves break in or steal " (Mt. vi. 20 M + Q). That some such passage once stood in Q is made probable by the fact that Lk. xii. 33 has the words, " Sell your belongings and give alms ; make yourselves purses that grow not old, an unfailing treasure in the heavens, where no thief approaches nor moth works ruin ". Both Evangelists conclude with almost identical words, " For where your treasure is, there will be your heart also " (Lk. xii. 34 = Mt. vi. 21 Q). The passage strongly recalls the words spoken to the Rich Ruler, " Go, sell whatsoever thou hast, and give to the poor ; and thou wilt have treasure in heaven : and come, follow me " (Mk. x. 21 = Lk. xviii. 22 = Mt. xix. 21). The future tense and eschatological tone of these promises encourage us to interpret eschatologically another reference to Heaven which we have already provision-

---

[1] Cf. Beyschlag, *Theol.* i. 84f, ; Muirhead, *Eschatol. of Jes.* 107 ; W. H. Dyson in H.*D.C.G.* i. 711f.

[2] Cf. C. J. Cadoux, *Cathol. and Christianity*, 377–379, 382.

ally quoted under the general heading of rewards. To the persecuted, Jesus says, " Rejoice on that day, and leap for joy ; for behold ! great is your reward in the heavens " (Lk. vi. 23 = Mt. v. 12 Q).[1] Akin to this promise is the saying addressed, according to L, to the seventy-two Disciples, on their return from their mission-tour : " Only, do not rejoice over this, that the spirits are submissive to you ; but rejoice because your names have been written in the heavens " (Lk. x. 20 L).[2]

(18) In describing the future punishment of the wicked, Jesus uses the terms " Hades " and " Gehenna ", the concept of fire, and the phrases " cast into the outer darkness " and " weeping and gnashing of teeth ". Yet when we come to sift his sayings, we are struck by the scantiness of well-attested and precise descriptions, over and above the evidence we have already examined in another connexion. " Hades " primarily meant simply the abode of the dead, and is used in this sense as an expression for the consequence of slaughter in Lk. x. 15 = Mt. xi. 23 Q (see below, p. 268) ; and " the Gates of Hades " in Mt. xvi. 18 M seem to designate the infliction of martyrdom on Jesus and his followers.[3] In Jewish parlance the word, as the recognized Greek equivalent of " She'ol ", had undergone and was undergoing a development of meaning ; and in certain circles it still stood in Jesus' day for the temporary abode of all, good and bad alike, between bodily death and the Last Judgment, and therefore as clearly distinguishable from Gehenna, the place of torment for the wicked.[4] But by Jesus' time no uniformity of usage had been established, as is clear from the different senses in which he employs the word, for in Lk. xvi. 23 L " Hades " clearly means the place in which the wicked suffer torment immediately after death (see above, pp. 221–223). We do not find him using this actual word for the place of punishment after the Last Judgment : but the word " Gehenna "

---

[1] Cf. Wellhausen, *Mt.* 15 ("' Euer Lohn ist im Himmel ' würde in einer jüdischen Schrift bedeuten: er ist im Himmel aufbewahrt, um von dort dermaleinst auf die Erde herabzukommen, mit dem Reiche Gottes und seinen Gütern. Ob dieser Sinn auch hier beabsichtigt ist, lässt sich nicht sicher entscheiden ") ; McNeile, *St. Matthew*, 54a (" ἐν τοῖς οὐρανοῖς does not locate the bliss of the coming age " ; it marks it as future and with God).

[2] On the idea and expression, cf. Strack-Billerbeck ii. 169–176.

[3] C. J. Cadoux, *Cathol. and Christianity*, 388 ; Manson in *Mission*, etc. 497.

[4] Cf. the very full collection of evidence concerning She'ol and Gehenna in Strack-Billerbeck i. 115f., 581, 606, ii. 228 (" ᾅδης = שאול, das Totenreich, wird im NT noch streng unterschieden von γέεννα = גיהנם, . . . , dem Ort der Qual oder der Hölle ; . . . "), iv. 1016–1118. Cf. Sharman, *Future*, 256–266 ; Moore, *Judaism*, ii. 289–291, 391f., iii. 196 : also the shorter notes on Gehenna in Swete, *St. Mark*, 210f., and Manson in *Mission*, etc. 399.

that *is* used is clearly an equivalent for "Hades" in the narrower sense seen in Lk. xvi. 23 L.

(**19**) In regard to Gehenna, as in regard to Hades, reference must be made to the passages discussed above in connexion with the punishment of the wicked immediately after death (Mk. ix. 43–48 = Mt. xviii. 8 f. = Mt. v. 29f. ; Lk. xii. 4f. = Mt. x. 28 Q ; Lk. xvi. 22–28 L : see above, pp. 221–223). We can be tolerably certain that the conditions visualized in those passages would hold good equally well for the fate of the wicked after the Last Judgment. The idea that the mission of the Messiah would lead up to a fiery judgment was emphatically expressed by John the Baptist. "The axe is already lying at the root of the trees : so every tree that does not produce fruit is cut down and thrown into (the) fire" (Lk. iii. 9 = Mt. iii. 10 Q). "There is coming after me the one who is stronger than I, . . . I have baptized you with water ; but he will baptize you with fire.[1] Whose winnowing-shovel is in his hand, and he will clean out his threshing-floor, and will collect the wheat into his store-house ; but the chaff he will burn up with unquenchable fire" (Lk. iii. 16f. = Mt. iii. 11f. Q, + Mk. i. 7f.).[2]

We note with interest, however, that the allusions made by Jesus to the fiery punishment of Gehenna, other than those already referred to, are all found in Mt. We must not too hastily infer that they are for that reason to be judged to be ungenuine : for it is arguable that the other and less Jewish Gospels Mk. and Lk. omitted these allusions as likely to offend Gentile readers. The Matthæan reports, however, rightly fall under some suspicion, because (a) the Matthæan Evangelist, on the whole, clearly allowed himself a very free hand in writing up his story (see above, p. 22), and (b) some of the special passages involved show clear signs of late origin. Thus Mt. vii. 19 m runs, "Every tree that does not produce sound fruit is cut down and thrown into (the) fire". Now this verse ascribes to Jesus exactly the same utterance as is earlier ascribed to John on the unimpeachable authority of Q : it is furthermore in Mt. vii. 19 irrelevant to the theme of its context (the likeness in quality of the tree and its fruit). Failure to distinguish between the sayings of Jesus and John is possibly again illustrated by Mt. iii. 2, where John is made to say, "The Kingdom of the Heavens has drawn

---

[1] Cf. Creed, *St. Luke*, 54a.

[2] On the fire of Gehenna, cf. Sharman, *Future*, 263–265 ; Leckie, *World to Come*, 113f., 140–143, 170f., 173 ; Strack-Billerbeck ii. 19, iv. 1075–1083.

near ! ", which Mk. (i. 15 = Mt. iv. 17) gives as the initial proclamation of Jesus (but see above, p. 108 n. 5). When therefore we find Mt. twice putting into Jesus' mouth (Mt. xii. 34, xxiii. 33) the phrase, " Offspring of vipers ! ", which Q (Lk. iii. 7 = Mt. iii. 7) assigns to John, we are justified in suspecting that the Matthæan report is not to be trusted in such passages where it is not supported by other sources. The phrases peculiar to Mt. probably represent the unauthorized glosses of m. We cannot therefore regard with confidence as a real saying of Jesus the words of Mt. xxiii. 33 m, " Serpents ! offspring of vipers ! how are ye to escape from the judgment of Gehenna ? "—i.e., the judgment which consigns to or punishes in Gehenna (see above, p. 228). The conclusion thus reached must needs throw doubt on the other Matthæan references to Gehenna, and goes far to justify the charge that the Evangelist has for reasons of his own increased the stress which his sources showed Jesus to have placed on the idea.[1]

The remaining passages are :

Mt. v. 22 fin. M : " And whoever says (to his brother), ' Mōré ! ' will be in danger ($\check{\epsilon}\nu o\chi os$) of the Gehenna of fire "—a passage the context of which is so obscure as to its meaning and its original form (see above, pp. 214 [3], 228 [5]) that we are unable to tell with any certainty what Jesus (if indeed the saying be his) intended to convey by it. It seems, however, like Mt. xxiii. 33 to link Gehenna definitely with " the Judgment ".

In Mt. xiii. 30 M, 40–42 M or m, the problematic Parable of the Tares and its still more dubious interpretation, the tares are collected in bundles and burnt, and similarly—at the consummation of the age—" all the hindrances and those who act lawlessly " will be collected by the angels out of the Kingdom, and cast " into the furnace of fire . . . ".

In Mt. xiii. 50 M or m, the dubious interpretation of the Parable of the Net uses precisely the same phrases in describing the fate of " the evil " ($\tau o\grave{v}s$ $\pi o\nu\eta\rho o\acute{v}s$).[2]

Mt. xxiii. 15 M : " Alas for you, Scribes and Pharisees, hypocrites ! for ye traverse sea and land to make one proselyte ; and when he has become (so), ye make him twice (as much) a son of Gehenna as yourselves ". The last two words (= $\acute{v}\mu\hat{\omega}\nu$) are textually doubtful : if they be omitted, we probably ought

---

[1] H. T. Andrews in *Congreg. Quart.* v. 267 (July 1927).
[2] On the furnace, cf. Strack-Billerbeck i. 673 ; Manson in *Mission*, etc. 487.

to understand " as he was before ".[1] This is perhaps the most likely of the group to be genuine.

In Mt. xxv. 46 M the dramatic picture of the Last Judgment concludes by saying of the condemned, " And these will go away into eternal punishment ($\epsilon\hat{i}s$ $\kappa\acute{o}\lambda a\sigma\iota\nu$ $a\hat{i}\acute{\omega}\nu\iota o\nu$), but the righteous into eternal life ". The punishment is described as " the eternal fire which has been prepared for the devil and his angels " (Mt. xxv. 41 M).

The fire mentioned in Mk. ix. 49 and in Lk. xii. 49 L is a metaphorical expression indicating painful discipline (such as persecution, and the like—cf. 1 Pet. iv. 12), and has no eschatological significance, though Mk. ix. 49 probably owes its position to the idea that it had.

(20) There was another phrase used by Jesus in his descriptions of final doom—" There there will be weeping and gnashing of teeth ". It appears in Q in a saying so differently reported in Lk. (xiii. 28f.) and Mt. (viii. 11f.) that we cannot be sure of its precise original form ; but it clearly depicted the admission of Gentiles to the Patriarchs' table in the future Kingdom, and the expulsion or departure from it of unworthy Jews. But the compiler of Mt. is fond of the phrase, as he is of references to Gehenna. In the passage just quoted, he combines it with another expression which he alone uses—" cast into the outer darkness " : and the same combination appears also in his Parable of the Man without the Wedding Garment (Mt. xxii. 13 M) and in his conclusion of the Parable of the Servants entrusted with Money (Mt. xxv. 30 M) : in both these cases the words seem to be put into the mouth of the principal character in the story, but in reality are appropriate only if spoken by the Divine Judge. " The weeping and gnashing of teeth " appears, without the reference to outer darkness, in Mt. xiii. 42, 50 M or m (in the probably-ungenuine interpretations of the Parables of the Tares and the Net) and in Mt. xxiv. 51 m (in the description of the punishment of the disloyal and disorderly head-slave : contrast Lk. xii. 46 Q). The " outer darkness " is a figure suggested by the darkness of a street at night outside a house the windows and doors of which face only the interior court.[2] The picture presupposed by these expressions, as indeed the context in several cases makes plain, is that of exclusion or explusion from a brightly-lighted hall, where

[1] Cf. Wellhausen, *Mt.* 117 ; McNeile, *St. Matthew*, 334a.
[2] B. T. D. Smith, *Parables*, 19 n.2. According to Carl Clemen (*Primitive Christianity*, 171) the idea is of Persian origin. J. H. Robertson (*Spiritual Pilgrimage*, 66, 195) thinks a reference to the howling of pariah-dogs may be intended.

guests are partaking of a joyous banquet. They are therefore more or less directly connected with the idea of the great Messianic Feast—to the consideration of which we must next turn.

(**21**) It was a very widely held Jewish belief that, either in the days of the Messiah, or (as some thought) in the Age to come which would follow those days, a magnificent banquet would be Divinely prepared and provided for the righteous, who would then be privileged to feed on the flesh of Leviathan and Behemoth.[1] The tacit popular assumption comes out in the observation once hazarded by a man who had been listening to Jesus at table : " Happy is he who will eat bread in the Kingdom of God ! " (Lk. xiv. 15 L). That prior to, and altogether independently of, any idea of his coming Passion, Jesus adopted this idea (without, however, any crude speculations regarding Leviathan and Behemoth) is clear from a number of indications in the Gospels. The crowd-feeding by the Lake-side, for instance (Mk. vi. 33–44 = Lk. ix. 11–17 = Mt. xiv. 13–21 ; Mk. viii. 1–9 = Mt. xv. 32–38), is to be regarded, not as a stupendous exhibition of incredible miraculous power, but as a common meal superintended by Jesus with solemn thanksgiving and bread-breaking as an acted anticipation of the Messianic Feast. The terms used to describe it resemble closely those used to describe the Last Supper, with which the language of the Fourth Gospel connects it (John vi), and which Jesus explicitly interpreted as an anticipation of this kind (Mk. xiv. 25 = Mt. xxvi. 29 ; Lk. xxii. 16, 18 L : see above, p. 58 [g]). He describes his presence with the Disciples as that of a bridegroom with his friends—no time for fasting ! (Mk. ii. 19 = Lk. v. 34 = Mt. ix. 15a : see above, pp. 189f. [**9**]). He evidently made a practice of reclining at table with all and sundry, so much so that unfriendly critics said of him, " Look ! a glutton and a tippler, a friend of tax-collectors and sinners ! " (Lk. vii. 34 = Mt. xi. 19 Q). He invites sinners to partake of his hospitality (Mk. ii. 17 fin. = Lk. v. 32 = Mt. ix. 13 fin : see above, p. 49 n.1). He pronounces the hungry happy, " for (they) will be satisfied " (Lk. vi. 21a = Mt. v. 6 Q [m : " those who hunger and thirst for righteousness "]). The reward which the man who is hospitable to the poor will receive at the

---

[1] Dalman, *W.J.* 110–113 ; Schürer, *G.J.V.* ii. 631f. n.56 (where the lit. on the subject is listed) ; Schweitzer, *Quest*, 377 n.1, and *L.J.F.* 311 ; Strack-Billerbeck i. 475f., 684 top, 992, iv. 840, 892, 1146f., 1154–1165 ; Moore, *Judaism*, ii. 363–365, iii. 203f. On the less-frequent notion of the Feast as a *Wedding*-feast, McNeile, *St. Matthew*, 314a ; Strack-Billerbeck i. 517f. For the Old-Testament basis of the idea, see Isa. xxv. 6–8, lv. 1–3, lxv. 13.

Resurrection of the righteous (Lk. xiv. 14 L) was probably thought of as a heavenly banquet, in place of the earthly banquets he had missed (Lk. xiv. 12 fin. L).

The most concrete picture of the Messianic Feast, however, is that given in Lk. xiii. 23–30. It seems to come in the main from Q, though the Matthæan parallels are scattered, and seem to be heavily glossed. In reply to one who asked if the saved were few, Jesus pictures a banqueting-hall, with a narrow entrance, through which many would-be guests strive to pass. The presiding host within shuts the door, and repudiates the plea of the undeserving applicants for admission by disowning acquaintance with them and sending them away. The banqueting-hall is the Kingdom of God : within at table are the Patriarchs and Prophets, and with them many Gentiles (and presumably many Jews also) from all over the world : those excluded as unworthy are Jews who as such might have been expected to be the principal guests. The Matthæan parallels are—Mt. vii. 13f. (the narrow gate and road, and the broad), Mt. xxv. 10–12 (the futile plea of the foolish virgins), Mt. vii. 22f. (the dismissal of the undeserving ones, who claim acquaintance with the host), Mt. viii. 11f. (a fairly-close parallel to Lk. xiii. 28f.), and Mt. xix. 30 = xx. 16 (last first, and first last). Lk. xiii. 26f. = Mt. vii. 22f. make it clear that Jesus thinks of himself as the Master of the Feast. Several of his apparently-eschatological Parables depict feasts—that of the Wise and Foolish Virgins (Mt. xxv. 1–13 M), the so-called Parable of the Great Feast (Lk. xiv. 16–24 Q ? [where it is spoken in reply to the man who said, " Happy is he who will eat bread in the Kingdom of God "] ; Mt. xxii. 1–10 Q + m), and that of the Man without the Wedding-Garment (Mt. xxii. 11–13 M). The first and third of these are wedding-banquets, and—according to m (Mt. xxii. 2)—the second also. We may note too the allusions to feasting in Lk. xv. 23–25 L (Prodigal Son), Lk. xvi. 22f. L (Lazarus in Abraham's bosom : see above, p. 221), and Mt. xxv. 21, 23 M (the Servants entrusted with Money).[1] Such then is the evidence for Jesus' thoughts concerning the Messianic Feast, in so far as they were unaffected by the prospect of the Passion. It is clear that he thought and spoke frequently about it as a future and final climax of completely-joyful fellowship, and about exclusion from it as utter and bitter punishment.[2] The ulterior questions which the

---

[1] Cf. Wellhausen, *Mt.* 132 ; McNeile, *St. Matthew*, 365b ; and Moffatt's translation.

[2] Cf. Manson, *Teaching*, 276f.

prediction raises—as to how far the picture was meant figuratively, and whether any thought of material reality was attached to it—had better be discussed later, when the final development of Jesus' anticipations regarding the future have also been studied (see below, pp. 326–328, 340–342).

(22) It remains only to quote the impressive simile with which Jesus concluded the Sermon on the Mount. It stood in Q ; and the Matthæan version seems in this case nearer to the original. " Every one therefore who listens to these words of mine, and does them, will be like a sensible man who builds his house on the rock. And the rain descended, and the rivers came, and the winds blew, and fell upon that house ; and it fell not, for it had been founded on the rock. And every one who listens to these words of mine, and does them not, will be like a foolish man, who built his house on the sand. And the rain descended, and the rivers came, and the winds blew, and struck against that house ; and it fell, and great was the fall thereof " (Mt. vii. 24–27 = Lk. vi. 47–49 Q). It is conceivable that the crisis here depicted is meant as an instance of the sort which may frequently recur to a man in the course of his life : [1] it seems to me, however, much more likely to be the great historical climax of the Coming of the Kingdom in power and the Divine Judgment of all.

[1] Dr. Manson (in *Mission*, etc. 353f.) inclines so to take it.

SUMMARY OF PART THREE

The reader who has toiled through Part Three in the hope of discovering those earlier beliefs of Jesus about the Future which must be distinguished from his later beliefs, may be tempted to feel that he has drawn a blank. Again and again he has had to be reminded that the data are scanty and often obscure, and that any conclusions we may frame are bound to be vague. These limitations are, no doubt, matter for regret : yet, having regard to the state of our evidence, we cannot but recognize that some vagueness in the reconstruction is inevitable.

Once the fact is admitted, however, that Jesus began his ministry expecting that Israel would as a nation receive, honour, and follow him, a great many conclusions follow naturally. The future " Coming " of the Kingdom (which in no way conflicts with its being in a sense already here) is a golden culmination of present effort : it is destined to be realized soon by God's power and in God's own time, yet not so as to dispense with the need of man's strenuous efforts and prayers, or so as to interfere with Israel's fulfilment of the duty of bringing reconciliation and the true faith to the Gentile world and the Roman Empire. The concrete features of the approaching end are determined according to certain eternal Divine principles of reward and punishment, under which eternal happiness is linked with the realization by men of the purpose which God desires them to realize, and utter misery with the frustration of that purpose. We can only dimly see how Jesus expected his historic mission to eventuate immediately. His predictions of the ulterior future are complicated by the fact that he mixes together those bearing on the life beyond the grave and those bearing on the Last Judgment and its consequences. On the whole, the way in which he fills in the details of his forecast of the future follows the broad outlines of Jewish eschatology. A sharp dualism characterizes the future lot of mankind: a man will be either inside or outside the Kingdom of God (at death, and after the Last Judgment), and his eternal happiness or misery will depend on which of these alternatives he is found to have incurred.

PART FOUR

THE FUTURE OF THE KINGDOM AS LAST ENVISAGED

CHAPTER I

THE CROSS FORESEEN, ACCEPTED, AND EXPLAINED

(1) Jesus voluntarily accepted death, (2) not for dogmatic eschatological reasons, but because it met him in the practical fulfilment of his Ministry among men, (3) as is clear from his deep disappointment at their rejection of him. (4) Opposition was offered to him on various grounds by the Pharisees, the Sadducees, and the populace ; (5) and Jesus came to see that, unless he fled or fought, this opposition would eventuate in his being put to death. (6) But he did not voice his anticipation of death until after Peter's Confession at Cæsarea-Philippi. (7) His three reported formal predictions of it may be based on only one utterance, (8) but in any case he made several other allusions to it from time to time. (9) The approach of it was the greatest of his many " temptations ", (10) and brought him the bitterest grief. (11) Yet he did not believe that his acceptance of death would prove fruitless ; (12) and on two occasions he spoke obscurely of the service it would render, (13) using sacrificial terms in doing so. (14) Various explanations of these sayings have been suggested ; (15) but the truth can be discovered only by drawing on Isaiah liii, a prophetic poem which makes it clear that the Suffering Servant of God triumphs by moving men to penitence for their sin. (16) Several considerations confirm the conclusion that this was also the true content of Jesus' own hope. (17) That hope was, however, set in the midst of most extreme sorrow.

(1) All sources of information and lines of argument concur in showing that, whatever was the cause of Jesus' death, and whatever its significance for him and others, his submission to it was on his part a voluntary act. His hand was not forced ; he made no attempt either to resist, or to escape from, his enemies. Opinions, however, diverge, not only as to the time at which the prospect of death became clear and certain to him, but also as to his motive and purpose in accepting it. These two questions are indeed not unconnected. Those who hold that Jesus came only gradually to foresee a violent death as certain, having first for a time hoped for national obedience, usually see the prime cause of his death in the ill-

will and opposition of his enemies; and they regard his acceptance of death at their hands as the supreme act of compliance
with the Father's Will, because it was the supreme manifestation of love for sinful men. Those, on the other hand, who
believe that Jesus clearly foresaw and accepted the Passion
from the time of his baptism at latest frequently assign the
initiative from which it eventuated not to his enemies, but to
himself, acting as he was in obedience to some idée fixe concerning what the Messiah would have to do and derived either
from the Old-Testament Scriptures [1] or from the currently-
accepted Messianic programme, modified through his disappointment at the non-irruption of the Kingdom. In support of this last-named view it has been urged that the Gospels
tell us nothing of any waning popularity of Jesus or growing
opposition to him such as would suffice to account for his
expectation of a violent death : we are therefore shut up, it is
claimed, to the necessity of explaining that expectation from
his own dogmatic beliefs.[2]

(2) We need, of course, to tread warily when we are trying
to discover the ways of an Eastern mind of ancient times. But
we can surely not be altogether unwarranted in supposing that,
with all the great differences in outlook and approach between
such a mind and ours, the great moral realities of life made
much the same impact then and there as they do here and
now. One may therefore hazard the conjecture that the
second of the two main views outlined in the last paragraph is
inherently the less probable. For a religious leader to frame
a life-scheme terminating in the infliction of death upon
himself by his fellow-countrymen, deliberately to go about to
get that scheme carried out, and to do so, primarily if not
solely, because he believed himself to be identical with one
prophetically described in an ancient book as so suffering, or
because his mind was dominated by some other dogmatic
prepossession, would surely be to act, both morally and
intellectually, in a very questionable way. Certainly the
Jewish habit of deterministic thought and speech does not
warrant any such theory. I hold it to be inherently almost
certain that, if Jesus accepted death, he accepted it because

[1] The best representative of this view is the late Sir Edwyn Hoskyns (see
above, p. 186 n.1).
[2] Cf. Schweitzer, *Mystery*, 84–86, 179, 223f., 261–266, *L.J.F.* 432, 438f. =
Quest, 385, 390 : see also above, pp. 4f., 16f. The idea that Jesus was disappointed and puzzled because the Kingdom did not break in miraculously
during his ministry was also defended by Burkitt in *H.C.L.M.K.* 225f., 229 =
Jesus Christ, etc. 29f., 33 (he speaks of " the determination of Jesus to bring
things to a crisis, to create a crisis by His own action . . . ").

others threatened him with it under conditions which made the acceptance of it morally nobler than any attempt to fight against them or to flee (see above, pp. 186f. [**3** and **4**], 188f. [**7**]).

(**3**) But in this matter we are not left to our modern calculations of inherent probability alone. The appeal lies to the evidence itself. How can it be maintained that Jesus calculated from the first on being rejected and martyred by his fellow-countrymen, and that he purposely made plans in order to be so martyred, when we find him passionately lamenting that Khorazin and Bethsaida and Kapharnaum had not repented at the sight of his deeds of power and that the children of Jerusalem had not gathered together under him or seen their true welfare in accepting his ministry as a Divine visitation ?[1] Why the tears shed and the agonized regret outpoured on the ride into Jerusalem (Lk. xix. 41–44 L), if the whole tragic event was from the first a foregone conclusion, which Jesus himself was, on his own initiative, going out of his way to bring about ? There are other supplementary considerations which support the view that the unresponsiveness of the nation and the plot against his life were a real frustration of his hopes (see above, pp. 183- 193) : but—unless we are to ascribe to him an attitude of mind inconsistent with all else that we know about him—the case is settled for us by this evidence, just adduced, of his real and profound disappointment.

(**4**) It hardly forms part of our task in this book to trace the story of the growing opposition which Jesus encountered (Lk. ii. 34f.) and to discuss at length his successive allusions to the fatal end to which it was to lead.[2] It is not as easy as it looks to specify the precise issue round which so desperate a conflict raged. The opposition was initiated by the Scribes and Pharisees ; in its latest stage it received the powerful support of the Sadducees, who were chiefly instrumental in carrying it through to a bloody end : it was only when these influential leaders had joined forces and decided on extreme measures that the mind of the populace was manœuvred into a repudiation of their former hero. A motive common to all these leaders was jealousy (Mk. xv. 10 = Mt. xxvii. 18) ; but the jealousy of the one group differed in content from that of the other. The Pharisees were badly upset by Jesus' independent and (as they would feel) shockingly-irreverent

---

[1] See the passages quoted and considered above, pp. 191–193.

[2] The development of the opposition is well sketched by Dr. A. T. Cadoux in *The Lord of Life* (e.g., 61, 63, 76, etc.). Cf. Meyer, *Ursprung*, i. 163.

attitude to the Law, and his telling way of appealing as a prophet to other parts of Scripture in justification of his free personal judgments and of his drastic criticism of themselves and their methods. Besides that, they could not fail to see that his teaching, for all his cautious adaptation of it to the prepossessions of his hearers, spelt the virtual abandonment of many exclusive privileges which the Jews assumed to be theirs as the Chosen People of God. In the very suggestion that the Gentiles should come into the Kingdom, they felt their nationalistic pride hurt to the quick.[1] In any case, their own prestige stood to suffer gravely from whatever success Jesus might attain. The Sadducees, too, were alarmed at the menace which his influence seemed to cast on their authority as the main custodians, under Rome, of the existing civil and religious régime ; and they regarded any serious claimant to Messiahship as a danger to law and order and therefore to their own privileges.

The rank and file of the people were for a long time and to a large extent friendly : they saw at close range his wonderful deeds of healing ; they heard him speak " as never man spake " ; they felt something of his personal spell. But they were ill-prepared to accept his universalism, and they admired him for so long a time only because his abandonment of exclusive nationalism was concealed from their notice partly by his reserve (see above, p. 162), and partly by the absorption of their interest in other things. But when at the end their leaders were able to exhibit him as a self-styled Messiah who yet did not intend to strike a blow or move a hand either to punish the Gentiles or even to keep himself out of chains, they quickly passed from admiration or at worst indifference to indignation and contempt. And the motives which led Judas to desert and betray him may have been very similar to those which led former admirers in the crowd to shout " Crucify him ! "[2]

(5) The Gospels contain numerous statements to the effect that Jesus foresaw and foretold his death at the hands of his enemies. We may admit the inherent probability that foreknowledge of whatever actually happened to him would in

---

[1] Liberty, *Political Relations*, 89–93, 102f.
[2] Cf. Menzies, *Earliest Gospel*, 210b, 218b, 228b, 266b, 274b ; Holtzmann ap. Schweitzer, *L.J.F.* 204f. n. 2 = *Quest*, 204f. n. 2 ; Moffatt, *Theol. of the Gospels*, 66f. ; Bartlet, *St. Mark*, 56, 230f., 315, 332 ; Klausner, *Jes. of Naz.* 318 ; Montefiore, *S.G.*² I. cxxiii ; A. T. Cadoux in *The Lord of Life*, 76 ; E. C. Essex in *The Atonement in History and in Life* (ed. Grenstead, 1929), 262 (" The refusal of Christ to claim an earthly kingdom is one of the chief reasons for His death ") ; Goguel, *Life of Jes.* 377 ; Otto, *Kingdom*, 58.

any case be almost certain to be later on ascribed to him : and the view has therefore been held that these predictions of the Passion which he is said to have uttered were probably just vaticinia post eventus.[1]   Yet it is inherently even more likely that Jesus would discern that the tension between himself and the most influential Jewish parties in the country could, if he persisted as he intended to persist, end only in their doing him to death : [2] and when once that upshot had been seen to be involved in the situation in which he actually stood, the picture in Isa. liii of the martyred Servant of the Lord would help to confirm his expectation of a similar fate for himself.[3]   While, however, Jesus must have foreseen his approaching death, it is not likely that he knew in advance the details of the fatal process.[4]   In this respect we ought undoubtedly to make allowance for the fact that Christian devotion would later enlarge his general anticipation of tragedy into an exact prevision of all its features.   If the conjecture be sound that certain passages in the Gospels indicate that he expected to suffer death by the characteristically-Jewish method of stoning,[5] then he clearly did not foreknow the details.   He may well have had both stoning and crucifixion (Mk. viii. 34 [= Lk. ix. 23 : see the variant reading] = Mt. xvi. 16 ; Lk. xiv. 27 = Mt. x. 38 Q) in mind as possible alternatives.

(6) Just as we cannot say with what degree of precision Jesus foresaw the manner and circumstances of his death, so we cannot say exactly when and by what stages the virtual certainty of his martyrdom came home to him.   He had the earlier of the Deutero-Isaianic Servant-passages in mind from the time of his baptism onwards ; and some have inferred from this fact that he must have applied the Passion-prophecy of Isa. liii to himself from an equally-early date.   But this is unlikely (see above, pp. 186f.).   The allusion in Mk. ii. 20 = Lk. v. 35 = Mt. ix. 15 to the removal of the bridegroom is similarly taken by many to prove that already at that early point in the Ministry Jesus was looking forward to his death.   But again, in view of the evidence as a whole, the inference must be pronounced unsound (see above, pp. 189–191 [9f.]).   Apart from other considerations regarding these two supposedly-

---

[1] See the lit. quoted in Holtzmann, *Theol.* i. 353f. n. 1 ; and cf. Montefiore, *S.G.*[2] I. 274f.

[2] Cf. Otto, *Kingdom*, 359 (4), 360 (6), 363 (6 fin.).

[3] Cf. K. L. Schmidt in *R.G.G.* iii (1929) 149 (E. 2).

[4] Cf. Bacon, *Beginnings*, 118 ; Otto, *Kingdom*, 359f. (5f.).

[5] Otto urges that Jesus' bread-breaking at the Last Supper and passages like Lk. xiii. 34 = Mt. xxiii. 37 Q indicate that he expected his own body to be broken by stoning (*Kingdom*, 303 [3], 314f. [1], 320f. [6], 361f.).

early indications, the fact that all the other prophecies of the Passion—and there are over twelve of them—are placed by the Evangelists after the Confession of Peter at Cæsarea-Philippi must surely tell against the likelihood of two such prophecies having been uttered before it.

(7) Mark is followed by the other two Synoptists in recording three distinct, explicit, and more or less detailed predictions of the Passion, the first of which is placed immediately after Peter's Confession ([a] Mk. viii. 31–33 = Lk. ix. 22 = Mt. xvi. 21–23 ; [b] Mk. ix. 30–32 = Lk. ix. 43–45 = Mt. xvii. 22f. [perhaps the simplest and most original of the three] ; and [c] Mk. x. 32–34 = Lk. xviii. 31–34 [cf. xxiv. 6f., 44] = Mt. xx. 17–19). Having regard to the similarity of the three predictions and to the degree of detail which they contain and to the fact that the topic is on the second and third occasions introduced as a new one and therefore creates perplexity, we may perhaps conjecture not unreasonably that we have here a triplication of a single prophecy.[1] But the determination of the date and precise contents of the one original utterance from which all three were in that case derived is beyond our power.

(8) It may be useful here just to enumerate the remaining allusions to the Passion.   . .

Lk. ix. 31 l: during the Transfiguration—a few days after Peter's Confession—Moses and Elijah speak with Jesus of " his departure, which he was about to carry out at Jerusalem ". The Marcan and Matthæan accounts omit this detail.

Mk. ix. 12 = Mt. xvii. 12, on descending from the Mount of Transfiguration, Jesus speaks to Peter, Jacob, and John about the coming suffering and humiliation of the Son of Man. Luke omits the section.

Lk. xii. 49f. L : " I have come to throw a fire upon the earth ; and what do I wish ? Would it were already kindled ! And I have a baptism to be baptized with ; and how troubled I am—until it is finished ! "[2]

Lk. xiii. 33 L : " . . . Only I must journey on to-day and to-morrow and the next day, for it is impossible that a prophet should perish outside Jerusalem ".

Lk. xiii. 34 = Mt. xxiii. 37 Q : " Jerusalem, Jerusalem !

---

[1] Cf. A. T. Cadoux in *Expos.* VIII. xv. 74–77 (Jan. 1918), and *Sources of the Second Gospel* (1935), 25f. (where the triplication serves as the basis of a theory of Marcan sources) : also Otto, *Kingdom*, 360–363.

[2] Cf. Otto, *Kingdom*, 360, on the genuineness and emotional depth of this utterance.

thou that killest the prophets, and stonest them that have
been sent to her, . . . ".

Lk. xiv. 26f. = Mt. x. 37f. Q : hatred of one's own life and
willingness to carry one's own cross are conditions of discipleship. The lesson is enforced in Lk. (xiv. 28–33 Q or L) by the
illustrations of the Tower-builder and the belligerent King.

Lk. xvii. 25 Q or l ? : " But first he must suffer many things,
and be rejected by this generation " (Mt. xxiv. 27 omits).

Mk. x. 45 = Mt. xx. 28 : " For even " (m put " just as ")
" the Son of Man came not to be served but to serve, and to
give his life (as) a ransom for many " (Lk. xxii. 26f. L omits).

Mk. xii. 1–12 = Lk. xx. 9–19 = Mt. xxi. 33–46 : the Parable
of the Wicked Vinedressers, the genuineness of which has been
doubted by some.[1]

Mt. xxvi. 2 m : " . . . and the Son of Man is, (at Passover,
to be) handed over to be crucified ".

Mk. xiv. 7f. = Mt. xxvi. 11f. : " For ye have the poor with
you always, . . . but me ye have not always. She has done
what she could. She has anointed my body in anticipation
for my burial ".

The other references to the Passion belong to the Passion-
story itself, and can therefore hardly be ranked as anticipations
in the same way as those just quoted.

(9) Though we cannot reconstruct in detail the movements
of Jesus' mind as the ordeal which he knew to be in store for
him drew slowly nearer, and can do little more than note his
several allusions to it according to the precarious chronology
of the Synoptic narratives, we can observe to some extent the
deep emotional distress which the prospect involved. This
frustration of the great enterprise of his life, and all the stinging
tokens of defeat that met him week by week as the situation
gradually developed in favour of his opponents, constituted
for him a set of " temptations " ($\pi\epsilon\iota\rho\alpha\sigma\mu\text{o}\iota$) as serious as that
which he had encountered immediately after his baptism. The
root-idea of $\pi\epsilon\iota\rho\alpha\sigma\mu\text{ò}\varsigma$ is not inducement to sin, but the
encountering of any situation which by its difficulty constitutes
a special " test " or " trial " of one's character and resources.
So in the Lucan interpretation of the Parable of the Sower, " a
time of $\pi\epsilon\iota\rho\alpha\sigma\mu\text{ó}\varsigma$ " is put as the equivalent of the Marcan
phrase " when affliction or persecution comes on account of the
Word " (Mk. iv. 17 = Lk. viii. 13 = Mt. xiii. 21). So it is
that at the Last Supper Jesus says to the eleven faithful

[1] E.g., B. T. D. Smith, *Parables*, 22f., 50, 59, 223f. Per contra, V. Taylor,
Sacrifice, 106f.

Disciples, after Judas—the offended one—had departed to betray him to his foes, " Ye are they who have stood by me throughout my trials " (Lk. xxii. 28 L : . . . οἱ διαμεμενηκότες μετ᾽ ἐμοῦ ἐν τοῖς πειρασμοῖς μου).[1]

The word πειρασμὸς is supposed by some to have had a technical signification as designating the tribulations which were expected to precede the coming of the Kingdom : and it has been suggested that when, in Gethsemane, Jesus warned his Disciples to watch and pray, that they should not come into " trial " (Mk. xiv. 38 = Mt. xxvi. 41 ; Lk. xxii. 40, 46 L), the reference is to the woes that would usher in the last great crisis.[2] Some go further, and make this reference a ground for denying that the warning was really spoken by Jesus ; and others think that even the petition in Jesus' model prayer, " Lead us not into trial " (Lk. xi. 4 L ; Mt. vi. 13 M), similarly refers to the eschatological tribulation. It is not easy to see the slightest reason for importing any such technical sense into either passage. " Trial " is a common experience of the religious life ; and that is sufficient to account for the petition in the model prayer. In regard to Gethsemane, Jesus knew that his own arrest and execution would involve the Disciples in the gravest danger, even if they did not go so far as to stand by him and share death with him (Mk. x. 38f. = Mt. xx. 22f. : cf. Mk. viii. 34 [= Lk. ix. 23 : see the variant reading] = Mt. xvi. 16 ; Lk. xiv. 27 = Mt. x. 38 Q). It was in view of that impending danger, which resulted from the circumstances, and had nothing technically eschatological about it, that Jesus urged them to pray. It would be a " trial " of the same kind as Jesus himself had met—a testing of the strength of one's loyalty to God through the threats and cruelty of persecutors.

(10) The unspeakably-profound anguish which Jesus endured in facing these trials comes out more than once in the way he speaks of them. " I have come to throw a fire upon the earth ; and what do I wish ? Would it were already kindled ! And I have a baptism to be baptized with ; and how troubled I am—until it is finished ! " (Lk. xii. 49f. L). The agonized lamentations and tears over Jerusalem (Lk. xiii. 34f. = Mt. xxiii. 37–39 Q ; Lk. xix. 41–44 L) testify to the depth of his grief. ' And they were on the road going up to Jerusalem ;

---

[1] Otto's argument (*Kingdom*, 273) that Lk. xxii. 28 is an awkward editorial gloss in the wrong place, because Jesus' πειρασμοὶ had not yet begun, seems to me highly arbitrary and improbable, and involves an unduly narrow idea of what the word might mean. Cf. V. Taylor, *Sacrifice*, 177, 188.

[2] Cf. Schweitzer, *L.J.F.* 411, 414, 421, 435f., 438f. = *Quest*, 362, 370, 375, 387, 390, *Mystery*, 257–259, 271f. ; Dodd, *Parables*, 166f. n.1.

and Jesus was in front of them, and he began to be appalled
(ἐθαμβεῖτο), and those who were following him grew afraid ',
and he went on to tell them of his approaching death (Mk. x.
32).[1] So long as his enemies had not struck their last fatal
blow, some margin of hope, however small, remained open.
But when in Gethsemane the time had come for him to witness
the final extinction of that margin of hope, unless by some
utterly-unforeseen possibility God Himself should intervene to
avert the worst, then at last did Jesus feel the whole crushing
weight of sorrow descend upon him (Mk. xiv. 33f. = Mt. xxvi.
37f. ; Lk. xxii. 43f. L). I borrow the words of another to tell
the story.

" As it is, we must view Jesus' feelings largely as the
outcome of his Messianic experience and consciousness.
We must see the rejection by God's People, and the death
virtually at its hands, from which he shrank with such
agony of soul, in the light of his representative function
as the bearer of the Father's message of good-will and love
to His erring children, His wandering sheep. So viewed,
their treatment of God's Anointed, His Son *par excellence*,
meant for Jesus their own self-condemnation as men
culpably blind, in virtue of long failure to respond as they
should have done to the higher aspects of the Law and the
Prophets, God's special revelation in its preparatory forms,
and one meant to lead up to recognition of the final or
Messianic message of Divine Love in the Gospel. To feel
that he, with his utter devotion alike to the Heavenly
Father's gracious will for Israel, and to the welfare of
Israel itself, was being turned by his own people's attitude
to himself, and to the Gospel entrusted to him, into the
means of bringing their corporate sin to a head in a
terrible crime, was, indeed, to have a bitter cup held to his
lips by the Father's hand. Fain would he be spared the
draining of it ; but . . . let the Father's will be done,
cost him what it might . . . "[2]

(11) In recoil from the unrelieved gloom of defeat and
despair, the mind of Jesus sought and found for itself, through
its instinctive trust in the invincibility of God, certain counter-
vailing assurances which rendered possible some sort of adjust-

---

[1] On the conjectural reading ἐθαμβεῖτο for the ἐθαμβοῦντο of the MSS., see
Turner, *Study of the N.T.* (1926), 62, and cf. Wellhausen, *Mc.* 83, and Bartlet,
St. Mark, 301.
[2] Bartlet, *St. Mark*, 398. Cf. the somewhat similar but longer account
given by Dr. A. T. Cadoux in *The Lord of Life*, 76–81 ; also Menzies, *Earliest
Gospel*, 258a, 260f.

ment to the unspeakably-tragic reverse which lay ahead. Some of these assurances were concerned with the future course of human history, and will come up for discussion a little later.   Others of them lay in a different field—that of the religious and moral experience of man as such.   Whether it is possible to present these two forecasts as aspects of a single whole it is hard to say.   But our immediate task is to investigate the latter group by itself, and to endeavour to find an answer to the question : What did Jesus himself expect the effect of his death to be on the lives of men as moral and spiritual beings ?

(12) Such an inquiry does not mean a discussion of the whole problem of the Atonement ; but it does mean the first part of such a discussion.   The meaning of Jesus himself, so far as we can discover it, must in the nature of things furnish the basis for any satisfactory doctrine of the Atonement ; and no doctrine will be entitled to acceptance which either contradicts, or even gives no essential place to, the thoughts of Jesus on the topics concerned.

Now it is well known that, while his teaching about God's willingness to forgive the repentant sinner is clear and abundant, his words regarding the significance of his death (as distinct from the certainty of its occurrence) are few and obscure.   There are only three passages which demand consideration in this connexion ; and of these only two are directly relevant.

(a) I take first the so-called Cry of Dereliction uttered by Jesus on the cross—Mk. xv. 34 = Mt. xxvii. 46.   The Gospel-report is full of obscurities.   It is not even certain in what language the Cry was uttered—though it was probably Aramaïc. It is still less certain what Jesus actually said.   One would indeed expect him, if he were really quoting Psalm xxii. 1, to keep closely to its wording, " . . . why hast thou forsaken me ? "   The supposition that he did so is confirmed by the Matthæan report ($\sigma a\beta a\chi\theta a\nu\epsilon i$ = Aramaïc שבקתני = $\mu\epsilon$ ἐγκατέλιπες ;) and the *possibility* that $\zeta a\phi\theta a\nu\epsilon i$, which is probably the correct reading in Mk., is meant to represent the original Hebrew of the Psalm (עזבתני).   On the other hand it has been plausibly argued [1] that the original text of Mark's translation ran . . . εἰς τί ὠνείδισάς με ; i.e., " . . . why hast Thou reproached me ? " ; and this would correspond to the Aramaïc עזפתני, whereof Mk's. $\zeta a\phi\theta a\nu\epsilon i$ may quite well be intended as a transliteration.

---

[1] See Harnack, *Studien* (1931), 98–103.

And most uncertain of all is the precise meaning we are to give to whatever words were used. Dale, for instance, declined to accept any interpretation of them which did not assume that they correctly expressed Jesus' actual condition at the moment : but in that case he ought to have inferred, not only that God had actually forsaken Jesus, but that Jesus did not know the reason for which He had done so—otherwise, why his question ? The very idea that the God revealed in Jesus should have *actually* either " forsaken " or " reproached " him when he was suffering for the sins of men is so inherently incredible that it would need some far less dubious evidence than we have here before it could be accepted. So obscure is the passage that, among those who insist on interpreting it theologically, there is no unanimity as to precisely what it was meant to convey.

It seems to me that the true explanation is to be sought on far simpler lines. It is well known that, under conditions of extreme physical pain, the human mind fails for the time being to function in its normal way. I suggest, therefore, that the words here ascribed to Jesus were simply a cry of sheer anguish, wrung from him when the unbearable agony of crucifixion was at its height, and were spontaneously cast into a form suggested by the opening words of a familiar Psalm. There is nothing in what we know of the human conditions of his life which makes such a view untenable or improbable ; and it has the advantage of not basing a staggering paradox on a very dubious foundation. Furthermore, it implies that we cannot derive from the Cry any clear light on the way in which Jesus himself viewed the purpose or meaning of his death. I pass on therefore to the other two passages.

(b) After urging on the Disciples the duty of humility and service, Jesus enforces his counsel by concluding, " for even " (m : puts " just as ") " the Son of Man came not to be served but to serve, and to give his life (as) a ransom for many " (Mk. x. 45 = Mt. xx. 28 : . . . λύτρον ἀντὶ πολλῶν).

(c) At the Last Supper, after handing round the cup of wine, he said, " This is my blood of the covenant, which is being poured out on behalf of many " (Mk. xiv. 24 = Mt. xxvi. 28 [m adding " unto remission of sins "]. Paul's earlier version of the saying in 1 Cor. xi. 25 [written about 55 A.D.] runs, " This cup is the new covenant in my blood : . . . "). In these two brief utterances we have virtually all that is preserved for us of the direct teaching of Jesus on the subject of our inquiry. What do these utterances mean ?

(13) The first thing that must strike us about them is that

they both recall to mind the sacrificial system of the Old Testament and the Jewish Temple. Λύτρον belongs to a group of Greek words which correspond to the Hebrew group clustering around the root כפר and expressing the ancient notion of atonement or propitiation. The surrender of the Son of Man's *life* as a λύτρον still more directly suggests the offering up of a propitiatory sacrifice.[1] The sacrificial suggestion in the reference to covenant-blood poured out (see Exod. xxiv. 8) is quite unmistakable.[2] It is therefore natural to infer that Jesus likened his death to the death of a sacrificial victim, the offering-up of which to God would effect—in the unexplained manner presupposed in the old Law—the needful adjustment of the relations between man and God, in so far as these had been impaired by human sin. And it must, indeed, be admitted that Jesus did at least use such language and therefore presumably to some extent entertain such thoughts.[3] But the urgent question remains over, Did this language and these thoughts convey his real meaning and the real interpretation he gave to his death, or were they possibly *the vehicle* of some deeper meaning and interpretation ? The difficulty of reconciling his other teaching about God's forgiveness with the sacrificial expressions about his death, when these latter are taken strictly at their face-value, gives a primâ-facie preference to the second alternative.[4]

(14) Alternative theories have, of course, not been lacking. The one advocated by the school of " konsequente Eschatologie " is to the effect that Jesus, sorely perplexed by the non-

[1] Cf. Holtzmann, *Theol.* i. 361–363 ; Otto, *Kingdom*, 256–261, 271f. ; V. Taylor, *Sacrifice*, 103f.; Macaulay, *Death of Jes.* 119–123, 127–130 ; Büchsel in *T.W.N.T.* iv. 341–351.

[2] Cf. Menzies, *Earliest Gospel*, 253f. ; V. Taylor, *Sacrifice*, 121, 127, 136–139.

[3] The Jews were familiar at this time with the idea that the sufferings of the righteous had atoning or propitiatory power (Moffatt, *Theol. of the Gospels*, 141 ; Moore, *Judaism*, i. 546–552, iii. 164–166 ; Otto, *Kingdom*, 253f., 297 [2], 306). On the general Jewish theory of ritual atonement, cf. Moore, *Judaism*, i. 497–506, iii. 151–155.

[4] Dr. V. Taylor, though himself favouring a sacrificial interpretation (*Sacrifice*, 74f., 261f., 269–271, 281–298, 304–306, 317), yet frankly recognizes that " the word ' ransom ' is used as a metaphor, and ought not to be treated as if it were a fixed scientific term . . . whether we find a sacrificial meaning in the saying depends ultimately upon other sayings of His . . . " (104).

An extreme form of the sacrificial interpretation of the death of Jesus is the view of it suggested by the late Sir E. Hoskyns in *Myst. Christi* (87), namely, that the sacrificial cultus of the Old Testament is consciously fulfilled in the death of the Messiah, and that the necessity of this fulfilment underlies the necessity of the Messiah's death, which consequently meets the need for " a new cultus centring round the sacrificial death of Jesus . . . ". This exegesis would seem like turning one's back finally on the possibility of giving any ethical interpretation to the traditional language.

appearance of the Kingdom, forced on his own death in the hope that he would thereby hasten the Kingdom's coming. But not to mention the grotesqueness of the idea that God's Servant could, by bringing about his own death, force God's hand and compel Him to take the next step in an imaginary eschatological programme, it is impossible to account on this theory for the testimony of the Gospels, in regard both to what it contains and to what it omits.[1] More recently the attempt has been made to find the really-original explanation of Jesus' death in the Pauline and Johannine idea that by means of it a victory was won over Satan and the demons (Col. ii. 15 ; John. xii. 31).[2] Now it is true that Jesus often pictured his life-task as a contest with Satan and Satan's realm (see above, pp. 65–68) : and it is therefore possible that, in so far as he was able to think of his death as a victory, he may have related it in thought to the great enemy over whom the victory was won. But here again, the evidence is lacking. Pauline and Johannine interpretations of the death of Jesus are not direct evidence of what Jesus himself thought : and though the idea of his death as a victory has commended itself to many Christian minds, and the patristic idea of a conquest of Satan has (to the darkening of counsel) been recently revived as if it helped us to the true doctrine of the Atonement, there is no clear evidence that Jesus ever looked at his approaching death from that angle. Moreover, the theory in question labours under the additional disadvantage of needlessly de-ethicizing the meaning of Jesus' death. The figure of a victory won suggests the forcible suppression of unwilling opponents, and can therefore in this connexion be at best but a very subsidiary illustration, and by no means the central truth.[3] Others, again, without pledging themselves to anything in the nature of a theory of substitutionary satisfaction, rest content with representing the death of Jesus as a providentially-ordained but otherwise-inexplicable transaction or device whereby man's reconciliation with God could be effected.

(15) If there be any possibility of discovering a deeper meaning beneath the two recorded utterances of Jesus, our quest must avail itself of the light indirectly thrown for us on his mind by the Servant-poem in Isa. lii. 13–liii. It has often been remarked that the notion of even a martyred and particularly

---

[1] Cf. Manson, *Teaching*, 206, 208.
[2] See above, pp. 67f. n. 4, and cf. Dodd, *Parables*, 76–80 ; V. Taylor. *Sacrifice*, 26of. (partial endorsement).
[3] Cf. Macaulay, *Death of Jes.* 170.

a crucified Messiah was totally alien from Jewish ideas.[1] But in Isaiah liii we have a passage which actually pictures the Servant of God as suffering death, and which we know to have been applied by Jesus to himself (see above, pp. 37f. [8]). Here, therefore, if anywhere, we may hope for further light on the meaning of his sufferings. At first sight, perhaps, it might appear as if even this new source of knowledge gives us little more than we have already from the Gospels themselves, namely, the general assurance that the Servant's death is the rendering of a vital service to men in that it provides a means for their redemption. Moreover, if we may trust the traditional text of Isa. liii. 10 a (which many regard as gravely corrupted), the service in question was likened to a guilt-offering (אשם)—an anticipation, it would seem, of the sacrificial expressions in the Gospels.[2] But if we ponder the poem further, and ask what precisely constitutes that triumph of the Servant which is metaphorically described as " the Lord's purpose prospering in his hand ", and as his getting a possession among the many, and dividing the spoil with the mighty (Isa. liii. 10, 12), we see that the triumph consists in " making the many righteous ", carrying away their sin and guilt, and interceding for the rebels (Isa. liii. 11, 12b : the text is again somewhat uncertain). Even these phrases are to some extent metaphorical : their essential meaning, however, is revealed to us when we study the deep change which the poet himself lets us see that he and his fellows went through as they contemplated the Servant's sufferings. They had begun with the self-satisfied view that those sufferings were a chastisement laid on him by God because he needed or deserved it (Is. liii. 3, 4b) ; but when they considered the matter further, they realized that the Servant himself was innocent, and that the transgressions which had caused his suffering were not his, but theirs (4a, 5–9). This discovery on the part of the poet and those for whom he speaks is the key to the whole mystery : by the Servant's sufferings they have been made conscious of their own sin—and penitently conscious of it ; they therefore are among " the many " whom the Servant is said to make righteous, and whose sins he carries away.[3]

(16) When now we remember that it was the great desire and purpose of Jesus to lead men to repentance and thereby to

[1] Schürer *G.J.V.* ii. 648–651 ; Strack-Billerbeck iv. 6 ; Otto, *Kingdom,* 254f.
[2] Cf. V. Taylor, *Sacrifice,* 41 n.
[3] Cf. V. Taylor, *Sacrifice,* 39–42.

that fellowship with God which he knew to be their supreme good, when too we realize that his death meant that hitherto he had failed in this effort, we cannot help seeing that, if his surrender to death was to effect in some way what his ministry among men had failed to effect, its natural fruit would have to be that it would move his former despisers to repentance. It is true that such a conclusion is nowhere explicitly formulated in the Synoptic Gospels ; but the Fourth Gospel (xii. 32) and the First Epistle of Clemens of Rome (vii. 4 : " the blood of Christ . . . brought to the whole world the grace of repentance ") show that it was present to the mind of the early Church, it follows inevitably on any real understanding of Isa. liii, and it is no harder to accept as an interpretation of *Jesus'* sacrificial expressions than is the analogous conclusion as an interpretation of the metaphorical expressions in that old poem.[1]

The acceptance of this view as probably representing Jesus' own interpretation of the meaning of the Cross opens up a number of other lines of thought. Did space permit, one could go further and show that this doctrine is not only required by Isaiah liii, and is historically probable as a conviction of

---

[1] The view that Jesus hoped that his death would generate a widespread movement of repentance in Israel, and through Israel in the world, and would be the means of bringing many into the Kingdom, is in some form or other accepted by many modern scholars as true : cf. Menzies, *Earliest Gospel*, 202ab ; Holtzmann, *Synopt.* 161 ; Moffatt, *Theol. of the Gospels*, 68f. ; Ranke quoted by Schweitzer, *L.J.F.* 221 (" . . . Jesus hat seinen Tod mit voller Bestimmtheit kommen sehen, aber er wusste, dass damit seine Lehre bekräftigt und gerettet würde ") ; Bartlet and Carlyle, *Christianity in Hist.* 62 ; Bartlet, *St. Mark*, 275, 308, 325f., 351, 398 (" Fain would he be spared the draining of it ; but if nothing short of this could suffice to effect the change of heart by which alone Israel's redemption from her crooked and sinful state might be achieved, and she rendered fit to fulfil her vocation as the medium of blessing to all nations, . . . then let the Father's will be done, cost him what it might ") ; H. G. Wood, quoted in *The Lord of Life*, 78 n.1 ; Manson, *Teaching*, 206–210 ; Otto, *Kingdom*, 258f. (" . . . The suffering of the master is propitiatory [sühnend], because its effect is to convert and unite . . . ").

The twofold reference to " many " in Isa. liii. 11f. and the echoes of it in the two Gospel-passages we are studying (see above, p. 38 [d]) would seem to refer to the fact that, while *all* are invited to repent, only *some* respond. I do not therefore see why Swete should say (*St. Mark*, 241a), " Jerome's comment ' non dixit . . . " pro omnibus ", sed " pro multis ", id est, pro his qui credere voluerint ' is quite unwarranted ".

Dr. Dodd rejects the view that Jesus died in order to bring about the repentance without which the Kingdom could not come, on the ground that Jesus had previously declared that the Kingdom had come already (*Parables*, 75). But this judgment rests on the opinion that, because *in some sense* the Kingdom had already come, there could be no other sense in which it was still to come (see above, pp. 133, 194ff.). And in any case did the fact that the Kingdom had already come mean that Jesus did *not* now want to bring about men's repentance, and therefore could *not* have thought that his death might be the means of doing so ?

Jesus himself, but that it is confirmed by the evangelical experience down the ages, when once it is realized that the traditional language in which that experience has been described is only the imperfect vehicle for expressing it, and not its very stuff and substance. We could also urge that a vital connexion can now be seen (as on the older views it never could be seen) between the moral grandeur of Jesus' own action in submitting to death and the moral grandeur of God's willingness to forgive, the clear dominating principle in both cases being love for sinful men. A vital relation is also established between the redemptive sufferings of the Saviour and the redemptive sufferings of his followers.[1] It is surely a great advantage to be able to establish such connexions, instead of being obliged to interpret Jesus' self-sacrifice in the light of primitive, enigmatic, and semi-magical (or at least unethical) ideas of atonement by blood, and to divorce it completely from that great sum-total of Christian self-sacrifice with which the New Testament so closely links it. At the same time, by recognizing in the forth-going love of God the root-cause whereby the sinner is moved to repentance, we are clearly not advancing (as is so often and so perversely suggested) a purely-subjective theory, but are positing an objective basis of redemption, namely, the willing-ness of God to meet out of His own resources the cost of the damage wrought by human sin.[2] This costliness and this willingness are the realities which the older propitiatory theories were endeavouring to express, but were expressing only very imperfectly. Thus the Cross conveys to him who will learn from it a new and revolutionizing conviction of the holiness and love of God.[3] In other words, the death of Jesus, being the manifestation in human terms of the reaction of Divine love to human sin, effects our salvation by first effecting our repentance.

(17) It must however be borne in mind that, while Jesus may have been persuaded that God would use the sufferings he was to endure to stir men to penitence, he could not possibly know how soon that penitence would come about and how far it would extend. It has been rightly urged that such hope as remained to him must have been well-nigh swallowed up in the

---

[1] Mk. x. 43–45 = Mt. xx. 26–28; Col. i. 24; 1 Peter ii. 21; 1 John iii. 16: cf. Manson, *Teaching*, 232f.; Otto, *Kingdom*, 308. V. Taylor (*Sacrifice*, 99) underrates, I feel, the link suggested by Mk. x. 43–45 = Mt. xx. 26–28. Yet even he accepts, though cautiously, the idea of a sharing of the Disciples in Jesus' redemptive work (*Sacrifice*, 120 top, 139, 265–269).

[2] Cf. Manson, *Teaching*, 310.

[3] So Wendt, *Teaching*, ii. 241.

greatness of his sorrow for the coming misery of Israel and the world. When the author of Hebrews said that Jesus endured the cross for (ἀντί) the joy that lay before him (Heb. xii. 2), he was counting on a very long view. Despite the fact that

" in the midmost heart of grief
His passion clasped a secret joy ",

the immediate experience must have been one of almost unrelieved darkness. " The Church has always seen here Jesus' descent to the utmost depth of woe, and in the very absoluteness of His sorrow has found the absoluteness of His love, and so of the salvation which He won by it ".[1]

[1] A. T. Cadoux in *The Lord of Life*, 78–82 : cf. id., *Theol. of Jes.* 283–298. Per contra, V. Taylor, *Sacrifice*, 90 (" He did not see His death as a catastrophe, but as an essential part of His Messianic achievement"), 255f., 262–265. On Jesus' thought of his death as pre-ordained, see above, pp. 184 bott., 250f., 253.

CHAPTER II

THE ROMAN INVASION AND CONQUEST

(1) Jesus foresaw that Israel's rejection of him, involving as it did a rejection of his policy of love for enemies, would lead eventually to revolt against Rome and to consequent conquest at Rome's hands. (2) Hence his grief for the Galilæan towns that did not repent, (3) his prediction of vengeance for the deaths of the martyred prophets, (4) and his sayings now collected in Lk. xii. 54—xiii. 9, (5) namely, his allusion to the signs of the times, (6) his appeal for an early settlement with one's creditor, (7) his words about the Galilæans slain by Pilate at sacrifice, (8) and his Parable about the Barren Fig-tree. (9) (10) Hence also his two lamentations over Jerusalem, (11) and several other sayings. (12) The great eschatological discourses contain references to the sufferings of war-time, (13) both the Q-discourse in Lk. xvii, (14) and the discourse in Mk. xiii. (15) Finally, we have Jesus' reply to the women who wept for him on his way to Golgotha. (16) It was his ethic of love (and therefore non-resistance) to enemies which caused the crowd to turn against him at the last. (17) The war of 66–71 A.D. was a Divine punishment of Israel for rejecting Jesus, but only in the sense that it resulted automatically and inevitably from Israel's choice, under those psychological Laws of Nature which so largely determine human conduct.

(1) Whatever might in the providence of God be the final outcome of Jesus' decision to go down into the dark valley, one of its more immediate results appeared to be beyond question —his long-cherished hope of being able to avert a bloody struggle between the Jews and the Roman Empire was destroyed.[1] We have taken account in an earlier chapter (see above, pp. 163–174) of the inflammable condition of Jewish feeling in regard to the Roman and Herodian rule, and of the desire of Jesus that his people should be peacefully reconciled to heathendom and Rome as a means of extending God's Kingdom throughout the world, and as the only alternative to a destructive war. For the success of that policy it was

---

[1] Cf. Weinel, *Stellung des Urchristentums zum Staat* (1908), 9 : " Sein ganzes Leben ist ein Kampf mit der politischen Frage seines Volkes gewesen, und er hat mit seinem Leben seine Stellung bezahlt ".

needful that the Jews generally should under his guidance learn how to love their enemies and return good for evil. In proportion as they refused to follow him and to adopt the policy he urged upon them, they became as a nation less peaceable and conciliatory in their relations with their rulers and their Gentile neighbours. Those Jews who became his followers would—if he were generally rejected—wield less and less influence in the counsels of the nation at large : Judaïsm would thus deteriorate, and be left more completely a prey to nationalistic passions of a narrow and vengeful kind. It was impossible, therefore, for Jesus not to foresee clearly that, if Israel should finally reject him, a violent collision with Rome was bound sooner or later to occur. In foreseeing that, he foresaw the appalling devastation of the land and the pitiless massacre of its inhabitants, innocent and guilty alike. The Roman armies would march slaughtering from place to place ; Jerusalem would be besieged and put to sack, the Temple desecrated and destroyed. In all this Jesus foresaw also the grievous frustration of his Father's plan that Israel should be a light to the Gentiles, that His salvation might be known unto the ends of the earth. Such a prospect was naturally more than sufficient to urge him to the most eager and strenuous efforts to avert the unspeakable calamity.

What made the anticipation of this all the more unbearable was the thought that it was really needless, and that it could be not only avoided, but changed for a healing and fruitful peace, if only Israel would listen to God's word as Jesus was proclaiming it. Notwithstanding his torturing realization that many of those engulfed in the coming disaster would be quite innocent people, he could not but think of the disaster on its national scale as a providentially-sent chastisement for the national sin of rejecting him.

Such were the thoughts which we shall find him clearly voicing, as we consider in succession the relevant passages in the Gospels, in the light of what we have already learned as to the political situation generally and as to his own attitude towards it.[1]

[1] On the whole subject, cf. Harnack, *Hist. of Dogma* (Eng. trans., 1894), i. 69 (deterioration of Israel) ; Dobschütz, *Eschatol.* 186f. (needlessly doubtful as to whether Jesus himself regarded the capture of Jerus. as a judgment) ; Sharman, *Future*, 107–109, 117 (9), 119f. (11), 352–355 ; Holtzmann, *Theol.* i. 387f. ; Bartlet, *St. Mark*, 405 ; Simkhovitch, *Understanding of Jes.* 38f., 42 ; Garstang in *H.C.L.M.K.* 135 (" . . . reading clearly the signs of the times, He warned His hearers repeatedly against the dire consequences of the impending breach with Rome ") ; A. T. Cadoux in *The Lord of Life*, 77f., and *Theol. of Jes.* 200–202, 285, 288f. ; H. G. Wood, *Christianity and the Nature of Hist.*

(2) Many sayings of Jesus usually regarded as the prediction of Messianic woes or Divine judgments in general, are much more intelligible if they are referred to the terrors of the forthcoming war with Rome. This is apparently the case with the first passage to be quoted—the woes over the Galilæan towns.[1] " Alas for thee, Khorazin ! Alas for thee, Bethsaida ! for if the deeds of power which have been done in you had been done in Tyre and Sidon, they would have repented long ago, sitting in sackcloth and ashes. But it will be more tolerable for Tyre and Sidon at the Judgment than for you. And thou, Kapharnaum, wilt thou be exalted up to heaven ? Thou shalt go down as far as Hades ! " (Lk. x. 13–15 = Mt. xi. 21–23a Q : Mt. completes the passage by adding : " for if the deeds of power which have been done in thee had been done in Sodom, it would have remained to this day [Mt. xi. 23b Q ?]. But, I tell you that it will be more bearable for the land of Sodom on the day of Judgment than for thee " [Mt. xi. 24 = x. 15 = Lk. x. 12 Q]). The passage is not free from difficulty, for the warnings addressed to Khorazin and Bethsaida resemble other more general predictions of judgment which contain no explicit reference to a coming war (see above, pp. 227f.). Nor is it easy to see clearly why Kapharnaum is accused of presuming to ascend to heaven : the warning seems to be a general one against overweening pride (see Isa. xiv. 13–15). But by far the simplest explanation of going down, or being brought down (Mt.), to Hades is to suppose that it refers to the massacre of the inhabitants by the Roman armies (cf. the precisely similar allusions to the pit and She'ol [= Hades] in Ezek. xxviii. 8, xxxi. 17f., xxxii. 17–32).[2] Galilee lay on the direct line of march from Antioch to Jerusalem : it had been before, and it would be again, traversed by the invading legions, who of course committed slaughter as they went.[3] If that interpretation is accepted for the words addressed to Kapharnaum, it probably ought to apply also to those addressed to Khorazin and Bethsaida.

(3) In Jesus' great denunciation of the religious leaders of

(1934), 105f. ; Dodd, *Parables*, 60–63, 66, 70–72, *Hist. and the Gosp.* 135f. Apart from Simkhovitch, however, hardly one of these writers recognizes adequately the connexion between the approaching disaster and the Jews' rejection of Jesus' teaching about returning good for evil.

[1] On the meaning of οὐαί, here translated " Alas ", see above, p. 42 n.1.

[2] On the meaning of Hades here, cf. Weinel, *Theol.* 60 ; it is used " nicht im Zusammenhang mit dem Gerichtsgedanken, wenn dieser auch in dem ganzen Satz liegt "

[3] Cf. Josephus, *Wars*, III. vi–x.

his time occur the words, " Therefore the Wisdom of God said, ' I will send to them prophets and messengers ; and some of them will they kill, and (some) chase out '—in order that from this generation there may be required the blood of all the prophets which has been shed ever since the foundation of the world . . . Truly I tell you, it will all be required from this generation ! " (Lk. xi. 49–51 = Mt. xxiii. 34–36 Q). There is no explicit mention here of a Roman war ; but the description of the final retribution as destined to fall upon the generation contemporary with himself points forward clearly to the great anticipated struggle.[1]

(4) We have next to consider a section which has usually been treated by New-Testament scholars as a group of un-related scraps, thrown together by the Evangelist largely because he did not know where else to put them, but which in point of fact form a close unity, being all of them animated by a single dominating motif. I refer to the passage Lk. xii. 54–xiii. 9 (mostly L).[2] This little block of sayings reflects throughout Jesus' sense of the most urgent need that, before it was too late, and the short interval still left for reconsideration was past, the Jews should repent, i.e., should turn from the course they had up till then been pursuing, a course bound to bring down upon them the avenging hand of Rome. The sayings look as if they were spoken in Jerusalem. Let us consider them in succession.

(5) " When ye see a cloud rising in the west, immediately ye say, ' A shower is coming ' ; and so it happens. And when ye see the south-wind blowing, ye say, ' There will be heat ' ; and so it happens. Hypocrites ! ye know how to discern the face of the earth and of the sky : but how (is it that) ye do not discern (the meaning of) this season ? " (Lk. xii. 54–56 L). If in these words Jesus was simply referring to the great eschatological Divine Judgment, what signs of the times were there from which the ordinary intelligent Jew could clearly tell that it was impending ? If however such a Jew were asked to say what in particular did the signs of the times forbode for Israel, he could hardly have failed to reply, " If we are not very careful, a war with Rome ! "

(6) " And why do ye not of yourselves judge what is right ? For as thou art going off with thine opponent to the magistrate,

---

[1] Cf. Winstanley 266 : " . . . Mt[36] and Lk[50f.] agree that the warning refers to a doom primarily political coming on that generation . . . ".

[2] Probably Lk. xii. 49f. L or Q, and Lk. xii. 51–53 = Mt. x. 34–36 Q, ought to be regarded as belonging to the same group of sayings as those that follow : but they are not directly relevant to our immediate quest.

do thy best on the road to get free from him, lest he drag thee before the judge ; and the judge will hand thee over to the officer, and the officer will cast thee into prison.   I tell thee, thou wilt by no means come out thence, until thou payest even the last mite " (Lk. xii. 57 1 ; Lk. xii. 58f. = Mt. v. 25f. Q).   The Lucan setting of the section is usually supposed to be superior to the Matthæan : and the aptness of the words as a warning to the nation confirms the conjecture that Luke has got them in the right place.   Israel is on the brink of a tussle with an inexorable foe : before the issue is finally joined, and escape from the extreme penalty is impossible, let the nation seek some means of averting the fatal collision.[1]

(7) We learn next that Jesus was told that the Roman Procurator Pilate had caused certain Galilæans to be slain when actually engaged in sacrifice.   We know nothing further of the circumstances : the men may have been killed in some perhaps needlessly-hasty effort on the part of the Roman soldiers to quell disorder in the Temple-area (possibly occasioned by an outburst of Jewish patriotic zeal).   Anyhow, the story raised in an acute form the problem of Jewish duty in face of Roman brutality ; and the narrator probably hoped to see Jesus rise in indignation at the ghastly news, and incite or even lead a movement of resistance.[2]   It is significant that Jesus chose this occasion to speak, not of the justice of revolting against Rome, but of the association of the innocent with the guilty in the war that was certain to come if Israel did not repent, as in the butchery wrought by Pilate and even as in the accidental fall of a building.   " Think ye that these Galilæans were (worse) sinners than all the (other) Galilæans, because they suffered this ?   No, I tell you : but unless ye repent, ye will all perish likewise.   Or those eighteen on whom the tower fell at Siloam, and killed them, think ye that they were (greater) debtors than all the men that inhabit Jerusalem? No, I tell you : but unless ye repent, ye will all perish like-wise " (Lk. xiii. 1–5 L).   Here again, if by " perishing likewise " Jesus means the dire condemnation which awaits the unrepen-tant at the Last Judgment,[3] why draw attention to the fact that those who perished in the Temple and at Siloam were not specially guilty ?   This stress on comparatively-innocent

---

[1] Cf. Simkhovitch, *Understanding of Jes.* 72f. ; A. T. Cadoux, *Parables*, 97f., 160, 162. B. T. D. Smith (*Parables*, 113f.) interprets it of the duty of the individual in view of " the great Assize ", Dodd (*Parables*, 136–139, 201) of his duty in face of the present challenge of the Kingdom.

[2] Cf. Manson in *Mission*, etc. 565.

[3] Cf. Easton, *Christ in the Gospels*, 138.

suffering gains immensely in significance if Jesus is alluding to the wild injustices of human warfare from which all and sundry will suffer, " unless ye " (i.e., the nation as a whole) " repent ", i.e., abandon your frenzied hatred of Rome.[1]

(8) Our group of sayings comes to an end with the Parable of the Barren Fig-tree, which it is not necessary to quote in extenso (Lk. xiii. 6–9 L). It is a mistake to try to allegorize it, and attach a pertinent meaning to each of its details. The point of it is that, when the tree was on the verge of being cut down because of its unfruitfulness, it was given a last chance— a brief additional space of time in which to show that it could do better. The tree of course is Israel : Israel has disappointed God so badly that the judgment of destruction is on the point of going forth ; still however there is a narrow margin left—let therefore this last chance be taken ere the nation calls down on itself the Divine condemnation in the form of the red ruin of Cæsar's anger.[2]

(9) The oft-quoted Lamentation over Jerusalem (Lk. xiii. 34f. = Mt. xxiii. 37–39 Q) presents difficulties when we attempt either to date it precisely (for its setting in neither Gospel is very good) or to interpret its closing sentences. It does not therefore tell us anything very clear regarding the nature of the coming crisis. But its testimony is nevertheless weighty, as it certainly comes from Q, and certainly foretells approaching disaster for Jerusalem, whether in the form of an abandonment of the city by God and all that that might mean, or possibly— if we read ἔρημος with Mt. xxiii. 38—in the form of a destruction by enemies.[3]

There is an explicit allusion to the approaching destruction of Jerusalem, viewed as a Divine punishment for the murder of Jesus and the Prophets, in Mt. xxii. 6f., part of the Matthæan

---

[1] So Holtzmann, *Synopt.* 376 : " Lässt das Volk von seinen politischen Messiasträumen nicht ab, so wird es in seiner Gesammtheit den Römern zum Schlachtopfer fallen, unter den Ruinen seiner Thürme und Festungen begraben werden ". Dr. Manson says, I think mistakenly, that Jesus " carries the whole matter *out of the political* into the religious sphere " (in *Mission*, etc. 565f.) : but he adds a little later, " So this generation, says Jesus in effect, is walking—*politically* and religiously—straight for disaster " (italics mine).

[2] " Im engen Zusammenhang damit " (i.e., with the danger referred to in the last n.) " steht das Gleichniss 6–9 . . . Das Gleichniss von dem ausnahms- weise geschonten, schliesslich um so sicherer umgehauenen Baum versinnbild- licht die Dringlichkeit der 13 3 und 5 geforderten Busse, da die Langmuth Gottes einmal ihr Ziel findet, Rm 2 3 4 " (Holtzmann, *Synopt.* 376). Dr. B. T. D. Smith (*Parables*, 114–116) interprets the parable as above, but without any reference to the Roman danger. The *story* about a fig-tree in Mk. xi. 12–14, 20f. = Mt. xxi. 18–20 is probably an unhistorical corruption of the parable recorded in Lk.

[3] See McNeile, *St. Matthew*, 342a.

version of the Parable of the Feast : but it is very clearly an unauthorized gloss inserted by m.

(10) Holding over the prophecies of trouble in Lk. xvii until we come to consider the great apocalyptic discourse of Mk. xiii = Lk. xxi = Mt. xxiv, we turn next to the Lucan report of Jesus' Triumphal Entry into Jerusalem. 'And as he drew near, having caught sight of the city, he wept over it, saying, " O if only thou hadst come to know, even at this (late) day, the things (needful) for thy peace ! But now they have been hidden from thine eyes ! For days will come upon thee when thine enemies will put a rampart around thee, and encircle thee, and shut thee in on all sides, and dash thee to the ground while thy children are within thee ; and they will not leave in thee one stone upon another—(all) because thou knewest not the season of thy visitation (from God) " ' (Lk. xix. 41–44 L). As these words do not come from Q, but have Lucan attestation only, they lie with some under suspicion of being a vaticinium post eventum, a prophecy shaped later in the light of what had actually happened.[1] We shall notice below, in connexion with the great apocalyptic discourse, the plea that in Lk. certain obscure prophecies of Jesus are transformed into concrete allusions to the coming siege of Jerusalem (see below, pp. 275f. n. 3). But if Jesus anticipated the siege at all (and there is abundant evidence that he did), there seems no reason why he should not have spoken of it in concrete terms. His words linked the approaching calamity with Israel's blindness to the Divine authority of his mission ; his choice of the unwarlike beast on which he was riding, with its tacit repudiation of all violent measures against the enemy, linked his mission with that ethic of gentleness which Israel was declining to follow.

(11) Brief mention will suffice for the following subsidiary pieces of evidence.

Lk. xix. 27 L : " But these enemies of mine who did not want me to be king over them—bring them hither and slaughter them before me ". This is the conclusion of the Lucan version of the Parable of the Servants entrusted with Money. That version seems to be an amalgamation of two parables, whereof one deals (like the Matthæan) with the Servants and the money, while the other describes a nobleman going abroad to receive a Kingdom. It is to the latter that our verse belongs. If it be a real parabolic saying of Jesus, we must treat it as conveying a general announcement of punitive justice to come, and as exemplifying rather strikingly his comparative unconcern over

[1] Cf. Dodd, *Parables*, 64, 70.

272

the concrete details of his parabolic stories. But the difficulty of reconciling its extremely-severe terms with the style of Jesus' warnings even of future judgment, together with the clear traces of literary amalgamation, justifies one in wondering whether the story about the nobleman and his kingdom may not be, not a parable at all, but a narrative drawn from the life of Archelaus [1] and told by Jesus as an example of Gentile tyranny (cf. Mk. x. 42 = Mt. xx. 24 ; Lk. xxii. 25 L).[2] It is difficult to say.

Mk. xii. 1–12 = Lk. xx. 9–19 = Mt. xxi. 33–46 : the Parable of the Wicked Vinedressers.[3] The apparently allegorical character of this Parable has caused some scholars to suspect its genuineness (see above, p. 255 n. 1). We may note, however, the doom predicted for the transgressors (Mk. xii. 9 = Lk. xx. 16 = Mt. xxi. 40), and the different ways in which in Lk. and Mt. this doom is described. In Lk. xx. 18 L we have the obscure allusion to the rock that damages both him who falls on it, and him on whom it falls (see above, p. 214) ; and in Mt. xxi. 43 M the threat, " Therefore I tell you, the Kingdom of God will be taken away from you, . . . ".

Mk. xii. 13–17 = Lk. xx. 20–26 = Mt. xxii. 15–22 : the dispute about tribute to Cæsar. The point of interest is that Jesus distinctly enjoins the peaceable payment of the tribute demanded by Rome, and sees in such payment nothing inconsistent with the Jew's fulfilment of his duty to God (see above, pp. 172f.).

(12) We come now to what is usually known as the great eschatological discourse contained in Mk. xiii = Lk. xxi = Mt. xxiv, along with which we may take what some regard as an alternative version of parts of it drawn from Q and preserved in Lk. xvii. 22–37 = Mt. xxiv. 26–28, 37–41, x. 39. The study of these passages is greatly complicated by (a) the possibility that Mk. xiii contains an early Jewish-Christian apocalypse, which did not emanate from Jesus (see above, pp. 11f.), and (b) by the fact—obvious in the case of Mk. xiii, and probable in the case of Lk. xvii—that the prophecies refer both to a war in Judæa and to the Parousia of the Son of Man, without the relation between them being made clear. We shall consider later the predictions of the Parousia and the significance of their being so closely interwoven with predictions of war (see below, pp. 318ff.). At the moment we may provisionally

---

[1] See Josephus, *Antiq.* XVII. xi, xiii.
[2] Cf. A. T. Cadoux, *Parables*, 67f. ; Creed, *St. Luke*, 235b.
[3] Cf. Liberty, *Political Relations*, 96.

assume that the interweaving has resulted in some measure
of confusion, with the result that some sayings which originally
referred to the wartime-experiences now look as if they were
meant to be prophecies of the End of the World.[1] Let us now
briefly survey the passages, beginning with the apocalypse of Q.

(13) Lk. xvii. 22 (no parallel in Mt.) foretells a time of
distress, when men shall long in vain for the days when the Son
of Man will be with them again.   Lk. xvii. 23f. = Mt. xxiv. 26f.
warns them against being misled by false reports of the Son of
Man's presence, which when it comes will be as conspicuous as
the lightning.   For Lk. xvii. 25 (no parallel in Mt.), see above,
p. 255.   Then comes a reference to the suddenness and unexpectedness of the destruction caused by the Flood (Lk. xvii. 26f.
= Mt. xxiv. 37–39), followed by a similar allusion to the
destruction of Sodom (Lk. xvii. 28f. : no parallel in Mt.).
Although both Gospels take the unforeseen calamity as
illustrating the revealing (Lk. xvii. 30 Q ?) or parousia (Mt.xxiv.
39b m) of the Son of Man, the description of the calamities
themselves would well fit the sudden and incalculable incidents
of war-time as affecting any particular group of persons.   Still
more so would the next verse in Lk. (xvii. 31 Q ?, which closely
resembles Lk. xxi. 21, and as such has parallels in Mk. xiii. 15f.
and Mt. xxiv. 17f.) : " On that day let not him who is on the
roof, while his goods are in the house, descend to fetch them ;
and likewise let not him who is in the field turn back ".   The
urgent need for flight when the enemy's troops are near seems
to be reinforced in Lk. xvii. 32 (no parallel in Mt.) : " Remember
Lot's wife ! " (yet see above, p. 159 n. 3).   After an allusion,
apparently out of place, to losing and preserving one's life
(Lk. xvii. 33 = Mt. x. 39 Q), there come what look like more
warnings about the arbitrary and uncertain horrors wrought
by an invading soldiery : " I tell you, on this night there will
be two on one bed ; one will be taken, and the other let go.
There will be two women grinding at the same place ; one will
be taken, and the other let go " (Lk. xvii. 34f. = Mt. xxiv. 40f.).
The discourse concludes with the Disciples' puzzled question,
" Where, Master ? ", and with Jesus' cryptic reply, " Where
the body is, there the eagles also will be assembled together "
(Lk. xvii. 37 = Mt. xxiv. 28 [Mt. omits the question] Q).   In
the general obscurity of the whole passage and what seems the
probability that much of it refers to a forthcoming war with
Rome, one is disposed to think that these last words of Jesus

---

[1] Cf. Simkhovitch, *Understanding of Jes.* 38f. ; Dodd in *Myst. Christi*,
61f., 62n.

contain an allusion to the familiar eagle-standards carried by
the Roman troops, together with a straight hint that Jerusalem
will in due time be ripe for Roman conquest, as a dead body is
ripe for birds of prey.[1]

(14) The sayings collected in Mk. xiii = Lk. xxi = Mt. xxiv
are to some extent even more explicit.   When his attention is
drawn by a Disciple to the magnificent masonry of the Temple,
Jesus replies, " Dost thou see these great buildings ?   There
will not be left one stone upon another, which will not be torn
down ! " (Mk. xiii. 1f. = Lk. xxi. 5f. = Mt. xxiv. 1f.).   Questioned privately on the Mount of Olives as to when " these
things will be " and as to the sign of their approaching
occurrence (Mk. xiii. 3f. [ὅταν μέλλῃ ταῦτα συντελεῖσθαι
πάντα] = Lk. xxi. 7 = Mt. xxiv. 3 [m wording it, " . . . the
sign of thy Parousia and (the) consummation (συντέλεια) of the
age "]), Jesus first gives a warning against their being misled,
very similar to that in Lk. xvii. 23 (Mk. xiii. 5f. = Lk. xxi. 8 =
Mt. xxiv. 4f.).   The next two verses, regarded by many as part
of " the Little Apocalypse ", run, " But whenever ye hear of
wars and rumours of wars, be not alarmed : it must needs be,
but the end is not yet.   For nation will rise against nation and
kingdom against kingdom . . . These things are the beginnings
of birth-pangs " (Mk. xiii. 7f. = Lk. xxi. 9–11 = Mt. xxiv. 6–8).
Then, after a paragraph on persecution, come descriptions of
the war, recalling in places those of Lk. xvii : " But when ye
see the desolating abomination standing where he ought
not, . . . then let those who are in Judæa flee to the
mountains " (Mk. xiii. 14 = Lk. xxi. 20f. = Mt. xxiv. 15f.).
" The desolating abomination " is borrowed from Daniel
(ix. 27, xii. 11), as m (who alters Mk's. masculine to neuter)
explicitly notes, and is clearly an allusion to a forthcoming
desecration of the Temple.[2]   Luke substitutes, " when ye see
Jerusalem encircled by camps, then know that her desolation
has drawn near ".[3]

---

[1] Cf. Dodd, *Parables*, 88.

[2] The late Canon Streeter argued (in *Camb. Ancient Hist.* xi. [1936] 259 n.)
that Mark was here referring, not to the destruction of the Temple in 70 A.D.,
but to its desecration by the personal Antichrist (hence his use of the masculine
ἑστηκότα).   But if he was (as Streeter rightly held) writing *before* 70 A.D.,
would he clearly distinguish the two coming calamities ?

[3] It is widely held that in these prophecies, wherever Luke has more
specific references to warfare and siege than Mark, he is freely re-editing the
material in his Marcan source in the light of what had actually happened in
66–71 A.D.   This may well have been so in places.   On the other hand it is
not impossible that he is giving us, at least at this point, a more-original form
of the prophecy, the Marcan having been modified in view of Caligula's

The next two verses in Mk. (Mk. xiii. 15f. = Lk. xxi. 21 =
Mt. xxiv. 17f.) are substantially the same as Lk. xvii. 31 Q ?,
for which see above, p. 274. Lk. xxi. 22 1 ? here inserts,
" because these are days of vengeance, for the fulfilment of all
things that have been written ". Then comes a word of pity
for pregnant women and nursing mothers (Mk. xiii. 17 =
Lk. xxi. 23a = Mt. xxiv. 19)—a very obvious allusion to the
state of things in war time—and a word of advice to pray that
the flight may not have to be made in winter-time (Mk. xiii. 18
= Mt. xxiv. 20 [m Jewishly adds, " or on a Sabbath," and
Lk. omits]). The unparalleled distress of the time is next
emphasized : had God not for the elects' sake decided to cut it
short, none would have survived (Mk. xiii. 19f. = Mt. xxiv.
21f. : Lk. xxi. 23b, 24 has instead, " For there will be great
anguish upon the land and wrath against this people ; and
they will fall by the sword, and be taken captive unto all the
Gentiles, and Jerusalem will be trodden down by the Gentiles,
until [the allotted] seasons of [the] Gentiles are fulfilled ").
The whole of the section Mk. xiii. 14–20 is usually taken to be
part of " the Little Apocalypse " ; but it contains very little
that Jesus himself could not have spoken. The rest of the
discourse deals with the Parousia, etc., and is not relevant to
this stage of our inquiry. But whatever may have to be
said about the Parousia-prophecies, Lk. xvii and Mk. xiii
surely put it beyond reasonable doubt that Jesus foresaw
and predicted with some detail the war between the Jews
and Rome as bound to occur in the not-distant future,
and therewith the sufferings of the population, the capture
of Jerusalem, and the desecration and destruction of the
Temple.

There may be a warning against the coming struggle also
in the words spoken by Jesus at his arrest : " Put back thy
sword into its place ; for all who take the sword will perish by
the sword " (Mt. xxvi. 52 M).

---

threatened desecration of the Temple in 40 A.D. (so Manson in *Mission*, etc.
621f. : cf. V. Taylor, *Third Gosp.* 118–124) : in any case he is only making
explicit what Mark expresses less concretely, and his operations cannot rightly
be taken as discrediting his reports when no Marcan parallel is in question
(see above, p. 272, and below, pp. 276f.).

It is certainly remarkable that so large a proportion of the evidence on the
political aspect of Jesus' Ministry and Passion should be found in Luke ; but
he only brings out more prominently what is certainly implicit in the other
sources : cf. Montefiore, *S.G.*² II. 580, and M. Kiddle on ' The Passion Narrative in St. Luke's Gospel ' in *J.T.S.* xxxvi. 267–280 (July 1935), and see
below, pp. 353f. On the general indifference of the Synoptists to politics, cf.
Sharman, *Future*, 103–106, 109.

(15) When he was on his way to be crucified, women in the crowd accompanying him wailed and beat their breasts. Jesus said to them, " Daughters of Jerusalem ! weep not for me, but weep for yourselves and your children. For behold ! days are coming when they will say, ' Happy are the barren, and the wombs that have not given birth, and breasts that have not given suck ! Then will men begin to say to the mountains, ' Fall on us ! ' and to the hills, ' Cover us ! ' For if men do these things when the tree is green, what will be done when it is dry ? " (Lk. xxiii. 27- 31 L). For the genuineness of the words reference may be made to what has been said above (see pp. 272, 275f. n. 3). The allusion to the approaching siege could not very well be plainer. The words about the green and the dry tree are an a fortiori argument, which may be paraphrased thus : If, in times of peace like this, the Romans will inflict this brutal penalty of crucifixion on an innocent man, how may they be expected to treat the population generally when peace has withered and their passions are roused because war has come ? [1]

(16) We have so far seen the approaching calamities represented mainly as a kind of providential consequence of Israel's failure to respond to Jesus' call for a nation-wide repentance. It is, however, important for a proper understanding of the position that we should realize the way in which that providential consequence came about. In rejecting Jesus, Israel rejected his ethic of love for enemies and forgiveness of wrongs, and his universalistic design for the peaceful enlightenment of the Gentile world. It was precisely this rejection of love and peace which was bound to eventuate, and did ultimately eventuate, in a war with Rome. That this ethic of love and peace had actually something to do with the fact of the nation's rejection of him seems to be a fair inference from Jesus' sudden loss of popularity on the eve of his death. He was in bonds

---

[1] The sense is not materially altered if, with most commentators, the green tree is identified with Jesus himself, the dry with guilty Judaism ; but that interpretation seems less likely. Cf. Fairbairn, *Studies in the Life of Christ* (1885), 319f. ; Wellhausen, *Lc.* 133f. ; Strack-Billerbeck ii. 263f. ; Montefiore, *S.G.*³ II. 623f. ; Creed, *St. Luke*, 286a ; Major in *Mission*, etc. 289 ; Manson in *Mission*, etc. 635.

It is noteworthy that Dr. V. Taylor, whose interpretation of the Passion follows different lines from those which commend themselves to me, feels that this passage " has no light to throw on the manner in which Jesus regarded His suffering beyond showing how He thought of the need of others in the very shadow of the cross. The language is apocalyptic in character, but it is doubtful if the thought is eschatological " (*Sacrifice*, 197). The important causal link between Israel's repudiation of Jesus in 30 A.D. and the calamity which came in 70 A.D. is thus missed.

because he would neither run away, nor hit back. We do not need to insist that those who cried out " Crucify him ! " were for the most part the same as those who a few days before had cheered him on his Triumphal Entry, though they may well have been so. But it is clear that at the last the authorities succeeded in inflaming the populace against him : and the most natural explanation of their success is that the sight of a claimant to Messiahship submitting unresistingly to bondage and maltreatment so shocked the nationalistic pride of the Jewish multitude that they broke forth into that frenzied indignation which political animus combined with oriental emotionalism was so well calculated to produce .[1]

(17) Postponing for the present the study of the relation, if any, between Jesus' predictions of war and his predictions of his own Return (see below, pp. 318 ff.), we may observe in conclusion how exactly Jesus' reading of the probable political consequences of Israel's unresponsiveness tallies with what actually happened and—as we have seen—was bound in the circumstances to happen. The obvious link we have observed between these consequences and a particular item in the ethical teaching of Jesus has been strangely overlooked both in ancient and modern times. The early Christian writers spoke baldly of the Fall of Jerusalem in 70 A.D. as the punishment directly inflicted on the Jews by God for crucifying His Messiah.[2] They sought for no other moral or psychological connexion between the two events. Even when we see what the real connexion was, we may still to-day speak of the Fall of Jerusalem as a Divine punishment,[3] but only in the sense that it was the inevitable result of the Jews' behaviour, inevitable under that system of psychological laws which so largely govern human conduct, which are necessarily regarded as a part of a Divinely-created system of Natural Law, and which in this instance meant that Roman passions were roused by what must have appeared as the perverse refractoriness of Israel. Finally, it must be insisted that Jesus' application of the ethic of love to the political situation rested, not on a sense

---

[1] Cf. Holtzmann, *Synopt.* 179 (the crowd " mag sich einen ohnmächtigen, in Fesseln dastehenden, Messias und König nicht gefallen lassen und geräth darob in Wuth, so dass die Priester leichtes Spiel haben, wenn sie die Loosung Barabbas ausgeben ") ; Liberty, *Political Relations*, 25 ; J. A. Findlay, *Jesus as they saw Him* (1920), 37 ; Bartlet, *St. Mark*, 320 ; Simkhovitch, *Understanding of Jes.* 41, 47f., 53f., 73f., 80, 82 ; Montefiore, *S.G.*[2] I. 320f., 375–377 ; and others. See also above, p. 252.
[2] Cf. C. J. Cadoux, *Early Christ. Attit. to War* (1919), 184–190 : also Strack-Billerbeck iv. 858, 865f. (God's use of the sword of men).
[3] Cf. Dodd, *Parables*, 76f.

of the certainty of failure if he led a revolt,[1] nor only on his pity for those whom he foresaw would suffer, but on his conviction that to love and serve one's enemies was the only way in which man could come to resemble in character the all-loving Father in heaven.

[1] On his chances of success, cf. Klausner, *Jes. of Naz.* 170 ; H. G. Wood quoted in *The Lord of Life,* 57 n.1 ; C. J. Cadoux in *Congreg. Quart.* xiv. 66 (Jan. 1936) ; Manson in *Mission,* etc. 337f.

CHAPTER III

THE RETURN OF THE SON OF MAN

(1) Jesus is believed by all to have been vindicated after Death by his Resurrection. (2) The Resurrection-appearances themselves are historically indubitable, (3) but are best regarded as Objective Visions. (4) This theory of their character well accounts for the disjointed condition of the records, (5) for the belief in the emptiness of the tomb, (6) and for the creation of the Ascension-story. (7) The early Church was not without its own difficulties and dissensions regarding the doctrine of the Resurrection. (8) It is remarkable that, though Jesus is said to have predicted his Resurrection, yet when the appearances occurred, they were totally unexpected. How was this ? (9) The three days, after which he said he would rise, might quite well stand for a short indefinite interval, (10) such as would elapse before that day—known precisely to God alone, but falling within the generation then living—on which Jesus expected a great event to happen. (11) His prophecies of that event—a personal return of himself in glory—are found in Q, (12–15) and still more frequently in Mark. (16) It is on several grounds probable that the Resurrection-prophecies ought to be identified in purport with them ; (17) such an identification, for instance, alone makes intelligible Jesus' words to the Penitent Brigand. (18) It is, in fact, virtually certain that Jesus looked forward to a simple period of absence in Paradise between his death and his Return in glory. (19) This theory implies that the wording of his Resurrection-prophecies has been subsequently modified in the light of the actual Resurrection-appearances. (20) Other conclusions also are involved, e.g., that Jesus expected to reappear as " the Son of Man ", i.e., in company with his redeemed and loyal community.

(1) In the course of the last two chapters, we have been studying two of those great assurances which came home to the mind of Jesus as it adjusted itself to the appalling prospect of earthly defeat and a torturing death. His death would be the means of moving many to repentance and so bringing them to God, and it would be followed by historical consequences which would unmistakably demonstrate Israel's folly in reject-

ing him, albeit by means so terrible as to overwhelm his heart with sorrow. But what now of Jesus himself ? What had the future in store for him personally, beside and beyond the death on the cross ? The prompt and natural answer which the Christian believer gives to this question is, of course, " the Resurrection ". Jesus rose from the dead on the third day— and knew beforehand that he would do so. That surely was the great vindicating reversal of his shameful death : he would by the power of God conquer death, when the sin of man had done its worst in slaying him.

(2) It is a well-established fact of history that, on the third day (as then counted) after his death and for several days following, various disciples and groups of disciples had visions of Jesus, risen and living, which convinced them that he had burst the bands of death, and which inspired them with a fearless longing to proclaim him to the world as the one Divine Saviour. Of the truth of that statement there is no room for the slightest doubt. But in regard to the questions how exactly the narratives of these appearances ought to be under-stood, how much of them is true and how much legendary, and what was the objective truth involved in such visions as are sufficiently well-attested—on these questions the widest differences of opinion prevail. The literature on the subject is of course enormous. The plan of the present book does not really call for a discussion of these questions, since we are primarily engaged in investigating, not the events of Jesus' life, but the thoughts of his mind. Having regard, however, to the position claimed for the Resurrection in Christian theology, and to the fact that Jesus is recorded to have foretold it, we shall find it worth while to touch briefly on the chief questions raised and the chief arguments involved, and to see whether a tenable if only tentative theory can be found.

(3) It is submitted, then, that the least-difficult theory regarding the Resurrection-appearances of Jesus is to think of them as objective visions, i.e., as real manifestations of himself given to the Disciples by the risen Lord, not by means of the presence of his resuscitated physical and material body, but by those mysterious means, the existence of which psychical research has been revealing to us, though we still remain ignorant of their precise nature. There is, I suggest, enough in the findings of modern psychical research, not to explain the Resurrection-appearances adequately, but at least to make credible the sufficiently well-attested declarations that Jesus was after death really present with certain of his early

followers, and that they were made aware of his presence by visual and auditory experiences roughly similar to the sense-experiences of normal life.[1]

Such a theory may rightly be criticized as leaving many interesting questions unanswered : but there is not a single theory on the matter against which the same objection could not be brought. The best we can do in any case is to adopt a theory which preserves the essential facts, and which for the rest is open to the fewest and least-serious objections. This theory, it will be seen, preserves intact what all Christians recognize as the core of the Resurrection-message—the precious and cardinal truth that Jesus' life was not utterly quenched on the Cross, but that he still lives and works among men. That, after all, is the one *religious* issue at stake.

It is, indeed, sometimes said that " mere " visions of Jesus, even if objective, might establish the fact that he had survived death, but not that he had conquered it. But if Jesus survived death in such a sort as to be able to energize and inspire his Disciples, he *had* conquered it ; nor would the resuscitation of his material body make the conquest any more real or glorious.

Further, by recognizing the visions to have been in some sense objective, we can still treat them as furnishing evidence in confirmation of the Disciples' faith in Jesus' continued life. It may be quite true that the Disciples were able to receive these visions only because they already had faith in Jesus as their Lord and Saviour ; but if we had to interpret their visions of him after his death as hallucinations produced by their peculiar psychological condition,[2] the visions themselves would cease to have any evidential value as regards the being of Jesus himself.

(4) The objective-vision-theory has, we may urge, the advantage, not only of preserving the essence of the Resurrection-faith, but of preserving it in a fashion that emancipates us from a number of intolerable intellectual burdens such as beset alternative theories. Thus, it provides a rational explanation of the confused condition of the New-Testament narratives.[3] If these narratives were wholly free from the admixture of error or legend or imaginative enlargements of the story, because they were all close transcripts of what was accurately

---

[1] See, e.g., L. J. Belton's art. on ' The Hypothesis of a Subtle Body ' in *Hibbert Journ.* xxxvii. 83–92 (Oct. 1938).

[2] See Martineau, *Seat of Authority* (ed. 1898), 375–377 ; Montefiore, *S.G.*[2] I. 398f. ; Major in *Mission*, etc. 217f.

[3] See the discussion of these in Meyer, *Ursprung*, i. 11–34, and in Prof. A. C. Morris's art. in *Hibbert Journ.* xxxix. 309–324 (Apl. 1941).

testified by first-hand witnesses, they could not possibly present the numerous and irreconcilable inconsistencies which we at present see in them. This is not the place in which to draw out and discuss these inconsistencies : but, although the attempt to harmonize the narratives has often been made, it may safely be said that no complete harmonization is possible. One cannot, that is to say, reconstruct the story of the appearances as a continuous series of credible or conceivable incidents, without many times contradicting the clear intimations of our informants. These latter differ radically from one another, for instance, on such cardinal questions as, Who first saw the risen Jesus ? Did the appearances take place in Judæa only, or also in Galilee ? Even Luke's own account in Acts of Jesus' appearances lasting forty days is so inconsistent with any natural understanding of his Gospel (see Lk. xxiv. 1, 13, 33, 36, 44, 50—mostly L), that we can acquit him of self-contradiction only by reading unwarrantably drastic modifications into the latter.[1] Whereas if, as our theory supposes, the visions were intermittent, sporadic, and of brief duration, it is easy to understand why their locality and their sequence should have been forgotten, and so the record of them have become confused. We should also have the explanation of Jesus' *sudden* appearance (e.g., Lk. xxiv. 36 L) and disappearance (Lk. xxiv. 31, 51 L), his passing through closed doors (John xx. 19, 26), and the occasional failure of the Disciples to recognize him (Lk. xxiv. 16, 31 L ; John xx. 14, xxi. 4). The theory also harmonizes well with the fact that in 1 Cor. xv. 4–8 Paul draws no other distinction between Jesus' appearance to Peter, the Twelve, his brother Jacob, etc., and his obviously-visionary appearance to himself on the road to Damascus, than is implied by his words " Last of all as unto one untimely-born . . . "

(5) Our theory, furthermore, satisfies those data of the problem which are concerned with the empty tomb and the disposal of the physical body. Whereas the evidence for the visions of the Risen Jesus is strong and incontrovertible, the evidence for his tomb being actually found empty is neither so early nor so convincing.[2] Paul may well have believed in the emptiness of the tomb ; but what he appeals to is not that, but the occurrence of the visions. The stories about the tomb are attended with all those incongruities and discrepancies which make the closing passages of all our Gospels so hard to

---

[1] Cf. Creed, *St. Luke*, 300ab. Ep. Barn. xv. 9 seems, like Lk. xxiv, to put the resurrection, manifestation, and ascension of Jesus all on the one day.
[2] Cf. Meyer, *Ursprung*, i. 16–22.

harmonize with one another. The key to the situation is that, once the Disciples were convinced by the visions they had had that Jesus was alive and active despite his death on the Cross, their belief that his tomb must therefore be empty would follow inevitably as the night the day, whether there was any actual evidence for it or not. Palestinian Jews, for the most part, had no idea—such as a Greek trained in the Platonic tradition would have had—of an immortal soul, shuffling off this mortal coil, and rising at once from the shackles of the flesh into a freer and more glorious life. For them it was either a resurrection of the flesh, or no resurrection at all. Having seen Jesus alive, the Disciples would therefore feel sure that his tomb was empty ; and narratives to the effect that it had been found empty would readily arise, and be readily accepted. That, it is submitted, is a sufficient defence of the objective-vision-theory as regards the tomb, even though the scantiness of our information prevents us from theorizing with any confidence or finality as to precisely what actually became of the *hastily*-buried body (John xix. 41f.), who, if any one, actually saw an empty grave, and whether the grave they saw was that in which Jesus had actually been laid and left.

(6) Perhaps the greatest relief which our theory affords is in regard to the Ascension. So long as it is insisted that the physical body of Jesus rose from the tomb, the necessity of accounting for its complete disappearance from the earth remains. That disappearance can, of course, be accounted for, if we are operating with the old idea of a three-storeyed universe, and are willing to accept the simple narrative embodied in Acts and hallowed in countless Christian pictures, to the effect that Jesus' body rose vertically off the surface of the earth, and disappeared into the sky. But such an occurrence is so hard to believe, that nothing save the most unimpeachable evidence could justify one in believing it. Yet what is that evidence ? The statement of a Christian author (Luke) who was not present, and who made the statement some fifty years after the event is supposed to have occurred ! Not unnaturally, therefore, conservative scholars who feel it is vital to maintain belief in the physical resurrection, have taken advantage of Paul's theory of " a spiritual body " (of which more in a moment) to adumbrate a variety of quite-unscriptural accounts of the Ascension which would release the mind of the modern believer from the severest strain imposed on it by the traditional version.[1] It is much simpler and more

[1] E.g., Rev. R. S. Moxon (*Modernism and Orthodoxy* [1924], 149f.) suggests

satisfying to abandon altogether the idea of an Ascension of Jesus' body into the sky, and to regard the belief in such an Ascension and Luke's description of it as resulting naturally and inevitably from the need of explaining why the series of visions (themselves interpreted, as we have seen, in a physical sense) came to an end.[1]

(7) Earnest modern Christians sometimes imagine that those who question the physical character of the resurrection of Jesus are guilty of needlessly and sceptically innovating in regard to a matter which all real Christians from the first unanimously believed. This is very far from being the case. It is true that there grew up and was by a fairly-early date generally accepted a simple version of the facts which furnishes no solution of the difficulties felt by thoughtful students of Scripture to-day. But that does not mean that no dissent ever existed, and that no inconsistencies were ever admitted into the Church's teaching. Intelligent Christian disciples not trained on the soil of Palestinian Judaism must have felt considerable difficulty over the doctrine of the resurrection of the flesh, both as regards Jesus and also as regards themselves. Unlike the primitive Palestinian disciples, they had no need of such a doctrine to help them believe in the future life, and many of them must have felt it to be a grave hindrance. We get a trace of their criticism in the complaint of Paul (1 Cor. xv. 12) that there were some members of the church at Corinth who said that there was no resurrection of the dead. Polycarp of Smyrna (about 117 A.D.) knew of certain errorists who said that there was neither resurrection nor judgment.[2] In the Pastoral Epistles we read of some who said that the resurrection had occurred already (2 Tim. ii. 18), apparently identifying resurrection in a spiritual way with conversion. Polycarp and the Pastoral author deal with such views, not by argument, but by harsh censure. Paul, himself a Jew of the Diaspora and feeling therefore some sympathy with Greek thought, did better than that : he met the Greek scepticism half-way with his theory of a " spiritual body "— a theory which enabled him to insist, along with the primitive

---

that Jesus' body simply rose a short distance into an overhanging cloud ! With this specious conjecture we may compare the view of the late Dr. Jas. Denney, who, after confidently declaring that " if we cannot speak of a bodily resurrection we should not speak of resurrection at all " (*Jes. and the Gosp.* [1913], 113), yet refuses to believe the Lucan statement to the effect that the risen Jesus *ate food* (*ib.* 146).

[1] Cf. Meyer, *Ursprung*, i. 39–42.
[2] Polyc. *Ep.* vii. 1.

Church, on the term and the idea of " Resurrection ", but allowed him to declare (in words that must have shocked the Palestinian mind) that " flesh and blood cannot inherit the Kingdom of God " (1 Cor. xv. 50). But how could such a statement be defended regarding the body of which some of the Resurrection-narratives speak ? The Johannine Gospel, again, stands by the primitive Palestinian version of the Resurrection-appearances : but it pronounces a blessing on those who did not need sensual evidence as a condition of their believing in the Lord's risen life (John xx. 29 ; cf. Lk. xvi. 31 L) ; and it largely abandons the Synoptic eschatology in favour of a spiritualized and mystical view of the Judgment and of the Lord's presence. The inclusion of both the Pauline and the Johannine theories in the Church's Scriptures should serve to remind us that bold modifications of current Christian beliefs have sometimes been made by very loyal disciples and with very helpful results.

(8) We must leave now our discussion of the character of the Resurrection-appearances of Jesus, and turn back to the question of his own prophecies and expectations regarding them. And here we are at once struck by the very clear fact that these appearances of Jesus on and after the first Easter-Sunday were wholly unexpected by those who witnessed them. In every case, the presence of the risen Lord caused astonishment and bewilderment as soon as it was observed. The fact that women went to the tomb with materials for embalming the body proves of itself how little expectation there then was in any Christian minds that the Lord would rise so soon. Yet, according to the Synoptic record, Jesus had three times over distinctly and explicitly told his friends that he would rise from the dead " after three days " (so Mk. : Lk. and Mt. substitute " on the third day ", the two expressions being, it would seem, roughly equivalent [1]—Mk. viii. 31 = Lk. ix. 22 = Mt. xvi. 21 ; Mk. ix. 31 [= Lk. ix. 44] = Mt. xvii. 23 ; Mk. x. 34 = Lk. xviii. 33 = Mt. xx. 19). If he spoke thus, they could hardly have forgotten so startling a prophecy ; nor is it satisfactory to say that they were so incapable of believing it that its fulfilment took them completely by surprise. The fact that they *were* completely taken by surprise forces us to ask whether Jesus did really say and mean that he would rise from the dead on the third day, in the literal sense of the words.[2]

---

[1] Swete, *St. Mark*, 179b.

[2] Holtzmann, *Synopt.* 84, *Theol.* i. 380 ; *Beginnings of Christianity*, i. 381f. ; A. E. Morris in *Hibbert Journ.* xxx. 95–97 (Oct. 1931) ; V. Taylor, *Sacrifice*, 88f.

(9) It is natural to suspect that a prophecy which it is difficult to believe to have been actually uttered was really a vaticinium post eventum, i.e., was composed in the light of what actually happened, and was subsequently put into the prophet's mouth. Before we draw this conclusion regarding Jesus' prediction of his Resurrection, however, let us see whether there may not have been some misunderstanding as regards its real meaning. Ought the phrase " after three days " or " on the third day ", for instance, to be taken in its literal sense ? Those familiar with the Bible must have been struck by the frequency with which this interval is mentioned in it (see, e.g., Gen. xxii. 4, xlii. 17 ; Exod. xix. 15 ; Josh. i. 11, ii. 16, 22, iii. 2, ix. 16 ; 1 Sam. ix. 20, xxx. 13 ; 2 Kings xx. 8 ; Jonah i. 17 ; John ii. 1 ; Mk. viii. 2 = Mt. xv. 32 ; Acts ix. 9, xxviii. 7, 12, 17). If the number is meant always to be taken in its literal sense, it is extraordinary that it should be mentioned with such disproportionate frequency.[1] Students of the Old Testament in the original will remember that the normal Hebrew expression for the indefinite and particularly the recent past is " yesterday (and the) third (day) ".[2] It looks as if " three days " really stood for any short indefinite interval, and " on the third day " meant " after a short time ". Jesus seems to be using the phrase in that sense when he sent his reply to Herod Antipas (Lk. xiii. 32f. L), and when he spoke cryptically of restoring in three days the demolished temple (Mk. xiv. 58 = Mt. xxvi. 61 ; Mk. xv. 29 = Mt. xxvii. 40 ; John ii. 19f.). Modern analogies are not wanting. The Palestinian Arab says " ba'd bukra " (i.e., " the day after to-morrow "), when he means " some time soon ".[3] The German word " paar " designates " a few ", though its literal meaning is " a couple ".[4] If therefore Jesus spoke of rising again after three days, is it not probable that he was referring to something which he expected to happen not on what would be literally the third day, but after a short indefinite interval ?[5] The likelihood that this is so is increased by the fact that in Hosea (vi. 1f.) there is actually an allusion to being raised up on the third day :

[1] Cf. Strack-Billerbeck i. 760.

[2] Cf. Herodotus' use of the similar phrase " yesterday and the day before, so to speak " (πρώην τε καὶ χθές, ὡς εἰπεῖν λόγῳ, ii. 53) when he means " within the last few centuries ".

[3] Cf. Strack-Billerbeck ii. 201f. for the analogous use of " the morrow " in Rabbinic.

[4] Sir F. W. L. Butterfield (My West Riding Experiences [1927], 189) explains that in his line " O Parliament, thrice self-prolonged " he is using the word " Not in the literal sense of ' three ', but in the general sense of ' many times ' ".

[5] Cf. V. Taylor, Sacrifice, 89.

" After two days will He revive us : on the third day He will raise us up, and we shall live before Him ".[1]

(10) Now Jesus did, in point of fact, speak of a certain important event as destined to occur on a future day known to none, not even to the angels, nor to himself as unique Son, but to God the Father only (Mk. xiii. 32 = Mt. xxiv. 36). We also find him saying explicitly that a great event will take place before the generation among whom he is living dies out (Mk. ix. 1 = Lk. ix. 27 = Mt. xvi. 28 ; Mk. xiii. 30 = Lk. xxi. 32 = Mt. xxiv. 34) : the same determination of time is implied by the frequent tacit assumption that the men to whom he is speaking will themselves witness the event in question. What precisely this great event would be, and whether Jesus regarded it as identical with that whereof no one knew the day or the hour, might be thought to have been rendered doubtful by our ignorance as to the limits and character of " the Little Apocalypse " (see above, pp. 11f.). There is, however, little ground for hesitation. Even supposing that Mk. xiii. 30f. = Lk. xxi. 32 f. = Mt. xxiv. 34f. have to be separated, as a portion of " the Little Apocalypse ", from Mk. xiii. 32 = Mt. xxiv. 36,[2] there is plenty of other evidence for Jesus'

---

[1] Difficulties, indeed, remain. (a) If Jesus really referred to three days, he could not (strangely enough) have been understood by his hearers to be meaning the words in their literal sense. Again, (b) while his first *appearances* took place on Sunday (the third day after his death, according to the ancient method of counting), the Gospels do not explicitly say that he actually *rose from the dead* on that day. These two facts have led scholars to seek for the origin of the phrase " on the third day " (which was supposed to have Scriptural warrant : see 1 Cor. xv. 4) in some other quarter than Jesus' own prediction or the Disciples' knowledge of when he actually rose. Solutions have been sought in the words of Hosea vi. 1f., in the time for the offering of the first-fruit sheaf at Passover (Lev. xxiii. 5–15), in the Rabbinical belief that the soul hovered about its dead body for three days after death (cf. John xi. 39), and in pagan myths narrating the resurrection of a dead god, Tammuz or other, sometimes in connexion with astronomical considerations. But it is perhaps least difficult to suppose that the day of the resurrection was from the first tacitly identified with " the third day " on which the first and most memorable visions had been seen, and that either (a) Jesus so framed his predictions of resurrection as to prevent his reference to three days being understood in a literal sense, or (b) that this reference, and perhaps also the choice of the term " rise again ", were carried back from the Easter-experience into the record of his speech (but see below, pp. 293f., 297f.). Cf., on the various points here raised, Edersheim, *Life . . . of Jes.* . . . , ii. 631 ; Holtzmann, *Theol.* i. 382f. ; Clemen, *Primitive Christianity,* 187–198 ; Bartlet, *St. Mark*, 250f., 253f. ; Strack-Billerbeck i. 649, 747, 760, ii. 544f. ; Weinel, *Theol.* 237 ; Bacon in *Expos.* VIII. xxvi. 426–441 (Dec. 1923) ; Bousset, *Relig. des. Jud.* (1926), 297 n.1, 518 ; Von Gall, Βασιλεία, 111, 154f. ; Montefiore, *S.G.*[3] I. 193f. ; S. V. McCasland in *Journ. of Bibl. Lit.* xlviii (1929) 124–137 ; Johannes Weiss, *Hist. of Prim. Christianity* (Eng. trans. 1937), i. 92–98.

[2] See Manson, *Teaching*, 262 n. 1.

expectation of a great event due to occur before that generation
died out ; there is no real difficulty in reconciling that note of
time with his ignorance as to the precise day or hour ; [1] and
it would be importing needless complexity into the data of our
problem not to assume at least provisionally that the two
future events are the same.   Is it possible that the rising-again
of the Son of Man " after three days ", seeing that there are
objections to understanding that interval in the literal sense,
ought also to be identified with the great event that was to
happen on some day known to none, but falling somewhere
within say the next thirty or forty years ? (see below,
pp. 299–301).

(**11**) Our different Gospel-documents speak with different
degrees of emphasis and clarity regarding this great coming
event ; but together they leave us in no doubt as to its general
character : Jesus (the Son of Man) will—some time after his
death—return to the earth in visible glory and royal power. [2]

The Lamentation over Jerusalem preserved in Q concludes
with the words, " I tell you, ye will by no means see me (again)
until (the time) comes when ye say, ' Blessed (be) he who comes
in the name of the Lord ! ' " (Lk. xiii. 35 = Mt. xxiii. 39 Q).
The words are obscure, but they seem to contain an allusion
to a future coming.

In Q's eschatological discourse preserved in Lk. xvii, Jesus
foretells a time when the Disciples will vainly long " to see one
of the days of the Son of Man " (Lk. xvii. 22 Q or l). [3]   He then
says that, as with the suddenness of lightning and the
unexpectedness of Noah's Deluge or the destruction of Sodom,
" so will be the Son of Man " (Lk. xvii. 24 = Mt. xxiv. 27
[" so will be the Parousia of the Son of Man "] Q), " so will it
be in the days of the Son of Man " (Lk. xvii. 26 = Mt. xxiv. 37,
39 [" so will be the Parousia of the Son of Man "] Q), or
" after the same fashion will it be on the day on which the Son
of Man is revealed " (Lk. xvii. 30, probably Q ; no parallel in
Mt.).   The prophecies are intermingled with what look like
warnings against the terrors of foreign invasion (see above,

---

[1] Beyschlag (*Theol.* i. 197), Muirhead (*Eschatol. of Jes.* 50, 118f., 125f.),
Charles (*Crit. Hist.* [1913], 380), Denney (*Jes. and the Gosp.* [1913], 355 n.),
and Leckie (*World to Come*, 58) regard this combination as incredible—I
think, needlessly.   Cf. Dobschütz, *Eschatol.* 116 ; Manson, *Teaching*, 277f.

[2] Cf. Wellhausen, *Mt.* 124 ; Holtzmann, *Theol.* i. 383–392 ; McNeile, *St.
Matthew*, 344f. ; Gloege, *Reich Gottes*, 173–179 ; Manson, *Teaching*, 134–141.
On the necessity of being removed from the earth (by death ?) before returning
to it in glory, cf. Schweitzer, *L.J.F.* 412f. = *Quest*, 363.

[3] Creed, *St. Luke*, 220a : " i.e. one of the days of the new age after the Son
of Man has been revealed . . . ".

pp. 273—275) ; and it is only Mt. who introduces (perhaps without the authority of Q) the technical term for the Lord's Second
Advent, " the Parousia ". But it seems impossible to draw
any other conclusion than that, with or without the use of the
word " Parousia ", Q represented Jesus as foretelling his future
reappearance before men.[1]

In another saying, preserved independently in L and M,
Jesus tells his Disciples, when within near prospect of the
Passion, that they will sit on thrones judging the twelve tribes
of Israel. In the Lucan version (Lk. xxii. 29f. L) he also
assigns to them—as his Father has assigned to him—royal
rank, and places at his table in his Kingdom ; in the Matthæan
version (Mt. xix. 28b M) he speaks of the Son of Man sitting on
his glorious throne.

In the Parable of the Servants entrusted with Money, which
is similarly preserved in apparently-independent versions in
L and M, the return of the Master for a reckoning after a period
of absence (Lk. xix. 15 L ; Mt. xxv. 19 M) suggests the future
return of Jesus himself ; and the account in the Lucan version
of the King's execution of those who did not want him to be
king (Lk. xix. 27 L) looks like a reference to the punishment of
the wicked at the future Judgment (but see above, pp. 272f.).
But as the passages are parabolic, and the interpretation of
them in a measure obscure, too much weight cannot be put
upon them.[2] And the same applies to the Parable of the Wise
and Foolish Virgins (Mt. xxv. 1–13 M).[3]

(12) We must turn next to a series of passages contained
in Mk.

" Whoever is ashamed of me and of my (follower)s in this
adulterous and sinful generation, the Son of Man will in his
turn be ashamed of him whensoever he comes in the glory of
his Father, with the holy angels " (Mk. viii. 38 = Lk. ix. 26 =
Mt. xvi. 27). ' And he said to them, " Truly I tell you that there
are some here of those standing (round me) who will certainly
not taste of death until they see that the Kingdom of God has
come with power " ' (Mk. ix. 1 = Lk. ix. 27 = Mt. xvi. 28).
The Matthæan variations in both verses are of interest.
Mt. xvi. 27 runs, " The Son of Man is destined to come in the

[1] Cf. Sharman, *Future*, 129–135 ; Winstanley, *Future*, 144–148, 158 ;
Dodd, *Parables*, 83–88, 108 n. 1.

[2] Dr. Dodd (*Parables*, 146–153) thinks that, in its original form, the Parable
had no eschatological reference, but was meant as a protest against the
exclusive and unadventurous legalism of many pious Jews.

[3] Dr. Dodd again takes this Parable as an injunction of " preparedness . . .
for the developments actually in process in the ministry of Jesus " (*Parables*,
172).

glory of his Father, with his angels, and then he will repay each
man according to his conduct "—a formula and theme strikingly re-echoed in Mt. xxv. 31ff. The thought of the Marcan
verse is thus reproduced, with the modification that the Son
of Man is represented, not simply as witness, but as judge (see
above, pp. 228f. [6], and below, pp. 321–323). Mt. xvi. 28
concludes, ". . . until they see the Son of Man coming in
his Kingdom ". I have argued above (pp. 199f.). that the
Kingdom's coming with power referred to by Mark is thought
of as certainly preceding, but not by a long interval, the
realization of the fact by some men of that generation, i.e.,
that the Kingdom's coming is destined to occur at some time
within the next thirty or forty years.[1]

Further, although I have used the passage (see above,
pp. 199f.) as possible evidence to the effect that, altogether
independently of the prospect of the Passion, Jesus looked
forward to a future coming of the Kingdom with power, I
must observe that it is still more unquestionably usable as
evidence of his expectation of a return of himself in power at
some time after his death : for (a) all the Synoptists place the
verse immediately after an unambiguous reference to the
Parousia, (b) the Matthæan paraphrase, " the Son of Man
coming in his Kingdom ", has value as an early interpretation
of Mark's words, and (c) it is more likely that Jesus should have
in mind *one* great spectacular event in the future, than several
disconnected ones.

(**13**) When Jacob and John came to Jesus with the request,
" Grant to us that we may sit, one on thy right hand, and one
on thy left, in thy glory ", Jesus declined to usurp the Father's
function of making this award (Mk. x. 35–40 = Mt. xx. 20–23) ;
but he tacitly admitted that there *would* be such glory and such
places, after he and his followers had undergone the baptism
and drunk the cup of martyrdom.

(**14**) The great eschatological discourse in Mk. xiii = Lk. xxi
=Mt. xxiv helps us less than we could hope, on account of the
uncertainty of the literary origin and mutual relationship of its
several parts. It cannot however for that reason be neglected ;

---

[1] I can see no reason for the conjecture that the saying originally referred
to *all* who were standing round, and that this was altered later to " some "
because, at the time when Mark wrote, only " some " of Jesus' hearers survived
(Montefiore *S.G.*[2] I. 200 : cf. Holtzmann, *Theol.* i. 386). A saying referring to
all the bystanders would have had to be quite differently framed. On the
identity of the coming of the Son of Man with the coming of the Kingdom,
see Holtzmann, *Theol.* i. 391f., Gloege, *Reich Gottes*, 173f. ; H-D. Wendland,
Eschatologie, 45f. : per contra, cf. Sharman, *Future*, 81f. ; V. Taylor, *Sacrifice*,
10, 31 ; Flew, *Church*, 44 ; and A. T. Cadoux, *Theol. of Jes.*, 26–31, 47, 198–213.

and we shall find that, on the main point, its evidence is in line with that which is abundantly provided elsewhere. We note, to begin with, that it is spoken in response to the Disciples' enquiry, " When will these things be ? and what will be the sign when all these things are about to be consummated ? " (Mk. xiii. 4 = Lk. xxi. 7 = Mt. xxiv. 3). To judge from the context, " these things " are the destruction of the Temple : but the sequel shows that a wider range of topics is in mind ; and the Matthæan version of the Disciples' question runs, " When will these things be ? and what will be the sign of thy Parousia and of (the) consummation of the age ? " (Mt. xxiv. 3).[1]

The section of the discourse which explicitly foretells the Parousia is reckoned by most scholars to belong to the detach-able " Little Apocalypse ", and is as follows : " But in those days, after that affliction, the sun will be darkened, and the moon will not give her light, and the stars will be falling from heaven, and the powers which are in the heavens will be shaken ; and then will men see the Son of Man coming in clouds with great power and glory ; and then will he send forth the angels, and will gather together the elect from the four winds, from the furthest point of earth to the furthest point of heaven " (Mk. xiii. 24-27 = Lk. xxi. 25-28 [where the wording is very different, but the prophecy of the Son of Man's coming is retained] = Mt. xxiv. 29-31 [repeats and elaborates Mk.]). Whether the immediately-ensuing verses originally stood in the same context is uncertain ; but they state that, as fig-leaves foreshadow summer-time, so will " these things " forewarn men that the Son of Man is near (Mk. xiii. 28f. = Lk. xxi. 29-31 [" . . . the Kingdom of God is near "] = Mt. xxiv. 32f.),[2] that " this generation shall in no wise pass away until all these things happen " (Mk. xiii. 30 = Lk. xxi. 32 = Mt. xxiv. 34), that " heaven and earth will pass away, but my words will not pass away " (Mk. xiii. 31 = Lk. xxi. 33 = Mt. xxiv. 35), and lastly that only the Father knows the precise day and hour (Mk. xiii. 32 = Mt. xxiv. 36 : see above, p. 289 top).[3] We may append here as further dubious allusions to the Parousia a

[1] On this last phrase, ἡ συντέλεια τοῦ αἰῶνος, which in the Gospels occurs only in Mt. xiii. (39), 40, 49, xxiv. 3, xxviii. 20 (cf. Heb. ix. 26), see Strack-Billerbeck i. 671.

[2] Dr. Dodd (*Parables*, 137 n. 1) thinks " the Parable " of the Figtree is " more pointed if Jesus was calling upon men to recognize the significance of the situation in which, at that moment, they stood ".

[3] Rev. T. Nicklin (in *E.T.* xl. 475f. [July 1929]) thinks we can distinguish sharply in Mk. xiii between the Fall of Jerusalem (which Jesus knew would occur within a generation) and the end of the world (the time of which he did not know).

reference to Mt. x. 23b M and to Lk. xviii. 8b L (see above, p. 95).

(15) When Jesus was directly asked by the High Priest in the Sanhedrin whether he were the Messiah or not, he replied, " I am ", and then added, quoting Dan. vii. 13, " and ye will see the Son of Man sitting on the right hand of the Power " (i.e., at God's right hand) " and coming with the clouds of the heaven " (Mk. xiv. 61f. [see above, p. 60 n. 1 for possible variant reading] = Lk. xxii. 67–70 = Mt. xxvi. 63f.). It is important to note here that the qualifying clause " from now (onwards) " is added in different forms in both Lk. and Mt., Lk. reading " from now (onwards) (ἀπὸ τοῦ νῦν) the Son of Man will be sitting . . . ", and Mt., " from now (onwards) (ἀπ’ ἄρτι) ye will see . . . ". Ought this qualification to be regarded as part of the original saying of Jesus ? Despite the striking agreement of Lk. and Mt., we should probably answer, No. Luke indeed, as elsewhere in his Passion-story, seems to be drawing on a non-Marcan source ; but his omission of the reference to Jesus coming on the clouds and to his enemies " seeing " him betrays a desire to describe his heavenly glory rather than his Parousia. This desire however operates unhistorically, for the words " and ye will see . . . " are needed as part of Jesus' actual retort. It is unlikely that Mt. either knew Lk., or had any other source for his Passion-narrative than Mk. : his modification of Mk. therefore is simply a gloss (m), which distorts Jesus' real reply in somewhat the same way as Lk. does.

There is a final allusion to Jesus' coming in (or with) his Kingdom in the words addressed to him by the Penitent Brigand who was crucified with him (Lk. xxiii. 42 L). We may perhaps presume that, although the words are not those of Jesus himself, they were based on what he had been heard to say, and represent his meaning accurately.[1]

(16) Let us now try-out the theory that, when Jesus prophesied that the Son of Man would rise from the dead after three days, he had in mind the same triumphant appearance as he is elsewhere said to have designated " the Parousia " and to have stated to be destined to happen on some day unknown within the generation then living.[2] The theory immediately

[1] On their meaning, cf. Wellhausen, *Lc.* 134 mid.

[2] This theory was held by Weiffenbach (Schweitzer, *Quest*, 232f.), Schweitzer himself (*L.J.F.* 385 n. 1 = *Quest*, 344f. n. 1 ; *Quest*, 364 n. 1 ; *Mystery*, 204, 208), Bartlet (*St. Mark*, 65, 252–254, 351), Cadman (*Last Journey*, 78–80), and tentatively by C. H. Dodd (*Parables*, 98–101). See also the summary of a paper by W. S. Bradley in *Oxford Society of Historical Theology : Abstract of*

solves the difficulty occasioned by the unexpectedness of Jesus'
appearances after his death : they were unexpected because,
whatever he may have actually said about his Resurrection,
he did not convey and never meant to convey the idea that
he would emerge from the tomb on what was *literally* the third
day after his death. A further advantage gained is that we
now see why, in his recorded sayings, he never connects
Parousia with Resurrection or relates them to one another, as
he surely would have done, had he thought of them as separate
events. The Resurrection-prophecies say nothing of an
ensuing ascension to and return from heaven ; and the
Parousia-prophecies leave no room for a visible reappearance
of Jesus and intercourse with his Disciples between death and
Parousia, but always imply that the interval will be a simple
blank of absence. If, for instance, Jesus expected to rise in
two days' time, why did he at the Last Supper limit himself to
an allusion to the Messianic Feast in the coming Kingdom ?
There is indeed a reference to the Resurrection in the Marcan
account of the walk to Gethsemane (Mk. xiv. 28 = Mt. xxvi.
32) ; but its historicity is doubtful,[1] and in any case it says
nothing about the third day, and is quite unrelated to the
anticipation just uttered at the Supper-table.[2]

(17) The expectation of a Resurrection from the tomb,
destined to occur a few days after death and before the
Parousia, is also hard to reconcile with Jesus' words to the
Penitent Brigand who was crucified beside him, " To-day shalt
thou be with me in Paradise " (Lk. xxiii. 43 L). The attempt
has indeed been made to harmonize these words with an
expectation on Jesus' part that he would descend for a couple
of days to She'ol or Hades before rising : it has been supposed
that Paradise was actually a section of Hades, in which those
destined for ultimate bliss were temporarily detained pending
the final Resurrection and Judgment. In the absence, however, of any suggestion of temporariness either here or elsewhere in the Gospel-references to the future abode of the dead,

---

Proceedings . . . 1915–1916, 58–63. The theory is rejected by Wendt
(*Teaching*, ii. 266–269 [he thinks Jesus meant by Resurrection, not a reappearance on earth, but a very early (invisible) ascent to heavenly life : but if so,
why " the third day " ?]), Holtzmann (*Theol.* i. 383–386), and Rawlinson
(*St. Mark*, 114).

[1] McNeile, *St. Matthew*, 387f.

[2] It is interesting to observe that Professor R. H. Lightfoot, who believes
that the original ending to Mk. is *not* lost, holds that this Gospel leaves the
reader anticipating, not a resurrection-appearance distinct from the Parousia,
but some event possessing that quality of climax and finality which we usually
associate with the latter (*Locality and Doctrine in the Gospels*, 59–65, 73–77).

we are bound to understand " Paradise " as the final home of bliss (see above, pp. 222f.). If Jesus, therefore, expected to go thither on the very day of his death, he could hardly have also expected to rise from the dead (in the usually-understood sense) two days later.[1]

(18) We shall discuss later the comparison Jesus draws between his Disciples before his Parousia and a household of Servants waiting for their Master's return (see below, pp. 311–313). It is alluded to here only in order to show that, so far as the comparison goes, it is much more apt if Jesus has in mind a simple period of absence from his friends between his death and his Parousia than if that period is broken up by an intermediate Resurrection followed by a short time of intercourse which ends with the Ascension. And even if we did not possess these pictures of the waiting Servants, must we not feel that the scheme—death, absence, return—is much simpler and more natural, and therefore more likely to have been Jesus' real forecast, than a series complicated by a descent to and resurrection out of Hades, an ascent to heaven, and a later descent thence to earth ? Jesus realizes that, since Israel is stiff-necked, it is the Father's will that he should pass through the dark portals of death into the unseen world. Such a prospect was one of mingled terror and faith.

> " If I stoop
> Into a dark tremendous sea of cloud,
> It is but for a time ; I press God's lamp
> Close to my breast ; its splendour, soon or late,
> Will pierce the gloom : I shall emerge one day ".[2]

He will drink the cup of sorrow to the dregs. But God will vindicate him against the rebellious disregard of his fellow-countrymen, by bringing him back in great power and glory. Nothing less than such a vindication was involved in the conviction that, though men were free to be sinners if they chose, God's own cause could not be finally defeated.[3] No doubt an integral part of this vindication would be the winning of many to repentance through his death (see above, pp. 262f. [16]) ; but that it should include some convincing manifestation of God's full approval and favour resting upon himself was also for Jesus a necessity of thought ; and the picture of a return

---

[1] Cf. Bickermann in *Z.N.W.* xxiii (1924) 292 ; Montefiore, *S.G.*[2] II. 627 ; J. A. MacCulloch, *Harrowing of Hell* (1930), 313–315, 344f.; Otto, *Kingdom*, 237–240.

[2] Browning, *Paracelsus*, fin.

[3] Cf. Moffatt, *Theol. of the Gospels*, 76f. ; Easton, *Christ in the Gospels*, 192.

in visible glory—before the generation that had rejected him should have died out, but at a time known precisely to God alone—was the most natural vehicle of expression that could be found for it.[1] And the evidence just collected from the Gospels (see above, pp. 288–293), supported as it is by the well-nigh unanimous belief and expectation of the Church of the first century,[2] establishes beyond reasonable doubt the conclusion that Jesus both looked forward to and predicted a triumph in that form.[3]

[1] Cf. Holtzmann, *Synopt.* 84f., *Theol.* i. 379, 390–392, 411f. See, however, below, pp. 343–345.

[2] See Manson, *Teaching*, 139–141.

[3] Dr. C. H. Dodd, in his recent books, has treated Jesus' declaration that the Kingdom of God had already come (Lk. xi. 20 = Mt. xii. 28 Q), and the early Christians' joyful sense of living under the power of it, as if they virtually disproved the existence of any futurist eschatology in the teaching of Jesus. I have already discussed (see above, pp. 194–207) certain aspects of his argument; but further reference is needed here to the question of the Parousia. Dr. Dodd admits that at least in Mk. xiv. 62 there is a prediction of a Second Coming (*Parables*, 96f. ; cf. also 185f.) : but he would, I imagine, refer this to the transcendent order beyond time and space. At all events, he interprets the eschatological Parables generally as misunderstood efforts made by Jesus to get men to realize that, in the presence of the Kingdom, they were faced with a tremendous crisis then and there (*Parables*, 174, 193f., 197f.) ; and he regards the Church's expectation of a *future* return of Jesus in glory as a misunderstanding of his real meaning—a misunderstanding which misled the more ignorant Christians into such apocalyptic extravagances as we find in "the Little Apocalypse" embedded in Mk. xiii and in the Apocalypse of John, but from which the Church as a whole was delivered by certain " finer minds " (*Apost. Preaching*, 91f. : cf. *Parables*, 132–134) such as Paul and the Fourth Evangelist, who made possible " an interpretation which did justice to the deeper meaning of the teaching of Jesus ".

I submit, however, that, in face of the evidence, this elimination of futurist eschatology from the teaching of Jesus must, undoubtedly be regarded as erroneous. It is not, as I have shown (see above, pp. 133, 194–196), necessitated by Jesus' feeling that, in his Person and work, the Kingdom had *in some sense* already come. The belief that the Lord would come again pervades the whole of the New Testament, with the partial exception of the Fourth Gospel. It is not invariably associated with such extravagances as we find in the Apocalypse of John. It is impossible to account satisfactorily for its existence by treating it as a misunderstanding of Jesus' real meaning. Certainly Paul, "finer mind " though he was, did nothing to emancipate his converts from it, for it was one of his own most precious and constant thoughts (see Manson, *Teaching*, 139). The frequently-held view that, towards the end of his life, Paul outgrew his belief in the Parousia is not justified by the evidence of his Epistles. Moreover, this belief is so strongly attested in the Gospel-records of Jesus' teaching that it cannot, on any reasonable theory of interpretation, be set on one side. Not only so, but it is necessitated also by the very fact of the Passion. In Dr. Dodd's scheme, the rejection of Jesus (which is not recognized as in any sense a disappointment or frustration of his initial purpose—*Parables*, 78–80) gets its needed compensation in his Resurrection from the dead. But, as we have seen, Jesus could not have predicted the Resurrection-appearances as these actually took place ; for in that case his friends would not have been so taken aback by them. Presumably, therefore, if he predicted a vindication of himself in time at all, he must have predicted some such Parousia as the records actually report him to have predicted.

(19) It is not, of course, contended that the theory that all Jesus' predictions of his Resurrection after three days were in reality intended to be predictions of his Parousia is wholly free from difficulty.   No hypothetical synthesis of our data could be claimed as lying open to no objections whatever.   It has, for instance, been plausibly urged that Jesus could not have looked forward to any other victorious sequel to his death than Resurrection,[1] and that rising from the dead is a very different process from coming on the clouds of heaven in great power and glory.   In reply to this, we may say that the actual occurrence of the appearances of Jesus from Easter-Sunday onwards would be bound to exercise considerable influence on the form in which his words about the future were preserved in the Gospels ; and this influence is not disproved by our inability to delimit its effects with precision.   It is indeed arguable that Jesus never actually spoke of rising from the dead at all, and that the several prophecies of Resurrection are all vaticinia post eventus. Incidentally, they are all, with one exception, either dependent on Mk. or else later than Mk.   They are found in the three formal predictions of the Passion (Mk. viii. 31 = Lk. ix. 22 = Mt. xvi. 21 ; Mk. ix. 31 [= Lk. ix. 44] = Mt. xvii. 23 ; Mk. x. 34 = Lk. xviii. 33 = Mt. xx. 19), in the conversation immediately after the Transfiguration (Mk. ix. 9f. = Mt. xvii. 9), in the conversation on the walk to Gethsemane (Mk. xiv. 28 = Mt. xxvi. 32 : see above, p. 294 [16]), in the historically-ungenuine Matthæan version of the sign of Jonah (Mt. xii. 40 m ; see above, p. 94), in the historically-dubious Matthæan story of the guard of soldiers at the tomb (Mt. xxvii. 63f. m), and in the Marcan account of Easter-Day (Mk. xvi. 6f. = Lk. xxiv. 6f. = Mt. xxviii. 6f.).   The only other allusion to a prophecy of the Resurrection is Lk. xxiv. 44–46 L ?, which however does not go beyond the general and somewhat-indirect observation that the Passion and Resurrection had been anticipated by Jesus because foretold in Scripture.   We are not, however, bound to go so far as to suppose that all Jesus' references to his Resurrection were created by the early Church in the light of the Easter-experience.   It is possible that he actually spoke of rising from the dead with reference to his passage to Paradise immediately after death,[2] and that the three days originally referred not to this Resurrection but to the future coming, and later got mistakenly attached to the Resurrection-sayings : alternatively we might suppose that he did really foretell

---

[1] Holtzmann, *Theol.* i. 381 n. 1.
[2] So Wendt, *Teaching*, ii. 266–269.

Resurrection from the dead after three days, meaning thereby his return to the earth after a short indefinite period, and that his predictions were later, in the light of the Easter-Day experiences, made more precise and therefore (for us) more obscure, in ways which it is no longer possible for us to trace in detail.[1]

(20) There are some other questions connected, not so much with the identification of the Resurrection-prophecies and the Parousia-prophecies, but with the precise meaning of the latter. Why, for instance, does Jesus always refer to the " Coming " (" Parousia ") and not to the " Coming-again " of the Son of Man ? And why does he always speak of the Son of Man in this connexion, and not use the first person singular ? Also, why in some passages is the Parousia spoken of as destined to occur with unexpected suddenness (e.g., Lk. xvii. 23–31 = Mt. xxiv. 26f., 37–39 Q), whereas in others its approach is heralded by a whole series of premonitory signs (e.g., Mk. xiii. 28f. = Lk. xxi. 29–31 = Mt. xxiv. 32f.) ? We can get a certain way by suggesting plausible answers to these questions. Thus we may say that, since the word " Parousia " is used only in Mt. among the Gospels, it, or rather its Aramaïc equivalent, was perhaps not used by Jesus himself, but was an early Christian coinage.[2] The use of the phrase " the Son of Man " instead of the first person singular is probably due to the influence of the language and meaning of Dan. vii. 13, Jesus thinking of his triumph not as confined to himself alone, but as shared by him with his loyal community, " the people of the saints of the Most High ".[3] The discrepancy about the premonitory signs is harder to solve : it may be due to the ungenuineness of parts of " the Little Apocalypse " and of other passages, to confusion between the Parousia and the Fall of Jerusalem, or even to changes occurring from time to time in Jesus' own outlook and point of view.[4] But interesting and important as these questions are, they do not seem to affect adversely the main conclusions to which the discussions of this chapter have led us.

[1] Cf. Holtzmann, *Synopt.* 84 ; Winstanley, *Future*, 218 ; *Beginnings of Christianity*, i. 381 ; Bartlet, *St. Mark*, 254 ; Dodd, *Parables*, 96. See also above, p. 288 n. 1.

[2] See Holtzmann, *Theol.* i. 385 ; McNeile, *St. Matthew*, 344f.

[3] See above, pp. 99–101, and cf. Manson, *Teaching*, 266–269.

[4] Cf. Holtzmann, *Theol.* i. 399 ; Manson, *Teaching*, 264–266, 269, 277, and in *Mission*, etc. 628f.

CHAPTER IV

THE DISCIPLES IN THE INTERVAL

(1) While Jesus spoke vaguely concerning the interval that was to elapse between his death and his return, he occasionally intimated that it might be as long as thirty or even more years. (2) He probably envisaged the Disciples as during that interval preaching about him up and down the lands ; (3) and he certainly warned them that they would meet with persecution. He had realized that this might occur even during the period of his Ministry ; (4) but he was more explicit regarding what might befall after his death. (5) He referred to the grounds on which the Disciples would incur persecution, the forms it would take, and the ways in which it was to be met. (6) He certainly "founded a Church " in the sense of establishing a community of those who believed in himself ; (7) but the Matthæan sayings in which he is represented as speaking of " the " or " my Church " are probably not genuine. (8) He does not seem to have expressly enjoined the practice of Baptism, (9) and we cannot be certain that he commanded the repetition of " the Lord's Supper ", though both of these were observed in the Church from the first. (10–12) He pictured his Disciples as servants left in charge of the house by an absent Master, who expects on his return to find that they have been, and still are, loyally doing their duty. (13) The enjoyment of his mystical presence was an experience which came to some Christians in the first century, but was probably not actually promised by him.

(1) If the main argument of the preceding chapter can be accepted as sound, Jesus described the great climax both as the coming of the Kingdom of God with power and as the arrival in glory of the Son of Man, i.e., of himself and his faithful community, and spoke of it as destined to occur (a) " after three days ", in the sense of " after a short indefinite interval ", (b) on a day known to God only, (c) within that generation, and (d) before some at least of his contemporaries should have died. It is not easy to say with any confidence and precision to what interval of time these indications point. It is most likely that Jesus had no even approximately-definite interval in mind, and that his anticipation swayed about between a very

near and a remoter future. The Fall of Jerusalem took place forty years after the Crucifixion. It has been urged that the generations were more short-lived in those days than they are now; [1] and certainly the phrase "after three days", however indefinite it be, seems hardly to suggest as much as two or three decades. On the other hand, in so far as Jesus' expectation was governed by the historical situation as between the Jews and Rome, his knowledge of recent and contemporary history would furnish no clear likelihood or certainty that the coming clash of arms would occur immediately or in the very early future. Moreover, as has been argued above (p. 291 n. 1), there is no good reason for doubting the genuineness of Mk. ix. 1 = Lk. ix. 27 = Mt. xvi. 28 as a saying of Jesus; and certainly when he uttered that saying, he was thinking of something at least some years ahead, perhaps as much as thirty or even forty years ahead. We do not need to maintain that he inclined even then to the furthest limit consistent with the formula he used, still less that he regularly had so long an interval in mind : but the words here used, and the inherent historical probabilities combine to show that he then expected that an interval of at least several years, possibly as much as two or three or even four decades, might elapse after his death and before either the war with Rome or his own reappearance. [2]

(2) It is therefore more probable than not that he occasionally spoke to his Disciples concerning their duties and their lot during this interval, and this in spite of (a) his apparent expectation, at least at one stage, that they would probably have to suffer martyrdom along with him (Mk. viii. 34f. = Lk. ix. 23f. = Mt. xvi. 24f. ; Lk. xiv. 27 = Mt. x. 38 Q ; Lk. xiv. 33 Q or l ; Mk. x. 38f. = Mt. xx. 22f. ; Mk. xiv. 27 = Mt. xxvi. 31), (b) his at least occasional inclination to expect only a very brief interval to elapse before the great climax, and (c) the inevitable tendency on the part of the early Church to ascribe to him unhistorically (especially to the post-Resurrection period—a blank space very convenient for the purpose) certain needful directions and admonitions regarding the conduct of the affairs of his community. We may consider first as a typically-problematic piece of teaching under this heading

---

[1] Dodd, *Parables*, 67f., 100–105. He says, "We must suppose that historical exigencies have led to a certain expansion of the interim period, and that Jesus actually expected the tribulation of Judæa to follow more closely upon His own death ". Cf. Holtzmann, *Theol.* i. 386f.

[2] Dr. R. N. Flew (*Church*, 15f., 41, 46, 121) argues that Jesus may have anticipated an interval of considerable length. Cf. also Sharman, *Future*, 197, 353f.

the references ascribed to Jesus by Mark to the preaching of
the Christian Gospel throughout the world—first in Mk. xiii. 10
= Mt. xxiv. 14 (a verse not usually assigned to " the Little
Apocalypse "), " And the Gospel must first be proclaimed to all
the nations " ; and second, at the conclusion of the story of the
anointing at Bethany, " Truly I tell you, wherever the Gospel
is proclaimed throughout the whole world, that also which this
woman has done will be spoken of in her memory " (Mk. xiv. 9
= Mt. xxvi. 13). It has been argued above (pp. 142, 158,
176) that, in view of the conflict in the early Church between
Paul and the Jerusalem-authorities—or at least of the unconcern of the latter—as to whether or not the evangelization of
the Gentiles (technically known as " the nations ") ought to be
undertaken, it is not easy to believe that Jesus was remembered to have explicitly referred to such an enterprise.[1] On
the other hand, these two sayings possess considerably-higher
historical value than the missionary-injunctions put by M or m
(Mt. xxviii. 19) and l or L (Lk. xxiv. 47) into the mouth of the
Risen Jesus. Preaching had been one of Jesus' main activities
during his ministry, and he had commissioned his Disciples to
go out on preaching-tours as well : if therefore he thought at all
of their activities during any considerable period after his
death (and we have seen that it is probable that he did), he may
quite well have pictured them as preaching about him then
even in other lands, though he may not have made it as clear
as the texts now suggest that the preaching was to be world-
wide and was to include the Gentiles.[2]

(3) Somewhat less problematic is the evidence of our sources
to the effect that Jesus forewarned his Disciples and his
followers generally that they would suffer severe persecution,
though here again we may reasonably suspect that the Church's
actual experience of persecution may to some extent have
coloured her record of what the Lord had actually said. These
warnings of Jesus were apparently not confined to any
particular part of his ministry, though—as we should expect—
they apparently became more frequent towards its close. But
in several of the sources they appear fairly early in the story :
and this distribution is in keeping with the supposition (see
above, pp. 185, 187 top, 218, 235 n. 2) that, although Jesus hoped

[1] Cf. A. T. Cadoux, *Parables*, 177, 179f. Dr. Flew (*Church*, 85) does not
seem to realize that the controversy between Paul and Jerusalem constitutes
any objection to the authenticity of the words.
[2] In particular, there is no necessity to regard (with Beyschlag [*Theol.* i.
197f.]) this world-wide preaching as intended especially to follow the Fall of
Jerusalem (Holtzmann, *Theol.* i. 388 n. 3).

at first to win over the nation at large without suffering death at its hands, he did not hope to do so without self-denying service and a measure of suffering connected therewith.[1]

Nor is it always made clear to us when the persecution itself is expected to befall the Disciples. Some of the allusions are perfectly general, and bear no definite indication of time. Thus, " Happy are those who have been persecuted for righteousness' sake, for theirs is the Kingdom of the Heavens " (Mt. v. 10 M) : " Happy are ye when men start hating you and excommunicating and reviling you, and publishing abroad your name as evil—for my sake. Rejoice on that day and leap for joy ; for behold ! great is your reward in the heaven : for after the same fashion did their fathers act towards the prophets " (Lk. vi. 22f. = Mt. v. 11f. Q : see above, pp. 95 top, 239 top : for the Jews and particularly Jerusalem as the habitual slayers of the prophets, cf. Lk. xi. 47–51 = Mt. xxiii. 29–36 Q ; Lk. xiii. 33 L ; Lk. xiii. 34 = Mt. xxiii. 37 Q) : " Love your enemies, do good to those who hate you, bless those who curse you, pray for those who insult you, . . . " (Lk. vi. 27f. = Mt. v. 44 Q) —words possibly spoken with reference to heathen or Herodian oppression (see above, pp. 171f.). The casual reference to persecution in the interpretation of the Parable of the Sower (Mk. iv. 17 [=Lk. viii. '13 fin.] = Mt. xiii. 21) occurs in what was probably not an actual discourse of Jesus (see above, pp. 48, 212). There is another quite general allusion to persecution as the lot of Jesus' followers in Mk. x. 29f. = Lk. xviii. 29 = Mt. xix. 29 (see above, p. 235).

But the fact that some of these predictions are included in the instructions Jesus is reported to have given to the Disciples, when sending them out on their mission-tour, seems to show that, even as they travelled about Palestine during their Master's own lifetime, they might expect to meet with opposition and maltreatment. " Behold ! I send you out like lambs into the midst of wolves . . . " (Lk. x. 3 = Mt. x. 16 Q). Where they were not listened to, they were to shake the dust of the place off their feet (Mk. vi. 11 = Lk. ix. 5 = Mt. x. 14 ; Lk. x. 10f. Q ?). " But whenever they persecute you in this city, flee to the other " (Mt. x. 23a M).[2]

---

[1] Cf. A. T. Cadoux in *The Lord of Life*, 63 : " If God's people repented and received His truth, it was still through danger and suffering that He would have to lead them to their destiny ".

[2] The compiler of the Gospel of Mt. made a practice of massing the teaching of Jesus in great blocks, each of which was marked by some unifying characteristic of style or content, and apparently of disregarding for the purpose the arrangement in which the sayings were placed in Q (Streeter, *Four Gospels*,

(4) While, however, Jesus speaks of persecution as something his followers must be ready to meet at any time, most of his allusions to it which contain any discernible time-reference refer to the conditions they would have to face when he should no longer be with them. As he came to realize that he would himself almost certainly be called on to die a violent death, his expectation that they would thereafter be likely to meet with unpopularity and ill-treatment naturally led him to warn them about it more frequently.[1] When, for instance, he says, " Days will come when ye will long to see one of the days of the Son of Man, and will not see it " (Lk. xvii. 22 Q or l), the reference to the interval between his death and his return seems clear. The same applies to the lesson drawn from the Parable of the Unrighteous Judge (Lk. xviii. 2–5 L) : " Listen to what the unrighteous judge says ! And will not God inflict vengeance for his elect, who cry to Him day and night ? and does He have patience regarding them (with their oppressors) ? I tell you, He will inflict vengeance for them speedily " (Lk. xviii. 6–8a, probably l). In this case, however, the words make the impression of being an explanatory gloss, produced during a time of persecution, and expressing what the glossator (perhaps Luke himself) felt the true purport of the Parable to be.[2] Certain verses in the great eschatological discourse in Mk. xiii also, which are not usually assigned to " the Little Apocalypse ", apparently refer to persecution destined to follow Jesus' death. " They will hand you over

---

261–265). He has accordingly included in his report of Jesus' mission-charge (Mt. x) a great deal of material which in his sources was assigned to other and later occasions in Jesus' ministry. Much of this material deals with persecution ; and one passage in it (Mt. x. 23b M : " . . . ye will by no means finish the cities of Israel until the Son of Man comes ") was almost certainly framed under the stress of the controversy between Paul and the Jerusalem-church (see above, p. 95). Ignoring these documentary considerations, and treating the whole of Mt. x as an historical unity, Schweitzer argued that, inasmuch as there was at that time no real danger of the Disciples being persecuted, and as in point of fact they were not then persecuted, the prophecies of persecution must have sprung simply from Jesus' own dogmatic conviction that, since the Parousia of the Messiah was imminent, and since—according to the accepted eschatological programme—tribulation (the " pangs of the Messiah ") must precede the Parousia, therefore the Disciples must be on the very point of incurring persecution (Schweitzer, L.J.F. 405–411 = Quest, 356–362). I have already argued (see above, pp. 16–18, 249–251) that it is inherently improbable that Jesus' thoughts moved along these rigid a priori dogmatic lines. We now see that the theory that they did so is based on a reading of Mt. x which, on entirely-independent grounds, must, from the literary and historical point of view, be judged to be in all probability mistaken.

[1] Dodd, Parables, 58, 60, 70. The somewhat obscure words of Lk. xxii. 35–38 L seem to be a prediction of this worsening of the situation.

[2] Cf. B. T. D. Smith, Parables, 152f.

unto sanhedrins, and in synagogues will ye be beaten, and before governors and kings will ye be made to stand for my sake, for a testimony unto them " (Mk. xiii. 9 = Lk. xxi. 12f. = Mt. x. 17f. = Mt. xxiv. 9a). " And ye will be hated by all men on account of my name " (Mk. xiii. 13a = Lk. xxi. 17 = Mt. x. 22a = Mt. xxiv. 9c). " And then will many be made to stumble, and will hand over one another and hate one another. And many false prophets will arise, and will mislead many. And on account of the increase of lawlessness, the love of many will grow cold " (Mt. xxiv. 10–12 M).

(5) It is not a matter of very great difficulty to understand why, even as early as Jesus' own lifetime, his followers should become exposed to persecution. The tension that sprang up between him and the authorities would be liable to reproduce itself wherever men who counted themselves his adherents were to be found. Several times did Jesus hint that those who followed him must expect to encounter the same sort of treatment that he was encountering himself—to be called " Beelzebul " as he had been (Mt. x. 25 M), to follow him bearing the cross (Mk. viii. 34 [= Lk. ix. 23] = Mt. xvi. 24 ; Lk. xiv. 27 = Mt. x. 38 Q), to drink his cup and be baptized with his baptism (Mk. x. 38f. = Mt. xx. 22f.). He speaks of men being " persecuted for righteousness' sake " (Mt. v. 10 M) and "for my sake " (Lk. vi. 22 = Mt. v. 11 Q: see above, pp. 95 top, 239 top). And in the nature of things, practical obedience to his teaching, and the advocacy of the truths he pleaded for, would be bound to arouse the same sort of opposition as he himself had aroused.[1] The opposition would naturally be first manifested in the painful antipathies which loyalty to Jesus would evoke on the part of the near relatives of his followers : members of the same family-circle would speedily find themselves in opposite camps. Jesus himself had apparently experienced misunderstanding and opposition on the part of his mother and his brothers (Mk. iii. 21 ; John vii. 1–8). It was therefore in every way natural that he should warn the Disciples of the fierce strain which their devotion to him would put upon the affections of their kith and kin (Lk. xii. 51–53 = Mt. x. 34–36 Q ; Lk. xiv. 26 = Mt. x. 37 Q ; Mk. x. 29f. = Lk. xviii. 29 = Mt. xix. 29 [see above, p. 235.] ; Mk. xiii. 12 = Lk. xxi. 16 = Mt. x. 21).[2] But his references to the possi-

---

[1] Cf. Simkhovitch, *Understanding of Jes.* 55 (the certainty that nationalistic zealots, e.g., would dislike Jesus' teaching) ; A. T. Cadoux, *Parables*, 177 ; Dodd, *Parables*, 57.

[2] Cf. Dodd, *Parables*, 68f.

bility that they might lose their lives (Mk. viii. 34f. [= Lk. ix. 23 f.] = Mt. xvi. 24f. ; Lk. xii. 4–9 = Mt. x. 28–33 Q ; Lk. xiv. 27 = Mt. x. 38 Q ; Lk. xiv. 33 Q or L or l ; Lk. xvii. 33 = Mt. x. 39 Q ; Mk. x. 38f. = Mt. xx. 22f. ; Mk. xiii. 12 = Lk. xxi. 16 = Mt. x. 21 = Mt. xxiv. 9) suggest the fear that some of them might incur the punishment of crucifixion at the hands of Roman soldiers or meet with violent death in some other way.[1]

But whatever peril they might encounter, either during Jesus' own life on earth, or during the interval between his death and his reappearance in glory, was to be met with unflinching patience and courage : not even the peril of death was to frighten them into denying their loyalty to him (Mk. viii. 34–38 = Lk. ix. 23–26 = Mt. xvi. 24–27 ; Lk. xii. 4–9 = Mt. x. 28–33 Q ; Lk. xvii. 33 = Mk. x. 39 Q). Their eternal destiny hung upon their faithfulness in the hour of trial : only " he that endures unto the end—he will be saved " (Mk. xiii. 13b [= Lk. xxi. 19] = Mt. x. 22b = Mt. xxiv. 13).[2] They would further need to be as prudent and cunning as snakes, though as innocent as doves (Mt. x. 16 [not in Lk. x. 3] Q or M or m). They must be on their guard against misleading rumours as to the presence and whereabouts of the returned Master. " They will say to you, ' Behold ! he is there ! ' and ' Behold ! he is here ! ' Do not go away (thither), and do not pursue him " (Lk. xvii. 23 = Mt. xxiv. 26 Q). " See that no one misleads you. Many will come in my name, saying, ' I am he ', and will mislead many " (Mk. xiii. 5f. = Lk. xxi. 8 = Mt. xxiv. 4f.). " And then, if any one say to you, Behold ! here is the Christ ! ' ' Behold ! there (he is) ! ', do not believe it. But false prophets will arise, and will do signs and portents, in order if possible to mislead the elect. But see ye (to it) ; I have told you all in advance " (Mk. xiii. 21–23 = Mt. xxiv. 23–25).[3] Finally, they were not to worry about how to defend themselves when standing on trial : they were to rely confidently on being guided by the Spirit of God when the moment came (Lk. xii. 11f. = Mt. x. 19f. Q ; Mk. xiii. 11 = Lk. xxi. 14f. = Mt. x. 19f.). As Jesus probably foresaw, and as the event proved, the experience of persecution became the Disciples' opportunity for a wider missionary-activity.[4]

(6) When the question is raised, Did Jesus intend to found

---

[1] Cf. Dodd, *Parables*, 58–60.
[2] Cf. Manson, *Teaching*, 263.
[3] Cf. Sharman, *Future*, 124–128, 161–165.
[4] Acts viii. 4 ff., xi. 19ff. : A. T. Cadoux, *Parables*, 180f. ; Flew, *Church*, 179.

the Christian Church ? we need to make quite clear what we mean by the question, in order to avoid being at cross-purposes with others in discussing the answers given. On the Roman Catholic and fundamentalist views, no word ascribed to Jesus in the Gospels is wrongly so ascribed, and no development of his work in the future was unknown to him. Hence the conclusion has to be drawn that Jesus did intend, in the fullest sense of the words, to found the Church. Roman Catholics go further, and ascribe to him detailed regulations regarding its organization and procedure, even to the point of the personal institution of all the seven Sacraments. Such theories rest on presuppositions regarding his foreknowledge, regarding the origin of the Church, and regarding the character of the Gospel-documents, which are unwarranted by such historical evidence as we possess, and which therefore must be set aside.

In setting them aside, however, many have hastily over-pressed the argument that, because Jesus expected to return in glory within a comparatively-short time, therefore he could not have contemplated at all the establishment or existence of an organized body of followers destined to last for a period of several years, that is to say, he could not have intended to found anything in the nature of a Church.[1] But as we have already shown, Jesus did not profess to know precisely when he would come again, and sometimes spoke of the interval that was to elapse as if it might be as long as three or four decades (see above, pp. 299f.). We cannot therefore treat his expectation of the approaching climax as a proof that he could not have contemplated the establishment of a Church.

It has also been argued that Jesus could not have thought of forming a special community attached to himself without renouncing his hope of winning the whole nation, and that, as he never did renounce that hope, so he never thought of establishing a special community.[2] Now it is certainly true that Jesus at first expected to be able to win the whole nation (see above, pp. 136ff.), and that right on almost to the end he clung to the hope that possibly he might succeed. At the same time, he was not blind to the numerous indications which experience from time to time gave him of the improbability—or virtual impossibility—of his hope being realized ; and he must have been familiar, through his knowledge of the Old Testament, with the prophetic idea of the Righteous Remnant,

---

[1] So, e.g., Weinel, *Theol.* 120f.
[2] See Holtzmann, *Theol.*i . 269.

the nucleus of loyal Israelites who were " Israelites indeed ", and through whom alone God's purpose for his Chosen People would be realized.[1] Indeed, there is good reason for believing that, in fusing together the two conceptions of " the Son of Man " and the suffering " Servant of the Lord ", he was envisaging as " the Son of Man " a corporate or social unit, consisting of the saved and saving Remnant of Israel with himself as its leader.[2] In any case there would be nothing impossible in his deliberately contemplating and forming such a social group, while at the same time keeping hold of the hope that it might possibly come to consist of the nation as a whole. Certain it is that Jesus constantly thought of his followers in terms of a community ; and in so doing and in planning for its corporate life during his absence, he may in a certain sense of the words be described as deliberately founding a Church.[3]

(7) It is, however, another matter to determine how concretely Jesus envisaged the organization of this community, whether he actually called it a Kahal or an 'edhah (i.e., ἐκκλησία, " Church "), and whether he prescribed any sacramental rites to be observed by its members. That he should have pictured them living together, treasuring his memory, watching for his return, loyally observing his precepts, and defending his claims—so much indeed is readily believable. But that, wearied by the strain and tension of his enterprise, immersed in the struggle against the manifold " temptations " that beset him, and appalled by the prospect of defeat and death, he should have had the leisure and detachment to prescribe details of organization and procedure for his group of followers after his death, is inherently far less likely and less easily credible. And when we turn to the Gospels in order to see how much organizational teaching is actually ascribed to him, we are met by the extraordinary facts, firstly, that very little of that sort is ascribed to him, and secondly, that what little there is is nearly all contained in the Matthæan Gospel. It has often been remarked that in this Gospel Jesus is represented as speaking of the Kingdom of God as if he really meant the Christian Church.[4] It is furthermore only in this Gospel that the word ἐκκλησία (" Church ") occurs. In Mt. xvi.

---

[1] Cf. Gloege, *Reich Gottes*, 209–219.

[2] See above, p. 100, and cf. Manson, *Teaching*, 230–236.

[3] This is the great argument of the first part of Dr. R. N. Flew's book, *Jes. and His Church* (e.g., 52–58, 122, 135f., 180, 214). Cf. also Gloege, *Reich Gottes*, 224–229, 241–249 ; H.-D. Wendland, *Eschatologie*, 135–163.

[4] Montefiore, *S.G.*[1] I. lvif. (quoting Wellhausen, *Einleitung* [1905], 105f. [= (1911), 94]).

17f. M (or m) Jesus, in commending Simon Peter for having acknowledged him as the Messiah, calls him the Rock on which he will build his Church, against which the Gates of Hades shall not prevail. In 19 he gives Peter " the keys of the Kingdom of the Heavens ", so that whatever he binds or looses on earth shall have been bound or loosed respectively in the Heavens. The words have nothing parallel to them in either Mk. or Lk. In Mt. xviii. 15–17 M or m (a passage of which a shorter and simpler version apparently stood in Q— see Lk. xvii. 3b), Jesus enjoins that an offending brother who is unmoved both by private remonstrance and by the persuasion of two or three other friends, is to be reported " to the Church ; and if he refuse to listen to the Church, let him be to thee like the Gentile and the tax-collector ". Then in Mt. xviii. 18 M or m the same promise about binding and loosing which was made in xvi. 19 to Peter alone is uttered in the second person plural.

Now it is this curious fact of exclusively-Matthæan attestation which tells so heavily against the originality of these ecclesiastical passages. It is not simply the rarity of the sayings which discredits them.[1] Were it only that, one might not unreasonably plead that their rarity speaks for their genuineness : if the Evangelists, it might be argued, were *inventing* sayings of this sort at all, they would have invented more. But what are we to say when all the ecclesiastical sayings of Jesus happen to be found in a gospel which, wherever we can compare it closely with its sources, is seen to be quite ready to depart from historical accuracy in the interests of what was considered edifying ?[2] If, notwithstanding their rarity, these sayings are really actual sayings of Jesus, why are none of them found in the other Gospels which are, by comparison with Mt., far less prone to abandon history for edification ? Certainty indeed is impossible, and dogmatism consequently out of place ; for a case can undoubtedly be made out in defence of these sayings, on the ground of their Jewish tone, and so forth.[3] But in view of their being exclusively found in a Gospel of the character of Mt., I hold that the balance of probability is in favour of the view that they do not represent with any closeness anything that Jesus actually said, but are

[1] This is the " argument from statistics " which Dr. R. N. Flew (*Church*, 123–125) labours to refute in the case of Mt. xvi. 17–19.

[2] Dr. Flew's recent defence of the Church-sayings (*Church*, 123–136) does not touch on this important point.

[3] They are accepted by Schweitzer (*L.J.F.* 416: cf. *Quest*, 369 n.), who interprets them eschatologically. K. L. Schmidt also defends the genuineness of Mt. xvi. 18 (in *R.G.G.* iii [1929] 148f. [E. I]). Cf. also Gloege, *Reich Gottes*, 261–276 ; H.-D. Wendland, *Eschatologie*, 164–187.

late enlargements of his teaching, constructed in the interests of the right management of Church-affairs (see above, p. 22).[1]

(8) The question as to whether Jesus explicitly instructed his Disciples to baptize new adherents to their body, and to take bread and wine together in memory of him (for these are the only two " Sacraments " that need to be considered in this connexion), is of great interest and importance, and is not irrelevant to the subject of the present study. But it is a question so problematic in character and consequently so prolific in literary discussion that adequate treatment of it in this place would demand so much space as to throw the rest of what is here offered to the reader out of focus. It must therefore suffice to indicate very briefly a few salient points.

The evidence that Jesus himself ever baptized converts is found only in the Fourth Gospel (John iii. 5, 26, iv. 1-3). If Jesus made anything like a regular practice of baptizing,[2] it is very curious that there should not be a single reference to it in the Synoptic Gospels. Waiving this objection, however, and accepting at least tentatively the statements of the Johannine narrative, we should gather that the baptism practised by Jesus (through the hands of his followers) was one similar, parallel, and supplementary to that of John the Baptist, and was practised only during the days before the Galilæan Ministry began.[3] It is in any case certain that the community of John the Baptist's followers remained quite distinct from Jesus' group of Disciples. The allusion to baptism in Jesus' words to Nicodemus (John iii. 5) cannot be depended on as a true saying of Jesus (see above, pp. 12f.) : it is a reflection of Christian practice at the time when the Fourth Gospel was written.[4] The only evidence that Jesus bade his Disciples baptize others after his death is the post-Resurrection saying reported in Mt. xxviii. 19 M or m. Apart from any doubts arising from the fact that this is a post-Resurrection saying, doubts do arise regarding an utterance on Church-procedure reported only in Mt., and especially regarding one cast (as this is) in a non-primitive form.[5] If the Church knew of any instruction to baptize

---

[1] Cf. Holtzmann, *Theol.* i. 268-270 ; Weinel, *Theol.* 120f. There is a full discussion of the " Church-sayings " in C. J. Cadoux's *Cathol. and Christianity*, 372-390.

[2] As Seeley in *Ecce Homo* (ch. v) assumes.

[3] Cf. Moody, *Purpose of Jes.* 36f., and see also above, p. 139 n.2.

[4] Another reflection, alluding cryptically to the problem of the pardon of post-baptismal sins, is probably to be seen in John xiii. 10a.

[5] Baptism elsewhere in the New Testament is always said to be in the Name, not of the Father, Son, and Holy Spirit (which is elsewhere first found in the *Didache* [vii. 1]), but of the Lord Jesus (e.g., Acts viii. 16, xix. 5 ; 1 Cor. i. 13).

actually uttered by Jesus, it would almost certainly have stronger attestation than this.[1] On the other hand, if Jesus said nothing about it, it is less easy to understand why from the Day of Pentecost onwards all new adherents who believed in him as the Messiah, and desired to identify themselves with the company of his Disciples, were subjected to baptism. Possibly, however, we ought to conclude that Christian baptism was due to the spontaneous and unanimous adoption, on the occasion of Pentecost, of a Jewish custom (the baptism of proselytes), which had already been adapted to a fresh use by John the Baptist, had as such received some measure of approval by Jesus himself, and commended itself as a solemn and fitting accompaniment of adherence to his cause.[2] It is not after all impossible that such a step may have appealed so strongly to the sense of the community that it was allowed to determine the future practice of the Church in an absolute manner, even though Jesus himself had given no instructions for its regular observance.

(9) The Lord's Supper is still more relevant to our subject, and still more problematic, than Baptism. Here the two burning questions are : (a) What precisely did Jesus mean by the " words of institution " ?, and (b) Did the words of institution include an injunction that the rite was to be repeated ?

(a) I must, for the reasons already given, refrain from attempting to investigate here the question as to what precisely were the thoughts in Jesus' mind when he said, " This is my body . . . ", " This is my blood of the Covenant . . . ". Volumes have been written on the topic, and even yet certainty is not attained.[3] It cannot be reasonably doubted that Jesus was thinking of his approaching death, and thinking of it as a redemptive service which he was rendering at great cost on

---

The argument that the original text of Mt. xxviii. 19 had ἐν τῷ ὀνόματί μου, instead of the Trinitarian formula, is based on a few readings in Eusebius, and is probably incorrect (McNeile, *St. Matthew*, 436f.).

[1] " Perhaps the very fact that it was ascribed to the *risen* Jesus betrays the realisation that it was not directly instituted by Jesus during His life upon earth " (A. E. J. Rawlinson, *Authority and Freedom* [1924], 144). Cf. Weinel, *Theol.* 70.

[2] Cf. Lake in Hastings' *Encyclop. of Relig. and Ethics*, ii (1909) 381b ; *Beginnings of Christianity*, i. 332–344 ; Moody, *Purpose of Jes.* 134–136 ; Oepke in *T.W.N.T.* i. 536f. ; Flew, *Church*, 164–167.

[3] Recent discussions may be seen in Otto, *Kingdom*, 263–330 ; in *Christian Worship*, 44–49 (T. W. Manson), 68–82 (C. H. Dodd) ; in V. Taylor, *Sacrifice*, 114–142, 201–217, 313f., 322 ; in Flew, *Church*, 99–106 ; and in much other recent lit. There is a survey of the lit. in Lohmeyer's arts. in *Theolog. Rundschau*, ix (1937) 168–227, 273–312.

behalf of others ; and it may reasonably be pleaded that in that respect his words ought to be interpreted along with, and in the light of, the rest of his teaching about his death and about redemption (see above, pp. 259–265).[1] Another aspect of the subject, which has been almost wholly ignored in later Christian interpretations of the Supper, but which is unmistakably recorded in the Gospels, is that for Jesus this partaking of bread and wine together was a foretaste of the Messianic Feast in the Kingdom of Heaven, which he was expecting to enjoy in the very near future (Mk. xiv. 25 = Mt. xxvi. 29 ; Lk. xxii. 16, 18 L ? : 1 Cor. xi. 26 fin.). Of this expectation we must speak again presently (see below, pp. 326f.

(b) In regard to the question whether Jesus gave instructions for the rite to be repeated, the difficulty lies in the fact that, while such instructions are reported by Paul (1 Cor. xi. 24 fin., 25 fin.) and in the ungenuine text of Lk. xxii. 19 fin., they are omitted in Mk. and (most strangely) in Mt. It is almost equally hard to believe that (i) the Disciples would have practised the rite constantly and Paul have twice written, " Do this in remembrance of me ", if Jesus had not given any such injunction, and (ii) that Mk. and Mt. would have omitted this injunction if he had. We must, for the reasons given, leave the question undiscussed and undecided here, observing only that the act of Jesus in distributing the bread and wine was emphatically a communal act, and that, if he was known among his Disciples and friends by his special manner of breaking bread and sharing wine when at table with them (Lk. xxiv. 30f., 35 L ; 1 Cor. xi. 24f. [" This do ", not " This eat ", " This drink "]), the solemn circumstances of the Last Supper might suggest to the Disciples the repetition of the act in his memory, even if Jesus himself had not explicitly enjoined such repetition in actual words.

(10) In perfect agreement with the anticipation of his absence from his Disciples for an interval of uncertain length between his death and his triumphant return, Jesus several times, both in set parables and in parabolic exhortations, depicts them in the likeness of a household of servants left to themselves, not

---

[1] It is, perhaps, worth observing that the verbal copula suggested by the original Aramaïc, and necessitated by the translation of it into Greek and English, would—in the Hebraïc milieu within which the words were first spoken—mean " stands for ", "typifies ", " represents " (cf. Ezek. v. 1–5, and other passages quoted in my *Cathol. and Christianity*, 399), not "is identical with " or "has been changed into." These latter meanings were read into the words only after the story had been transferred to Greek soil, and its original Hebraïc background forgotten.

knowing exactly when their Master is to return, but expected
by him to be found when he does return to have been attending
to their duty and so to be in all respects ready to receive him.
We quote first a passage in Q : "Who then is the trustworthy,
prudent steward, whom the master will set over his troop of
servants, to give out their rations at the proper time ?   Happy
will that slave be, whom his master when he comes will find so
doing !   Truly I tell you, he will set him over all he possesses.
But if that slave say in his heart, ' My master is a long time
coming ', and begin to beat the boys and the slave-girls, and
to eat and drink and get drunk, the master of that slave will
come on a day he does not expect, and at an hour he does not
know, and will cut him apart, and appoint him his lot among
the untrustworthy " (Lk. xii. 42–46 = Mt. xxiv. 45–51 Q : see
below, p. 325 n.1).   Next, from Mk.: "See (to it) : be wakeful,
for ye know not when the time is coming—as (when) a man (is)
abroad, after leaving his house, and giving authority to his
slaves—to each his own work ; and the doorkeeper he instructed to watch.   Watch therefore, for ye know not when
the Lord of the house is coming, whether late (in the evening),
or at midnight, or at cockcrow, or next morning—lest he come
suddenly and find you sleeping.   And what I say to you, I say
to all men—watch ! " (Mk. xiii. 33–37 ; cf. Mt. xxiv. 42).   L has
three passages of the same general purport.   " Let your loins
be girt and your lamps burning ; and be yourselves like men
waiting for their master, whenever he may come away from
the marriage-festivities, in order that, when he comes and
knocks, they may immediately open (the door) to him.   Happy
will those slaves be, whom their master, when he comes, shall
find awake !   Truly I tell you, he will gird himself, and make
them recline at table, and come up and serve them !   And even
if he comes during the second watch, or even during the third
watch, and finds (them) thus, happy are they ! " (Lk. xii.
35–38 L).   " That slave who knew his master's will, but did not
make preparation according to his will, will be beaten with
many (strokes) : but he who did not know his master's will,
and (therefore) did things deserving strokes, will be beaten
with few . . . " (Lk. xii. 47f. L).   " Take heed to yourselves,
lest your hearts become weighed down with surfeiting and
drunkenness and worldly anxieties, and that day come upon
you suddenly like a trap : for it will come upon all who dwell
on the face of all the earth.   But keep awake at every season,
praying that ye may succeed in escaping all these things that
are destined to happen, and in standing before the Son of Man "

(Lk. xxi. 34–36 L). In one Q-passage, the picture is altered to that of a householder not knowing at what hour the burglar would come. " But know this, that if the householder had known at what hour the thief was coming, he would not have allowed his house to be broken into. Do ye also get ready, because in an hour which ye do not expect the Son of Man comes " (Lk. xii. 39f. = Mt. xxiv. 43f. Q). The Parable of the Servants entrusted with Money, which has come down to us in what are apparently two independent recensions (Lk. xix. 12–27 L ; Mt. xxv. 14–30 M), involves the same motif of a staff of servants charged with certain responsibilities pending the return of their master after a period of absence. And finally the Parable of the Wise and Foolish Virgins (Mt. xxv. 1–13 M) also illustrates the need of readiness for the arrival of an important person, the length of whose absence is unfore-known ; and it does so in terms that somewhat resemble those of Lk. xii. 35–38 L, quoted above.

(11) When we consider the independent evidence accumu-lated above (pp. 288–296) to the effect that Jesus expected to return in glory at some interval after his death, and when we take account of the frequency of these allusions to a houseful of waiting servants responsible for being ready for the return of a master absent for an uncertain period, we can really have little doubt that these pictures were intended by Jesus to refer to the condition and duties of his Disciples during the interval between his death and his Parousia. On that interpretation, the whole of the evidence hangs admirably together. The dangers of slackness, self-indulgence, dissension, and unwisdom would obviously be exactly the sort of evils to threaten men living under such conditions : we do not need therefore to postpone the framing of these warnings against them to the days of the early Church, when actual experience was providing practical instances of the need for such warnings.

Attempts have however been recently made to give these passages another interpretation. It has been argued that the reference of them to the Parousia does not go back to the purpose of Jesus himself in uttering them, but is due to the later exegesis of the early Church. Jesus, it is supposed, had in mind the urgent need for men to be alert and ready to respond worthily to the searching crisis with which the coming of the Kingdom (as represented by his own presence and message) was facing them : [1] they belonged therefore originally " within

[1] Cf. Dodd, *Parables*, 165–167 : for his treatment of the Parables of the Servants entrusted with Money, see above, p. 290 n. 2. Colani had inter-

the context of the ministry of Jesus " ; [1] the absent master was simply a pictorial means of providing a situation in which alertness would be called for, and had at first no other significance than that.[2] It was only later, when the actual circumstances of the Ministry no longer prevailed, that the Church found in these descriptions warnings applicable to the period when the Parousia was being awaited.[3]

(12) The first objection to such a view has already been indicated at the commencement of the last section. It is that the more customary interpretation of these parables, according to which they are taken to refer to the Disciples waiting for the Parousia, not only has the support of the Evangelists, but also fits in with—one might almost say, is demanded by—the situation which much other evidence proves to have been foreseen by Jesus himself. If he intended by these descriptions to teach only the duty of alertness in a crisis, it is surely very extraordinary that he should have felt it necessary to throw on to the screen so often the same scene of servants whose absent master has left them in charge, who do not know when he will return, but do know that, when he returns, he will expect to find not only that they are then ready to receive him, but that they have been loyally doing their duty in his absence. The theory labours under other difficulties also. It purports to explain as a *present* crisis the crisis for which the hearers must be prepared, whereas the passages all suggest on the contrary a crisis near at hand, but not yet actually present.[4] It is unsatisfactory, from the point of view of the theory we are considering, to have to say with reference to this, " The crisis which He brought about was not a single momentary event but a developing situation . . . ", and to explain that the parables " were originally intended to refer to a situation already existing, but subject to unexpected developments at

---

preted the eschatological parables as meant to enforce simply the human sense of responsibility (Schweitzer, *L.J.F.* 229 = *Quest*, 230). A. T. Cadoux (*Parables*, 185–193) applies them to the need of seizing opportunities rather than to the Last Judgment.

[1] Dodd, *Parables*, 174.

[2] Dodd, *Parables*, 150, 159, 165, 172.

[3] Dodd, *Parables*, 152f., 157f., 160, 162f., etc......

[4] Dr. Dodd seems to admit this. " Jesus ", he says (*Parables*, 171), " is all through concerned to prepare His followers for the time of stress. The parables, rightly understood, take their place in that series of warnings and appeals ". Again, " This was the moral situation which found dramatic expression in the tragic forebodings of the ruin of the Jewish community and the destruction of the Temple " (200). " . . . So Jesus was concerned to prepare His hearers for the unexpected . . . " (202).

any moment . . . ".[1] To grant so much as that, especially if one goes further and includes the destruction of Jerusalem among the possible developments, is virtually to abandon the plea that the parables can all be given an application within the context of the ministry of Jesus, and to withdraw the contention that the reference of them to the expected Parousia was not part of the speaker's original purpose.[2]

It is therefore on several counts preferable to give these passages their natural and primâ facie meaning, not refusing of course to recognize the possibility that the wording of them may have been edited and enlarged at certain points in the light of the experiences of the early Church, but seeing in them on the whole the admonitions given in advance by Jesus himself regarding the steadfastness, diligence, and unity of spirit of which his Disciples would obviously stand in constant need during the difficult period of such uncertain length which must elapse until his coming-again.

(13) The evidence does not allow us to assert with any confidence that Jesus expected, and told his Disciples, that, after death had removed him from their earthly sight, he would be present with them either individually or in their corporate gatherings in a spiritual or mystical way. There is, indeed, good ground for believing that he thought of himself as genuinely *represented* by any who, because they were in need of help, or because they were appealing on his behalf, had the same sort of claim on the sympathy and attention of men as he himself had. Thus, " whoever receives one of such little children in my name receives me ; and whoever receives me receives not me, but Him who sent me " (Mk. ix. 37 = Lk. ix. 48 = Mt. xviii. 5). " He who listens to you listens to me ; and he who rejects you rejects me ; but he who rejects me rejects Him who sent me " (Lk. x. 16 = Mt. x. 40 Q). These are well-attested sayings ; and there is no reason to doubt their substantial genuineness. The pictorial description of the Last Judgment (Mt. xxv. 31–46 M) rests upon less-good documentary

---

[1] Dodd, *Parables*, 165f., 170f.

[2] Dr. Dodd acknowledges that this eschatological application may be at least as early as a very few years after the Resurrection (*Parables*, 168–170).

Among his subsidiary arguments is the plea that verbs γρηγορέω and ἀγρυπνέω mean to "keep awake", not to "watch". "The change in meaning in the English word ' watch ' makes it a most misleading translation " (*Parables*, 155 n. 1). But, even supposing the conception of watching is one not necesarily implied by verbs meaning " ' to keep awake ', with the implication of alertness ", the two ideas are not far apart : and even on Dr. Dodd's own interpretation of the Parables, the notion of " watching " is as much required as on the more usual exegesis.

authority, and lies open to certain critical difficulties affecting its structure and contents : but its assumption of the identity of the Master with his needy followers only puts a little more strikingly what the better-attested passages assert in substance. " The King " welcomes those on his right hand into the Kingdom because of their personal services to him when in need of food, drink, hospitality, clothing, or comfort in sickness or in prison ; and when they ask in surprise when it was that these services were rendered, the King replies, " Truly I tell you, inasmuch as ye did it to one of these least brothers of mine, ye did it to me ". Those on the left hand are correspondingly told, " Truly I tell you, inasmuch as ye did it not to one of these least, neither did ye do it to me ! " (Mt. xxv. 40, 45 M). Such an imaginative extension on Jesus' part of his representative presence would not be too alien from Hebraïc modes of thought for him to be likely to make it ; and as we have seen, there is good documentary evidence to show that he did so.

But the idea that he would be spiritually or mystically present with his followers belongs to a different range of thought, one remote from Palestinian habits, and hardly likely to have dwelt in the same mind alongside the notion of a period of absence to be terminated by a triumphant and glorious visible return. True it is that in the first century certain Christians (notably Paul and the Fourth Evangelist) had experiences which led them to think of the risen Lord holding mystical communion with themselves and with other Christians and groups of Christians. This idea is one of the most striking characteristics of Paul's religion, whereas in the Fourth Gospel it has developed so far as almost wholly to supplant the Synoptic idea of the Lord's personal return. Doubtless too there were many others who were privileged to enjoy the same sense of Christ's unseen presence, though we are not in a position to say that the experience was a general one, common to all or even to most Christians. There would be many, of course, who would believe in its reality simply on the strength of others' testimony, especially as regards the Lord's presence with his Disciples when met together in a group in his name. But the passages in which Jesus himself promises such a privilege are—among the Synoptic Gospels— confined to Mt. " Again I truly tell you, that if two of you shall agree on earth concerning anything for which they shall ask, it shall come to them from my Father Who is in the heavens. For there are not two or three assembled together

in my name, with whom I am not—in the midst of them "
(Mt. xviii. 19f. M or m). " Go ye and make disciples of all the
nations, baptizing them into the name of the Father and of the
Son and of the Holy Spirit, teaching them 'to observe all the
injunctions I have laid upon you. And behold ! I am with
you all the days until the consummation of the age ! "
(Mt. xxviii. 19f. M or m).

Here we have another exemplification of what we have
already observed in the case of " the Church ", namely, that in
Mt. we find sayings ascribed to Jesus, not on the basis of some
early and satisfactory record, but because the experience and
needs of the Evangelist's contemporaries led him to regard them
as an edifying expression of what all imagined must have
been the Lord's meaning (see above, pp. 22, 307–310).
Sayings (particularly post-Resurrection sayings) which have
exclusively-Matthæan attestation, and which furthermore
reflect a different order of thought from that which we know
on much better authority to have been customary with Jesus,
are not supported by evidence strong enough to warrant our
accepting them as historically-genuine,[1] though of course they
may still be religiously true and of great spiritual value. On
the other hand, when once the Church had learned to recognize
and to treasure the idea of spiritual or mystical fellowship
between the believer and the Lord, it was only natural that
sayings foreshadowing such fellowship should come to be
ascribed to him in the less-strictly historical records of his
teaching. Among the Agrapha (see above, p. 14) there is preserved a saying of this character, couched in almost pantheistic
terms. " Wherever there are two, they are not without God ;
and where there is one alone, I tell you I am with him. Raise
the stone, and there thou wilt find me : cleave the wood and I
am there ".[2]

[1] Cf. Weinel, *Theol.* 67f.
[2] Preuschen, *Antilegomena*, 22 (4), 31 (39) ; James, *Apocr. N.T.* 27 (x).
J. H. Ropes (in H.*D.B*. extra vol. 344b [b], 347a [30]) thinks that a case can
be made out in favour of the genuineness of this saying, though not
conclusively.

CHAPTER V

THE CONSUMMATION

(1) Various views have been held regarding the relation
which Jesus believed to exist between the Fall of Jerusalem
and his own Parousia. (2) He clearly thought of the former
as preceding the latter, and of both alike as following from
Israel's rejection of him ; but otherwise he did not directly
relate them to one another. (3) His views regarding the
Last Judgment were to some extent affected by the Parousia-
prophecy ; (4) in particular, this prophecy tended to foster
the conception of himself as the Judge. (5) He used a
variety of terms and figures in order to set forth the rewards
(6) and punishments which would be meted out. (7) He
made frequent use of the picture of the great Messianic Feast,
(8) providing a practical anticipation of it at the Last Supper,
(9) and finally depicting it as a scene of gladness, dominion,
and glory for himself and his faithful followers.

(1) We have seen that Jesus foretold the siege and destruction of Jerusalem and also his own return in glory. We have
now to consider how in his own mind he related these two
future events to one another. As the records of his sayings
about them now lie before us in the Gospels, the sayings seem
to be inextricably intermixed (see above, pp. 273–277) ; and
we are compelled to disentangle one series from the other in
order to get anything approaching a coherent picture. In the
nature of things, however, we should expect some positive and
definite relationship to have existed between the two anticipations, seeing that both arose out of Jesus' certainty that his
enemies would compass his death, and both were expected to
materialize before the generation then living had died out. A
very generally accepted treatment of the question as to how
the two stood in relation to one another is to take advantage
of the supposed habitual practice of Jewish prophets to put
closely alongside of one another predictions concerning future
events destined to be separated by wide intervals of time.[1]
Such a theory relieved one of all necessity, either of supposing
Jesus or the Evangelists to have been mistaken, or of seeking
for some recondite interpretation of the Parousia-prophecies,

[1] So, e.g., Salmond in H.D.B. i. 750b.

because nineteen centuries have elapsed without any Parousia of the kind apparently foretold having occurred. It is impossible, however, not to feel that the advantages of the theory are secured at too high a price; for it must be obvious to any one who reads the Gospels with an unprejudiced mind that Jesus did not intend to foretell events so far distant from his own age as our own or the times posterior to it. The evidence, both direct and inferential, leaves us no option but to conclude that he gave his hearers to understand that both of the two great consequences of his rejection would come about within the lifetime of that generation. Nor are we much better off if we attempt to interpret the time-connexion apparently intended in our sources as simply a logical or causal connexion,[1] and ascribe to the predictions a certain timeless significance, taking the Fall of Jerusalem as a mere exemplification of the Divine Judgment involved in the very existence of the Kingdom. The great particularity and emphasis with which the actual occurrence of the Parousia is foretold makes it impossible to regard it as other than a particular event expected to occur within the next forty years at most, and completely rules out as alien to the thought of Jesus himself any attempt to interpret his Parousia as a gradual process of world-history.[2] A still more desperate effort to solve the problem without abandoning any main traditional assumption regarding the authority of Scripture is the idea that, shortly or immediately after the Fall of Jerusalem in 70 A.D., Jesus did actually return to earth, as he had (to all appearance) said that he would.[3]

A somewhat less-difficult, but still unsatisfying, solution is to identify the Parousia with some event which is known to have actually happened. Events conceivably so identifiable are the Transfiguration, Pentecost (with the ensuing triumphant propagation of the Gospel), and the Fall of Jerusalem itself—particularly the last of these.[4] For it would obviously be a great simplification of our problem if the two events, the

---

[1] Cf. A. E. Taylor in *Hibbert Journ.* xii. 459 (Jan. 1914); H. H. Farmer in *Congreg. Quart.* viii (1930) 276; Dodd, *Parables*, 71.

[2] Holtzmann, *Theol.* i. 389f.

[3] This was the contention of E. Hampden-Cook's treatise, *The Christ has come. The Second Advent an Event of the Past*, 1894 : second edition, 1895 ; third, 1905.

[4] Cf. Farrar, *Early Days of Christianity* (1882), 489 (" It is strange that these distinct limitations " [as to the time of the Second Advent] " should not be regarded as a decisive proof that the Fall of Jerusalem was, in the fullest sense, the Second Advent of the Son of Man which was primarily contemplated by the earliest voices of prophecy ") ; Muirhead, *Eschatol. of Jes.* 139 ; Manson, *Teaching*, 279.

Gospel-references to which are so bewilderingly interlocked, should prove after all to have been really meant to be one. Attractive, however, as the theory is on this account, we ought to recognize that much unnatural forcing of the plain meaning of the terms is required, if we are to plead that, when Jesus spoke of the coming of the Son of Man, he really had in mind nothing more than one aspect, or significant phase, of the events of 70 A.D.[1]

(2) The fact of the matter would seem to be that Jesus did not directly relate the approaching doom of Jerusalem to his own expected Parousia, beyond picturing both as the consequences of Israel's rejection of himself, and indirectly suggesting that the Parousia would follow shortly after the destruction of Jerusalem (for, while both were to occur within that generation, it was inconceivable that the Parousia should *precede* the war between Israel and Rome). Whether he placed them imaginatively in such chronological proximity as really to justify that extremely-close juxtaposition seen in certain parts of the Gospels may be reasonably doubted : it is, however, curious to note that, while the Evangelists on the one hand link the two events very closely together, they also evince at certain points a desire to explain (through the medium of sayings ascribed to Jesus) why it was that, though Jerusalem had now fallen, the Messiah had not come.[2]

It is finally legitimate to observe that, while Jesus certainly did not identify his Coming or the Coming of the Kingdom with the destruction of Jerusalem, this destruction was in point of fact a historical proof of Israel's folly in rejecting him—in more Biblical language, a sign of the judgment of God (see above, pp. 278f.) : as such it did stand in a positive relationship to the future triumph of himself and his cause which he foreshadowed in the form of an apocalyptic Parousia.[3]

(3) We have considered above in some detail the thoughts of Jesus regarding the coming Judgment, and the Rewards

[1] Cf. Muirhead, *Eschatol. of Jes.* 132f. ; Manson, *Teaching*, 281.

[2] Cf. Holtzmann, *Synopt.* 283 (with reference to [Mk. xiii. 10 =] Mt. xxiv. 14 [" And this Gospel of the Kingdom will be proclaimed throughout the whole world for a testimony to all the nations ; and then will the end come "] he says, " . . . Solche Eintragungen dienen aber nur dazu, den Gang der zu rasch ablaufenden Weltuhr in den rein apokalyptischen Stücken einigermaassen zu hemmen . . . "), *Theol.* i. 388f. ; Bacon, *Matthew*, 68f., 77 ; Major in *Mission*, etc. 160 ; Manson in *Mission*, etc. 628.

[3] It is not therefore correct to dissociate them as completely as Dr. T. W. Manson does (*Teaching*, 281 : " . . . The ruthless suppression by a great military empire of an insane rebellion in an outlying part of its territory has as much—or as little—to do with the coming of the Kingdom of God in power as the suppresion of the Indian Mutiny "). Cf. Dodd, *Parables*, 71, 76f., 88, 170.

and Punishments to be therein meted out to men. We studied in the first place his general conceptions about reward (as "life" or "salvation") and punishment (as "loss" or "destruction") (see above, pp. 208–218), then his application of these conceptions to the conditions of the life after death (pp. 220–223) ; and in the third place we studied his utterances regarding the Resurrection of the Dead, the Last Judgment, and the forms which reward and punishment would then take (pp. 224–245), in so far as these utterances did not seem to be directly connected with his expectation of death, absence, and return. We have now to take account of certain special ideas regarding these topics which *are* more or less directly related to the Parousia-prospect : but in doing so, we must bear in mind that Jesus' general words on the subject form the constant background of the more specific references, and that these latter are purely supplementary to the teaching that has already been studied. The uncertainties of exegesis will probably involve us in a little overlapping of the evidence to be adduced : and we shall find that this evidence does not give us a unified and self-consistent programme, but is made up of a number of disparate items, the mutual relations of which are largely left undetermined.

In regard to the institution of the Judgment itself, the only evidence we have is of a secondary character. Of the more-explicit passages, one occurs in the somewhat-dubious context called " the Little Apocalypse " : " Then will men see the Son of Man coming in clouds with great power and glory : and then will he send forth the angels, and will gather together the elect from the four winds from the furthest point of earth to the furthest point of heaven " (Mk. xiii. 26f. [=Lk. xxi. 27f.] = Mt. xxiv. 30f.). The language recalls some still more dubious passages in the interpretation of the Parables of the Tares and the Net (Mt. xiii. 40–42 M ; Mt. xiii. 49f. M : see above, p. 241). Here too we must place the detailed picture of the Judgment of " all the Gentiles " (Mt. xxv. 31–46 M), a picture difficult to estimate and expound,[1] not only because of its exclusively-Matthæan attestation, but also because the distinction it draws between " the Son of Man " and " the King " (see above, p. 100) and the specification of " the Gentiles " as the ones judged raise the question as to how this Judgment is to be related to the universal Judgment (which of course must include Jesus' own followers and other Jews).

(4) It has been argued above (pp. 228f. [6]) that, in those

---

[1] Cf. Holtzmann, *Theol.* i. 393–395.

references to the Judgment which seem to be independent of the Parousia-prospect, Jesus always assumed that the Judge would be God the Father, and assigned to the Son of Man the function of witness only. The Son of Man, when he comes in his glory, will acknowledge before God any one who has acknowledged Jesus and his followers before men, but will be ashamed of and disown any one who has been ashamed of or disowned Jesus and his followers before men (Mk. viii. 38 = Lk. ix. 26 [= Mt. xvi. 27] ; Lk. xii. 8f. = Mt. x. 32f. Q). Possibly an echo of the same thought is to be heard in the words of the Penitent Brigand, " Jesus, remember me when thou comest in " (or " with ") " thy Kingdom " (Lk. xxiii. 42 L).

But while normally in Jesus' mind God figured as the future Judge, the whole picture was sufficiently fluid to allow the idea to form itself that Judgment would be exercised by Jesus himself. It was easy to pass from the conviction that men's eternal destiny would depend on the attitude they took up towards him (see above, p. 78 [18]), to the idea that he would himself be their judge.[1] Hence—beside the picture already noted (pp. 228f.) of Jesus as householder shutting the door on the unworthy—we get allusions to him sitting in glory with his chief friends on his right and left hand (Mk. x. 37, 40 = Mt. xx. 21 [" in thy Kingdom "], 23), to these friends sitting on thrones " judging " (i.e., governing) the twelve tribes of Israel (Lk. xxii. 30b L ; Mt. xix. 28b M), and to persons " standing before the Son of Man " (Lk. xxi. 36 L).[2] The frequent employment of the illustration of a householder or master returning after a period of absence to investigate the conduct of his servants, for the purpose of enforcing the need of loyalty pending the Parousia, again naturally suggested the idea that the returning Lord would himself be the judge. This suggestion comes out most sharply in the termination of the Lucan version of the Parable of the Servants entrusted with Money : " These enemies of mine who did not want me to be king over them, bring them hither and slaughter them before me " (Lk. xix. 27 L : see above, pp. 272f.) : but it is implicit in several other Parables about Servants (e.g., Lk. xii. 35-38 L ; Lk. xii. 42-46 = Mt. xxiv. 45-51 Q).

[1] Cf. Holtzmann, *Theol.* i. 395 ; Von Gall, Βασιλεία, 425-430 ; V. J. K. Brook in *The Bible and Modern Religious Thought*, II. iii. 33f. (Mar. 1928).

[2] I doubt whether the references to " the Day " or " Days " of the Son of Man in Lk. xvii. 22, 24 (cf. the variant reading), 26, 30 (=Mt. xxiv. 27, 37, 39) can reasonably be brought into close connexion with the idea of the Judgment (cf. Holtzmann, *Theol.* i. 393 top : " . . . zum ' Tag ' (im Sinne eines gerichtlichen Termins) ".

Not only may the idea of himself as judge have thus naturally occurred to Jesus' mind, but it was bound to be accentuated in the thought of the early Church as a ready and obvious means of expressing the exalted glory of the Risen Lord. The Gospels give us two perfectly-clear instances of the process, both (as we might expect) in Mt. In the interpretations of the Parables of the Tares and the Net, the Son of Man through his angels inflicts punishment on the unworthy (Mt. xiii. 39–43, 49f. : the gathering of the elect by the Son of Man in Mk. xiii. 26f. [= Lk. xxi. 27f.] = Mt. xxiv. 30f. does indeed *suggest* that he is to judge, but very much less directly than do the purely-Matthæan passages). And the Matthæan version of Mk. viii. 38, in which Jesus speaks of the Son of Man being ashamed of certain persons " when he comes in the glory of his Father, with *the* holy angels ", runs, " For the Son of Man is destined to come in the glory of his Father, with *his* angels ; and then will he repay each man according to his conduct " (Mt. xvi. 27 m, echoing Psa. lxii. 12 and Prov. xxiv. 12). All this adds to our hesitation in accepting Mt. xxv. 31–46 M, in which " the King " (i.e., Jesus) himself fulfils all the concrete functions of judgeship, as a close report of what he had explicitly said (see above, p. 321).

(5) The nature of the reward to be meted out to those who at the Judgment receive a sentence of acquittal and commendation is indicated only with much vagueness by the use of a number of different terms. How vague indeed the conception was is revealed by the fact that the Penitent Brigand is apparently promised the full measure of heavenly reward on the day of his death, irrespective of any final Judgment whatever : " To-day shalt thou be with me in Paradise " (Lk. xxiii. 43 L : see above, pp. 294f.). The acquitted are variously described as being acknowledged by the Son of Man " before the angels of God " (Lk. xii. 8 = Mt. x. 32 Q), being remembered by Jesus when he comes in (or with) his Kingdom (Lk. xxiii. 42 L), and " standing before the Son of Man " (Lk. xxi. 36 L). " He that has endured to the end ", i.e., despite the fierce persecutions that will occur during the Lord's absence, " he will be saved " (Mk. xiii. 13b [= Lk. xxi. 19 : " In your endurance will ye gain possession of your souls "] = Mt. x. 22b = Mt. xxiv. 13 : *not* " the Little Apocalypse "). From the picture of the Waiting Servants comes the idea of joyful promotion to a moe extended and responsible service (Lk. xii. 43f. = Mt. xxiv. 46f. Q [" . . . Truly I tell you, he will set him over all he possesses "] : cf. Lk. xix. 17, 19 L = Mt. xxv. 21, 23 M).

Another touch from the same quarter is the description of the pleased master making his well-behaved menials recline at the table, and girding up his own loins and himself waiting upon them (Lk. xii. 37 L). This last scene links up with the great idea of the Messianic Feast, with which we must deal presently. It is hinted at also in those allusions, already quoted (p. 322), to Jesus sitting with his friends in glory : in one of them, in fact, Jesus promises the Twelve that they shall " eat and drink at my table in my Kingdom " (Lk. xxii. 30 L : not in Mt. xix. 28b M). In the descriptive scene in Mt. xxv. 31-46 M, the righteous are thus addressed, " Come hither, ye blessed of my Father ; inherit the Kingdom that has been prepared for you ever since the foundation of the world . . . " (Mt. xxv. 34 M) ; and at the close of the proceedings they " go away into eternal life " (Mt. xxv. 46 M). Side by side with this description we may set the conclusion of the probably-ungenuine interpretation of the Parable of the Tares : " Then will the righteous shine out like the sun in the Kingdom of their Father " (Mt. xiii. 43 M or m). Nor must we forget that all that has been said above about rewards in general (pp. 208-211 [2]), about eternal life (pp. 214f. [4], pp. 234-236 [14]), about salvation (pp. 215-217 [5], 236f. [15f.]), about the Kingdom (pp. 229-234 [7-13]), about Paradise (pp. 220f. [2]), and about Heaven (pp. 237-239 [17]), forms a body of teaching on the subject of final rewards to which these additional pieces of evidence here quoted are but supplementary.

(6) Conversely, " he who has disowned me in the presence of men will be disowned " (i.e., by the Son of Man) " in the presence of the angels of God " (Lk. xii. 9 [cf. 8] = Mt. x. 33 [cf. 32]). " Whoever is ashamed of me and of my (follower)s in this adulterous and sinful generation, of him will the Son of Man in his turn be ashamed, whensoever he comes in the glory of his Father with the holy angels " (Mk. viii. 38 = Lk. ix. 26 [= Mt. xvi. 27]). Some of the predictions of woe which have been quoted above as referring to the calamities incidental to the Roman conquest (see above, pp. 272-276 [11-14]) would either, like the Parable of the Wicked Vinedressers (Mk. xii. 1-12 = Lk. xx. 9-19 = Mt. xxi. 33-46), lend themselves to a more-general eschatological interpretation, or, like the sayings in the great discourses of Lk. xvii and Mk. xiii and their parallels, are closely interwoven with allusions to the Parousia (see above, pp. 318-320), so that they are taken by some to be descriptions of the final doom of the wicked at or after the Last Judgment. The various pictures of the Watching Servants

supply various accounts of the punishments inflicted on the disloyal. "But if that slave say in his heart, ' My master is a long time coming ', and begin to beat the boys and the slave-girls, and to eat and drink and get drunk, the master of that slave will come on a day he does not expect, and at an hour he does not know, and will cut him apart,[1] and appoint him his lot among the untrustworthy " (Lk. xii. 45f. = Mt. xxiv. 48–51 Q [m adds, " There there will be weeping and gnashing of teeth "]). " That slave who knew his master's will, but did not make preparation according to his will, will be beaten with many (strokes) : but he who did not know his master's will, and (therefore) did things deserving strokes, will be beaten with few. And everyone to whom much has been given—much will be demanded from him : and he to whom men have committed much—from him will they ask more " (Lk. xii. 47f. L)—possibly a hint of what might happen to the Gentiles as distinct from the more-enlightened Jews (see above, p. 159 top). The Parable of the Servants entrusted with Money illustrates the principle whereby the idle and unproductive are deprived of such opportunities of service as they had been given, but had neglected to use (Lk. xix. 24, 26 L = Mt. xxv. 28f. M). The Matthæan version of it concludes, " And cast ye the unprofitable slave into the outer darkness : there there will be weeping and gnashing of teeth " (Mt. xxv. 30 M) ; while the Lucan concludes, " These enemies of mine who did not want me to be king over them, bring them hither and slaughter them before me " (Lk. xix. 27 L : see above, pp. 272f.). In the description of the Judgment in Mt. xxv. 31–46 M, the uncharitable Gentiles are told, " Depart from me, ye cursed, into the eternal fire prepared for the devil and his angels . . . " (Mt. xxv. 41 M) ; and at the end " these will go away into eternal punishment " (Mt. xxv. 46 M : see below, pp. 338–345). In the lesson drawn from the Parable of the Unjust Judge, we read of the vengeance which God is expected speedily to inflict upon those who have oppressed the elect (Lk. xviii. 6–8a, probably l) ; but it is doubtful whether this addition to the Parable actually comes from the lips of Jesus. Finally we must note that the evidence

---

[1] Διχοτομήσει αὐτόν can hardly mean literally " will cut him in two " (for what purpose would then be served by appointing him his lot among the untrustworthy ?), but *either* " will severely scourge him " (a conjectural rendering, but one supported by the analogy of δέρω, which means literally " I flay ", but can mean simply " I buffet " [John xviii. 23]), *or* " will separate him " from his fellows (see Burkitt, *Evang. Da-Meph.* ii. 296, and *Jesus Christ*, etc. 72f. ; Littmann in *Z.N.W.* xxxiv [1935] 24 ; Manson in *Mission*, etc. 410 [the latter rendering rests on a supposed confusion between two very similar Aramaic words]).

collected above regarding the teaching of Jesus about punishment in general (pp. 211–214 [3]), about loss or destruction (pp. 217f. [6], 236f. [15f.]), about Hades, Gehenna, and the outer darkness (pp. 221f. [3], 239–243 [18–20]), must also be added to what has been quoted in this section, in order to complete the sum of the material for the study of Jesus' beliefs regarding the future punishment of the wicked.

(7) It will be remembered that, in enumerating the forms in which Jesus cast his anticipation of the final rewards in the Kingdom of God, we noted his frequent references to the great Messianic Feast (see above, pp. 243–245). There is clear evidence that he had this joyful climax constantly in mind as representing the ultimate and supreme bliss in store for man, and that he frequently warned his hearers against the peril of being excluded from it as the most appalling punishment that could befall them. It is clear too that this picture of final happiness was not dependent on any expectation he might have had of his own death at the hands of men. Yet when that expectation shaped itself, the anticipation of the Messianic Feast naturally became, if anything, even more prominent and concrete. I have included in the evidence collected above a reference to Mt. xxv. 21, 23 M—from the Parable of the Servants entrusted with Money—as containing a parabolic hint at the future banquet : " Come and share your master's enjoyment " (see above, p. 244 n. 1). That Parable presupposes the Parousia (and therefore the Passion also) ; and if so, it really falls to be considered here—along with the Parable of the Wise and Foolish Virgins at the wedding-feast (Mt. xxv. 1–13 M), and the description of the master, on his return from wedding-festivities, making his servants take their places at table and himself waiting upon them (Lk. xii. 36f .: see above, p. 324 top).

(8) It was consonant with his spirit and method to bring this particular piece of teaching home to the minds of himself and his Disciples and hearers by symbolic action as well as by the spoken word : and we have already seen (p. 243) that, when he fed the crowd, he was presenting a symbolic anticipation in dramatic form of the happy Feast of the future.

The other great occasion on which he gave an object-lesson of this kind was at the Last Supper, when the thought of his approaching departure and of what was to follow it weighed heavily upon his mind. Amid much that is obscure in connexion with what took place and what was said and meant at that last meal, this at least is clear : for Jesus it was a solemn anticipation of the Messianic Feast in the Kingdom of Heaven, which he was apparently expecting to enjoy in the very near future. According to Mk. xiv. 25 = Mt. xxvi. 29, after distributing the bread and the wine, he added, " Truly I tell you, I shall by no means ever drink again of the produce of the vine, until that day when I drink it new in the Kingdom of God ". In Lk. we have what looks like an independent version of the story : ' And he said to them, " With longing have I longed to eat this Passover with you before I suffered. For I tell you, I shall by no means eat of it until it is fulfilled in the Kingdom of God " ' (Lk. xxii. 15f. L). After giving thanks for the cup, he bids them divide it among themselves (Lk. xxii. 17 L), adding, " For I tell you, I shall by no means drink henceforth of the produce of the vine until the Kingdom of God comes " (Lk. xxii. 18 L) : then follows in Lk. xxii. 19 the distribution of the loaf. Judging from what we have seen elsewhere, Jesus expected to pass immediately at death to Paradise, where presumably the heavenly banquet awaited him. His Disciples could not join him there until after his Parousia : hence the words " with you " in Mt. xxvi. 29 are probably a gratuitous insertion of m. Yet, as we shall see in a moment, Jesus seems at this point to have been thinking of the interval that was to pass as only a very brief one. He looks beyond the tragedy and gloom of the immediate future to that brighter scene into which he is confident he will soon be Divinely translated, and in which the wine he will drink will therefore be new wine (cf. Isa. xxv. 6) : and as the Passover symbolized for Israel deliverance from Egypt, so the meal in the upper room symbolized his deliverance from the bondage of his earthly sorrow.[1]

(9) According to the Lucan arrangement, Jesus made yet one more allusion to the coming feast that night, before they went out to the Mount of Olives. " Ye are the men ", he said, " who have stood by me throughout my trials : and I assign to you—just as my Father has assigned to me—royal rank, that ye may eat and drink at my table in my Kingdom ; and ye shall sit on thrones, judging the twelve tribes of Israel " (Lk. xxii. 28–30 L).[2] The passage recalls in its general tone

---

[1] Holtzmann, *Synopt.* 174 ; Schweitzer, *Mystery*, 271 ; Montefiore, *S.G.*² I. 339, II. 587 ; D. C. Simpson, in *H.C.L.M.K.* 164 ; Dodd, *Parables*, 56 with n. 1 ; Otto, *Kingdom*, 286–290.

[2] Possibly we ought to translate, " I assign to you—just as my Father has assigned royal rank to me—the (privilege) of eating and drinking ", etc. (see V. Taylor, *Sacrifice*, 188f.). The Matthæan parallel (Mt. xix. 28b M) says nothing about the feast, and by saying " twelve thrones " specifically limits the promise to the Twelve.

the earlier allusion to the places on Jesus' right and left hand when he sits in his glory (Mk. x. 37, 40 = Mt. xx. 21 [m substitutes " Kingdom " for " glory "], 23).[1]

[1] On Lk. xxii. 28–30 and Mt. xix. 28b, cf. Holtzmann, *Synopt.* 412 ; Manson, *Teaching*, 268 ; Otto, *Kingdom*, 274f., 317 ; Dodd, *Parables*, 72–74, 95f.

The most obvious and immediate implicate of Israel's refusal to follow Jesus was Israel's contrivance of his execution. Jesus foresaw this fatal issue, and made no attempt to escape it. He believed that, by submissively yielding himself to death, he would, like the suffering Servant described in Isa. liii, be the means of bringing about that widespread repentance which men had, despite his teaching and his works, so far failed to show. Yet even so, the sorrow and tragedy of his rejection were unspeakably deep : for not only was it impossible for him to foresee how early or how complete this repentance might be, but it was clear that, in repudiating Jesus as Messiah, the Jews were repudiating the only policy which would save them from revolting against Rome, and thus save them from the horrors of a Roman conquest. To the last, Jesus struggled passionately to prevail upon them to heed his warnings.

He expected that immediately after his death he would depart into Paradise, whence—after the lapse of an undefined interval (now estimated as comparatively short, now lengthened to nearly the lifetime of a generation)—to return to earth in glory by the power of God. Pending this Return, his Disciples were to proclaim the Good News of the Kingdom, as he had proclaimed it, to all and sundry, though he did not *explicitly* enjoin a missionizing of the Gentile peoples : they were bravely and loyally to endure persecution in his name, to remain in loving fellowship with one another, and above all to keep themselves prepared, by steady obedience to his teaching, for his reappearance, whensover that might befall.

He seems to have expected the Roman conquest and the destruction of Jerusalem to occur in the fairly-near future, and his own return to follow it after the lapse of some years. His Return would inaugurate the great " Coming " of the Kingdom of God, involving the Resurrection of the Dead and the Last Judgment. At this last the final punishments and rewards would be meted out to all according to each man's personal desert. The place of punishment would be the fiery Gehenna ; the place of reward the Kingdom of the Heavens. Jesus' favourite picture of the reward of the righteous was that of the great Messianic Feast, at which he himself would preside in royal power and glory, with the Patriarchs and his own redeemed ones reclining at table beside him.

CONCLUSION

CONCLUSION

All human knowledge of reality is a product of two factors. One of these is constituted by the objective data which make up the reality to be known ; the other consists of the conditions imposed by the structure of the mind that knows. To disentangle the contributions made by each of these factors in our cognitive experience is assuredly a philosophical task of no little difficulty : but it does not need a great deal of penetration to realize that every such experience does involve the presence of these two elements—the subjective or a priori, and the empirical, objective, or a posteriori.

In the case of historical knowledge, the objective consists ideally of the past events themselves : but inasmuch as these, because they *are* past, cannot be directly witnessed afresh, the records which have been made of them and are still accessible constitute the objective data : the subjective is provided by the historian's love of truth and his intellectual power to assess, to compare, to combine, and to interpret the sundry probabilities concerning what lies behind the extant records.

In the case of religious knowledge, the objective is given in the Nature and Will of God and in His revelation of Himself in the experience which others have had of Him : the subjective lies in the ethical and spiritual insight of the theologian, and his general aptitude for and responsiveness to the things of the Spirit.

Now it is generally acknowledged and indeed a patent fact that Christianity is an historical religion ; and as such the understanding and exposition of it involve as it were two types of objective data and two distinguishable if closely-related subjective capacities. The interrelation and mutual adjustment of these four factors constitute a problem of very considerable complexity.

In the Middle Ages early Christian history was dealt with only on certain fixed lines laid down by the supposedly-inerrant tradition of the Roman Catholic Church. The Renaissance revealed the fact that the observance of these limits had involved, and was in the nature of things bound to involve, the acceptance of numerous errors as if they were truths. The German Aufklärung served itself heir to the convictions of

333

the Renaissance in this respect, and took it for granted that historical inquiry, even that concerned with Holy Scripture and with the Christian beginnings, must be conducted in obedience to the simple laws of evidence, irrespective of all religious and theological preference for this conclusion or for that. Liberal Protestantism, making the same assumption, popularized what came to be known as " the historical method ", and produced with its aid that rich crop of conclusions affecting Biblical history and literature which are designated generally as " Higher Criticism ". Winning decisive victories first in the field of Old-Testament study, and convincing nearly all competent and open minds of its reliability and its value, Liberal Protestantism saw no reason why the same method should not be equally valid for the treatment of New-Testament matters. And so, by its help, large strides were made towards the solution of the Synoptic Problem, and valuable light was thrown on early Christian history and literature.

When, however, this same method came to be applied to the life and teaching of Jesus, questions of graver import began to emerge. The criticism levelled at the liberal version of the Gospel-story by Schweitzer and other writers of the eschatological school, and the consequent and subsequent courses followed by Christian thinkers, have been briefly outlined in the Introduction (see above, pp. 3–9). As there explained, our own study in these pages has, in intention at least, been carried on in loyal regard for the objective evidence, so far as this is available and can be subjected to comparative scrutiny. Before, however, we proceed to base our concluding comments on the results at which we have arrived, a further word must be said in vindication of the method that has here been adopted.

The general post-War reaction against liberalism has within the last fifteen years been showing itself in various theological quarters in the form of an enhanced " recoil from historicism ". It is not very easy to describe precisely the viewpoint of this recoil : but in general the ground of it seems to be a conviction that the early records of Jesus' life should be approached only as an integral part of the whole early Christian message, a message which embodies a unique and final revelation of God centred in the Incarnation, Death, Resurrection, Ascension, and Heavenly Lordship of Jesus Christ. Those who thus recoil have repeatedly pointed out that none of the authors of our various Gospel-documents wrote in order to supply merely-biographical information concerning Jesus of Nazareth :

they wrote to create and sustain Christian faith in him as the Son of God, through whom alone salvation may be had. That being so, arguments based on the contents of the Synoptic Gospels alone, without regard to the primitive Christian exaltation of Jesus as Lord, will (it is contended) give distorted or erroneous results : nay more, the very attempt to get behind the Gospel-records to a real " historic Jesus ", distinguishable from the Christ of faith, is itself an illegitimate attempt, because it means transporting the records to an alien atmosphere, and ignoring the only interpretation of them in which their authors and first readers were interested.[1]

Now let it be willingly conceded that the historical data concerning Jesus embrace more than the Synoptic Gospels, that they embrace the creation of the Christian Church from an impulse which he imparted,[2] that they embrace furthermore the impression made by him upon the first generations of his followers—an impression so profound that such a work as the Fourth Gospel could be written about him, and Divine rank assigned to him, within three-quarters of a century after his death. Let us also grant that these considerations, taken together, call for a theological, i.e., a metaphysical, explanation, and that neither this nor any other historical or theological quest can be pursued except under the influence and control of subjective factors which, in conditioning, may possibly hinder as well as help the acquisition of truth. Let it moreover be recognized that reverence for Jesus is one of the conditions for rightly understanding him, a fact ignored by some scholars, who treat any manifestation of personal religious or moral interest in his story as apologetic and therefore unscientific.[3]

Yet all these considerations do not alter the fact that, unless we use to the very utmost our best powers of examining and weighing the evidence, and of drawing inferences from it

[1] As illustrations of the tendency here alluded to, cf. H.-D. Wendland, *Eschatologie*, 2–4, and Dodd, *Hist. and the Gosp.* 11ff., 36 ; and for a sketch of the situation, Windisch, *Bergpredigt*, 1–5. Dr. A. E. J. Rawlinson's curious disapproval of the effort to get at the facts behind the miracle-stories in the Gospels, on the ground that it " is wholly foreign to the standpoint of antiquity ", " utterly foreign to the spirit of the narrative ", and so forth (*St. Mark*, 59f., 68, 70, 84, 88, 243), is a special example of the same general attitude, which to some extent characterizes also Dr. C. H. Dodd's thoughtful article on ' Miracles in the Gospels ' in *E.T.* xliv. 504–509 (Aug. 1933), and still more the Rev. Alan Richardson's recent volume, entitled *The Miracle-Stories of the Gospels* (1941).

[2] " Their (the German critics') theories seemed to explain everything except the existence of the Christian religion and of the Christian Church . . ." (Blunt, *The Gospels and the Critic*, 15).

[3] As an example of this over-intellectualistic attitude, cf. the article by Dr. D. W. Riddle in *J.R.* xiv (1934) 162f., etc.

without conscious bias in favour of one historical conclusion
rather than another, our results will be needlessly and avoidably
untrue, and our acceptance of them therefore inconsistent in
the long run with really veracious and healthy discipleship.
In reply to those who urge that no investigation of the history
of Jesus can be salutary and fruitful unless one accepts at
the outset the entire New Testament as a Divine Revelation
and the general New-Testament estimate of Jesus as right alike
in its assertions and in its distribution of the stress—nay, unless
one drops as "liberal" and therefore wrongheaded any
attempt to get at the real Jesus behind and in distinction from
the kerygma of the early Church—we would say that, be it
hard or be it easy to harmonize "historicism" with the
conditions conceded in the foregoing paragraph, the claims of
history cannot be politely bowed out of court in the interests of
"revelation" and tradition, without opening the door to
obscurantism, error, and untruth. If there be any ancient
interpretation of the Person of Jesus that is really entitled to
our acceptance, we may rest assured that a deeper and more
thorough probing of the historical facts concerning him will in
the long run do it no harm, but will serve to bring out its truth
more thoroughly. To warn men off such a probing suggests
very strongly that the apologetic interests for the sake of which
such warning is given are unconsciously felt to rest on histori-
cally-insecure foundations. Let us again recall the wise words
of Canon Moberly: "Councils, we admit, and Creeds cannot go
behind, but must wholly rest upon the history of our Lord
Jesus Christ".[1] To claim that a man is psychologically
incapable of studying that history until he has accepted the
teaching of the Councils and Creeds, even if it be only that of
the creed of the first century, is to put the cart before the horse.
Every one acquainted with the facts knows that, behind the
early Christian kerygma about Christ as heavenly Lord,
several successive strata in the growth of the traditions concerning his earthly life are more or less clearly distinguishable:
and that being so, there is no real reason why these should not
be investigated to the full. The essential condition for
investigating them properly is not the acceptance of the early
Christian kerygma as an infallible interpretation of the facts;
it is a real and humble reverence for truth, coupled of course
with some competence in the assessment of historical evidence.
Such is, reasonably enough, the sole condition demanded by
Barthians and non-fundamentalist conservatives generally,

[1] In *Lux Mundi* (ed. 1891), 177.

when it is a question of dealing with, say, the Synoptic Problem. Why should the case be otherwise when it is a question of investigating the contents of the Gospel-story ? The investigation needs, certainly, to be extended so as to include the study of the revolutionary effects of Jesus' earthly life on the experience of the early Church : but the investigation itself is nevertheless an indispensable necessity, and its findings have an indefeasible right to be embodied in the Church's Christology. Like the proffered solution of a problem in mathematics which fails to utilize all the data of the problem, the Church's Christology will certainly be at fault if it does not provide an integral place for what historical research, working freely in loyalty to its own well-tried laws, has to tell us about the facts of his life and teaching.[1]

That point established, it may perhaps with all due modesty be claimed that the foregoing description of the way in which Jesus viewed his mission is for all practical purposes a tolerably complete and accurate version of the account of the matter preserved in the Synoptic Gospels. The discrimination that has been made in the documentary sources from which the several pieces of evidence have been drawn will have enabled the reader to estimate and compare the varying degrees of authority on which these different pieces of evidence rest. We have been careful to note which items are certainly or almost certainly editorial glosses : but although these latter are numerous, it is fairly easy to see which of them are tendencious additions, and as such devoid of value as witnesses to Jesus' real meaning, and which of them are early and valuable comments on, or paraphrases of, his actual words, and therefore helpful sources of information (see above, pp. 14f). Setting glosses of the former type aside, we may say of the remaining evidence as a whole that the general coherence of the resultant picture is no small confirmation of the historical reliability of those Gospel-documents which are already taken (on literary grounds) to be the oldest (see above, pp. 21f.), and also of the conclusions we have arrived at by comparing and collating their contents.

[1] Cf. Windisch, *Bergpredigt*, 4, 119, 124, etc.; Héring, *Royaume*, 2. Windisch's book is a fine protest against the attempt to hamper historical investigation by doctrinal presuppositions. Rev. W. L. Knox says, in reviewing the 1937-edition of it (in *J.T.S.* xxxix. 173 [Apl. 1938]), "The great value of the book . . . lies in its protest against the confusion of critical scholarship with theological exegesis . . . It must . . . be recognized that there is a real need to preserve English no less than German theology from an attempt to subordinate critical scholarship to the supposed needs of theology, . . . ".

This encouraging result, however, does not quite settle the question as to whether our conclusions, besides representing the actual contents of the Synoptic Gospels, truly reflect also the mind of Jesus himself. For one thing, the Synoptic material does not quite exhaust our sources of information. Some recollections and echoes of what Jesus said and meant are to be found outside its limits. The Epistles of the New Testament, the Fourth Gospel, the experience of the early Church, the non-canonical sayings, all have something to teach us regarding the real Jesus, and would therefore all need careful sifting and scrutiny if our study of the available material had to be quite exhaustive. Conclusions based on the Synoptic Gospels alone can for this reason never be absolutely final in every detail. On the other hand, these Gospels are so very much the main sources of information, that an historical foundation constructed out of their whole contents could hardly leave much more to be added to it and could hardly need correcting in any material particular.

But a deeper question still remains to be faced. It is that which concerns the relation between the teaching of Jesus (as reported by the Synoptists) and absolute truth. For this teaching contains certain elements which are to all appearance incompatible with beliefs which we cannot help regarding— under the guidance of the Divine Spirit—as indubitably true. The Lord's Return, for instance, did not actually take place at the time at which he is reported to have said it would (see above, p. 319 n. 3). The fiery Gehenna, as depicted in the records, the ultimate " loss " of great numbers of men, and the eternity of future punishment, seem—as Divinely-ordained inflictions — incapable of being harmonized with Jesus' picture of God as the *Father* of men or as the Shepherd who goes out to search for a single straying sheep. The idea that man carries his physical blemishes with him into the future life beyond the grave has become incredible for most of us, as also has the belief that illness and insanity are due to the malignant operation of evil spirits. The question as to the right way in which a Christian ought to view these apparent incompatibilities is one over which a great deal of unnecessary heat had been generated : but nonetheless, despite the impatience with which apologists are prone to demand belief each in his own solution, as the obvious and only tenable one, the question is worthy of careful reconsideration.

The first course that suggests itself to a devout Christian is

338

that he ought reverently to accept the reported teaching of
Jesus as a Divine revelation of the actual truth of things. That
was, indeed, the line normally taken by our pious ancestors ;
and it is still taken by some to-day, especially (though not
exclusively) by Fundamentalists and Roman Catholics. Thus
there are many serious and indeed well-informed Christians
who still expect to see Christ return to earth in a glorious
Second Advent.[1] But the method as a whole lies open to the
fatal objection that it compels us (a) either to force our minds
to dismiss certain indubitable facts or firm convictions of our
own as erroneous because incompatible with Divine revelation,
or (b) to shut our eyes to the incompatibility in question,
or (c) so to force the plain meaning of the supposed revelation
as to cause the incompatibility to disappear.

A second course is to suppose that Jesus has been inaccurately reported, whenever he is reported to have said anything
which conflicts gravely with the facts or convictions to which
allusion has just been made. The assumption is somewhat
as follows : Jesus, being Divine, could have said nothing but
what is true ; if therefore he is *reported* to have said anything
which we to-day cannot believe to be true, then the report
must be incorrect.[2] But this is hardly the way to arrive
at the truth. The evidence that Jesus said these difficult
things is exactly the same in objective strength and inherent
credibility as that on which our whole knowledge of him (and
therefore also our belief in his Divinity) rests. We are, up to a
point, entitled to hold that this or that utterance, if it means
what it seems to mean, is incredible or untrue : but we are
not entitled to treat this conviction of ours as a ground for
declaring that Jesus could not have made the utterance in
question. To do so would be to violate a prime canon of
historical study in order to maintain our own a priori dogma of
Jesus' intellectual infallibility.

A third course is to accept the record at its face-value, but
to believe that Jesus was deliberately using the thought and
language of contemporary Judaism as a convenient vehicle
for certain deep spiritual truths, without himself believing
that this thought and language were in point of fact true.
This view is very widely accepted as a way-out by many
intelligent Protestants to-day.[3] But it is really no better

---

[1] E.g., Dr. F. A. M. Spencer in *The Church Quarterly Review*, cxxvi. 16–18
(Apl.–June 1938). Cf. the interpretation offered by Mr. Kenneth Ingram
in his book, *And He shall come again* (1938).

[2] E.g., Leckie, *World to Come*, 109f., 113.

[3] Cf., e.g., Winstanley, *Future*, 283 ; and see above, p. 61.

than the last-named alternative. It has no inherent probability to commend it (beyond the arbitrary assumption that all Jesus' utterances must have been rigidly consistent with each other and with absolute truth) ; and it labours under the additional disadvantage of ascribing to him a course of action which we should shrink from defending ethically if it were taken by another man. For it would not merely mean that he chose simple picture-language for simple people, much as one feeds an infant on milk ; it would mean that he consciously indoctrinated his hearers with a number of very serious beliefs about God which he himself believed to be false.

A fourth alternative is simply to omit the difficult eschatological elements from our study of the teaching of Jesus, on the ground that, by comparison with his ethics and his revelation of the love of God, his eschatology is for men to-day religiously unimportant. Such was the tendency of the Ritschlian School ; and many " liberal " exponents of the teaching of Jesus have laid themselves open to the same reproach. Schweitzer, despite his excesses, succeeded in convincing men that to disregard Jesus' eschatology was gravely to misrepresent his outlook ; and certain of the newer schools of thought that have been born out of the reaction against liberalism endeavour to find a central significance of some sort in the eschatological teaching. Whatever may have to be said about the theories of Schweitzer and of these modern schools of thought, they are right at least in refusing to ignore what is clearly a very important part of the data.

A fifth course is to take advantage of the manifest difference between an imaginative Oriental mind, working with pictures or visions, and a western mind endeavouring to be scientific and precise. It is not easy for us to say exactly how far the Jewish Apocalyptist seriously meant his predictions and descriptions to be accepted at their face-value. It is probable that the question rarely if ever crossed either his mind or the minds of his readers, while we moderns, on the contrary, cannot feel ourselves entitled to evade it. Reasons can indeed be found for supposing that these pictorial apocalyptic descriptions were not in all cases seriously intended as close transcripts of reality.[1] The Apostle Peter, for instance, is reported to have found in the events of the Day of Pentecost a fulfilment of the prophecy of Joel, " . . . And I will produce portents in the heaven above, and signs on the earth beneath—blood and fire and smoky mist. The sun will be changed into darkness

---

[1] Cf. Leckie, *World to Come*, 17-19.

and the moon into blood, before the great and manifest day of the Lord comes ! . . . " (Acts ii. 19f. : Joel ii. 30f.).[1] Nay more, it has been urged that the language of apocalyptic is always and necessarily poetical and imaginative, and must therefore be understood not dogmatically but figuratively.[2] It would seem, therefore, to be only reasonable, in dealing with the Gospel-sayings, to allow for this method of speech, and to interpret them freely as orientally-figurative references to spiritual realities, such as, in their more prosaïc setting, we moderns need feel no difficulty in accepting. The Parousia would thus be simply the extension of Christ's sway throughout the world ; " the clouds of the heaven " would mean " heaven " understood in a purely spiritual sense as God's sphere ; [3] the Last Judgment is really the present, perpetual, and automatic exhibition and segregation of the good and the bad, just as it is represented to be in the Fourth Gospel (e.g., John iii. 18–21) ; [4] the seats on Jesus' right and left hand, about which he spoke to Jacob and John, are to be interpreted just as metaphorically as are the Cup and the Baptism which stand for his death (Mk. x. 37–40 = Mt. xx. 21–23) ; [5] the Messianic Feast is simply a vivid symbol for joyous spiritual fellowship with others in the future life.[6] The adoption of this spiritualizing interpretation of Jesus' eschatology has seemed to many— and for long seemed to the present writer—the true solution of the puzzle.[7]

It is by no means easy to assess it at its true value. One rightly hesitates to reject it out-of-hand. For the employment of poetical language, of metaphor, and of pictorial illustration quite clearly not meant in its literal sense (e.g., the Danielic beasts, and Joel's prophecy), is indubitable ; and it is impossible for us to define the limits beyond which it would certainly or probably not go. But the conviction forces itself persistently upon the mind that, even so, such limits must have

---

[1] Cf. Stevens, *Theol. of the N.T.* 162.
[2] Cf. Gould, *Bibl. Theol. of the N.T.* (1900), 45 ; Leckie, *World to Come*, 49–51, 53f., 58f., 66f., 109, 111, 115, 129, 151f., 153, 156, 160, 174, 204.
[3] Cf. Muirhead, *Eschatol. of Jes.* 52f.
[4] Cf. Ottley in *Lux Mundi* (ed. 1891), 352, 377 ; Dobschütz, *Eschatol.* 196f. ; Charles, *Crit. Hist.* (1913), 422–425.
[5] Cf. Streeter in *Stud. in the Syn. Prob.* 435.
[6] Cf. Wendt, *Teaching*, i. 221 ; Menzies, *Earliest Gospel*, 223 ab ; Dobschütz, *Eschatol.* 119f. ; Charles, *Crit. Hist.* (1913), 396 : also Rom. xiv. 17. Gehenna " only a metaphor after all " (Andrews in *Congreg. Quart.* v. 268 [July 1927]).
[7] See above, pp. 18f. The method is best represented in German by Erich Haupt's *Die eschatologischen Aussagen Jesu* (1895), and in English by G. B. Stevens' *Theol. of the N.T.* (1899). For other literature reflecting this method and that last described (p. 340), see Holtzmann, *Theol.* i. 388–390, 397 n. 2.

existed, and that some of the passages in question cannot naturally be brought within them. I doubt whether we can rightly conclude that the Apocalyptists, for all their love of pure imagery, did not on occasions mean precisely what they said. Such doubt is confirmed when we recall the striking and habitual realism of their words. It will perhaps be said that, even if this were the case with the Apocalyptists, it would not necessarily be the same with Jesus, who clearly differed from them in many important ways, and in particular towered immeasurably above them in spiritual insight.[1] That, of course, is true ; but it does not alter the fact that we can discover his real meaning only by learning humbly from the most reliable records we have of what he actually said, not by imposing on those records an a priori canon of our own in the shape of an insistence on his intellectual infallibility and complete self-consistency. Nor does it demolish the probability that, since he must have chosen his words with a view to being understood by his hearers, he meant by such expressions as Abraham's bosom, Gehenna of fire, outer darkness, and so on, approximately what his Jewish contemporaries would have meant by them.[2] We are right then in allowing for the use of metaphor and poetry ; we are right in believing that Jesus knew better than the Apocalyptists : but we are not right either in assuming that all his realistic sayings must be purely figurative because otherwise our belief in his infallibility is threatened, or in assigning to his words a widely-different meaning from that which they would naturally and inevitably have conveyed to his hearers.[3]

[1] Weinel (*Theol.* 62–66) has compiled a list of seven important respects in which Jesus certainly differed from the typical Jewish Apocalyptist : (1) he did not write pseudonymously ; (2) he spoke comfort as well as doom ; (3) his pictures of the future were comparatively simple ; (4) the eschatology was subordinate to the prophetical element in his teaching (cf. Montefiore, *S.G.*[2] I. cxii) ; (5) he constructed no numerical calculations as to the time of the End ; (6) he was free from Jewish particularism ; (7) he preached a present as well as a future Kingdom. On Jesus' intellectual superiority to apocalypticism, cf. Simkhovitch, *Understanding of Jes.* 73.
[2] Cf. Bacon, *Matthew*, 417 : " In reality Jesus' actual words can only have been of the type to which his hearers were accustomed. More than that ; his thoughts, to be sincerely in harmony with his words, and to give to his words *that ring of sincerity and conviction which no mere allegory or symbolism can take on*, must have moved in the conventional channels of the time . . ." (italics mine).
[3] Cf. the discussion in Gloege, *Reich Gottes*, 187–200. On the question whether after all the Messianic Feast was not understood by Jesus in a more or less literal and physcial sense, cf. Holtzmann, *Synopt.* 174 (on Mk. xiv. 25 : " Vergebliche Frage . . . , was hier Bild . . . , was Sache sei ! "), *Theol.* i. 396–398 (" . . . Bild und Sache in den Reden Jesu zu unterscheiden . . . wird zur völligen Unmöglickeit, wo unkontrollierbare Jenseitigkeiten zur

Unless, therefore, we are prepared to give a forced and unnatural interpretation to many of the well-attested sayings of Jesus, and to assume in advance his necessary infallibility (an assumption which ultimately presupposes our own, and is moreover contradicted by Jesus himself),[1] we are shut up to a sixth solution of our problem—the conclusion, namely, that Jesus' own knowledge was to some extent limited by the conditions of his race and education, that his eschatological teaching contains an element of human ignorance and error, that he uttered predictions which were never fulfilled in the sense in which he uttered them, and that he assumed, as true, descriptions of the life after death which, resting ultimately on Jewish imagination, cannot rightly be so regarded. We must, of course, be careful not to over-estimate the extent of that element of error, as some have indeed overestimated it : but nothing is to be gained by piously shutting one's eyes to the fact or by endeavouring to prove that it is not a fact. Such proof can be had by artificially forcing the evidence, but at no cheaper price.[2]

Of those Christians who see that the intellectual infallibility of Jesus cannot be maintained, many try to guard themselves by urging that the limitations of his knowledge affected only those matters which are of no moral or religious importance.[3] The supposition is arbitrary. For the limitations in question arose from the impression made upon his thoughts by the teaching to which as a Jewish boy he had been subjected. That teaching clearly embodied ideas concerning the character of God as well as beliefs concerning the authorship of the Pentateuch and the Psalms and concerning the life after death. We must, of course, recognize that Jesus himself immensely modified and transformed this body of traditional teaching by his own inspiration and insight: but we cannot in reason profess to believe that he had a truly-human nature and

---

Sprache kommen wie Stühle und Tische im Reiche Gottes . . . ") ; Dalman, *W.J.* 110–113 ; Schweitzer, *Quest*, 377 n. (" Jesus' references to the Messianic feast are therefore not merely images, but point to a reality " [not in *L.J.F.*]) ; Montefiore, *S.G.*[2] I. 334 (" . . . we cannot be sure that it [drinking wine in the Kingdom] was merely a metaphor to him . . . ").

[1] Cf. C. J. Cadoux, *The Case for Evangel. Modernism* (1938), 85–89.

[2] That Jesus' eschatological teaching was, in part at least, erroneous is now recognized by many scholars who regard themselves and are regarded by others as orthodox, though the recognition is usually (and perhaps rightly) couched in extremely-cautious words. Cf. Winstanley, *Future*, 357–360, 383, 386f. ; Charles, *Crit. Hist.* (1913), 387f. ; Manson, *Teaching*, 282f. ; Kümmel, *Eschatologie*, 29f. ; Héring, *Royaume*, 49.

[3] E.g., Charles, as last quoted.

" increased in widsom " as in stature, and at the same time assume that he had wholly emancipated himself from every existing flaw in the current religious beliefs of his people.

The clearest example of the manner in which he shared the intellectual limitations of his age and race is given in the physical features he ascribed to the life after death and to his own future triumph. This element of error does not touch his faith in the future life as such, with its accompanying rewards and punishments, nor his anticipation of a coming triumph, whereby he would through God's power be vindicated in the eyes of men : it concerns only the physical forms with which he believed these realities would be clothed.

But further. I do not think it can be denied that, in taking over (as under the conditions of his incarnate life he was bound to do) the main Jewish beliefs of his time, he also took over certain elements which did not entirely match—in point of ethical and spiritual quality—the revelation of the Divine character clearly visible in his own Person. That revelation is most plainly seen in his portrayal of the fatherly love of God, of the generosity with which the returning Prodigal is welcomed, and of the Shepherd's concern as he tracks down the straying sheep, in his startling injunction to love one's enemies in imitation of the Most High, and finally in his endurance of the torture of the Cross that men might be moved to repentance by this manifestation of God's holy love. Perhaps the reader may wish to intervene at this point with reminders that love is not just kindly sentiment, but that it is compatible with discipline and severity, and that God's wrath against sin is as prominent in the New Testament as His love for the sinner. Such reminders are quite justified : but do they really suffice to make Jesus' special revelation of the character of God consistent with " eternal punishment ", with the destruction of soul and body in Gehenna, with the final loss of great numbers of men (Lk. xiii. 23f. Q ? : cf. Mt. vii. 13f. and see above, p. 237 [16]), with the unpardonability of blasphemy against the Holy Spirit, or with the terrible words, " These enemies of mine who did not want me to be king over them, bring them hither and slaughter them before me " (Lk. xix. 27 L) ? A revered Christian senior with whom I was once discussing this question observed that what we have to do is to judge Christ by Christ. The Spirit of God, responsiveness to which we largely owe to Jesus himself, warrants us in tentatively drawing these distinctions between one part of his teaching and another. On the strength of what he himself has revealed about God, the modern Christian conscience has definitely given up its belief in fiery and eternal punishment, and demands the right at least to trust that at long last all men will be saved. Efforts have naturally been made in all sorts of ways to prove that Jesus did not believe in eternal fire and that he did believe in the final salvation of all. But the efforts are futile, and, if pursued beyond a certain point, dishonest. Our modern convictions on these matters can appeal for authority to what is *implied* in those teachings of his which we feel to be most characteristic of him and most lofty : they cannot appeal to what, so far as we can judge, he explicitly taught.[1]

Apart from the question as to the character and duration of future punishment, it may also be asked whether the employment of the apocalyptic picture of a miraculous Parousia as the form in which Jesus cast his sureness of a future vindication did not involve a partial obscuring of the full glory of his characteristic revelation of God. For this picture was not only inconsistent with what was actually destined to happen, but, unless it be purely figurative, it seems to suggest a less-ethical means of victory than that set forth in the Sermon on the Mount, in the personal ministry of Jesus, and in his death at Golgotha.[2]

It is such difficulties as those which we have just been discussing that have led many modern Christian thinkers to draw a more or less sharp distinction between Jesus' apocalyptic teaching (the accuracy of which, *in the form given to it in the record*, can no longer be defended) and some essentially-valuable truth of which that teaching may be regarded as the vehicle. These " vehicle-theories ", if we may so designate them, present us with a great variety of suggestions when it becomes a question of stating precisely what *is* the essential truth or value which eschatology serves to express ; and some

---

[1] Cf. Wendt, *Teaching*, ii. 87f. ; Holtzmann, *Theol.* i. 415f. ; Winstanley, *Future*, 316f., 378 ; Montefiore, *S.G.*[2] I. 245f., II. 121–123. For efforts to prove that Gehenna was not *quite* so black as it is painted, cf. Rawlinson, *St. Mark*, 131 ; Major in *Mission*, etc. 123. Dr. Charles is very outspoken regarding the unethical character of the Jewish doctrine of Hades (*Crit. Hist.* [1913], 366–368).

[2] See this point forcibly put by Mr. Eric W. Philip in *Reconciliation*, April 1931, 303f. : " . . . But there is nothing moral about the appeal of a transcendental Messiah coming in visible appearance on the clouds. That would be to use the method of coercion, the refusal to use which had led Jesus to the Cross . . ." He concludes accordingly that Jesus did not really anticipate a Parousia of the sort expected by the early Church. See, however, above, pp. 289ff., 295f.

of them are highly subtle. It has, for instance, been pointed out that an intellectually-unsystematized religion, when it rouses a man to earnest concern for his fellows, usually takes the form of a prediction of an imminent final catastrophe.[1] The apocalyptic beliefs are said to have " provided the categories in which " Jesus delivered his conceptions of the moral law, of our new relation to God, of his own personality, and of the meaning of his death, and from which these conceptions are easily separable.[2] It has also been claimed that the eschatology of Jesus, with its insistence on the element of suddenness and discontinuity in history, is in line with the latest scientific and philosophical thought, which has drawn new attention to the unforeseeable and the catastrophic in nature and in existence generally.[3] On another view, the permanently-valuable element in Jesus' teaching is the heroism with which he willed and sought the Coming of the Kingdom, notwithstanding the erroneous character of his " Vorstellungsmaterial ", which makes it quite impossible for us to modernize him.[4] Eschatology is said to have been of value to the early Christians because it gave them a firm grip on history, preserved their social outlook, guarded their belief in the value and significance of human effort, and maintained the balance between worldliness and otherworldliness.[5] True ideas regarding the nature of God's redemptive world-rule have been declared to constitute " the abiding significance of the Apocalyptic ".[6] Another suggested equivalent for the eschatological attitude of the New Testament is " der Wille zur Lebensvollendung ".[7] Yet again, the core of New-Testament eschatology is said to be God's redeeming act in the historic coming of Christ.[8] Lastly, by the aid of a special interpreta-

[1] Harnack, *What is Christianity ?* (1901), 41–43.
[2] E. F. Scott, *The Kingdom and the Messiah* (1911), 254f. Cf. also Holtzmann, *Theol.* i. 410–414 (' Kern und Schale '), 413–418 (' Zeitliches und Zeitloses ') ; W. Manson, *Christ's View*, 168.
[3] Cf. W. L. Sperry in *H.T.R.* v (1912) 385–395.
[4] So Schweitzer, in the ' Schlussbetrachtung ' of his *L.J.F.* 631–642 (greatly enlarged from *Quest*, 396–401) : cf. also *Mystery*, 274f., and C. C. McCown in *J.R.* xvi (1936) 46.
[5] C. H. Dodd in *Interpreter*, xx. 14–24 (Oct. 1923).
[6] See a somewhat obscure paper by the late Dr. J. W. Oman with this title in *The Churchman*, xlvi. 184–191 (July 1932). H. H. Farmer (in *Congreg. Quart.* viii [1930] 276–278) links apocalyptic with the new Barthian stress on the initiative and transcendence of God.
[7] So F. Buri, *Die Bedeutung der neutestamentlichen Eschatologie für die neuere protestantische Theologie* (1935). Cf. Preisker in *T.L.Z.*, lxi. 137–139 (Apl., 1936), Kümmel, *Eschatologie*, 29. I have not been able to see A. N. Wilder's *Eschatology and Ethics in the Teaching of Jesus*, New York (Harper), 1939.
[8] So Kümmel, *Eschatologie*, 29–32.

tion of the eschatology of Jesus as a " realized eschatology " which never became " futurist " until it was misunderstood by the early Church, the effort has been made to treat this eschatology of the New-Testament period as a more or less imperfect method of expressing the absoluteness and timeless validity of the revelation and redemption brought by Jesus.[1]

Such are some of the theories in which the effort is made to exhibit the eschatological teaching of Jesus, recorded for us in the Synoptic Gospels, as the temporary and necessary, but comparatively-unessential vehicle of some indispensable item or other of Christian truth. Though there is a certain similarity between the account of the central item given in one theory and that given in some of the other theories, the variety of the statements offered testifies to the difficulty of the interpreter's task, when he endeavours to do justice to all the data relevant to the problem he is set to solve. Perhaps the baffling complexity of the problem and the wide variety of the solutions offered indicate that a stop should be made at this point, and that I should rest content with having laid out and surveyed the material, and stated in outline some of the conditions attendant on its full and proper interpretation, and should now just leave the matter of interpretation to be taken over by abler hands.

Yet I should be loth to lay down my pen without adding a few more lines, in however halting and tentative a style, regarding the significance of the great enterprise I have been at such pains to delineate correctly. And my first concern is to reaffirm the faith I professed in my Introduction (see above, pp. 19f.), namely, that a blessing is linked with every real advance

[1] Such, very roughly put, is the theory advanced by Dr. C. H. Dodd in *Apost. Preaching*, 193–240 (= *Oxford Society of Historical Theology : Abstract of Proceedings* . . . 1934–1936, 5–23), in *Parables*, 202–210, and in *Hist. and the Gosp.* 149–182. A form of Dr. Dodd's theory, modified by fresh stress on the future life and on social reform, is presented by Prof. H. Cunliffe-Jones in *E.T.* li. 231–235 (Feb. 1940).

In *Present Task*, 38–40, Dr. Dodd deprecates as superficial any attempt to disengage the permanent element in the New Testament from its temporary setting, on the ground apparently that truth must not be " disengaged from a context with which it forms a living whole ". He instances the old habit of writing off the New-Testament eschatology as " temporary ". " Our task is not thus to pick and choose, but to grasp the whole first-century Gospel in its temporary, historical, and therefore actual, reality, and then to make the bold and even perilous attempt to translate the whole into contemporary terms ". I agree that the eschatology cannot be simply omitted from our interpretation of the New-Testament teaching : but I submit that the needful task of " translating " it into contemporary terms is bound to involve some measure of that very " picking and choosing " which Dr. Dodd deprecates.

in our knowledge of Jesus' earthly life, that his life is of so Divine a quality that the more we learn of it by the aid of bold critical scrutiny the more we are conscious of owing him a debt as our Saviour in the full experiential sense of the word, despite the somewhat alarming discovery of previously-unrealized limitations whereby his ministry to men was conditioned. However hard some of my friends may find it to understand, the fact remains that my sense of absolute indebtedness to him for that poor measure of spiritual and moral health that is mine is not a whit impaired by my realization that in some measure he shared the ignorance common to the Jews of his day.[1] In reality, however, the friends in question ought not to be surprised at this. For the whole Christian Church sprang from the life Jesus had lived on earth : if therefore historical science can, as we claim, give us a truer picture of him than is otherwise obtainable, the sense of an enhanced indebtedness to him is only what one ought to expect as the result of a keener historical quest. Jesus is so great that the noblest religious movement of all history began with his earthly life, that even man's misinterpretations of him do not suffice to quench his redeeming power in those who love him, and that, whenever we get to learn more about him, the conditions and limitations which newly come to light are abundantly counterbalanced by our closer contact with the mighty reality. " The divine obedience of Jesus is the fountain among remote hills whence has flowed down in a never-interrupted stream that loyalty of heart to the divine which is the living principle of the Christian faith ".[2]

When, therefore, I come to ask myself what precisely does his eschatology mean to me, or what permanent value is discernible in it, one thing at least I can say is that it registers the crucial urgency of those great life-values for which Jesus stood. I confess I find it beyond my power to produce a satisfactory account of the meaning of the time-factor for Christian faith, and satisfactory answers to the questions whether world-progress in social, economic, and international relations is or is not a worthy standard by which the success of Christianity may be measured, and whether a right estimate of the value of utopian ideals is or is not a good means of setting forth the Kingdom of God.[3] I am just as much at

---

[1] See some wise words written by the late Dr. J. Estlin Carpenter in his little book, *The Relation of Jesus to his Age and our own* (1895), 61–63.

[2] P. Gardner, *A Historic View of the New Test.* (ed. 1904), 88.

[3] These great questions are learnedly and lengthily discussed in the com-

sea as were the Jewish Apocalyptists generally in regard to the relation between the life after death and the future of the race. I would only observe with due caution that, despite all the discouragements with which contemporary history faces us, I find myself unable to join in the chorus of derision with which many Christian thinkers are now repudiating the liberal and Victorian belief in human progress.[1] If God is evermore at work, in the way which Jesus revealed, seeking and saving that which was lost, how can mankind do other than progress ?

However that may be, the eschatology of Jesus can at least be regarded as expressing the absoluteness and vital urgency of God's demand on us through him. And it is well to remind ourselves that, though our view of the course of human history is necessarily different from that which Jesus held, yet our modern life is not entirely devoid of eschatological conditions. For physical death awaits us all : in that respect we stand on the same ground as the first-century Jew ; and the very mixture which we find in the Gospels between the life beyond the grave and the Coming of the Kingdom of God (see above, pp. 218f.) should teach us that our necessary independence of Jesus' eschatology is by no means total.[2] Now the prospect of physical death—a prospect from which none born of woman is free—forces on the mind, if the general experience of life has not previously forced it, a grave sense of moral responsibility. At the near prospect of death, if never before, a man becomes deeply conscious of the unchangeability of the past, of the cutting-off of all further opportunities of earthly amendment, of the sort of record he will leave behind him, and of the reckoning to which he goes. In Biblical words, he becomes acutely aware that he stands before the Judgment-Seat of God. Then it is that the terrific significance of the moral quality of his past life comes home to him, and

---

posite volume entitled *The Kingdom of God and History* (1938), " wherein " (as the author of the second Epistle of Peter felt with regard to the letters of Paul) " are some things hard to be understood ".

[1] Cf., e.g., the words of Dr. Martin Dibelius in *Church. Community, and State* iv. (1938) 42.

[2] For a discussion of the suggestive equivalence death and the end of the world, see Bartlet and Carlyle, *Christianity in Hist.* 125 ; Bultmann, *Jesus*, 52f., 82f. ; Frick in *Myst. Christi*, 261–265 ; Raven, *Is War Obsolete ?* (1935), 133–135 ; Otto, *Kingdom*, 52f. Cf. Augustine, *Epist.* cxcix. 2 (in the Vienna *Corpus*, lvii. [1911], 246: " in quo enim quemque inuenerit suus novissimus dies, in hoc eum comprehendet mundi novissimus dies: quoniam, qualis in die isto quisque moritur, talis in die illo iudicabitur "), and Thomas à Kempis, *Imitation of Christ*, I. xxiii. 1 (" Many die suddenly and when they look not for it ; for ' at an hour when we think not the Son of Man will come ' ").

perhaps for the first time he sees the eternal issues that hang upon the character of each man's doings. Then it is that that " new way of life " to which Jesus called men both by precept and by influence stands out before the mind as the one absolutely and perpetually valid way. In that sense the Kingdom of God may rightly be said to challenge us as His inescapable judgment,[1] and its ethics may rightly be regarded as necessarily " interim ethics ".[2]

Furthermore, the menacing instability of the international position is thrusting upon all men a new sense of imminent peril, a terror of a kind not previously known to the race even in its savage state. The character of such a war as that which the civilized world is now waging is an appalling revelation of the plight into which humanity has fallen. The causes of the plight are many and various, and to enumerate them all would be to tell a very long story. None of the nations—perhaps no individual—is quite free from a share of responsibility for the present state of affairs. But the crisis does reveal to us at least in broad outline the real nature of the trouble. The war arose in the first place from the deification of nationalism without regard to the moral rights of others—a glaring repudiation of the very way to which Jesus called his fellow-countrymen as the way of their greatest glory. But behind the immediate political crisis there lie the recent years of successive and unmitigated horrors—the detestable and iniquitous cruelties inflicted by the Axis-powers on Jews and Abyssinians, Libyans and Czechs, democrats and Christians. The heart turns sick when we are reminded of the concentration-camps of Central Europe and the firing squads of Spain. Is there not some vital connexion between the revolting character of these horrors and their total and flagrant incongruity with the values for the sake of which Jesus undertook his great enterprise ? Surely it is in substance the deliberate abandonment of those values that leads on the Dictators and their henchman to cover with lasting infamy the countries they profess to love and to do deeds that stink in the nostrils of Heaven.[3]   But heavy as is the sin of the Dictator-governments, it is not theirs exclusively : for, at least in the case of Germany, the Dictatorship was made possible by the vindictive cruelty

---

[1] Cf. Dodd, *Parables*, 76f., *Hist. and the Gosp.* 168–175.
[2] Cf. H.-D. Wendland, *Eschatologie*, 104–107.
[3] Cf. H. G. Wood in *Kingdom of God and Hist.* 9 : " The Christian objects to modern dictatorships . . . because they seek to gain their ends by disregarding the commandments : ' Thou shalt do no murder ; thou shalt not steal ; thou shalt not bear false witness against thy neighbour ' . .

with which the country was deliberately treated by the Allies in the years succeeding the Armistice of November 1918. Hitler is in no small measure the nemesis for the continued starvation of surrendered Germany (in spite of the terms of the Armistice), the quartering of black troops on the Rhine, and the occupation of the Ruhr.[1] Just as clearly as the excesses of National Socialism are wrong, was this post-Armistice policy of the Allies wrong : both alike are the fruit of a contempt for Christian standards. One might look at other countries, like Turkey or China, or at other days like those preceding the Great War, to draw everywhere the same conclusion. The acts which by their stupidity, their selfishness, their cruelty, have helped to bring mankind to its present parlous state, are all reducible, in one form or another, to a revolt, not against the dogmas of the Church, but against the moral authority of Jesus. Hence the great Judgment with which we are all now faced.

The agony which Jesus felt as he watched the people of Israel turning away from that rôle of forgiveness and healing for which God had destined them, and slipping steadily down to the indescribable calamity of 66–71 A.D., seems in many ways similar to the agony which has been weighing on many a Christian's heart as he has watched civilized humanity drifting towards the present inevitable conflict. Not that we ought to put on the same level all who take part in so unchristian a proceeding as war. Unselfish motive, respect for treaties, and a conviction that wanton aggression ought to be resisted, raise those who so fight far above all who are simply animated by crass national self-centredness. And it may be that, as in the days of Napoleon, so in our day, mankind really needs—in a certain sense of the word " need "—to pass again through the storms and throes of war, if so be that by this sharp lesson the most elementary moral duties may be brought home to peoples and rulers who have been pleased to forget them. But even so, the use of this terrible corrective, in order, as Irenæus once put it, to " smite down the manifold wrong-doing of the Gentiles ",[2] is but a partial contribution to the problem ; in fact—notwithstanding all its relative necessity as a temporary check—it is a confession of inability to solve it.

---

[1] Perhaps I may refer to my recent book, *Christian Pacifism Re-examined* (1940), 159–163, for a vindication of this statement, if such be needed.

[2] Iren. *Adv. Haer.* V. xxiv. 2 : " Ad utilitatem ergo gentilium terrenum regnum positum est a Deo, . . . ut timentes regnum hominum, non se alterutrum homines vice piscium consumant, sed per legum positiones repercutiant multiplicem gentilium injustitiam ".

351

While contemplating the approaching war with Rome as in a certain relative sense a necessity, Jesus shrank in horror from the prospect, and himself urged persistently the adoption of the nobler path of forgiveness and love as alone capable of healing the open sore of international strife. So we, although we are in the midst of a war on behalf of the decencies of inter-racial conduct, can break the vicious circle of ceaseless enmity only by introducing a new spirit and policy which shall more truly reflect the ethic of the Kingdom of God. Hard indeed is it to see the precise steps which even now statesmen might take by way of at least approaching so true an appeasement : hard too for many a Christian man to see his way through the cruel dilemma of either sharing in the sub-christian corrective of war-measures or, by adhering personally to the standards of Jesus, to seem to give up for the time being any direct participation in the immediate practical problem. He who takes the former alternative, if he can take it with a clear conscience, may be believed to be making some worth-while contribution to the world's need ; but it is a contribution that has many a time proved as harmful as the evil it was meant to remove. On a long view, and on a true understanding (I would submit) of our Lord's mind, the second alternative alone promises to bring about a really-radical solution of the problem : and on those who feel called to take it there lies the heavy responsibility of grappling so far as may be, directly and positively, with the immediate situation, as well as of being ready to bear the Cross, as their Master bore it, in loyalty to the claims of God.

Both for the grave international problem, then, and for the wider and more general question of social redemption, the teaching of Jesus is of central and fundamental significance.[1] Only in so far as individuals are seized with a great and passionate loyalty to Jesus—a loyalty passionate and great enough to commit them wholly to his way of life—and only in so far as such individuals can multiply themselves into groups which will exploit to the full their opportunities of affecting their fellows, can human society be led through to a condition of righteousness and peace.[2] Despite all the problems which historical scrutiny generates in connexion

---

[1] Cf. W. L. Knox in *J.T.S.* xxxix. 173 (Apl. 1938) : " We must accept the Sermon on the Mount and the whole ethical teaching of Jesus as ethical teaching, or, if we use the word, as law, which Christians are intended to obey, and not reject the whole concept of ethical religion as alien to the Gospel in order to substitute for it a system of redemption based entirely on St Paul's teaching in Romans and Galatians ".

[2] Cf. Shailer Mathews, *Social Teaching of Jes.* (ed. 1910), 217–219.

with Jesus' view of the world, the larger understanding of him which it generates serves to confirm our faith in him as the only Name given under heaven among men whereby they may be saved. The Kingdom of God is still at hand : it is still the Father's good pleasure to give it to us, to welcome us into it, and to bestow upon us its unmeasured blessings. We are still summoned to enter it, to receive the Divine gift, to shoulder the Divine yoke. We may still be sure that by so doing we are taking the only course by which human relationships can be purified and redeemed. The prospect of the Coming Kingdom still remains the lode-star of all healthy human effort.[1]

It may perhaps appear to some readers that insufficient attention has hitherto been given in this discussion to what the Christian Church has had to say on all these great and difficult themes. One might, for instance, ask why, if the mission of Jesus was of the kind which we have deduced from the Synoptic record, his Church seems to have shown, even from the first, so little interest in its political and social aspects. Does not the apparent unconcern of the early Christian community for some of the schemes that bulk so largely in our version of Jesus' own teaching suggest that that version may be sadly astray from the real facts ? The answer is that, firstly, the bitter hostility of Judaïsm to the Christian sect, and secondly, the complete disappearance of Israel as a political entity in 70–1 A.D., so drastically altered the conditions of the world-problem as it had faced Jesus himself, that any further direct efforts to get his plan put into effect were out of the question.[2] There was the additional fact that the early Christians found it to be increasingly necessary to convince the Roman authorities everywhere that they were politically inoffensive. It is interesting in this connexion to note that Luke, in whose Gospel we find the political interest of Jesus more clearly represented than it is in Mk. or ' Mt. ' (see above, pp. 275f. n. 2), reveals very clearly, especially in Acts (e.g., xvi. 19–24, 35–39, xvii. 5–9, xviii. 12–17, xix. 37–41, xxiv. 12f., xxv. 8–12 : cf. Lk. xxiii. 2, 4f., 14f. L) his desire to bring out the political harmlessness of the Christian movement.[3]

[1] Cf. Héring, *Royaume*, 49f.
[2] Cf. A. T. Cadoux, *Theol. of Jes.* 262 : " it is interesting to note that when Matthew (xxi. 13) and Luke (xix. 46) take over the account from Mark (xi. 17), they, writing after the destruction of the temple, omit ' for all the nations ' ".
[3] Cf. Montefiore, *S.G.*[2] I. 277.

But it is only fair to remember that the early Church, under the new and special and somewhat limiting circumstances in which its life had to be lived, did make a very gallant effort to apply to the world of its time, as an inevitable implicate of its adoration of Jesus as Lord, the moral principles for which he had pleaded and striven. It succeeded in planting throughout the Mediterranean lands that lofty monotheistic faith which Israel had refused, or at least failed, to plant; and it brought into pagan society an ethical standard immeasurably purer and loftier than that of paganism as a whole, however true it be that there was a good side to paganism and that there were points to criticize in Christian practice.[1] There is thus something to be said for regarding Pentecost—the birthday of the missionary-Church—as a sort of fulfilment, in certain respects, of Jesus' promise of the future Kingdom. The more precise assessment of the value and defects of the contribution of the early Church is a task of great interest and importance; but the further discussion of it in this place would take us beyond our proper limits.

I have hitherto said little or nothing about the place which Jesus came to take in the devotional life and in the theological speculations of the Church. These questions again, like the problem just referred to, have a great claim on our concern and attention; and I should regret it if any reader were to draw from my omission to treat them fully here the inference that I regard them as uninteresting or of no great consequence. I take the opportunity therefore of acknowledging clearly and emphatically my sense of the great place filled in Christian life by the privileged believers' sense of devotional or mystical fellowship with the Risen Christ (see above, pp. 315-317) and by the development of Christian thinking on the subject of the Lord's Person and redeeming work. I am not prepared to say that I regard the proportion of attention bestowed by the early Church on Christology as having been determined with perfect wisdom, or the Christological conclusions reached in the fifth and sixth centuries as having been in all respects satisfactory or final. But I recognize that the issue did need to be faced, and that the efforts made to settle it are of historic importance and cannot be ignored without distorting our own doctrine of his Person. The reason why I have not said more

[1] Cf. Liberty, *Political Relations*, 131-140; C. J. Cadoux, *The Early Church and the World* (1925), 611-619.

about them is simply the fact that, for all their importance, they really lie beyond the proper limits of my subject. My concern has been to make a valid historical contribution to the problem of Christology : and beyond insisting that due regard to the findings of history is essential to a right handling of that problem, I do not venture in this place further to handle it.

In bringing this Conclusion to an end, I am painfully aware that I have in the course of it raised a number of very urgent and important questions to which I have been unable to give final answers. I feel somewhat like a cartographer who has prepared a detailed plan of a city, the importance of which largely consists in its connexion by a network of roads with a wide area of surrounding country. Having completed to the best of my ability my plan of the city itself, I have taken the student round its outer rim, and showed him the points whence there issue from it great thoroughfares linking it with distant places, the life of which is intimately connected with its own. We have noted the direction which each road takes, looked along it into the far distance ; here and there we have travelled a little way along it. But in the case of them all we have had to forgo the exploration of the regions through which these highways pass and the positions to which they ultimately lead. So with our study of the historical Jesus. We have laid out systematically the main bulk of the evidence : and, passing beyond the strict limits of that task, we have touched on some of the great ulterior questions which arise naturally from such an exposition. We have noted how important and how difficult many of those questions are, and have realized how they branch out and extend into still further realms of thought. But we have been unable to pursue any one of them for more than a short distance. Our defence must be that this impression of unlimited range is due to the greatness of the central story from which these numerous lines of thought flow out. The ramifications of the issues raised are endless, because the majesty of Jesus himself is immeasurably great. Just because he is the fertile centre of such vast outgrowths of interest and value, it is worth our while to know him as he really was to the fullest extent that is possible to us. And as through the lens of history we focus our gaze on him

355

afresh, until his image is visible to us with perceptibly-sharper definition, we discern, it is true, a few features of very human limitation which tradition had obliterated and the sight of which at first perhaps disquiets us ; but, what matters to us far more, we can see all the better the Divine quality of the life, and can decipher with all the greater clearness that holy message inscribed for us therein by the finger of God.

O Thou great Friend to all the sons of men,
  Who once didst come in humblest guise below,
Sin to rebuke, to break the captive's chain,
  And call Thy brethren forth from want and woe—

We look to Thee ; Thy truth is still the light
  Which guides the nations, groping on their way,
Stumbling and falling in disastrous night,
  Yet hoping ever for the perfect day.

Yes !   Thou art still the Life ; Thou art the Way
  The holiest know ; Light, Life, and Way of heaven !
And they who dearest hope and deepest pray,
  Toil by the Light, Life, Way, which Thou hast given.

(Theodore Parker)

INDICES

In the ensuing indices, the letter n. added to a page-number, but with no footnote-number following it, represents the latter portion of a footnote carried over from the preceding page.

Bracketed page- and footnote-numbers represent places where the indexed item is referred to allusively, but not by the precise title under which the reference is entered.

I

INDEX OF SCRIPTURAL PASSAGES QUOTED OR REFERRED TO

OLD TESTAMENT

358

SUBJECT-INDEX

The true key to the contents of this book is to be found in the Detailed Table of Contents (pp. vii–xvi.), along with the foregoing Index of Scriptural Passages quoted or referred to. The Subject-Index here provided is intended to be used only as a supplement to these, and not as a complete guide to all the subjects discussed. Otherwise it would have had to be much larger and more elaborate than was feasible. It does not therefore contain entries for such great topics as could have been represented only by an unmanageably-long list of page-numbers, such as 'Disciples', 'Eschatology', 'God', 'Israel', 'Jesus', 'Jews', 'Kingdom', 'Messiah', 'Synoptists', 'Parable(s)', 'Teaching'.

Nor have I indexed all the authorities quoted. A few such references are included in certain cases where I have felt bound to express disagreement, or where for some other reason the allusion was noteworthy.